Discussion of the Åland question in the League of Nations, Switzerland, Geneva, on 27 June 1921. "Het eerste geschil beschlecht", volkenbondplaat met handleiding van J. M. Wansink. Naar een schilderij van F. Rackwitz. Uitgave: D.A. Daamens uitgevers My. n.v. Den Haag. Printed with kind permission of the Finnish Heritage Agency.

The Autonomy of the Åland Islands

Constitutional and International Law Challenges

Edited by

Gudmundur Alfredsson
Göran Lindholm

BRILL | NIJHOFF

LEIDEN | BOSTON

Library of Congress Cataloging-in-Publication Data

Names: Gudmundur Alfredsson, editor. | Lindholm, Göran, editor.
Title: The autonomy of the Åland islands : constitutional and international law challenges / [edited] by Gudmundur Alfredsson, Göran Lindholm.
Description: Leiden ; Boston : Brill/Nijhoff, 2024. | Series: Studies in international minority and group rights, 2210-2132 ; 18 | Includes bibliographical references and index.
Identifiers: LCCN 2024033743 | ISBN 9789004691100 (hardback) | ISBN 9789004691117 (ebook)
Subjects: LCSH: Åland (Finland)—International status. | Self-determination, National—Finland--Åland. | Constitutional law—Finland—Åland. | Neutrality—Finland—Åland. | Demilitarization (International law) | Åland (Finland)—Politics and government.
Classification: LCC KZ4214 .A98 2024 | DDC 342.4897/2—dc23/eng/20240724
LC record available at https://lccn.loc.gov/2024033743

Typeface for the Latin, Greek, and Cyrillic scripts: "Brill". See and download: brill.com/brill-typeface.

ISSN 2210-2132
ISBN 978-90-04-69110-0 (hardback)
ISBN 978-90-04-69111-7 (e-book)
DOI 10.1163/9789004691117

This book is printed on acid-free paper and produced in a sustainable manner.

Contents

Notes on Contributors

Gudmundur Alfredsson
is an Icelandic lawyer, holds the degree Doctor of Juridical Science from Harvard Law School (1982). He is Senior Associate at the Stefansson Arctic Institute in Akureyri, Editor-in-Chief of the *International Journal on Minority and Group Rights*, Co-Editor-in-Chief of the Yearbook of Polar Law, and former Law Professor at Lund University. He chaired the UN Working Group on Minorities (2006) as well as the expert meetings that drafted the OSCE/HCNM Lund Recommendations on the Effective Participation of National Minorities in Public Life (1998–99).

Ove Bring
is Professor Emeritus of International Law at Stockholm University. He served as Legal Adviser at the Swedish Ministry for Foreign Affairs (1987–1993) and then represented Sweden in the Sixth (Legal) Committee of the UN General Assembly. He has participated in human rights missions to former Yugoslavia, Vietnam, China and Tibet and been a member of the International Humanitarian Fact-Finding Commission (IHFFC) in Geneva. He has for many years served as Head of the Swedish Branch of the International Law Association (ILA) and was until 2021 a member of the Executive Council of the ILA in London.

Krzysztof Drzewicki
is an LL.D., Dr Habil., Professor of Public International Law, University of Gdańsk, Poland (ret.). He has written extensively on the international protection of human rights and international humanitarian law (over 130 publications). From 1989 to 1994 he was an adviser on international labour standards and human rights for the National Commission of Trade Union 'Solidarność'. In 1994–2003 he was appointed by the Minister of Foreign Affairs an Agent of the Government of Poland before the European Court of Human Rights. In this capacity he served as a minister counselor to the Permanent Representation of Poland to the Council of Europe. In 2003–2010 he was a Senior Legal Adviser to the OSCE High Commissioner on National Minorities, The Hague. Since 2015 he has been a member of the Advisory Legal Committee for the Minister of Foreign Affairs.

Bogi Eliasen
is the Director of Health at the Copenhagen Institute for Futures Studies, with a background in political science and international law from the University of Aarhus where is specialized in the right of self-determination. He went on to work in the Faroese Prime-Minister and Foreign office, had his own weekly radio program on foreign relations for 4 years before entering into working specifically with the future of health, first with establishing genomics in the Faroes and later as director of health at Copenhagen Institute for Futures studies and fellow at the Robert Bosch Academy.

Lauri Hannikainen
is Professor of International Law, Emeritus. His professorship is from Turku University but as Emeritus he does research at Helsinki University. In international law his main themes have been questions relating to Finland; basic principles of international law (esp. the prohibition of use of armed force and the principle of self-determination); and international human rights (esp. minority rights). His principal publication, however, is from general theory of international law, analyzing international jus cogens (1988, 781 pages). He was member of the European Commission against Racism and Intolerance at Council of Europe, in 2000–14.

Alexander Heger
Dipl.-Jur., is a research assistant and doctoral candidate at the Chair of Public Law, Public International Law and European Law of Professor Rainer Hofmann at the Goethe University Frankfurt (Germany). His research focuses on European Law and German Constitutional Law.

Axel Hjo
is a Ph.D. Candidate in Comparative Constitutional Law at the University of Bergen researching different styles of Constitutional Preview in the Nordic countries. Former member of the Åland parliament, Ålands lagting.

Rainer Hofmann
Prof. Dr. Dr., is Senior Professor of Public Law, International Public Law and European Law at Goethe University Frankfurt (Germany). He is the President of the German Association of International Law and Treasurer of the International Law Association. He was a Member and President of the Advisory Committee on the Council of Europe Framework Convention for the Protection of National Minorities (1998–2004, 2008–2012) and represented the Council

of Europe on the Executive and Management Boards of the European Union Fundamental Rights Agency (2015–2020).

Bárður Larsen
is an associate professor in law at the University of the Faroe Islands since late 2022. Before that he was assistant professor since late 2014. He has taught courses and engaged in research on topics as Jurisprudence, Faroese Administrative law, Case Analysis, Comparative Law and Legal History. He was secretary to the Faroese Constitutional Committee 2002–2004, member from 2005–2006, and later an occasional advisor.

Göran Lindholm
LL.B., formerly Lawdrafting Department at Åland Government (1979–1980), Junior Research fellow in Public International Law at University of Bergen (1981), Legal Director at Åland Lagting (1982), Head of Administration at Åland Government (1983–1987), Deputy member of the Åland Delegation (1983–).

Gun-Mari Lindholm
is a Nurse, Politician, and Party leader (2001–2013). She was elected to the Åland Legislative Assembly (1999–2019), served as Environment and Health Minister (2003–2005), and was Minister of Civil Affairs with responsibility for i.a. police and self-government issues (2011–2013). She was a member of the self-government policy committee (2007–2011), the Deputy Speaker of the Åland Legislature (2007–2011), a member of the law and culture committee (2013–2015), acted as Speaker of the Åland Legislative Assembly (2017–2019), and was Chairman of the self-governance policy committee (2017–2019). She is currently a leading politician at municipal level (1991–).

Julia Lindholm
is a political scientist from Åland. Lindholm has a background as a political advisor in the European Parliament and as the Åland Government's representative to the EU. She holds a degree in public administration from Hertie School of Government and is the founder of the Åland-based think tank Policylabbet Granit.

Bjarne Lindström
is an independent researcher and consultant, living in Åland. He has been director of ÅSUB, *Statistics and Research Åland*, head of the *Nordic Institute of Regional Research* (NordREFO) and assistant professor at the Department

of Regional Planning, *Royal Institute of Technology* (KTH). He has also been employed by the international consulting company *Sweco Society Ltd* as a senior consultant.

Lars-Erik Lundin
Ph.D. in political science/international relations 1980, is a former Swedish diplomat (1976–1996) focusing on security policy, including on CSCE/OSCE 1984–86 and 1990–1996. He served in the European Commission (1996–2009) and as EU Ambassador to the OSCE (2009–2011). He was distinguished Associate Fellow at SIPRI. He was an elected member of the Swedish Royal Academy of War Sciences and Coordinator of Academy research. He is the author of a Handbook on EU and Security in 2015. He concluded official inquiry in Sweden into the Treaty on the Prohibition of Nuclear Weapons 2019. He is the coauthor of several books on the Southern dimension of European security (2020) and Swedish security policy (2021, 2023).

Moritz Malkmus
Dipl.-Jur., is a research assistant and doctoral candidate at the Chair of Public Law, Public International Law and European Law of Professor Rainer Hofmann at the Goethe University Frankfurt, Germany. His research focuses on minority rights in international law.

Elisabeth F. Rasmussen
is the head of the Mission of the Faroe Islands to the EU. She holds a law degree from the University in Copenhagen and has prior to her current position been a member of the Foreign Service in the Faroese Government.

Allan Rosas
Dr.Jur., Dr.Jur. h.c., Dr.Pol.Sc. h.c.; is visiting Professor, College of Europe, Catolica Global School of Law (Lisbon) and University of Helsinki ("docent"); President of the Article 255 TFEU Panel; Chair of the Independent Ethical Committee of the European Commission; he is a former Professor of Law, University of Turku (1978–81) and Åbo Akademi University (1981–95) and Director of the latter University's Institute for Human Rights (1985–95); he was a Principal Legal Adviser and later Deputy Director-General of the Legal Service of the European Commission (1995–2002); and he was a Judge at the European Court of Justice (2002–2019). His writings cover various areas of international law, constitutional law, administrative law and, since the 1990s, EU law. Among his most recent works are A Rosas and L Armati, *EU Constitutional Law: An Introduction*, 3rd rev edn (Oxford, Hart Publishing, 2018); A Rosas, J Raitio and

P Pohjankoski (eds), *The Rule of Law's Anatomy in the EU: Foundations and Protections* (Oxford, Hart Publishing, 2023); A Rosas, *EU Law and National Law: A Common Legal System* (Florence, European University Institute, Academy of European Law, Working Paper 1/2024).

Susann Simolin
is Director of the Åland Islands Peace Institute and Doctoral Researcher in Political Science at Åbo Akademi University in Finland. Her research has mainly concerned territorial autonomy in relation to conflict resolution and the international relations of territorial autonomies.

Sia Spiliopoulou Åkermark
Jur. Dr., is Professor of Law at Åbo Akademi University (Finland). Former Director of the Åland Islands Peace Institute (2007–2023). Sia has worked in academia, non-governmental organisations and research institutions in Europe, East Africa and the USA focusing on pluralism, minorities, peaceful resolution of conflicts, territorial autonomy, and on legal restraints on securitization and the use of force. Served for many years as expert member and president of the *Advisory Committee on the Framework Convention on National Minorities* of the Council of Europe.

Markku Suksi
is Modeen Professor of Public Law at the Department of Law, Åbo Akademi University, in Finland (msuksi [at] abo.fi). He teaches within the areas of constitutional law, administrative law and comparative law. He has published, inter alia, the following books and edited volumes: *Sub-State Governance through Territorial Autonomy* (Springer, 2011), *Double Enumeration of Legislative Powers in a Sub-state Context – A Comparison between Canada, Denmark and Finland* (Springer, 2018) and *Autonomy – Applications and Implications* (Kluwer Law, 1998). He has authored a number of articles in the area autonomy, but in addition in, inter alia, in the area of linguistic rights and minority rights.

Fredrik Sundberg
is Director of the Institute for Public and International Law, Stockholm. He was a marine officer in the naval reserve. His law degree is from the University of Stockholm in 1981. He is a Master of Comparative Jurisprudence, New York University 1983. He was a researcher in market regulations, 1981–85. He was a visiting professor in human rights and minority rights, at the College of Europe, Natolin site, 1998–2001. He has held different positions linked with the functioning of the European Convention on Human Rights 1985–2020, notably

the Deputy Head and Head of the Department for the execution of the judgments of the European Court of Human Rights 2005–2020. He was an expert for the Council of Europe's Steering Committee for Human Rights 2020–2022. The main themes covered in articles he has published are market regulations and the functioning and role of the system of the European Convention of Human Rights in Europe.

Reetta Toivanen

Reetta Toivanen (PhD 2000 Humboldt University in Berlin) is since 2018 full professor in Sustainability Science (Indigenous Sustainabilities) at the Helsinki Institute for Sustainability Science (HELSUS) and Department of Cultures at the Faculty of Arts at the University of Helsinki, Finland. She is also a docent in social and cultural anthropology. She is the vice-director of the Centre of Excellence in Law, Identity and the European Narratives (EuroStorie) funded by the Academy of Finland (2018-2025). She is a non-resident senior research fellow at the Erik Castrén Institute of International Law and Human Rights at the University of Helsinki and at European Centre for Minority Issues (ECMI) in Flensburg (Germany). 2023-2025 she is a member of the Finnish Government's Expert Panel on Sustainability. In 2024, she was awarded the Richard von Weizsäcker Fellowship.

Alfred de Zayas

(US and Switzerland), retired lawyer with the OHCHR; He is former Secretary of the UN Human Rights Committee, an ex UN Independent Expert on International Order (2012–18), and the author of 12 books, including *Building a Just World Order* https://www.claritypress.com/book-author/alfred-de-zayas/.

Introduction

Gudmundur Alfredsson and Göran Lindholm

The recent 100 year anniversary of the autonomy of the Åland Islands is the occasion for the publication of this book. The autonomy arrangements are widely known and frequently quoted as an advanced model of self-government, not least when seen from the outside. From inside, however, demands for improvements and tensions if not cracks have from time to time appeared in the Åland relationship with Finland.

The purpose of the book is to provide an accessible and analytical overview of the legal and political issues that continue to generate debate about both the Åland autonomy as a working institution and as a model for others. The authors are from the Åland Islands and neighbouring States and most of them have previously written about the Åland autonomy or related issues in international and constitutional law and politics.

The authors seek to examine the history of the Åland autonomy, its current status in law and in fact and future prospects. They also address the series of legal, political, cultural, economic and security issues at global, regional, constitutional and other levels that affect both the autonomy and sovereign Finland. Despite a long history, it is interesting to note how many good questions remain unanswered.

Internally questions have arisen relating to both respect for the initial commitments dating back to the League of Nations and changing expectations and demands that have emerged over the past century. Do the current autonomy arrangements live up to the promises made in the original deal negotiated by the League? Has there been backtracking? Have the autonomous institutions and their powers grown along with similar bodies in Finnish society? Have they been given the opportunity to respond to the different political landscape within and beyond Finland?

External developments, such as the creation of sub-regional organisations like the Nordic Council and the Baltic Sea State Council, and more importantly Finland's membership in the European Union and NATO, have inevitably affected the autonomy arrangements. Are the autonomy institutions empowered and equipped to handle the additional issues and layers of governance which accompany these and other international undertakings? Have they been given the opportunity to participate in these organisations in a manner that continues to guarantee Åland's identity, culture and peaceful way of life?

Various actors, including sub-regional, regional and global intergovernmental and non-governmental organisations and other autonomies, are present at the table where Åland-related issues come up. More basically, while the origins of the Åland autonomy arrangements were with the League of Nations, it is unclear today whether the United Nations has replaced the League as the real or potential monitor and guarantor of the implementation of these arrangements. And if the UN has such a role, beyond its human rights monitoring mandates, which UN body or institution is responsible?

Not to forget the origins with the League of Nations and keeping in mind the Islands' location between Finland and Sweden, the Åland autonomy served to prevent, manage and resolve a potentially violent conflict. Indeed, the Organisation for Security and Co-Operation in Europe (OSCE) has identified autonomy as one of the useful tools available for conflict prevention.[1] Recommendations drafted under OSCE auspices clearly draw on human rights standards but they are based on a conflict prevention mandate. As far as autonomy is concerned, comparable international minority rights instruments do not exist.

Is autonomy a human right, that is do minorities have the right to autonomy? In the absence of express provisions in human rights instruments, is it possible that widespread autonomy practice by States has led to the emergence of international customary law? Does a human rights approach to minority rights somehow contradict the security approach? Can it really be the case that minorities stand a better chance of enjoying autonomy if threats of violence are involved?

What demands have been made by the Åland Islanders concerning substantive and procedural changes to the autonomy? Are such changes backed up by international standards, either those based on conflict prevention or human rights, or both? What lessons, if any, can the Åland Islanders draw from the autonomies and constitution-drafting in the Faroe Islands and Greenland? Should Åland draft a constitution of its own?

Why have the autonomy-related wishes of the Åland Islanders encountered Finnish resistance? Have negotiation positions of the Finnish Government at any point in time interrupted the holistic approach to the Åland solution, by placing uneven emphasis on autonomy, language and the security components? Does ongoing strengthening of the integration of the Finnish State stand in conflict with the Åland autonomy arrangements?

---

1 Paragraph 35 of the 1990 Document of the Copenhagen Meeting on the Human Dimension and Part III of the 1999 Lund Recommendations on the Effective Participation of Minorities in Public Life.

Which intergovernmental organisations (IGOs like for example UN system organisations, OSCE and the Council of Europe), and which bodies within them, are most suitable, able and willing to address issues relating to the Åland autonomy? Does the mandate of the OSCE High Commissioner on National Minorities (HCNM) extend to the peaceful Åland Islands, or is the threat of armed or violent conflict necessary for HCNM involvement? Asking again, is it really so that minority rights will get more attention by IGOs if or when their demands for change involve threats or acts of violence?

The membership of Finland in the European Union has brought both opportunities and challenges to Åland's autonomy, in relation to both applicable laws and representation. As to many of the European law issues, we are grateful to Rainer Hofmann, his co-authors and the Åland Government for allowing us to draw on their recent study.[2] Similar questions arise in regard to Finland's recent membership in NATO – will it in law or in fact affect Åland's demilitarisation and neutralisation?

The Åland autonomy has served and continues to serve as an example of what an international organisation can accomplish in the fields of conflict prevention, peace-making and minority rights. This is confirmed by the lessons from the Åland Islands and Finland concerning delegated powers, self-governing institutions and the mostly harmonious interplay between autonomy and sovereignty and between law and politics.

On the basis of the 100-year experience, it ought to be possible to make use of the Åland model in its holistic sense if either the OSCE Lund Recommendations on the political rights of minorities were to be revisited or a new instrument drafted, by the HCNM or other IGO bodies? By holistic we are referring to autonomy along with culture and language protection, demilitarisation and neutralisation. As to the minority rights approach, what is the interplay between equal rights, discrimination and special measures in the Åland situation? Should linguistic and religious minorities within the Åland population have their own minority rights?

Furthermore, is it realistic that Åland's autonomy can become a model for solving other minority situations? Should Åland, or for that matter Finland, take an active role in promoting the Åland autonomy model abroad? Could this model and the lengthy practical experience that comes with it constitute a serious positive contribution to actual situations currently in the news, for example Corsica and Nagorno-Karabakh?

Beyond what is already the case, should the Åland Islanders be represented in global, regional and sub-regional organisations and at what level? Should

---

2 The Åland Islands in International and European Union Law: Present Situation and (Potential) Problems, submitted to the Åland Government in 2023.

they have seats of their own in the European Parliament, the Nordic Council or other parliamentary bodies? What about international sports organisations and sports events – should the Åland Islanders be able to obtain membership and to compete under their own flag when they so want? In this context, one can also ask what is the role, if any, of the kin-State, in this case Sweden, in both sport-based and general terms?

What is the best method for promoting and strengthening minority rights? Special efforts relating to culture, education and employment, the adoption of national and international standards, emphasis on national implementation and international monitoring, and/or the enhanced role of domestic courts and international appeals? Again, one can ask whether the Åland Islanders should seek to contribute to such efforts and in the process become more of an actor in international affairs?

What is the likely further evolution of the rules concerning the right of self-determination, with emphasis on the internal dimension? Does it in any way offer benefits to the Åland Islands? What does the term 'a people' mean? Are the Sami, as an indigenous people of Finland, entitled to stronger autonomy and better protection than the Åland Islanders? Certainly, the 2007 UN Declaration on the Rights of Indigenous Peoples offers stronger language on autonomy than any minority rights instrument. How do the Sami and Åland autonomies compare?

It is our hope that this book can serve as a source of further debate and inspiration about autonomy and minority rights and related issues in the Åland Islands and beyond. We welcome all comments on the book's contents, both what might be missing and what can be improved. And we'd be pleased if this kind of debate leads to subsequent meetings and new editions of the book. Indeed, many issues and questions have come up in the preparatory process putting the book together, and the answers to some of the questions are pending.

By way of conclusion, we say many thanks to several persons and institutions which have made this book possible. In addition to the authors and unnamed peer reviewers, essential contributions have been made by the Olof M Janssons Foundation for covering the costs of Open Access, Lindy Melman and especially Bea Timmer at Brill for good advice and all the Brill staff involved in getting the book published, Alexandra Gäddnäs for editing and layout and Graham Robins and Elspeth Randelin for language editing. Librarian Hans-Erik Ramström at the Library of Ålands Lagting was very helpful with the bibliography. Of course, we the editors remain responsible for any missteps and mistakes that may have occurred during the preparation and presentation of the book.

CHAPTER 1

The Åland Islands Autonomy Paradox

Bjarne Lindström

1 Background and Geopolitical Context

The Åland Islands is a home-ruled archipelago with approximately 6,800 islands and 31,000 inhabitants in the northern-central part of the Baltic Sea. Following its separation from Sweden in conjunction with the Russian conquest of Finland in 1809, the archipelago was demilitarised by the middle of the nineteenth century. In connection with the peace negotiations after the First World War (1919–1920), the Ålanders demanded reunification with Sweden, appealing to the principle of people's right to self-determination. A referendum was suggested by the Ålanders, supported by Sweden, but Finland refused.

The 'Åland Question' was finally submitted to the League of Nations who solved the conflict by offering Finland sovereignty over the islands, while the Ålanders were granted political autonomy,[1] which included special safeguards for their Swedish language and culture.[2] To ensure this the Finnish Government promised the people of Åland "[…] the possibilities to themselves arrange their existence as freely as possible for a territory that does not constitute an independent state".[3]

The internationally agreed resolution of the conflict over Åland's political status thus rests on two closely linked prerequisites: (1) securing the Ålanders' Swedish language and culture, and the means to achieve this through (2) a territorial autonomy that gives the islanders the greatest possible legal and political home rule. The international dimension of this two-sided solution was further highlighted by the fact that the 19th century demilitarisation of the territory was confirmed by a separate, mutually binding treaty between the then-existing Baltic states (except the USSR).

1 In this chapter 'autonomy', 'home rule', and 'self-government' are in all essential respects synonymous.

2 P.M. Brown, 'The Åland Island Question' 15:2 *The American Journal of International Law* (1921) pp. 268–272; N.J. Padeldorf, & G.A. Anderson, 'The Åland Question', 33:3 *The American Journal of International Law*, (1939) pp. 465–487.

3 Finnish Government, 1919:73. *Proposition till Riksdagen angående lag om självstyrelse för Åland.* (Helsingfors, 1919).

DOI:10.1163/9789004691117_003

The international background, the original Finnish guarantees and the fact that the autonomy is confirmed in the Finnish constitution, have led to the perception that the autonomy must be exceptionally strong and extensive. Åland's home rule is often described – especially in official contexts – as unusually well-developed. Even in more scholarly contexts, it is a commonly held opinion that Åland's constitutional position is a guarantee for an extensive regional[4] autonomy, and thus also political and legal room for manoeuvre.[5]

2 Home rule – *de jure* and *de facto*

The question is, however, whether such a connection between constitutional (*de jure*) protection and (*de facto*) self-determination really exists? Does a strong constitutional position guarantee a well-developed and comprehensive autonomy? And does it therefore follow that the lack of a constitutionally secured home rule leads to a weak and undeveloped *de facto* autonomy?

A recent comparative analysis of six territorial autonomies in the EU/Europe provides no convincing support for this hypothesis.[6] The most developed autonomies in the study lacked an explicit constitutional guarantee, while the reverse was true for some of the more constitutionally protected autonomies. Although the constitutional status of these autonomies was not without significance, the national and geopolitical background of their home rule, their history of origin and – not least – the quality of the political partnership with the respective metropolitan state, proved to be significantly more important for the extent of their autonomy.

Åland's autonomy is an interesting example of the lack of a strong and clear link between constitutional status and the extent of self-determination. In recent years, several in-depth analyses of the content and scope of Åland's home rule have identified significant problems and shortcomings with negative

4 'Regional' and 'territorial' (in combination with autonomy/home rule) are, in this chapter, interchangeable.

5 J. Loughlin & F. Daftary, *Insular Regions and European Integration: Corsica and the Åland Islands Compared* (European Centre for Minority Issues, Helsinki & Mariehamn, 1999); P. Joenniemi, 'The Åland Islands: Neither local nor fully sovereign', 49:1 *Cooperation and Conflict*, (2014) pp. 80–97; D. Paci, 'The Åland Island Question: Irredentism and Autonomism in the Archipelago of Peace, 40:85 *Revista Brasiliera de História* (2020).

6 B. Lindström, 2020:2 *De legala och politiska förutsättningarna för Europas autonomier. En jämförande studie.* (Olof M. Janssons stiftelse, Mariehamn 2020).

impacts on its room for manoeuvre.[7] The archipelago's century-old autonomy is – despite its strong constitutional status – rather limited and lacks much of the legal and political dynamism that a more well-developed territorial autonomy requires.[8] Nordic comparisons have also shown that Åland's home rule is politically weaker, and its content less developed, than the Danish 'sister autonomy' Faroe Islands – a home-ruled North Atlantic archipelago with considerably weaker constitutional position than Åland.[9]

3 An Autonomy Put on Hold

Awareness of the limitations of the autonomy, and growing difficulties in further developing the home rule within the framework of the current Autonomy Act, caused the Åland Government to take an initiative to renew the Act in 2010.[10] A proposal to modernise the law with a focus on increased flexibility and greater room for legal and political manoeuvre, not least in the economic area (where home rule is severely limited), received broad political consensus in the Åland Parliament and was submitted to the Finnish Government.

After more than a decade of difficult negotiations, however, virtually all of Åland's wishes (apart from some technical improvements) have been eliminated in the Finnish Government's final proposal (2022) for a new Autonomy Act, a bill which the Åland Parliament could not accept. The door to a more modern and better functioning autonomy is thus, at least in the foreseeable future, closed.

---

7 M. Holm-Johansson, *Förhållandet mellan självstyrelselagen och grundlagen.* (Promemoria 2020-09-01, Ålands landskapsregering, Mariehamn, 2020); S. Palmgren, 'De statsrättsliga garantierna för Ålands självstyrelse', 6:20 *Tidskrift utgiven av Juridiska Föreningen i Finland* (2020) pp. 689–715; A. Jonsson, 'Konsten att olovligen ta makten av en nordisk autonomi', 2:21 *Tidskrift utgiven av juridiska Föreningen i Finland* (2021) pp. 87–110.

8 B. Lindström, 'State Integration vs. Minority Protection through Regional Self-Determination: The Åland Case. 30:1 *International Journal on Minority and Group Rights*' (2023), pp. 110–131; cf also J. Sundberg and S. Sjöblom, *Det åländska självstyrets kvaliteter. Demokrati, resurser och kompetens* (Svenska litteratursällskapet i Finland, Helsingfors, 2021).

9 M. Ackrén and B. Lindström, 'Autonomy development, irredentism and secessionism in a Nordic context', 50:4 *Commonwealth & Comparative Politics* (2012) pp. 494–511.

10 Åland Government, *Betänkande från parlamentariska kommittén om förslag till reformering av självstyrelsesystemet och självstyrelselagen för Åland* (Åländsk utredningsserie, Mariehamn, 2010:2);
Åland Government, *Slutrapport från parlamentariska kommittén för fortsatt arbete med ett nytt självstyrelsesystem.* (Åländsk utredningsserie, Mariehamn, 2013:2).

4 Two Important Questions

Despite its international background and constitutional safeguards, the development of Åland's home rule has thus reached a dead end. In practice, the islands' autonomy currently delivers less *de facto* self-determination than its *de jure* (constitutional) status and international background history seems to indicate.

This raises two important questions. First, which legal and political building blocks of Åland's home rule have led to this paradox? The second – in the context of this book even more interesting (and forward-looking) – question is whether there is an untapped potential in the autonomy's international background and/or in current international law-praxis that could be used in order to contribute to a positive solution to today's stalemate in the development of the home rule.

The first of these two questions is dealt with below. We will briefly return to the second question in the concluding section of this chapter.

5 Main Shortcomings of the Åland Autonomy Model[11]

The gap between Åland's constitutional status and *de facto* room for manoeuvre essentially stems from two crucially important flaws in the legal and political set up of the autonomy, namely:
- The autonomy's limited *de facto* legislative competence
- The asymmetrical partnership with the Finnish state

5.1 *The Autonomy's Limited Legal Competences*

The strict limitation of the legal room for manoeuvre shows itself in two different, albeit closely related, ways. These are evident upon a closer examination of the catalogues of legislative competence in the Åland Autonomy Act. First, there is a clear *quantitative* imbalance between the two parties' respective competences. The Finnish Parliament's competence comprises significantly more legal areas (48) than that of the Åland Parliament (27). The second characteristic feature of the autonomy's legal set-up is the *qualitative* imbalance in the division of competences. The Finnish Parliament's catalogue of competence

11 The below section on the main shortcomings of Åland's current self-government system is a partially revised and shortened version of section 5.2 in B. Lindström, 'State Integration vs. Minority Protection through Regional Self-Determination: The Åland Case', 30:1 *International Journal on Minority and Group Rights* (2023) pp. 110–131.

is not only significantly more extensive than that of the Åland Parliament, it also includes a number of legal areas that are fundamental for the island's economic and social development.

This includes procedural law, civil and criminal law, the main part of the taxation rights, more or less all legislation connected to companies and corporations, (including banking, insurance and shipping), legislation of labour markets and labour, pension legislation, as well as the technical norms and standardisation that affect occupational conditions within ever greater areas of the Åland society. Moreover, the entire court and legal system, so crucial to the interpretation of Åland's own legislation, is within Finnish jurisdiction.

In addition to the fact that the examples given above (a list which is not exhaustive) substantially limit the autonomy's extent and scope for action, their central role in the regulation of modern society means that they often tend to influence and restrict the possibilities to deviate from current Finnish legislation even within those legal areas where Åland, formally, has the legislative rights. The overpowering quantitative and qualitative nature of the state's legal competences tends to contribute to the existence of a number of overlapping areas and judicial grey areas, complicating the question of competence. In practice, the simplest way of solving these problems – which have a tendency to crop up within new legal areas as a consequence of general social development – is to use so-called 'form-legislation', i.e. legislation by copying a Finnish law.[12]

The result is that significant parts of Åland's own legislation is integrated into the Finnish state's legislative regime, with little possibility for genuine self-legislation based on Åland's needs and particular circumstances. Thus, almost one quarter of the legislation *within* the Åland autonomy's area of competence today comprises state laws, which through the method of 'form-legislation' have been adopted in a more or less unaltered state.

5.2 *The Asymmetrical Partnership*

The unequal partnership between the autonomy and the Finnish state manifests itself in how the limits of home rule are interpreted, as well as in the

12 This is the special Åland variant of what is usually referred to as 'legal transplants' in international legal research. See A.Watson, 'From Legal Transplants to Legal Formants', 43:3 *The American Journal of Comparative Law* (1995) pp. 469–476. Bardur Larsen has described this phenomenon in an international context, as well as the problems it has caused Faroese legislation in B. Larsen, 'Problemet med den ubekymrede retliga transplantation', 2022:6 *Juristen* (2022) pp. 251–263. Regarding the Faroe Islands, however, it should be noted that the copying of Danish legislation seems to contain more local adaptations, and thus does not appear to be as complete as Åland's 'rubber stamp' method.

long-term development of the autonomy. In both cases the Finnish state has the last say (interpretative prerogative) regarding the division of competences between Finland and Åland – something that has had a limiting effect on the autonomy's development and extent. A fundamental characteristic of the island's system of home rule is thus that one party (Åland) is dependent on the other party's co-operation and willingness to promote a development of the autonomy based on Åland's specific needs and local conditions. This dependency on the state's good will and active support for a flexible development of the home rule has led to several problems, each of which has negatively affected the way autonomy functions and – above all – its long-term development.

The *first* main problem is Åland's dependency on the Finnish Government's and Parliament's political priorities in revising the Autonomy Act. Originally, this is derived from the good intentions to guarantee that the Finnish Parliament could not unilaterally act to impair the contents and extent of the autonomy. However, the downside is that the autonomy's development is decided by the party that has the lowest ambitions and least wishes to instigate a revision, i.e. as a rule, the Finnish state. Dependence on the state's political goodwill when renewing the Autonomy Act is confirmed by the fact that the state decides the political parameters for the preparatory work that precedes a revision of the Autonomy Act. The unsuccessful, more than ten-years long, work and negotiations on the revision of the current Autonomy Act mentioned above highlights this problem.

A *second* issue is the dependency on information about, and possibility to influence, state legislation of importance to the Åland society. Indeed, there is a provision in the Autonomy Act regarding the right to information, and also the possibility to submit opinions intended to reduce the negative effects of state legislation poorly adapted to the needs and conditions of Åland society. However, important information is often lacking – or is provided so late that preparation time is cut unacceptably short. In addition, even when the autonomy has had the possibility to present its opinions regarding forthcoming legislation, these have seldom been given greater consideration. This applies not least to legislation within areas with unclear and/or mixed areas of competence. The pandemic legislation passed by the Finnish Government and Parliament during 2020 and 2021 is a clear example of how little the Autonomy Act's provision regarding advance information and the possibility to influence state legislation really means.[13]

13 B. Lindström and G. Lindholm, *The Future Conditions for the Åland Autonomy. A study of the legal and political development of Åland's self-determination* (Olof M. Janssons stiftelse, Mariehamn, 2021).

The *third* major problem is the dependency on the Finnish state's willingness to cooperate and to take into account the needs of home rule in the preparation and implementation of EU legislation. However, in this case the Autonomy Act gives a more explicit, and therefore stronger, support to Åland's active inclusion in the EU co-operation. Despite this, it has been difficult for Åland to make its opinions heard in the state's handling of EU questions and, not least, to be informed in time and to be able to influence the preparation of the Finnish EU-positions that concern Åland and its autonomy. Åland's role in Finland's EU politics has been further weakened by its lack of a representative in the EU Parliament.

The *fourth* problem is the dependency on state concessions and support to be able to play an active role in international bodies handling questions of particular importance for Åland. This especially applies to co-operation within the autonomy's core areas (education and culture), but also concerns large parts of other international co-operation of importance to Åland. However, a closer examination of several Nordic and European autonomies comparable to Åland shows that it is indeed quite possible to take part in international co-operation (which is not expressly reserved for sovereign states) – provided that permission and support is given by the autonomy's metropolitan state.[14] Because this, as a rule, has not been the case for Åland, it has resulted in a general absence from international forums handling questions where the autonomy has legislative competence, or where the co-operation is in some other way particularly important for Åland.

The Nordic co-operation, which is the exception to the general rule of Åland's absence from the international arena, sheds its own special light on the limitations in Åland's position, compared to that of the other two autonomies in this co-operation, the Faroe Islands and Greenland. It was not thanks to a productive and close interaction with the Finnish state that the doors of the Nordic co-operation were opened for Åland in the early 1970s. It was in fact the demand from the Faroe Islands, supported by Denmark, to be included in the co-operation that paved the way for Åland membership.[15]

6 Conclusion: the Need for a Comprehensive Autonomy Reform

Åland's autonomy is now more than a century old. It is one of the world's oldest territorial autonomies. It has a history of origin confirmed by international

14 B. Lindström, The political and legal prerequisites for autonomies in Europe: A comparative study. https://www.olofmjanssonsstiftelse.ax/app/uploads/2023/10 /cmc-11654-paper -autonomy-in-europe-061023.pdf.

15 B. Mattson-Eklund, *Folke om Folke. Folke Woivalin samtalar med Benita Mattsson-Eklund,* (Ålands Tidnings-Tryckeri AB Förlag, Mariehamn, 1998).

law, and constitutional protection within the framework of metropolitan Finland. Despite this, comparisons with several similar Nordic and European autonomies show that the actual content and scope of Åland's home rule has many surprisingly strong, legal as well as political, limitations. Somewhat simplified – but not entirely wrong – it can be said that the objective of securing the population's Swedish identity has been prioritised at the expense of long-term development of the material content of the autonomy. The original connection between the goal (language/nationality, League of Nations) and the means (greatest possible autonomy, Finland) thus tends to become increasingly diffuse.

There is, however, a structural link between the extent of the Åland autonomy and the possibilities to guarantee its linguistic and cultural goals. Limited competence in core legal and political areas tends to generate a gradually increasing integration into the overall, substantially Finnish-speaking, state structure. Solving the problem of too limited competence is therefore not only a key to realising the promise of greatest possible home rule, but also to guaranteeing the autonomy's original purpose regarding language and culture.

The overall conclusion is thus that the time is ripe for a comprehensive, in-depth reform of the Åland Autonomy Act. Without such reform, Åland's legal and political manoeuvrability will gradually erode, and the home rule will acquire the character of regional 'self-administration' rather than that of a qualified political autonomy with the tools needed to successfully deal with the integration pressure that being part of a unitary state like Finland – more or less by definition – tends to generate.

The increasingly complex legal situation and the current blocking of the much-needed Autonomy Act reform, are essentially *political* problems that can only be solved by the home rule system's two main political partners, i.e. Åland and Finland. Having said this, however, the second important question posed in the introduction above remains to be addressed: Could the autonomy's – according to international law scholars still valid[16] – international law guarantees be used to contribute to a break of the current stalemate in the development of Åland's home rule?

16 Ove Bring, *Ålands självstyrelse under 80 år: Erfarenheter och utmaningar.* (Ålands Landskapsstyrelse, Mariehamn, 2002); Lauri Hannikainen, *De folkrättsliga grunderna för Ålands självstyrelse* (Institutet för mänskliga rättigheter vid Åbo Akademi, Åbo, 2004); Markku Suksi, *Ålands konstitution – en sammanställning av material och tolkningar i anslutning till självstyrelselag för Åland* (Åbo Akademis Förlag, Åbo, 2005); Sia Spiliopoulou Åkermark (2011, ed.), *The Åland Example and Its Components – Relevance for Conflict Resolution* (Ålands Fredsinstitut, Mariehamn, 2011).

CHAPTER 2

Constitutional Status of the Åland Islands: Expectations and Demands

Göran Lindholm

1 Background

Given their geographical location in the northern part of the Baltic Sea, the Åland Islands have lain at the crossroads of the region's major trading routes ever since the Iron Age. Åland was a part of the Swedish Kingdom up until 1809, when the Russian Tsar claimed Finland and the Åland Islands in a peace treaty that ended a long series of wars between Russia and Sweden. In the aftermath of WWI and the Russian Revolution, Finland declared itself independent and Åland strove for a reunification with Sweden. The question of sovereignty escalated and was handed to the Paris Peace Conference (ending WWI) and later to the newly established League of Nations.

During the deliberations of the League, Finland passed a constitutional act for Åland that endowed the people of Åland with a right to self-government in internal matters in order to meet the international view on minority rights and to ensure the Ålanders' Swedish language, culture and local heritage. The proposition of 1919 emphasises that the given autonomy should be as far-reaching as possible for a region that lacks the status of a sovereign state. The movement for reunification with Sweden had started already in 1917, prior to the Finnish declaration of independence, when a common assembly for the Åland municipalities was created. This assembly rejected the Autonomy Act, referring to the right of self-determination and thus the right to hold a referendum on the issue of sovereignty.

The League decided in 1921 that Finland should have territorial sovereignty over Åland. The people of Åland should be consoled by reinforced guarantees, as an integrated part of the already-passed Autonomy Act, for their Swedish language, culture, and local heritage. These guarantees should be negotiated by Sweden and Finland and added to the constitutional Autonomy Act, which was otherwise considered to meet the then-present standards.[1] The Åland

1 Here the League could compare the governance of the Free City of Danzig and Memel Territory. J. Barros, The Aland Islands Question: Its settlement by the League of Nations (Yale University Press, New Haven and London, 1968), pp. 170 and 190.

DOI:10.1163/9789004691117_004

authorities also received the right to complain to the Council of the League of Nations in case Finland should not honour the guarantees. The Council Secretariat should also monitor if Finland was complying with the guarantees, as it was doing in other minority solutions established after WW1. Moreover, the Åland Servitude, a non-fortification treaty from 1856,[2] was to be reconfirmed and strengthened to include demilitarisation and neutralisation in order to secure the future peace of the Northern Baltic Sea and thus meet Sweden's security interests.

2 The Åland Legislative Competence Today

The people of Åland are governed under three jurisdictions: the Åland Islands with the Åland Lagting, i.e., the Parliament of Åland, adopting legislation; Finland with the Finnish Parliament and other state institutions; and the European Union with the Parliament, Council, Commission and the Court. The Åland Parliament enacts Åland laws within its legislative competence. Secondly, laws enacted by the Finnish Parliament apply to Åland within the legislative competence of the Finnish Parliament as defined in the Autonomy Act. And finally, laws enacted by the European Parliament apply to Åland to the extent that the legislative powers are delegated from the Åland Parliament through the accession treaty to the union.[3]

In the first Autonomy Act of 1921 the legislative powers of the Finnish Parliament were enumerated, including foreign policy, defence and other state prerogative matters, while all residual legal matters belonged to the Åland Parliament. This division of powers followed the set-up for a federal state and partly fulfilled the original intention to award Åland as far-reaching self-government as possible for a region that lacked the status of a sovereign state. In the following years of implementation, the provision stating that new legal areas belonged to Finnish competence proved to be problematic, as the Supreme Court implemented this provision in the constitutional control, applying strict interpretations that favoured the Finnish Parliament.[4]

Today's limited legislative authority is defined in two lists of enumerations, one for the autonomy and one for the state. The list for Åland includes 26 legal

2 The Convention of 1856 Between Great Britain, France and Russia on the Demilitarisation and Non-fortification of the Aland Islands.

3 The Accession Treaty to the European Community 1994 of Finland, Sweden and Austria, Protocol 2.

4 Ida Jansson, 2020:1 *Att sätta självstyrelsens gränser, Av laggranskarna underkänd åländsk lagstiftning* 1922–2018 (Olof M Janssons stiftelse, Mariehamn 2020).

areas, while the list for Finland includes 41. Each list concludes with a general clause stating that new legal areas shall be interpreted in accordance with the principles in the respective enumeration.

The system of enumeration of the legislative competence of each parliament was intended to be exhaustive and leave less room for disputable interpretations in the legislative control of Åland laws. However, the lists of enumerations have been found to be too detailed and not especially transparent, and many areas of mixed competence have appeared. In some cases, the individual citizen doesn't know which law is applicable, in which version, and to what extent in each instant. In practice, only someone with long-term experience of how the competence lists are applied is comfortable with the current system. A more transparent and simpler system for the distribution of legislative competence would have a democratic value. Knowledge of the distribution of legislative competence and its implementation needs to be improved.

Maybe the most negative effect of Åland's limited legislative competence is the large number of mixed competences. In addition to contributing to the problem of the growing number of "legal transplants" (i.e., laws copied from Finnish laws), they also give rise to a legal uncertainty that affects the individual citizen as well as the party imposing the law.[5]

When comparing other European autonomies,[6] it becomes evident that the autonomous territories that have the broadest legislative competence tend to have fewer areas of conflict with the metropolitan state and, as a result, often enjoy a relatively conflict-free and well-functioning partnership with the state.

3 Demand for a New Autonomy Act

The Autonomy Act has seen two major revisions, in 1951 and 1991, as well as a number of minor changes.

Åland politicians have on several occasions underlined the urgent need for a revision of the Autonomy Act, also referred to as the Åland Constitution. The Åland Government appointed a revisory committee already in 2010, and

5 The Alec Aalto group, established by the Finnish Government to comment on the proposals, also believes that the possibility of abandoning the current form-legislation technique and creating a new legislation technique that is more transparent and correct in view of the citizens' legal protection should be investigated. *Ålands självstyrelse i utveckling*. Ålandskommitténs 2013 delbetänkande. (Aalto-kommittén), Justitieministeriet 6/2015.

6 Bjarne Lindström, *De legala och politiska förutsättningarna för Europas autonomier* (Olof M Janssons stiftelse, Mariehamn 2/2020).

a second one in 2013. The main conclusions can be summarised as the official Åland's demands for necessary changes to the Autonomy Act.

The proposals from Åland have been scrutinised and negotiated in several exclusively Finnish committees, as well as in joint committees and working groups, comprising both politicians and experts. The few issues on which Helsinki and Åland could agree were not considered worthwhile by the Åland authorities to pursue further.

A recurring conclusion in the Åland committees' reports is that the autonomy's political and administrative potential is considerably more limited than its constitutional position provides scope for. The Åland autonomy tends to deliver a lesser degree of home rule than its legal set-up implies, and, paradoxically, less flexibility and scope for action than a number of other European autonomies with a weaker constitutional position than Åland's. The explanation of this paradox can be summarised in two critically important weaknesses in the Åland autonomy model, namely:

- The autonomy's limited legislative competence
- The asymmetrical partnership with the Finnish state[7]

Without a deeper structural reform, the autonomy risks stagnation and distancing from its original purpose. This insight was the key idea behind the suggestion to reform the present Autonomy Act, which was initiated by the Åland Government over ten years ago. The most significant component in the reform proposal was, with reference to the Danish model of autonomy, the introduction of a new form of division of competences, in which all areas of law – except for those that can be tied to the most fundamental conditions (prerogatives) of national sovereignty – can be transferred to the autonomy's jurisdiction without changes to the Autonomy Act.

There have been a few minor changes to the Autonomy Act since 1991 when the present Act came into force. The new Finnish Constitution from 2000 rendered a minor revision to the Autonomy Act but not to the required extent, as the Autonomy Act explicitly excludes provisions of the Finnish Constitution when needed to uphold the autonomy and the Swedish national identity of the people of Åland.

The main proposals of the Åland revisory committees are still valid as the demands of official Åland:

1. The Åland Autonomy is internationally embedded under the auspices of the Council of the League of Nations in 1921, when the sovereignty and

7 Bjarne Lindström, 'State Integration vs. Minority Protection through Regional Self-Determination: The Åland Case', 30:1 *International Journal on Minority and Group Rights* (2023) pp. 1–22.

certain guarantees for language, culture and local heritage were settled. These guarantees were concretized in the Åland Agreement between Sweden and Finland. Moreover, the Åland Servitude, a non-fortification treaty from 1856, was to be reconfirmed and strengthened to include demilitarisation and neutralisation in order to secure the future peace of the Northern Baltic Sea. The Åland authorities also received the right to complain to the Council in case Finland did not honour the guarantees. These provisions were to be included in the Autonomy Act for Åland, the Åland Constitution. The self-government system for Åland is therefore not exclusively of Finnish national interest.

2. The self-government shall be established as an agreement between Finland and Åland. The parties are equal in all stages of the preparation of a revision of the Autonomy Act, and a new act, or a revision of the present one, shall be ratified by consistent decisions by both the Finnish and the Åland parliaments.
3. Future relations between Åland and Finland must to a higher degree be based on respectful and developing negotiations. The system needs to be adjusted in this direction, and the practical implementation needs to be directed towards the original intentions of the self-government. However, this cannot be done at the expense of legal certainty and a clear regulation of the distribution of competence.

What the committees interestingly enough conclude in their reports is the quest for a better and more equal partnership between the metropolitan state and the autonomy that would be fruitful for both parties. Today's legal and constitutional stronghold has proven not so fruitful for the development and adjustment of the autonomy to today's society. To create the legal and political scope for action required to fulfil the ambitions behind the establishment of the autonomy (language guarantee and greatest possible degree of self-determination) demands a fundamental revision of the whole Åland autonomy arrangement. There is a need for a structural renewal of the home rule's conditions for development, which makes use of the experiences of similar autonomy arrangements in the Nordic region and Europe.

4 Main Demands

4.1 *New Principle for Division of Competence*

Here, the Åland proposals amount to a return to the residual principle of the first Autonomy Act, where only the core areas of Finland's state sovereignty are listed in the Autonomy Act as non-transferable. All other legislative and legal areas can be transferred to the Åland Parliament by means of a simplified procedure, with only the procedure and the timing being subject to negotiation.

The committees underlined that the strongest reasons for a change to the current construction of the competence lists can be found in the excessively high thresholds that must be crossed when changes in the distribution of competence are needed, as well as the limited scope for development that the current competence lists entail. Amendments to the Autonomy Act have proven to be a rather time-consuming and persistent process.

The committees proposed a system for the division of legislative powers that is more flexible and allows for successive development of the autonomy. Such a system would include a future potential for further takeovers of legislative areas that currently fall within the Finnish jurisdiction. This would presuppose that the Autonomy Act contains a list of legal areas belonging to Finland's jurisdiction that cannot be subject to a takeover by the Åland Parliament without an amendment to the Autonomy Act. Remaining legal areas would constitute a residual legal competence that could be taken over by the Åland Parliament with the support of various procedures.

Such a major change requires thorough consideration. Today's system is rather predictable, and the constitutional control is based on legal discretion when it comes to interpretation of the Autonomy Act. A change might pave the way for a new praxis where, e.g., a nationalistic president could use political discretion to the disadvantage of Åland, regardless of the Supreme Court's opinion. The Åland position nonetheless considers that the present difficulties relating to an amendment of the Autonomy Act, i.e., the lack of legislative competence to hinder the on-going (unintentional) state integration,[8] constitutes a greater threat to the Swedish language, culture and local heritage, as well as to the future existence of a real form of self-government.

The proposal from the committees didn't take a position on which areas should be reserved for the metropolitan state, but states that it is natural that areas that are particularly associated with national sovereignty remain with Finland. These include the legal areas enumerated in the introduction to section 27 of the current Autonomy Act: foreign affairs, defence, human freedoms and rights.

A corresponding system has, in principle, been implemented in Denmark. Through a Danish law that entered into force in 2005, the Faroe Islands have

8 Bjarne Lindström and Göran Lindholm, 2021:4 *The Future Conditions for the Åland Autonomy. A study of the legal and political development of Åland's self-determination* (Olof M. Janssons stiftelse, Mariehamn, 2021).

received additional powers for taking over legislative competence.[9] According to this law, only a few areas are excluded from a future takeover by the Faroese authorities without the need for further amendments.[10]

A system based on the idea that the Åland authorities are given the main responsibility for future transfers of legislative competence would mean that the national legislation in force at the time must apply until the transfer comes into force within a specific area. In a sense, it is a question of a power of attorney for the Åland Parliament to transfer legislative competence at a later stage. The transfer would come into force when Åland's Parliament passes legislation covering this area. This would create a smooth transferral of specific areas when needed to match the development of society. Such a system presupposes an equal and respectful partnership between the autonomy and the state.

If the proposed reform was to be implemented with consideration to the most important of Åland's proposals, many of the problems that have been identified in the cooperation between Mariehamn and Helsinki would, if not totally disappear, be significantly reduced.

4.2 *Clearer Relationship between the Autonomy Act and the Finnish Constitution*

The relationship between the Finnish Constitution and the Autonomy Act is in some respects problematic. Questions regarding the relationship between the two constitutional acts have arisen in various application situations. The provincial government has found it problematic that the Finnish Parliament, through amendments to the Finnish Constitution, can infringe on the Åland Parliament's legislative competence without its approval. The present Autonomy Act requires that certain constitutional amendments come into force in Åland only after the legislature's approval has been given. This mainly applies with regard to principles relating to the right of individuals to own real estate or assets belonging to business activities in Åland, provisions derived from the original nationality guarantees.

The Åland position is that a provision should be included in the Autonomy Act according to which legislative powers cannot be limited by establishing, amending or repealing the Finnish Constitution, or by deviating from the Constitution unless the Åland Parliament has consented to the measure in a qualified manner.

9 Lindström, *supra* note 7, p. 41.

10 Ibid, p. 42.

This recommendation is also strongly supported by a comprehensive study of all Supreme Court opinions of Åland Laws, 1923–2018.[11] The results show various interpretation problems with, and limitations to, the autonomy's competence resulting from the introduction of the new Finnish Constitution.

4.3 *Increased International Competence*

Due to a growing European integration and a general internationalisation of politics, international standardisation is increasing in scope. Because of the proposals for extended jurisdiction for the Åland Parliament in the exercising of public power, expanded treaty-legal capacity for Åland is also assumed.

Increased competence in treaty jurisdiction is also seen by the Åland committees as necessary to the long-term maintenance of Åland's international guarantees of nationality. Åland should be given the ability to influence the preparation of international agreements so that an unwelcome erosion of the Autonomy Act can be prevented.[12]

The problems relating to the autonomy's weak position in the implementation of EU legislation are also criticised by the two committees. Despite regulations in the current Autonomy Act, there is little opportunity for the Åland Parliament to influence the preparation of EU legislation within its own areas of competence. The responsibility for Åland to implement EU directives correctly has in many cases led to rejection in the constitutional control, as the Supreme Court has regarded the Åland Parliament's way of implementing a directive as "evidently" in violation of the EU directive. This practice has been questioned as it is up to the European Court of Justice to consider if there is a breach of EU legislation or not. The leakage of democracy needs to be rectified, according to the Åland proposals. Another question that needs addressing is the guaranteeing of a seat in the EU Parliament for Åland, a current issue as the present proposal regarding seats in the EU Parliament is offering Finland an extra seat.

It should also be noted that a change to the Autonomy Act that provides Åland with some form of limited treaty jurisdiction could advantageously be used in relations with Sweden concerning education, culture, and trade. Such relations are necessary to uphold the language guarantee, which is a Finnish commitment.

---

11 Ida Jansson, *supra* note 5.

12 According to 58 § Autonomy Act, the Åland Government shall be informed about international negotiations which concern the Åland jurisdiction. This provision is very scarcely used.

The Åland proposal also addresses the international guarantees. As the UN replaced the League of Nations, can the Åland authorities now complain to the UN? If that is possible, to which UN body should the complaint be made, beyond the human rights complaints' procedures: To the General Assembly, the Security Council, the ECOSOC, the Peacebuilding Commission or somewhere else? The proposal demands the right of appeal to an international body to be restored in accordance with the League of Nations' decision. The Åland Parliament would have the right to appeal if Finland in any way failed to comply with the guarantees. The Åland demand also includes that the Finnish Parliament should require the government to negotiate a sustainable monitoring system of the nationality guarantees.[13]

4.4 *Taxation Competence and Economic Scope for Action*

Both of the Åland committees found that the original intention of the taxation forms that were included in the Åland competence was to cover the costs of home rule. They deem it necessary, therefore, that Åland's current taxation competence be developed so that the original intention can be fulfilled.

Taxation competence is in practice closely associated with civil, labour and company law. These legal areas, together with increased taxation competence, provide the necessary prerequisites for a development of the autonomy according to the original ambition of "broadest possible home rule". It would also increase the possibility to guarantee that Swedish remains as the dominant language within the business sector.

The Åland tax jurisdiction has to some extent a foundation in international law in the Åland Agreement from 1921. According to the agreement, the Åland Islands shall have the right to 50 percent of the revenues of a then-existing land tax. When abolished in 1929, there was no substituting tax revenue awarded to the Åland Parliament.

The original tax forms existing when the autonomy was created were abolished, or their significance was reduced without being replaced in the Autonomy Act, and thus fell outside the competence of the Åland Parliament. This meant that large parts of the tax base that could provide income for the Åland administration were no longer of relevance to the Åland economy. Instead, a backup system came into place. Today, the funding of the autonomy is calculated as 0.47 percent[14] of the state budget, supplemented by the

13 This demand has been reoccurring at every revision of the Autonomy Act. In the first revision of 1951, it was suggested by the Finnish Government but diplomatically rejected by the Soviet Union as infringing on the peace treaty that ended WW2.

14 Almost corresponding to the population ratio.

possibility of extra grants under exceptional circumstances or to facilitate greater infrastructural investments.

The committees state that the original intention was that the tax forms that fell within the jurisdiction of the Åland Parliament would be sufficient to cover the costs of self-government. The Åland position is that the taxation competence should be developed to restore the original intention.

Technically, the committees believe that the area of taxes and fees should be included among the areas where legislative competence can be transferred to the region by the Åland Parliament. The procedures for transfer should consider the need for coordination with the national authorities and the extent of the consequences that the transfers entail.

However, the paramount economic issue of funding the self-government has been temporarily solved. The system based on a return of the tax income, calculated as a percentage of the state budget, prevails. The percentage was increased slightly as the population of Åland has grown since the system was established 30 years ago. The Finnish Ministry of Finance identified an urgent need to change the technical calculation of the sum received by Åland due to the budgetary solution of the comprehensive health reform in Finland, which would have seen Åland receive 40 million euros more than anticipated. This was instrumental in reaching an agreement.

4.5 *Improved Language and Nationality Guarantees*

The committees found that Finland's inability to satisfy the demands for Swedish language service is in itself a sufficient motive for increased legislative competence for Åland. The linguistic service is at the core of the international agreement concerning sovereignty over Åland and is supposed to function in all situations.

A recent study[15] has shown that the tendencies to territorial integration, which to varying degrees characterise all modern unitary state formations, will eventually erode not only the Åland nationality guarantees but also the autonomy's own scope for action. In the long run, this process can be most effectively counteracted through increased Åland competence within the legal and political areas that are central to societal development.

With reference to the results of this study, it is also recommended that the Autonomy Act is clarified regarding the protection of language so that laws, regulations, administrative authority decisions and legally binding, labour market and wage agreements only apply in Åland if they are in Swedish.

---

15 Lindström & Lindholm, *supra* note 9.

4.6 *Equal Legislative Control*

The committees suggest a more symmetrical legislative control, where the Finnish president can request an opinion from the Åland Delegation[16] concerning the compatibility of a Finnish Parliament law with the Autonomy Act.

This proposal emanates from the criticism of the legislative control's asymmetry; the Supreme Court should be tasked with checking if Finnish legislation exceeds its competence, as it already does with regard to Åland legislation. The situation has been shown to be problematic after the new Finnish Constitution came into force in 2000, and the president's power not to promulgate a law passed in the parliament was strongly limited. According to the new constitution, it is the Constitutional Committee in the Finnish Parliament that will decide if a proposed law is unconstitutional in any way, and, if so, suggest corrections before it is passed. The legal consideration in the committee, which is politically elected, will then be a legal source by which the judiciary system, including the Supreme Court, shall interpret the law. When a corresponding Åland law then comes to the Supreme Court for constitutional control, it is probable that the same legal source be applied, instead of stating that the Åland Autonomy is a *sui generis* ruling and that the purpose of home rule constitutes the primary source of law in the legislative control. This should be written into the Autonomy Act as an interpretive directive for the Supreme Court and the judiciary system in general. In this way, the Autonomy Act defining home rule would be interpreted independently, based on its own conditions and purpose, and not using the definitions and scope of corresponding Finnish material law.

4.7 *Increased Role for the Åland Delegation*

The bilaterally appointed Åland Delegation should be given a more comprehensive role, both in legislative issues and, more specifically, in the administrative conflicts that often arise due to mixed competences, thereby promoting trust between the partners in the relationship Åland-Finland.

In Åland's proposal concerning a simplified procedure for the transfer of legal areas to the autonomy (the residual principle), the Åland Delegation could give their opinion on the need for coordination between Finnish and Åland parliamentary laws, and could also suggest concrete amendments in both legislations. But also in other contexts, the presence of a balanced discriminatory body could prevent conflicts and establish long-term trust. Amongst

16 The Åland Delegation is a mediating organ between the autonomy and the state, with members appointed by each party, which i.a. is giving legal opinions on laws passed by the Lagting.

the other European autonomies, South Tyrol is a good example, with its well-functioning, bilaterally appointed, legislative commission.[17]

5 Summary

The main demands from the Åland Government, as expressed by the preparatory documents, can be summarised as follows:

- Åland society has thrived and kept its viability over a period of 100 years during some very challenging political, economic and social developments. The last decades have, though, shown a regression in the autonomy's room for manoeuvre. Looking ahead, in order to secure a sound societal development for the people of Åland in accordance with the original purpose of the autonomy, i.e., in a Swedish cultural and linguistic environment, the Autonomy Act urgently needs to be revised.
- The time is ripe to move to the next generation of autonomy that can meet the requirements of a developing society faced with issues of internationalisation and integration.
- The original right of the Åland Parliament to appeal to an international body if the guarantees are not followed should be reinforced.
- The legislative and administrative competence, especially within the economic sphere, should grow as the need for reform occurs. The transferral of competence should be executed through Åland legislation.
- The Autonomy Act needs to very clearly state the right to enact language clauses/provisions in Åland laws in accordance with the very foundation of the autonomy, thus avoiding interpretation conflicts with the Finnish Constitution.
- The strict legalistic view of the implementation of the autonomy needs to be changed to an equal partnership where distrust is replaced by trust and mutual respect, legal battle by negotiation, and control by political dialogue.

However, most of these reform proposals have been rejected by the Finnish state in the on-going political process. The path to a more fundamental renewal of the autonomy is therefore, at least in the short-term perspective, closed.

17 Markku Suksi, 'Lagstiftningskontroll och rättsskipning i autonomier – jämförande perspektiv på självstyrande områden' in 2015:1 *JFT/Tidsskrift utgiven Juridiska Föreningen i Finland* (2015); Lindström, *supra* note 7.

CHAPTER 3

The Legislative Control of Åland Laws

Göran Lindholm

1 The Åland Self-Government's Basic Purpose

The first Åland Autonomy Act was prepared in a very short space of time with the aim of guaranteeing the Åland population its Swedish language, culture and local customs under Finnish sovereignty. The law entered into force in 1921 after the League of Nations' decision to approve the nationality guarantees that Sweden and Finland agreed upon in the Åland Agreement. These guarantees under international law were confirmed in the Åland Protocol in connection with the accession of Finland and Åland to the EU.

The original purpose of the autonomy still applies today and constitutes an interpretative directive for relevant authorities, including the Finnish Supreme Court and the President of the Republic, and can be found in the preparatory works to § 1 of the present Autonomy Act: "When interpreting the basic statutes on self-government, e.g., the stipulations that intend to preserve the language and culture, the [Ålandsöverenskommelsen][1] forms the starting point."

2 An Asymmetric Legislative Control System

After a law has been passed by the Åland Parliament,[2] but before it can enter into force, it is submitted to a process of legislative control, where the main bodies are the President of Finland, the Finnish Supreme Court, the Åland Delegation[3] and the Finnish Ministry of Justice. There is no corresponding control of laws passed by the Finnish Parliament.

The primary purpose of the control is to ensure that new legislation does not infringe on the Finnish Parliament's areas of competence. In recent decades, this control of Åland laws has been extended to include the legislation's

1 Ålandsöverenskommelsen is the agreement between Sweden and Finland on the Ålanders' nationality guarantees, which the League of Nations adopted as an integral part of the sovereignty decision in 1921.

2 The Åland Lagting is the Åland Parliament.

3 See below.

DOI:10.1163/9789004691117_005

relationship to the Finnish Constitution and to EU legislation. The legislative control is also, to a certain degree, affected by considerations by the Finnish Parliament's Constitutional Committee when considering if a corresponding Finnish law is compliant to the constitution. These interpretations tend to be a source of law also in the control of Åland laws. In certain cases, the process of control has been widened from the strict examination of areas of competence to include the Åland legislation's goals and material contents. During the past two decades, this has resulted in an increase in the number of Åland laws and individual regulations that have been blocked by the legislative control with reference to EU legislation and the Finnish Constitution. In many rejected cases the legal norm is enacted technically on the wrong level. The constitution requires that all material regulations affecting human rights must be enacted by law and not by any ordinance, decision, or other lower norm.[4]

The legislative control of Finnish laws is vested with the Constitutional Committee, a political body, before they are finally passed by parliament, thus creating an asymmetrical constitutional control depending on which jurisdiction is concerned.[5] The Supreme Court, as constitutional court, is not involved in the control process of Finnish laws. The general principle of legal review, where a judicial body applying a legal norm is required to assess if it is in accordance with a legal norm of systematically higher level, applies to both Finnish and Åland laws.

3 The Legislative Control in Some Other European Autonomies

A system of legislative control similar to Åland's does not exist in most comparable European autonomies.[6] However, in the British autonomies a ratification by the head of state is required before legislation can enter into force. This is more a routine formality than a fundamental constitutional control. Regarding the Faroe Islands, South Tyrol and the Basque Country, there is no formal review prior to the entering into force of laws that the autonomous parliament

4 Ida Jansson, 2020:1 *Att sätta självstyrelsens gränser*, (Olof M Janssons Stiftelse, Mariehamn 2020) p. 178.

5 Markku Suksi, Lagstiftningskontroll och rättsskipning i autonomier – jämförande perspektiv på domstolsorganisationen i självstyrande områden, 2015:1 *Tidskrift för Juridiska Föreningen i Finland* (Åbo Akademi, 2020) pp. 27–55.

6 *Ibid.* Bjarne Lindström, 2020:2 *De legala förutsättningarna för Europas autonomier, En jämförande studie*. (Olof M Janssons stiftelse, Mariehamn 2020).

has passed. However, it is possible to submit the autonomies' legislation to a form of constitutional review in retrospect, but this is only done if a competent party has pronounced their dissatisfaction with the law. This sort of retrospective review can lead to a law being repealed.

The federal characteristics of the Belgian state formation mean that Flanders differs in this respect in relation to Åland and to other European autonomies. Belgian regulations demand a constitutional review of all legislation, both at the level of the federal state and that of the autonomous Flanders.

4 The Constitutional Control System and Its Main Actors

The President of Finland has the right to reject an Åland law within four months after it has been passed by the Parliament on two grounds; either if it isn't within the legal competence of Åland, or if it "endangers the security of the state". If a rejection is considered, the Supreme Court is required to give a legal opinion on the constitutionality of the law. The Åland Delegation submits a legal opinion on every passed law. The Finnish Ministry of Justice is responsible for the administration of the process.

The Åland Delegation shall always give its legal opinion on the constitutionality of the law in question according to the Autonomy Act. If the legislation is new, involves mixed competences, or if there are dissenting opinions in the Åland Delegation, an opinion is asked of the Supreme Court. The president usually follows the opinion of the Supreme Court but in the end, it is up to his or her own discretion.

When it comes to the second ground for rejecting a law, "endangers the security of the state", this is more of a political issue that rests with the president. This provision has been used once, concerning the flag of Åland. According to the president, the first proposals resembled the Swedish flag, and thus it was not until 1954 that the Åland Flag law was approved.

The Åland Delegation, the only body in the review process with Åland representation, is a mediatory organ between the autonomy and the state. The Finnish Government and the Åland Parliament appoint two members each. The Governor of Åland, appointed by the president in agreement with the Speaker of the Parliament, serves as the chairman. The delegation's main tasks today are to give legal opinion on every passed Åland law, adjudicate in matters of special state monetary contributions, and act as a mediator between the Helsinki and Åland administrations.

5 Development of the Control System

The practical design of the constitutional control of the Åland regional laws has undergone relatively large changes since the 1920 Autonomy Act was enacted. According to the first Autonomy Act, the Supreme Court was to give its opinion before the President of the Republic could reject an Åland law, either because it infringes on the competence of the Finnish Parliament or because the president considered the law to endanger "the public interest of the Republic". The ministry most closely involved was responsible for preparing and reporting the case to the president.

The Åland Delegation had no formal role in the process of legislative control in the first Autonomy Act. The delegation's responsibility primarily concerned the financial relations between the autonomy and the state power. The two-party Åland Delegation was nevertheless heard to varying degrees due to its generally recognized status as an expert body on Åland issues.

In practice, the first Autonomy Act gave the Supreme Court interpretative priority regarding the concrete delimitation of the autonomy's legal – and thus also, by extension of this practice, political – authority in relation to the prevailing Autonomy Act. The praxis of the Supreme Court was more or less directly codified into the enumeration lists of legislative competence in the 1951 Act, and prevail in the present Autonomy Act.

The Supreme Court's role has not changed in the following two autonomy acts. In practice, however, the opinion of the Supreme Court is only requested in some cases, mainly if the Åland Delegation considers a law to be problematic, if the Åland Delegation's decision is not unanimous, or if the Ministry of Justice otherwise considers that the Supreme Court needs to be involved in the control.

As the structure of the distribution of legislative authority was changed in the Autonomy Act of 1951 to an enumeration of the respective legislature's authority, the law reviewers' criteria for the constitutional control were also changed. The main issue requiring assessment was whether an Åland law belongs to a legal area that falls under the competence of the Finnish Parliament or of the Åland Parliament, though completely new legal areas would be assessed according to the basic principles in the respective catalogue of competences.

According to the 1951 Autonomy Act, the president could also veto a law affecting Finland's "internal or external security", replacing the previous wording "endangers the security of the state". This acted as a kind of safety valve if an Åland law endangered vital state interests.

In the Autonomy Act of 1991, the structure was maintained with an enumeration of the competences of the respective parliaments. The major change in the law review process was the possibility for the president to disapprove only a limited part (paragraph, section) of the Åland law in question. In 2004, the Autonomy Act was also amended so that budget laws can now enter into force immediately, and the control of them is exercised after their entry into force. The 1991 Autonomy Act added to and clarified the competence lists somewhat, and a few areas were added to the Åland list. Maybe, the most important clarification was that the Autonomy Act expressly requires that an individual should have knowledge of the Swedish language in order to acquire Åland *hembygdsrätt*.[7] The new Finnish Constitution (year 2000) has, however, indirectly affected the work of the relevant audit bodies.

As of Finland's and Åland's entry to the EU, the legislative control was extended to include an examination of whether an Åland law potentially conflicts with EU legislation. Since the Åland Delegation was not considered to have the necessary EU competence, the delegation requests as a rule an opinion from the EU-unit at the Ministry of Justice before delivering their opinion.

6 Strict Interpretation Practice

The legislative control by the Supreme Court and the president during the first decades of autonomy was characterised by a clear focus on ensuring that the Åland legislation would in no way infringe on the Finnish Parliament's areas of authority. This was achieved not least through a relatively restrictive interpretation of the many still relatively open, and therefore also "interpretable", provisions in the first Autonomy Act.

During the lifetime of the second Autonomy Act, a total of 1,445 Åland laws were processed by the president, of which 74 (5 percent) were rejected. This is a considerably lower percentage of failed laws than during the first Autonomy Act, when almost a fifth of the autonomy's laws were rejected by the president.[8] The significantly improved approval frequency indicates that the interpretation of authority and legal control under the second Autonomy Act has been stabilised because of the practice developed during the considerably more turbulent period of the first Autonomy Act. The introduction of

7 Åland citizenship, which on top of Finnish citizenship enables the bearer to vote, own real estate, and to run a business. Autonomy Act (ÅFS 1144/1991).

8 During Autonomy Act (AA) 1, between 1922–1951, SUPREME COURT (SC) rejected 21.5 percent of Åland laws, during AA 2, 1952–1991, SC rejected 6 percent, and during the present AA 3, 1992–2018, SC rejected 5.1 percent. Ida Jansson, 2020:1 *Att sätta självstyrelsens gränser*, (Olof M Janssons Stiftelse, Mariehamn 2020).

an Åland and Finland "competence catalogue" probably made the legislative process easier for the legislators as well as for the legislative control.

The Supreme Court has set a steady interpretation practice, and the Åland Delegation very seldom challenges its opinions. In some principal matters, such as taxation rights, individual members have submitted dissenting opinion but generally the Åland Delegation toes the line. This has led to a greater stability and predictability in the Åland legislative process, albeit with a reduced level of the factual self-government than was originally intended.

The Supreme Court's own view of the control shows a continuation of the strict lexical interpretation under current law: "an objective interpretation of the law and thus of the fact that the autonomy's concrete content at any time corresponds to the law".[9] The Supreme Court apparently refers to the legislator to clarify the wordings in the Autonomy Act that a literal exemption from the provisions in the Finnish Constitution exists in order to support an interpretation based on the purpose of the autonomy.

In summary, it can be stated that the restrictive interpretation of authority that the Supreme Court and the president introduced during the 1920s and 1930s was formalised and consolidated in the second and the present autonomy acts. The Supreme Court has in all important respects been allowed to keep a restrictive view of the legal limits of the autonomy.

7 EU Membership and a New Finnish Constitution

Åland's and Finland's EU membership has provided a new reason for rejection. This has resulted in the rejection of several Åland laws that, contrary to the view of the Åland Parliament, were in (obvious) conflict with EU legislation and, therefore, fell outside the autonomy's legislative authority. This practice is questionable from the Åland point of view as it is up to the European Court of Justice to deem if a national law is compatible with Union legislation or not.[10]

A significant reason for the rejection of these laws is the strengthened role that the Finnish Parliament's Constitutional Committee received in the new Finnish Constitution. The committee is expressly responsible for considering if a proposed bill (from the Finnish Government) is in accordance with the constitution. These considerations have become a legal source for the judiciary system. The fact that the Supreme Court has adopted a relatively broad interpretation of the constitution's limiting effects on similar Finnish laws has

9 *Ibid.* p. 178.

10 The process of control with regard to EU legislation has been included by the Supreme Court, rather than it being based on regulations in the Autonomy Act.

generally allowed the new constitution to take precedence over the Autonomy Act and has thus led to the rejection of several Åland laws. It would seem as if an express exemption is required in order to give the Autonomy Act precedence.

As mentioned, more than half of the passed laws, 31 in total, during the present Autonomy Act have been rejected with reference to the Finnish Constitution, in some cases also in combination with other reasons. This can be compared to a total of two rejected laws with the same reasoning during the first Autonomy Act, and three during the second.[11]

Otherwise, the total number of rejections has decreased over the years, from one fifth during the first Autonomy Act to 5–6 percent during the second and the present acts. This is a sharp reduction in both number and proportion, which indicates that the division into jurisdictional areas in the present Autonomy Act has been easier to interpret for the Åland Parliament. It is also possible that the development of technology has made it easier for the legislative process to stay up to date on changes in Finnish legislation, which must be considered when drafting Åland laws, as such changes have a great impact on the constitutional control.

Here, however, is also a very interesting case on the Law on order for the Åland Parliament from 2011, where the Parliament's proposal to adopt a statute citing the bill to the first Autonomy Act "The population organises its existence according to its own wishes and as freely as possible for a province that does not constitute its own state" – a clear marking of the Supreme Court's role as guardian of the "critical" borders for the Åland's autonomy.[12]

The previously dominant reasons for rejection, "provisions of a national legislative nature that deviate from the national legislation" and "infringement on the national area of competence", now only account for a quarter of all rejections.

Finally, it is worth mentioning that no law has been rejected with reference to the internal or external security of Finland during the present Autonomy Act, and that the president has gone against the Supreme Court's statement in only a single case.

8 Consequences of the New Finnish Constitution

The new constitution has influenced the process of legislative review to a much greater degree than the old one. Of particular interest is the catalogue

---

11 *Supra* note 8.

12 RP 24/1919; Tulenheimokommittén (1919), Förarbetena till 1920 och 1951 års självstyrelselagar Del II. Opublicerad stencil utgiven av Ålands landskapsarkiv, s 1.

of rights that was already included in 1995 as a result of Finland's ratification of the European Convention, but also other parts. Over half of the Åland laws passed between 1993 and 2018 have been rejected with reference to the Finnish Constitution.

This interpretative practice has restricted the ability of the Åland Parliament to develop its own jurisdiction under the authority given in the Autonomy Act. Legal definitions, concepts to regulate certain phenomena in society, and other legal "inventions" are rejected in most cases. This is done without regard to the fact that the Autonomy Act and the Finnish Constitution are systematically on the same level, and one would think it would be up to the Parliament to freely formulate the underlying level of legislation, i.e., the material law. Inter alia, the provision of "standardisation", which belongs to Finnish competence, is frequently used as grounds for rejection, also impinging on areas otherwise belonging to the Parliament.

Most people seem to agree that the self-government should not infringe too much on the individual's rights and freedoms as defined in the Finnish Constitution. Legislative control thus fulfils an important function from that point of view. But the constitution also contains a number of other provisions, and there may be reason to consider whether there are parts of the constitution that expressly should not apply to the Autonomy Act.

The most obvious case in this regard is the question of the voting age in 2017.[13] The Åland Parliament wanted to lower the voting age and thus expand the group entitled to vote. It was therefore not about limiting the rights protected by the constitution, but, on the contrary, about expanding them. The Supreme Court interpreted the right to vote as a fundamental right, thus under Finnish authority, and that the Åland Parliament had no right to deviate to 16 years. In contrast, the Parliament considered the provision in the Autonomy Act, stating that election to the Parliament and municipality councils is under Åland competence, which also includes the voting age.[14]

Another noteworthy case concerns the law on the right to run a business on Åland.[15] The Autonomy Act requires that an individual or member of the board has Åland citizenship or has been domiciled in Åland for five years. In connection with a reform of the business law, the Åland Parliament expressly stated that all services and information to consumers must be in Swedish. The Supreme Court rejected the law, referring to the individual's fundamental rights as belonging to Finnish authority, but not considering the very fundamentals

13 Ida Jansson, 2020:1 *Att sätta självstyrelsens gränser*, (Olof M Janssons Stiftelse, Mariehamn 2020) pp. 137–138.

14 Ålandsdelegationen, XIII Serien, pp. 311–313.

15 KKO-HD/1919/2022.

of the autonomy as decided in Geneva in 1921 and reiterated in 1994 in the accession protocol to the EU.

This updated law was passed by the Åland Parliament 25 April 2022. The purpose, as described in the preparatory works, was to make it easier to establish a business, to make the monitoring of newly established businesses more effective, and to codify established practice for 30 years. Moreover, the Parliament aspired to adjust the business law to suit the new Finnish Constitution and the Constitutional Committee's interpretation of the same, i.e. that any restrictions on individual's freedom of movement and freedom of business must be written into law.

The updated language requirements were central to the law reform against the background of the strict interpretation praxis of the legislative control. The Parliament refers to the basic provisions to guarantee the Swedish language, culture, and local customs of the Åland population, which can be found in the Geneva Decision of 1921, the Åland Agreement of 1921 and the Åland Protocol of 1994 to the Finnish accession treaty to the EU. The latter stipulates that the (nationality protection) provisions guaranteed by international law form part of the primary EU law and are not affected by Union legislation.

However, the president decided that certain provisions of the law would not come into force, mainly the updated language requirements. In its statement, the Supreme Court rejected the Business Law Act with reference to, among other things, the fact that the following provisions "are in manifest conflict with Union law", namely: that everyone has the right to be served in Swedish, and that essential and necessary information about goods or services must be in Swedish. According to the Supreme Court, the provisions constitute an extension of the language regulations that applied at the time of EU entry and are thus in violation of the "stand still" principle within Union law. The Supreme Court therefore considered that the Åland law constituted a form of "breach of treaty" in relation to the Union law. According to the Supreme Court's practice, a breach of treaty applies to the "relationship with foreign powers" (here interpreted as the EU) and is thus under Finnish jurisdiction according to § 27 subsection 2. Self-Government Act.

9 Conclusion

The strong constitutional and international "fortification" of the Åland autonomy is two-fold. On the one hand, the strict legal tradition protects the rights of the people of Åland, and on the other hand, it tends to obstruct, through the process of constitutional control, the necessary development of the autonomy. A negative political attitude to the Swedish language in general, and especially to unilingual Åland in the Finnish Parliament, cannot change the Autonomy Act without the consent of the Åland Parliament.

The constitutional control system is reliable and predictable but cannot easily adjust to changes in local or international society. To enable this, the Autonomy Act must be revised by mutually equal decisions in the Finnish and Åland parliaments. As a constitutional law in Finland, any revision to the Autonomy Act requires a qualified majority in two consecutive parliaments, with an election in between. A qualified majority in the Åland Parliament consenting to the revised Autonomy Act is also needed. It goes without saying that this is a long and complicated process, with many years of preparatory work before a bill can be presented to the parliaments by the Finnish Government. In addition, the process is vulnerable to possible changes in the political landscape.

Moreover, many experts underline the fact that the Åland people enjoy strong legal protection for their Swedish language, culture, and local traditions. However, as we have seen, the material application/protection laws, based on decisions that are more than 100 years old, have been questioned as not compliant with today's human rights. So far, they have prevailed but any attempt to update the material legislation has been rejected in the constitutional control, as such changes must be realised in the Autonomy Act.

Another problem is the limited legal authority of the autonomy. Thus, important legislative areas, such as company law, banking, and insurance legislation, contract and labour market legislation, regulations governing technical standards, professional certification, the judiciary system and, to a greater degree, taxation, are vested with the state. The catalogue of legislative competence vested with the Åland Parliament is quite limited, as the restrictive practice in the constitutional system has been codified in the two revisions of the Autonomy Act and has increased since the new Finnish Constitution came into force.

The number of rejections of Åland laws will most likely decrease as the controlling bodies and the law-drafting unit of the Åland Government adjust to the current restrictive practice of the Supreme Court. A further consequence of this development, which has been more apparent during the last twenty years, is the adjustment of Åland laws to the corresponding Finnish material laws. So, although Åland has the power to enact legislation customised to its own needs and circumstances, the Åland Government chooses to compromise in order to minimise upcoming problems in the constitutional control. Only seldomly does the law-drafting unit challenge the existent practice, and more frequently uses 'form legislation', i.e., when a Finnish law is more or less copied and passed as an Åland law. In this way, interpretation problems with regard to split legislative competence and the mixed interaction between two jurisdictions, can be avoided.

Åland's autonomy thus delivers less *de facto* scope for action than what it *de jure* promises. This is underlined by the fact that Åland is dependent on the Finnish Government's and the Finnish Parliament's priorities in revising or amending the current Autonomy Act; on the Finnish state's desire and ability to provide information about state legislation that is of great importance to Åland; on the Finnish state's handling of Åland's wishes in the implementation of EU legislation and in the preparation of Finland's EU positions, and in treaty negotiations where Åland legislative competence is involved.

The overall conclusion is therefore that the autonomy's greatest structural failing is its lack of competence within several legal and political areas important for societal development; and not least the regulation of the more fundamental conditions for economy, trade and labour markets that are so central for societal development. Åland's limited legal competence and scope for action within these political areas also, in the long run, undermines what has always been seen as the core of the Åland autonomy model, i.e., the protection of the archipelago's Swedish culture and linguistic identity.

The overall picture of the autonomy's status that has emerged during the last 100 years clarifies the need to move the focal point of the autonomy from reactionary monitoring of the *status quo* to a more proactively aligned expansion of Åland's legal and political scope for action – a development toward the type of autonomy models seen in several comparable autonomies with significantly broader legal and political competence.

The asymmetrical partnership, with its one-sided competence control that is based on the state's priorities and needs, must be replaced with a more equal partnership between autonomy and state. This is difficult to achieve within the framework of the current Autonomy Act and the practice that has been created by the Åland autonomy model.

However, this does not mean that there is no room for improvement, e.g., concerning the exchange of information and engagement from both parties in a more active partnership.

CHAPTER 4

Legislative Competence in Matters Not Mentioned in Enumerations

Markku Suksi

1 Introduction

According to Section 17 of the 1991 Self-Government Act for the Åland Islands Act (1144/1991; hereinafter: the SGA), the Legislative Assembly of the Åland Islands enacts acts for the Åland Islands, so-called Ålandic Acts. It is this legislative power that is referred to in Section 75(2) of the Constitution of Finland (731/1999). Section 18 of the SGA specifies the areas of law in which the Åland Islands has legislative competence. The provision contains an enumeration of competences to the extent that the Legislative Assembly has the right to exercise legislative power regarding the territory of the Åland Islands according to the legislative procedure established in the SGA and in norms of the Åland Islands. This enumeration of competence delimits Åland's legislative power on the territory of Åland in relation to the legislative power exercised by the Parliament of Finland in view of the same territory. Therefore, the corresponding provisions on the legislative competence of the Parliament with regard to the Åland Islands are included in Section 27 of the Autonomy Act in the form of a list. Within the legislative competence of the Parliament, legal norms are enacted in the manner prescribed by the Constitution. [1]

The distribution of legislative powers between the Legislative Assembly and the Parliament is based on an enumeration of both legislative competences so that they are, in principle, exclusive in relation to each other. In areas where the Legislative Assembly is competent, the Parliament does not have legislative power, and in areas where the Parliament is competent, the Legislative Assembly does not have legislative power. The legislative competences are thus exclusive in relation to each other. This strict distribution of legislative competences can be described as watertight compartments between the legislative competences of the Legislative Assembly and the Parliament that

1 This article is based on Markku Suksi, 'Självstyrelselagens generalklausuler om fördelning av lagstiftningsmakt mellan Ålands lagting och riksdagen', 158:5–6 *Tidskrift utgiven av Juridiska Föreningen i Finland* (JFT) (2022) pp. 558–586.

 | DOI:10.1163/9789004691117_006

do not allow overlaps in such a way that both legislative bodies would have legislative power simultaneously over the same matter in the territory of the Åland Islands. A matter that is the subject of legislative measures belongs, with regard to the exercise of legislative power within Åland's borders, either to the legislative competence of the Legislative Assembly or of the Parliament. This also applies to those materially uniform areas where legislative power is in part held by the Legislative Assembly and in part by the Parliament.[2]

The starting point for this distribution of legislative power in the Åland Islands is the two lists or enumerations of legislative powers included in Sections 18 and 27 of the SGA. Section 18 lists the powers of the Legislative Assembly and Section 27 of the Parliament, the latter supplemented by a specification in Section 29 concerning competences that the Parliament may, by ordinary law and with the consent of the Legislative Assembly, transfer in whole or in part to the Legislative Assembly. The enumerations of both legislative competences consist of detailed listings of legislative matters.[3] However, at the end of the lists in both Sections, 18 and 27, there is a similarly worded provision which aims to allocate to either legislative competence those legislative matters which do not fall within the specific points of the lists. Section 18(27) of the SGA refers to 'other matters which, according to the principles of this Act, shall fall within the legislative competence of the *Legislative Assembly*', while Section 27(42) of the Act refers to 'other matters which, according to the principles of this Act, shall fall within the legislative competence of the *Parliament*'.[4]

The starting point is therefore that matters which are the subject of legislative measures and which are not mentioned among the listed legislative competences can be assigned either to the Legislative Assembly or to the Parliament on the basis of these two general clauses. Thus, additional legislative matters and perhaps also legislative areas can be added by interpretation to the explicit legislative powers listed in the two provisions. In such situations, it is either

2 However, legislative competence between the Legislative Assembly and the Parliament is never divided in the way competence is divided between the European Union and a Member State, where both can have competence over the same matter and the Member State can legislate as long as the EU has not used its competence. From the point of view of EU law, the Legislative Assembly is part of the legislative power of the Member State of Finland.

3 For the enumerations, please see the Self-Government Act for Åland in English, <finlex.fi/sv/laki/kaannokset/1991/en19911144_20200098.pdf>, visited on 18 July 2023.

4 The Swedish-language authentic version of Section 18(27) refers to "landskapet", that is, the region or province, and Section 27(42) to "riket", that is, the realm. To avoid confusion, in this article, the Ålandic law-making powers in Section 18(27) of the SGA are referred to as those of the *Legislative Assembly* of the Åland Islands, while the national law-making powers in Section 27(42) are referred to as those of the *Parliament* of Finland.

the Legislative Assembly or the Parliament that makes the law. However, the SGA's system of *ex-post* verification of legislative competence before the entry into force of an Ålandic Act requires, as far as the Legislative Assembly is concerned, that the legislature has first made a decision on the approval of the Ålandic Act, which decision then becomes subjected to the examination of competence, ultimately at the Supreme Court (hereinafter: the SC). For the Parliament, the system is not as clear but dependent on coincidences.

What is the system of general clauses or open points of jurisdiction based on, and why have these clauses been included in the SGA in terms of legal history? How have the SC's interpretations developed in the opinions on the last item of each of the list of competences, i.e., how do the principles determine where, for example, a new area of law belongs? How has this system of general clauses worked over the last three decades? Our examination concerns the development of the system of self-government from 1920 to the present day, but the examination of practice is limited mainly to those interpretations of the general clauses given during the period when the enumerations of powers of the current SGA indicated what might be beyond the explicit legislative powers of each of the legislative bodies. The review does not cover the interpretative practice that has arisen within the Åland Delegation,[5] nor the interpretation practices that the courts may have developed when deciding concrete cases concerning the general clauses. It is possible and even probable that such instances of interpretative practice exist, but they may be examined in some other context.

2 In the Beginning: a Different System for Distribution of Competences

Åland's legislative competence has changed during the existence of the autonomy arrangement, and the angle has shifted considerably, especially with regard to the transition from the 1920 SGA to the 1951 SGA. According to the 1920 SGA, the distribution of legislative powers was structured in such a way that Section 9 of the 1920 SGA listed the powers of the Parliament. These included

5 However, it is very likely that the Åland Delegation, an adjudication body with representatives of the Åland Islands and the State of Finland, has adopted positions on the general clauses and on the allocation of legislative powers on the basis of them. *See*, for example, Statement No 31/12 of the Åland Delegation of 29 October 2012 (equal treatment falls within the competence of both the Legislative Assembly and the and the Parliament) and Statement No 3/22 of the Åland Delegation of 28 January 2022 (domain name belongs to the jurisdiction of the Parliament).

constitutional matters, matters requiring Parliament's assent and legislation of a general nature and the issuing of decrees referred to in Section 9(2). The subject areas listed, including the subject matter governed by international treaties and subject matter 'which has not hitherto been required by law'. On the other hand, Åland's legislative competence was not listed, but the Legislative Assembly would have the right, by virtue of Section 12(1) of the SGA, to adopt Ålandic laws in matters other than those that fell within the competence of the Parliament under Section 9 of the SGA. The legislative competence of the Parliament was thus primarily of an enumerated nature, while the legislative competence of the Åland Islands was of a residual nature. Moreover, the two legislative powers were intended to be mutually exclusive in such a way that a new law which had entered into force in mainland Finland would not apply to the Åland Islands until it had been adopted by the Legislative Assembly, or else that the Legislative Assembly would be competent to adopt, in these matters, laws intended for the Åland Islands.[6]

Thus, the system of self-government was originally formulated in a way that characterizes most federations: the federal level has enumerated legislative powers, while the competences of the states are residual. This is the case, for example, in the USA and the Federal Republic of Germany. The original structure of legislative competence thus constituted the basic starting point for the development of competence: enumeration for the Parliament and residual powers for the Legislative Assembly.[7] It would appear that this starting point gave Åland a very strong position in the legislative work and that it contained a great promise in principle with regard to the possibilities of drafting its own legislation.[8]

---

6 Committee report No 24/1919 to the Government from the Committee on the Drafting of Proposals for County Self-Government, Administrative Courts of Lower Instance, and re-districting of current counties and administration, p. 21.

7 *See* Markku Suksi, *Sub-State Governance through Territorial Autonomy* (Springer Verlag, Heidelberg, 2011) pp. 125–132.

8 Esko Hakkila, *Suomen tasavallan perustuslait sekä eräitä niihin liittyviä lakeja, asetuksia ja säännöstöjä* (Werner Söderström Osakeyhtiö, Helsinki, 1939) p. 691 *et seq.*, states that the area of Åland's legislative competence under the 1920 SGA was so extensive that the League of Nations did not consider it necessary to extend the competence. According to Rafael Erich, *Suomen valtio-oikeus, II osa* (Werner Söderström Osakeyhtiö, Helsinki, 1925) pp. 369, 376–382, Åland's legislative competence was extensive and clearly exclusive in relation to the legislative competence of the Parliament and that a national act in no case would be in a hierarchically superior position in relation to Ålandic law. According to Antero Jyränki, 'Autonomy of the Åland Islands: A Federal Element in the Constitution of a Unitary State?' in Kirsi Pohjolainen (ed.), *Constitutionalism in Finland – Reality and Perspectives* (Finnish Society of Constitutional Law, Helsinki, 1995) p. 13, however, during the 1920s and 1930s there was a lack of clarity about the relationship between national and Ålandic laws: it had been

It should be noted, however, that paragraphs 12 and 13 of Section 9(2) of the 1920 SGA can be considered to have imposed severe restrictions on the Åland legislature with regard to the freedom to make use of this fundamental point of departure. Paragraph 12 referred to the Parliament's competence areas regulated by international treaties, something that in today's situation with an increasingly internationalized normative environment could have seriously threatened Åland's own legislative competence and transferred Åland's legislative power to the Parliament.[9] Paragraph 13 included in the legislative competence of the Parliament those areas which, at the time of the creation of the 1920 SGA, had not yet been the subject of legislative measures. This, in turn, had affected large parts of such modern activities that emerged much later and would have placed the regulation of these activities automatically within the competence of the Parliament.[10]

In retrospect, it can be stated that Åland's legislative competence would have been severely curtailed and subjected to a continuous leakage of powers in the direction of the Parliament, if this principle of the distribution of competences had applied until today. The area of Åland's legislative competence would have been considerably narrower and the legislative competence of the Parliament much more extensive than they currently are under the 1991 SGA. In addition, the original distribution of competences was perceived as problematic, because it was not considered to have been established with the necessary clarity, and measures were proposed by the Åland Islands in this regard.[11]

---

possible to consider that a national enactment would, in the event of a conflict of jurisdiction, take precedence over Ålandic law. *See* for example Hakkila, *supra* note 8, pp. 682, 690. However, this ambiguity has since been dispelled.

9 According to Arthur Tollet & John Uggla, *Lagstiftningen angående självstyrelse för Åland, jämte tillhörande författningar* (Holger Schildts förlag, Helsingfors, 1930) p. 70, paragraph 9(2)(12) of the SGA was adopted to avoid such misconception that treaties with a foreign power, when they relate to the legal provisions of national law, would require the consent of the Legislative Assembly. However, such an assent procedure was later introduced and is now part of Section 59 of the SGA, where it protects the Legislative Assembly's competence.

10 However, a mitigating interpretation of Section 9(2)(13) of the 1920 SGA is included in Tollet & Uggla, *supra* note 9, p. 71, where it is stated that the provision does not have such a broad meaning that any new question of law that arises or any development or extension of existing legal standards would be excluded from the competence of the Legislative Assembly. However, according to Hakkila, *supra* note 8, p. 692, the idea of 'new question of law' expresses the primary nature of national competence and the secondary nature of Ålandic jurisdiction.

11 *See* 'Committee report on the revision of the autonomy legislation for Åland 1946' (von Hellén-Committee Report), p. 252 (in *Preparatory work for the 1920 and 1951 Autonomy Acts for the Åland Islands*, Part III, Alandica Saml.).

3 Transition to Double Enumeration

The original starting point for the distribution of competences underwent an important change in connection with the reform of the autonomy legislation initiated by Government Bill RP 38/1948 rd. Instead of enumeration for the Parliament and residual competences for the Legislative Assembly, enumerated competences were now proposed for both the Parliament and the Legislative Assembly. However, both proposed lists of competencies were concluded in the bill with a reference to a residual category of affairs. As far as the Parliament is concerned, these were matters referred to in Section 11(2) of the 1951 Self-Government Act (670/1951). Paragraph 20 referred to matters which fell within 'areas hitherto not provided for by legislation and which, by virtue of the principles contained in this Section, fall within the legislative competence of the Parliament'. As far as Åland is concerned, these matters were defined in Section 13(1) of the 1951 SGA. Paragraph 21 refers to 'other matters which have not been reserved to the legislation of the Parliament and which, by virtue of the principles contained in this Section, fall within the legislative competence of the Legislative Assembly'. The content of the residual category would therefore be interpreted from the point of view of some kind of principle of reciprocity, but it should be noted that the two provisions on the residual category were not entirely symmetrical.

Although the 1951 SGA introduced a detailed enumeration of the competences of both legislatures, the assumption nonetheless was that in spite of this detail, 'numerous difficulties of interpretation caused by the general wording of the provisions in force' could already be foreseen. Thus, even a move towards enumerating the competences of both legislatures might 'lead to new differences of interpretation'.[12]

This fundamentally important change gave the distribution of competences between the Parliament and the Legislative Assembly a similar structure as applies in Canada through provisions in Articles 91 and 92 respectively in Canada's Constitution Act of 1867. Despite the fact that Canada is usually classified among federations, one can thus discern a similar exclusive idea of double enumeration as for Åland since 1951.[13] However, it is not clear from the

12 Statement of the Constitutional Committee of the Parliament GrUB 36/1950, p. 5.

13 Double enumeration also occurs in Denmark with respect to the Faroe Islands with the support of 1948 *Hjemmestyreloven* (the Home Rule Act) in combination with the determination of a minimum of the legislative power of the Danish Parliament and the right of transfer which the Faroese Legislative Assembly has by virtue of the so-called Transfer Act of 2005. *See* Markku Suksi, *Double Enumeration of Legislative Powers in a Sub-state Context – A Comparison between Canada, Denmark and Finland* (Springer,

legislative history of the 1951 SGA that the Canadian model was presented to the Parliament when the double enumeration solution was introduced.[14]

The preparatory work carried out in the 1980s with the aim of producing a new Self-Government Act for Åland was intended to extend the legislative competence of the Legislative Assembly. Although a gradual increase in Åland's legislative competence can be discerned since 1920, one of the intentions of the drafting was to further increase Åland's competence to enact Ålandic Acts. It was therefore proposed that legislative powers should be transferred as far as possible "to the Legislative Assembly in all areas which have a significant connection with autonomy and where reasons of expediency justify such regulation". New or extended powers for Åland were therefore proposed with regard to the use of the flag of Åland, rent and rent control, antiquities, social welfare, the serving of alcoholic beverages, the archives, the postal service, radio and television, and provisions of criminal law. In addition, the bill included a proposal for the flexible transfer of competence from the Parliament to the Legislative Assembly in the fields of population registration, registration of trade, associations and ships, work-related pension and other social insurance, some areas of alcohol legislation, banking and credits, employment contracts and cooperation within companies. At the same time, a transfer in the opposite

Heidelberg, 2018) pp. 13–15. In addition, double enumeration occurs in France with respect to New Caledonia. *See* Markku Suksi, 'Self-Determination through Autonomy or Independence? – On the Current and Future Position of New Caledonia', in 15 *Vienna Journal on International Constitutional Law* (2021) pp. 67–105.

14 A reference to Canada can be found in the committee report Kom.bet. 24/1919, p. 16, so it is conceivable that the Canadian double enumeration was known for the drafters at the time of the enactment of the first SGA in 1920. The preamble of Article 91 of the Canadian Constitution creates a relatively well-defined right for the Federation to legislate for "peace, order and good governance" in Canada that may apply to new areas of legislation. However, it has been used to fill gaps that have arisen between explicit federal legislative powers and, in particular, for legislation on war measures during the two World Wars. However, Canada's Supreme Court has rejected several of the attempts made by the Federation to use this provision. As far as the provinces are concerned, there is a provision in Article 92(16) which similarly confers on the provinces legislative competence in respect of "generally all matters of a purely local or private nature in the province". Thus, the Canadian version of double enumeration provides some scope for developing legislation outside the two enumerations, but the two enumerations clearly show exclusivity in relation to each other, even though the Supreme Court's interpretations have in some respects softened the edges of the jurisdictional divisions. At the same time, it should be noted that the Canadian residual categories are not formulated in a symmetrical way but show an asymmetry between the federation and the provinces. On the interpretation of these two provisions, *see* Suksi, *supra* note 13, pp. 81–85, 104.

direction was also proposed, as competence under employment contract legislation would be transferred to Parliament.[15]

The basis for the distribution of competences in the 1991 SGA remained the same as in the previous SGA, i.e., the distribution of competences is based on the enumeration of the competences of both legislative bodies and contains a general clause at the end of each of the lists of competences, allowing a certain development of competences within each competence area. The general clauses may be construed as references to implied powers of some kind accorded by legislation to both legislative bodies. The content of these powers depends on interpretation in the context of the relevant jurisdiction. The difference between the residual provisions of the 1951 SGA and the 1991 SGA is that the general clauses of the 1991 SGA are symmetrical for both legislators by using the same wording.

According to the legislative history of the 1991 SGA, the enumerations in Sections 18 and 27 are intended to specify which matters fall within the competence of the Legislative Assembly, on the one hand, and which ones fall within the competence of the Parliament, on the other. In addition, however, it is stated that 'not all areas of law have been indicated, nor can they be listed'. This is a recognition that enumerations of this kind cannot be made completely comprehensive for all conceivable situations. Therefore, the bill goes on to state that 'the proposal also contains general clauses, which are decisive for legislative competence, inter alia, for new areas of law'.[16]

According to the proposal for the 1991 SGA, areas of law not specifically mentioned in Sections 18 and 27 must be assessed in terms of competence on the basis of the principles followed in the Act as a whole, which means that it is not only the basic principles set out in the two enumerations that should be taken into account in the interpretation, but the whole of the SGA. This general framework based on the SGA could therefore be attributed, for example, to the provisions on the right of domicile in Sections 6 to 8, the right of trade in Section 11 and possibly also land acquisition on the basis of Section 10 of the SGA.[17]

In the preparation of new autonomy legislation to replace the 1991 SGA, certain characteristics of the general clauses of the current SGA have been put forward. According to the Åland Committee's 2013 final report, new areas of law,

15 Government Bill on the SGA, RP 73/1990 rd, p. 6.

16 RP 73/1990 rd., *supra* note 17, pp. 42, 63, 69, 73, 78. As stated on p. 41, one reason for the renewal of the distribution of competences was the uncertainty about the extent of jurisdiction caused by divided areas of law.

17 RP 73/1990 rd., *supra* note 17, p. 79.

when they arise, belong to either the Legislative Assembly's or the Parliament's area of competence. The basic principle of the 1991 SGA would thus be followed regarding how a new area is to be assessed in terms of competence is that it is to be attributed to the area to which it has the strongest links. None of the lists in Section 18 of the current Act on the competence of the Legislative Assembly and Section 27 on the competence of Parliament have more weight than the other in the assessment. This is a principal statement on the general clauses which is in many ways corroborated by the more detailed review of the various relevant opinions below.[18]

4 Interpretations of the Current General Clauses

Although the general clause is worded symmetrically for both legislators, the procedure for interpreting the content of the two provisions is asymmetrical. The general clause linked to the legislative competence of the Legislative Assembly is interpreted by the SC, while it is in principle the Constitutional Law Committee of the Parliament that could give an opinion on the interpretation of the general clause linked to the legislative competence of the Parliament with regard to the Åland Islands' area. The Constitutional Law Committee sometimes expresses an opinion on the relationship between national legislation and Åland's legislative competence, but it is not systematically examining the legislative competence of the Parliament under the SGA. An assessment of the legislative competence of the Parliament is usually given in relation to the explicit legislative competences.

It is not known to the author that the Constitutional Law Committee would have tested the Parliament's legislative power to any great extent in relation to the general clauses in Section 18(27) of the SGA in relation to the legislative competence of the Legislative Assembly, or Section 27(42), which concerns the legislative competence of the Parliament. An educated guess in this context is that such assessments are fairly rare, but at least one case, the Lotteries Act, exists. On the other hand, there are some interpretations concerning the legislative competence of the Legislative Assembly under Section 18(27) of the SGA and the legislative competence of the Parliament under Section 27(42) given by the SC in the context of the review of jurisdiction concerning Ålandic laws.

18 Ålands självstyrelse i utveckling – Ålandskommitténs 2013 slutbetänkande. Justitieministeriet, Betänkanden och utlåtanden 14/2018 (Justitieministeriet, Helsingfors, 2018) p. 153.

The SC's interpretations regarding Åland's general clause contain the referendum on EU accession (Opinion of 9 September 1994), the creation of indirect public administration (Opinion of 19 December 1996), emissions excess charge (Opinion of 29 June 2005), independent auditing office under the Legislative Assembly (Opinion of 15 February 2013), application of national statutes on data protection to Åland (Opinion of 1 August 2019), application of national non-discrimination legislation in the Åland Islands, with some modifications (Opinion of 16 September 2020), and legislation on the openness of official activities in the Åland Islands (Opinion of 1 June 2021).

Interpretations of the SC and the Constitutional Law Committee regarding the general clause of the Parliament include fewer examples, namely genetically modified organisms (Opinion of 21 March 1996; hereinafter GMO), lottery legislation (Constitutional Law Committee, Statement GrUU 22/2001 rd, and Statement of the SC in HD 2001:79) and criminal provisions on drunkenness at sea (Opinion of 25 February 2003).

Based on the SC's Statement HD 2001:79 regarding the Lotteries Act, it is possible to ask what a new area of legislation is, what is meant by the object of regulation and classification of objects in the regulation and what constitutes a whole of cases with regard to something falling within either the competence of the Legislative Assembly or the Parliament. A first step in the application of the general clause is a review of the subject matter of the proposed legislation against the existing competences in either list of competences. If no basis is found in either list of competences by which the subject matter of the legislation can be linked to a substantive basis of competence, a second step consists of an examination of whether the proposed legislation could be classified as belonging to the competence of the Legislative Assembly or the Parliament in view of the subject matter of the regulation. If the classification of objects suggests a connection to one of the areas of competence, the third step is a reasoned finding that the subject matter of the legislation belongs to one of the two areas of competence, that of the Legislative Assembly or the Parliament.

Since, roughly speaking, the material competences of the Legislative Assembly largely concern areas of public law, while the substantive competences of the Parliament are to a greater extent of a private law nature, it is generally conceivable that the regulation of vertical legal relationships, i.e. those concerning the relationship between authority and private individuals, may fall within the competence of the Legislative Assembly, whereas the regulation of horizontal legal relations, i.e. those relating to the relationship between two individuals, may fall within the competence of the Parliament. Competence in criminal matters can also be considered to follow from this division, since the

Legislative Assembly's competence in the area of criminal law depends on the public law nature of the other competences of the Legislative Assembly. The general competence of the Parliament in the area of criminal law, on the other hand, is not as clearly linked to this division.[19]

In the field of GMO regulation, the creation of units of indirect public administration and the establishment of the auditing office as an independent authority, a new area of legislation has been discovered. Admittedly, this is not entirely obvious for the auditing office, as the auditing previously operated under the Government of the Åland Islands. Thereafter, a classification of objects has been carried out and, on the basis of this, a determination of the matter as a matter that falls within the legislative competence of either the Legislative Assembly or the Parliament has been made. The interpretations of these Ålandic acts appear to follow the interpretative instruction developed by the SC in HD 2001:79 on the Lotteries Act for mainland Finland, because the SC has examined the provisions in terms of content to determine the entity to which the provisions are to be assigned and decided according to this classification of objects of the regulation whether the provision or regulation in question falls within the competence of the Legislative Assembly or the Parliament. With regard to the auditing office and to units of indirect public administration, the SC came to the conclusion on the basis of the general clauses that competence belongs to the Legislative Assembly, which can be considered to be in harmony with the idea that the regulation of public law issues, especially vertical legal relations, falls within the competence of the Legislative Assembly. The SC referred GMO to the competence of the Parliament, which means that the opinion is in harmony with the principles of the legislative competence of the Parliament, since the Gene Technology Act primarily concerns the regulation of the market, products and the position of the operator, although the authority organization is also involved in this legislation.

On the basis of the SC Statement HD 2001:79 on the Lotteries Act for mainland Finland, it appears that the jurisdictional interpretations, where a category of competence has been found in the lists and strengthened by reference to the general clause, are those where a classification of objects has been taken as a starting point and a matter has been found to which the Ålandic Act

19 Markku Suksi, *Ålands konstitution* (Åbo Akademi, Åbo, 2005) pp. 191–192. In addition to the general clause of the Parliament, there is in fact a 'general private law clause' in Section 27(41) of the SGA, which gives the Parliament legislative competence in other private law matters than those specifically referred to in this Section, unless they relate directly to a field of law which, according to the SGA, falls within the legislative competence of the Legislative Assembly. This general private law clause strengthens the private law character of national competences.

can be attributed. Then the interpretation has been consolidated by a check against the general clause. It is not necessarily a very established procedure as the interpretations are fairly fresh, but it seems to be a possible approach in the light of the SC's description of the interpretative steps. In these situations, the general clause for allocating legislative competence between the two legislatures has not really been applied, but what has been applied is the existing material competence in the actual enumerations.

Also, there are two interpretations where it can be said that the interpreter of the general clause is mistaken about the premises for the use of either general clause.

In the light of the SC Statement HD 2001:79 on the Lotteries Act, the Constitutional Law Committee's interpretation with regard to the Lotteries Act seems to consist of a misunderstanding of how the division of competence between the Legislative Assembly and the Parliament is structured and of how the general clause can be used. The Committee advocated an interpretation of the legislative competence of the Parliament that would have allowed the then Åland Provincial Administrative Board, which is a state body in the Åland Islands, to exercise administrative competence in Åland in a field where legislative competence and thus also administrative competence belongs to the Legislative Assembly. There were no other matters relating to the Lotteries Act which would have fallen outside the substantive definitions of the Legislative Assembly's competence and which would thus have created a need to remove a normative ambiguity by interpreting the general clause relating to the legislative competence of the Parliament.

Regarding the EU referendum, the wording of a core material provision of the enactment should have caused the SC to treat the issue as a binding referendum which does not fall within the scope of any substantive competence in Section 18 of the Autonomy Act, nor does it fall within the scope of the application of the general clause as a new area of legislation. However, it actually gives rise to an amendment to the SGA. It is possible that counterarguments can be presented in this regard, such as that the intention was always to arrange a consultative referendum, which is also reflected in the name of the law, but the wording of the content of the law is nevertheless binding on the Legislative Assembly. There is clearly a new area of legislation here, but the subject of the regulation, the creation of a binding referendum procedure according, falls outside the framework of the SGA. The matter should, actually have led to a formal amendment of the SGA. Perhaps a sense of expediency overshadowed the referendum issue, for it was natural to imagine that a referendum would be held in Åland on Åland's entry into the European Union together with the rest of Finland.

Attempts to renew the autonomy legislation and to change its structure by passing a new autonomy act to replace the 1991 SGA have been going on for 15 years. Without going into the content of these plans, however, it can be stated that even in a system with the possibility to transfer national competences to the Legislative Assembly through decisions of the Legislative Assembly, it is envisaged that a system of two enumerations will continue and thus also the need for two general clauses.[20]

5 Conclusions

The system of general clauses or open points of competence at the end of the lists of competences of the Legislative Assembly and the Parliament is a consequence of the fact that it has been considered impossible to determine, once and for all, which matters belong to which legislator. The system is based on the original division of competences in the 1920 SGA, which in principle placed a residual part of the competences with the Legislative Assembly, but opened the way for the exercise of legislative power by the Parliament in new legislative areas that arose in a way that automatically attributed them to the competence of the Parliament. It is possible to imagine that the original situation for Åland was similar to a federal distribution of legislative power, where it is typical that the state loses legislative competence to the federation through the application of a federal principle of precedence.

In order to stop the leakage of competence of this kind, the 1951 SGA created a system of double enumeration, i.e., two lists of competences for the exercise of legislative power for the Åland Islands. One list of competences gave legislative power to the Legislative Assembly and another list of competences to the Parliament. Even with double enumeration, new areas of law could not find their place in the explicit substantive competences, which prompted the need to formulate a residual category, a general clause, at the end of both lists of competences. This system was in principle transferred to the current SGA, but the general clauses were made symmetrical so that, on the basis of a similar wording, they can bring about a symmetrical distribution of new legislative matter to either legislature without any of them benefiting from the system. The idea is that this system would also apply in a prospective new autonomy act, which would admittedly be somewhat different in nature due to the planned possibility for the Legislative Assembly to decide through its

20 Draft of 2 July 2021 for the Government's proposal for a new Self-Government Act, <api.hankeikkuna.fi/asiakirjat/43e0520d-248e-4fc6-98f6-77c74e3be669/5f76b164-bfa7-4464-87fd-e056123bdc44/LAUSUNTOPYYNTO_20210706122322.PDF>, visited on 2 June 2022.

own decisions on the transfer of legislative powers from the Parliament to the Legislative Assembly.

It is relatively rare that the general clauses have been used as a basis for the examination of competence. This can be understood to mean that the rather detailed explicit substantive lists of competences work relatively well even in situations where legislative competence is not entirely obvious and given. In the last 30 years, only relatively few legislative matters have arisen which have not been possible to place in the existing substantive matters. The best example here is probably GMO regulation, which undeniably represents a new area of legislation. Most of the opinions on Ålandic laws issued by the SC have therefore been based on the substantive points in the lists of competences, which can be seen as meaning that the explicit enumerations have worked well, perhaps better than anticipated when the current SGA was passed.

The SC has thus had to rely on arguments about the principles of the general clauses in relatively few situations. This has taken place in approximately the same number of situations for both the Legislative Assembly's and the Parliament's competences. On the basis of the general clause of the Legislative Assembly legislative competence has been given with regard to the creation of units within indirect public administration and the establishment of the auditing office as a separate authority under the Legislative Assembly, while Parliament has been given legislative competence based on "its" general clause for GMO. It is possible to argue that the two competences which have been considered to belong to the Legislative Assembly by virtue of "its" general clause are clearer, whereas the question of GMO was genuinely new and created a less clear situation in view of the placement of GMO in either of the two areas of competence. It seems to me that the issue of GMO regulation has been the best example so far of how the assessment and interpretation of jurisdiction should be carried out on the basis of the general clauses. In situations where the general clauses have been used to distribute legislative power between the Legislative Assembly and the Parliament, the SC has maintained the clear dividing line between the powers of the two legislators established by the SGA: the general clauses do not lead to overlap of legislative powers, but legislative powers are distributed to either the Legislative Assembly or the Parliament and remain exclusive to both legislators. In a manner similar to the situation in Canada, the general clauses of the SGA do not introduce a principle of precedence for the national legislature as would be common in federations. This shows that the distribution of competences can be successfully created on a basis other than the traditional federal division of competences.

The SC may sometimes use the general clauses to support placing a subject area among the substantive areas of law mentioned in the lists of competences. This seems to have been the case for the Legislative Assembly in the case of the fees for exceeding emission rights, while the general clause's support for national competence may have been put forward for drunkenness at sea. It has happened that the SC, without explicit reference to the general clause, has argued along the lines of the tenets of the clauses in such a way that appears to reinforce the placement of a particular subject area within a substantive competence. This is a fairly recent development in the area of data protection and of discrimination. Interestingly, even the Constitutional Law Committee of the Parliament at least once felt compelled to rely on the general clause of the Parliament, but on that occasion, regarding the Lotteries Act, the SC had to step in and explain that the general clause cannot be used in the way that the Constitutional Law Committee intended. At the same time, in one case, the EU referendum in Åland, the SC has probably erred in deciding to apply the Legislative Assembly's general clause when the issue had actually required an amendment of the SGA so that referendums that bind the Legislative Assembly's decision-making power become possible.

Based on the application of the general clauses, it can be concluded at this stage in the life cycle of the current SGA that so far, there are relatively few situations of interpretation and that such issues have not really arisen during the last decade, following the assessment of the legislation on the auditing office. Thus, no completely settled practice can be deduced from the opinions of the SC issued so far, except that the Court stated in its Statement HD 2001:79 concerning the Lotteries Act in a fairly clear way how the classification and interpretation of the objects and matters should take place. In this context, an important interpretation was created which can be regarded as protecting the distribution of competences of the current autonomy arrangement.

Since private law issues do not arise to any great extent within the scope of the Legislative Assembly's competence, it is conceivable that the general clause at the end of the Legislative Assembly's list of competences is very rarely activated with regard to private-law oriented enactments of the Legislative Assembly. As far as the Parliament is concerned, the application of the general clause of the Parliament may be relevant in the field of public law, except in the case of certain typical areas of public law which fall within the legislative competence of the Legislative Assembly, but in particular, private law is an area of competence for the Parliament, so also general criminal law. An outside observer might get the impression that the distribution of competence between the Legislative Assembly and the Parliament does not show a good balance. However, in the light of the above analysis, it is submitted that there is a good balance in the distribution of legislative power through the general clauses: in the key areas of public law (education, social and health care, environment, etc.) where the Legislative Assembly has extensive competences, the general clause in Section 18(27) of the SGA works in favour of the Legislative Assembly, while the general clause in Section 27(42) of the SGA works in the area of private law in favour of the Parliament, in both cases on the basis of the principles of the SGA. It is also apparent that the nature of the general clauses at the end of each list of competences is such that, in comparison with the subject-specific points of competence, they not only invite more in-depth and general considerations, including the use of a step-by-step procedure for assessing competence, but lead to a more general interpretation of the normative environment of the provisions.

CHAPTER 5

Finland's Specific Obligations Relating to Åland's Autonomy under International and National Law

Lauri Hannikainen

1 The Creation of Åland's Autonomy in Legal Terms

The international legal basis of Åland's autonomy is formed by the decisions of the Council of the League of Nations on 24 and 27 June 1921. A dispute had developed between Finland and Sweden on the future of Åland. The newly-emerged, independent state, Finland, was of the opinion that Åland, which had been a part of the Finnish Grand Duchy in the Russian Empire, should naturally remain as a part of Finland. The great majority of the Swedish-speaking Ålanders were of the opinion that the Åland people should have the right to decide their future status, i.e. to become a part of Sweden. Sweden argued in favour of the right of Ålanders to determine their future status.

When those Nordic States were not able to settle their dispute, they agreed to submit the case of Åland to the League Council – ultimately for its binding decision. In order to improve its chances before the Council, Finland enacted an Act on the Autonomy of Åland (No. 124/1920), which provided for a regional parliament with limited legislative powers and for a regional government. In addition, Swedish was made the sole official language in Åland.

The League Council's decision was favourable for Finland: Åland was to remain under the sovereignty of Finland. However, Finland was to agree to certain guarantees in support of the autonomy and Swedish character of Åland:

> The new guarantees to be inserted in the autonomy law should specially aim at preservation of the Swedish language in the schools, at the maintenance of landed property in the hands of the Islanders, at the restriction, within reasonable limits, of the exercise of the franchise by new-comers, and at ensuring the appointment of a Governor who will possess the confidence of the population.[1]

1 Resolution of 24 June. LNOJ 699, IV Geneva (1921).

The Council was of the opinion that the guarantees would most likely achieve their purpose, if they were agreed by the parties to the dispute – Finland and Sweden. Indeed, after a few days, the negotiators of these states reached an agreement which was then added to the Council's Resolution of 27 June. According to the agreement, Finland undertook to introduce the following guarantees to the Autonomy Act:

- Åland was in no case obliged to support any other schools than those in which the language of instruction was Swedish. In the state schools, instruction was to be given in Swedish. The Finnish language could not be taught in those primary schools which were supported or subsidised by the state or by the municipalities, without the approval of the municipality concerned.
- When real property situated in Åland was sold to a person who was not legally domiciled in Åland, any person legally domiciled in Åland, or the Åland Government or the municipality in which the estate was situated, had the right to redeem the estate.
- Immigrants to Åland who had Finnish citizenship could acquire provincial and municipal franchise of Åland only after five years' legal domicile therein.
- The Governor of Åland was to be nominated by the President of Finland in agreement with the Speaker of the Legislative Assembly of Åland.
- Åland had the right to use for its own needs 50 per cent of the revenue of the land tax.

Finland faithfully incorporated the agreed text, not in the Autonomy Act, but in a specific Åland Guarantees Act.[2]

The Act on the Autonomy of Åland is of course the basic national legal source of the autonomy. In the first decades, the Guarantees Act was the second basic source, but since 1951, when the second Act on the Autonomy of Åland replaced the acts of 1920 and 1922, the Autonomy Act was the sole basic source.

2 The New Autonomy Acts of 1951 and 1991

The League of Nations was dissolved in the 1940s. With regard to the minority regimes created by the League, the United Nations did not become the League's successor as supervisor. Knowing this, Finland could have tried to weaken Åland's autonomy but it did not do so. On the contrary, the 1951 Autonomy Act[3]

2 FFS 189/1922.

3 FFS 670/1951.

reinforced the autonomy and preservation of the Swedish character of Åland, as compared with the settlement of the early 1920s.

First, the jurisdiction of the Legislative Assembly was enlarged and specified. Second, a specific regional citizenship – right to domicile – was created for persons who had acquired the right of permanent residence in Åland.[4] Only people with the right to domicile had full rights – i.e. voting rights, freedom of enterprise, and the right to own real property. Third, according to a new rule, if a treaty ratified by Finland contained a provision which was in conflict with the Autonomy Act, the provision was to enter into force only if the Legislative Assembly gave its consent.[5]

The Autonomy Act of 1991 replaced the Act of 1951. The new Act continues the same trend as seen with the previous Act: it further develops Åland's autonomy. First, in order to acquire the right to domicile the applicant also needs to be sufficiently proficient in the Swedish language.[6] Second, the right of persons not having the right to domicile to acquire and own real property is further restricted. Third, new provisions concerning the appointment of the Governor are made more favourable to Åland than before.[7] Fourth, Åland can have a role in Finland's treaty negotiations with other states.[8]

However, there is one provision in the 1991 Act which deviates from the 1921 settlement formally to the detriment of Åland. Namely, Section 40 improves the position of the Finnish language in schools. Originally, Finnish could not be taught in those primary and secondary schools which were supported or subsidised by the Åland administration or by the municipalities, without the approval of the municipality concerned. Section 40 no longer subjects all teaching of Finnish to such an approval procedure.

The modification created in Section 40 has a pertinent ground: the trend in Europe is towards multicultural societies with increased use of different languages. Åland has a greater need than before to have persons able to master Finnish. A great majority of Åland's pupils nowadays study Finnish at school as a foreign language. Besides, there was substantial opposition in the Finnish Parliament towards the strict attitude to teaching Finnish. Thus, I submit that the provision of Section 40 is actually not detrimental to Åland.

4 *Ibid.* §§ 3–5.
5 *Ibid.* § 11:19.
6 *Ibid.* § 7.
7 *Ibid.* § 52.
8 *Ibid.* § 58.

3 The Division of Competences between Åland and the State

The purpose of granting autonomy to Åland was to enable it to control its Swedish language and culture in a long-term manner. The division of competences is naturally a matter of prime importance.

In the list of the competences of Åland, there are 26 items in the Autonomy Act (Section 18). They include municipal administration and taxation, local public order and security, lease of land, protection of nature and the environment, health care and medical treatment, social welfare, education, culture and sport, hunting and fishing, the postal service, the right to broadcast by radio and cable in Åland, and trade (with certain exceptions).

The list of competences of the State includes 41 items (Section 27). This list makes it plain that the sphere of Åland's autonomy is not broad. The state list includes foreign relations, national defence and security, the right to reside and move in Finnish territory, company law, shipping lanes for merchant shipping, nuclear energy, labour law, criminal law, the judiciary and judicial proceedings, citizenship, passport, legislation on aliens, civil defence, taxes and dues (with certain exceptions).

At the end of the Åland and State lists there is a general clause according to which Åland/the State has legislative competence in other matters deemed to be within the legislative power of Åland/the State in accordance with the principles underlying the Autonomy Act.

It should be pointed out that the division of legislative power between the State and Åland is exclusive in principle in the sense that a state law or a treaty ratified by Finland is not in force in Åland if Åland has legislative power in that particular matter, not even subsidiarily in force.

When Finland became a member of the EU, it surrendered a part of its powers to the EU and the same was done by Åland when it joined Finland's membership.

4 The Opinion of the European Union

When Finland was negotiating with the EU on becoming a member of the EU, it was recognised that Åland was entitled to decide for itself whether it wanted to join Finland's membership or not. When Finland had agreed to join, Åland decided to join Finland's membership. A special protocol was added to Finland's membership treaty Protocol 2 on the Åland Islands in the Accession Treaty to the European Community 1994 of Finland, Sweden and Austria.

This short protocol begins by recognising that the Åland Islands have a special status in international law. During the negotiations Finland also recognised the special status of Åland. Thus, there was full agreement in this matter.

According to Article 1 of the Protocol, the provisions of the EC Treaty shall not preclude restrictions on the right of natural persons who do not enjoy regional citizenship (*hembygdsrätt*) and for legal persons, to acquire and hold real property in Åland without permission. A similar statement follows concerning the right of natural persons to provide services.

Article 2 states that the territory of Åland being considered as a third territory shall be excluded from the territorial application of the EC provisions in the fields of harmonisation of the Members on turnover taxes, and on excise duties and other forms of indirect taxation. This derogation is aimed at maintaining a viable local economy. Depending on future developments, this derogation may be only of limited duration.

The last Article 3 obligates Finland to ensure that the same treatment applies to all natural and legal persons of the member states.

5 Taxation Powers

An autonomous territory's legislative autonomy would be very limited if the territory did not have a given economic autonomy. In the past, Åland's use of its finances was strictly controlled by the state. The 1991 Autonomy Act brought a radical extension to Åland's economic autonomy; Åland now has significant powers to decide how it uses the finances it has acquired.

However, Åland does not have any extensive powers of taxation, the Åland authorities having the right to levy only municipal and some minor taxes. With those exceptions, the state levies taxes in Åland as in other parts of Finland. These taxes are 'returned' to Åland in the form of an equalisation sum from the state budget. The amount of equalisation is at present 0.45 per cent of the Finnish state budget. This system gives a certain economic security to the small economic entity that Åland is – especially during times of economic recession. However, Åland is a prosperous region that has managed its economy well, even in times of recession. Åland and the region of Uusimaa, where Helsinki is located, are the most prosperous regions in Finland.

Åland would like to have a more diversified tax legislation. Åland's joining in Finland's membership of the EU has increased its autonomy in tax matters. It may well be that in future Åland's autonomy in the field of taxation will continue to increase.

6 Strong Factors of Åland's Autonomy

When one compares the autonomy of Åland with other existing regional autonomies, the outcome is that Åland's autonomy is not a very broad one. One reason appears to be that the population of Åland is relatively small – about 30,000. One hundred years ago, when the autonomy system was established, the number was about 20,000. Those years were turbulent years in Europe and the newly independent Finland preferred to agree to a limited autonomy.

However, when speaking about the scope of the Åland autonomy as a limited one I do not mean that as a whole it is relatively modest. There are several aspects in this autonomy which are strong. The reader has already learned from previous chapters that the constitutional guarantees of Åland's autonomy are strong. There are also certain other factors which appear to successfully implement the goal of the Åland autonomy, namely to preserve the character of Åland as a Swedish-speaking community – which includes, beside the Swedish language, even the Swedish culture.

Those strong factors are the right to domicile and the clear predominance of the Swedish language. Concerning the right to domicile, only persons having it are full-powered members of the community; only they have full rights in the regional elections, to own and possess real property, and to exercise a trade of profession. A Finnish citizen is free to move to Åland but without the right of domicile it might not be easy to earn a living there . He/she has to live in Åland for five years before being able to acquire the right of domicile. The other requirement – to be satisfactorily proficient in the Swedish language – should not be difficult for a Finn who has lived five years in Swedish-speaking Åland.

In Finland there are two national languages, Finnish and Swedish, equal before the law. However, in fact the Swedish-speaking population of some five per cent is only a national minority. The Finnish and Swedish languages are structurally very different from each other, belonging to different language 'families'. Åland makes a monolingual difference since it has only one official language – Swedish. This is the case in all organs of the Åland autonomy. However, before State authorities in Åland, for example, before the courts, everyone is entitled to also use Finnish.

A telling example of the strong position of *the Swedish language* in the case of Åland is the provision in the Autonomy Act according to which the language used in communication and correspondence between the State and Åland authorities shall be Swedish. This is an indication that, in its relations with Åland, Finland displays a bona fide attitude.

As regards the school languages, the position of Swedish is strong and the position of Finnish is weak. Since the number of Finnish-speaking persons in Åland is relatively low, they have not demanded the establishment of a state-funded school where the language of instruction should be Finnish. Nor have they established a private Finnish-speaking school. It appears that Finnish-speaking pupils have managed quite well in the Åland school system.

In any case, the rules concerning the right to domicile and the strong position of the Swedish language in Åland have achieved their purpose. In the 2020s, one hundred years after the establishment of the autonomy system in Åland, in the population of circa 30,000 persons the number of Swedish-speaking persons is about 90 per cent. Finnish-speaking persons make up about five per cent, as also the number of persons having other mother tongues.

It should be pointed out that of the 200 seats in the Finnish Parliament one seat is reserved for Åland. The Åland parliamentarian is elected by the Åland voters in the course of Finland's parliamentary elections. However, Åland has not succeeded in getting a seat in the European Parliament. It has been considered to be too small to have a seat.

7 Concluding Observations

The circumstances have been favourable to Åland's autonomy. As an archipelago Åland is a distinct geographical entity with a homogenous population of about 90 per cent Swedish-speakers. Åland is a part of the Nordic region where the states have well-functioning democracies. From its beginning, the Åland autonomy has been a democracy with legislative assembly, government and regular, fair elections.

The guarantees for Åland's autonomy are strong in Finland's constitutional law, and in international law Åland's autonomous status has not been challenged. Its basis is the decision of the Council of the League of Nations, recognized by the EU.

During its hundred years' existence the Åland autonomy system has established itself in practice and has functioned quite smoothly. There have been disagreements between the Åland authorities and State authorities but they have been solved within the existing procedure of settling disputes – primarily according to legal criteria.

It can be presumed that either a new autonomy law will be enacted during the coming decades or further amendments meeting societal developments will be made to the existing Autonomy Act. A notable example of the need for amendments would come from developments within the EU system. Another example could come from the demilitarised and neutral status of Åland, i.e. if it were subjected to changes.

CHAPTER 6

International Procedural Safeguards for the Åland Islands' Autonomy? Some Reflections on the (Re-)Activation of a League of Nations Mechanism

Rainer Hofmann and Moritz Malkmus

1 Introduction

In 1920, the Council of the League of Nations was asked to resolve the sovereignty dispute between Finland and Sweden over the Åland Islands archipelago.[1] In an Agreement[2] later annexed to the Council Decision of 24 June 1921,[3] which ultimately confirmed Finnish sovereignty over the archipelago and laid important foundations for its autonomous and demilitarised[4] status, Finland gave far-reaching guarantees to protect the Swedish character of the islands, including in procedural terms to:

1 On the historical and legal background, cf. T. Modeen, Völkerrechtliche Probleme der Åland-Inseln, *Zeitschrift für ausländisches öffentliches Recht und Völkerrecht* 37 (1977), pp. 604–619; L. Hannikainen, The International Legal Basis of the Autonomy and Swedish Character of the Åland Islands, in L. Hannikainen and F. Horn (eds), *Autonomy and Demilitarisation in International Law: The Åland Islands in a Changing Europe* (Kluwer, The Hague et al., 1997), pp. 57–83; S. Harck, Åland Islands, in A. Peters (ed.), *Max Planck Encyclopedia of Public International Law* (online edn., OUP, January 2008); M. Suksi, *Sub-State Governance through Territorial Autonomy* (Springer, Heidelberg 2011), pp. 142 et seq.; M. Suksi, Autonomy, in A. Peters (ed.), *Max Planck Encyclopedia of Public International Law* (Online edn., OUP, April 2021), para. 10; M. Ackrén, The Åland Islands: 100 years of stability, in B.C.H. Fong and A. Ichijo (eds.), *The Routledge Handbook of Comparative Territorial Autonomies* (London, Routledge, 2022), pp. 107–118; G. Nolte, Some Observations on the 1920 and 1921 Expert Reports Regarding the Åland Islands Question, in P.B. Donath et al. (eds), *Der Schutz des Individuums durch das Recht* (Springer, Berlin, Heidelberg, 2023), pp. 93–100.

2 The Agreement of 27 June 1921 is reprinted in Hannikainen and Horn, *supra* note 1, p. 298.

3 The Resolution is reprinted in Hannikainen and Horn, *supra* note 1, p. 297.

4 It should be recalled that the demilitarised status of the islands was already enshrined in the *Convention between France and Great Britain and Russia respecting the Aaland Islands* of 30 March 1856, which, according to the Council's Resolution of 24 June 1921, "should be replaced by a broader regime [...]" (para. 5). This broader regime entered into force with the *Convention Relating to the Non-Fortification and Neutralisation of the Aaland Islands* of 20 October 1921, which is reprinted in Hannikainen and Horn, *supra* note 1, p. 299.

> 7. [...] forward to the Council of the League of Nations, with its observations, any petitions or claims of the Landsting of Aaland in connection with the application of the guarantees in question, and the Council shall, in any case where the question is of a juridical character, consult the Permanent Court of International Justice [PCIJ].[5]

Although corresponding provisions, including those concerning the abovementioned mechanism, were subsequently introduced into Finnish law, the formal complaints procedure, unlike the minority regimes brought before the PCIJ,[6] was not activated until the League of Nations collapsed and thereby corresponding domestic provisions disappeared.[7] While these events have not impaired the emergence of an international customary norm[8] safeguarding Åland's autonomy in substance, the question arises as to whether it would be possible to restore such a procedural mechanism for resolving disputes over certain aspects of Åland's special status, since the islands (as an autonomous sub-state entity) would not have standing[9] before the International Court of

---

5 *Supra* note 2. Cf. L. Hannikainen, The International Legal Basis of the Autonomy and Swedish Character of the Åland Islands, *supra* note 1, pp. 58 et seq.; Suksi, *Sub-State Governance through Territorial Autonomy* (Springer, Heidelberg, 2011), p. 151.

6 See, e.g. *Access to German Minority Schools in Upper Silesia*, Advisory Opinion, 12 February 1927 PCIJ Series A/B No 40; *Minority Schools in Albania*, Advisory Opinion, 6 April 1935, PCIJ Series A/B No 64. In the *Albanian* case, Article 7 of the 1921 Declaration Concerning the Protection of Minorities in Albania (League of Nations, Treaty Series, vol. 9, 1922, pp. 175–9) contains a clause under which a matter can be referred to the PCIJ. In the *Upper Silesian* Case, Article 12 of the Minorities Treaty between the Principal Allied and Associated Powers and Poland provides a similar clause. The advisory jurisdiction of the PCIJ results from Article 14, sentence 3 of the Covenant of League of Nations. Cf. G. Alfredsson, German Minorities in Poland, Cases concerning the, in A. Peters (ed.), *Max Planck Encyclopedia of Public International Law* (Online edn., OUP, April 2010); M.G. Samson, D. Guilfoyle, The Permanent Court of International Justice and the "Invention" of the International Advisory Jurisdiction, in C.J. Tams, M. Fitzmaurice (eds.), *Legacies of the Permanent Court of International Justice* (Brill, Nijhoff, Leiden, Boston, 2013), pp. 41 et seq.; C. Brölmann, The PCIJ and International Rights of Groups and Individuals, in C.J. Tams, M. Fitzmaurice (eds.), *Legacies of the Permanent Court of International Justice* (Brill, Nijhoff, Leiden, Boston, 2013), pp. 127 et seq.; H.C. Scheu, The heritage of the League of Nations' minority protection system, *Hungarian Journal of Legal Studies 61* (2020), pp. 356–371.

7 Cf. Section 6 of the Act containing Special Provisions concerning the Population of the Åland Islands (SoF 189/1922). This special complaint mechanism ultimately disappeared from Finnish domestic law when the Autonomy Act of 1951 came into force. Cf. Modeen, *supra* note 1, pp. 610–1; Hannikainen, *supra* note 5, p. 60; Suksi, *supra* note 5, p. 153.

8 Hannikainen, *supra* note 5, p. 65, 67; Suksi, *supra* note 5, p. 153.

9 Article 34 para. 1 of the ICJ Statute. Cf. G. Gaja, Standing: International Court of Justice (ICJ), in A. Peters (ed.) *Max Planck Encyclopedia of International Procedural Law* (online edn., OUP,

Justice (ICJ). The most recent proposals to this effect were made during the preparatory work for the legislative procedure to revise the autonomy legislation in Åland, most notably by a parliamentary committee chaired by Gunnar Jansson in 2010.[10]

2 Disputed Nature of the Agreement of 27 June 1921

Part of the complexity of this issue lies in the disputed legal nature[11] of the Finnish guarantees annexed to the Council Decision of 24 June 1921. The debate centred on whether the separate agreement between the Finnish and Swedish negotiators of 27 June 1921 qualifies as a bilateral treaty and to whom Finland is obliged to guarantee the Swedish character of the islands (e.g., Sweden, the League of Nations, the international community as such). Objections to the treaty nature of the agreement were based on the formal lack of signature and ratification, respectively the difficulty of demonstrating that Finland and Sweden nevertheless intended to be bound by a bilateral treaty.[12] The matter is further complicated by the fact that both states have taken varying positions on this issue over time.[13] The United Nations[14] in particular, followed by some legal scholars, considered the result of the negotiations between Finnish and Swedish representatives to be an "agreement" which was "approved"[15] by the Council of the League of Nations on 27 June 1921.[16] While further clarification

June 2018), para. 8 et seq.; M. Suksi, Autonomy, in A. Peters (ed.), *Max Planck Encyclopedia of Public International Law* (Online edn., OUP, April 2021), para. 23.

10 See the *Betänkande från parlamentariska kommittén om förslag till reformering av självstyrelse systemet och självstyrelselagen för Åland*, Åländsk Utredning Serie 2010:2, p. 37. This idea was later endorsed by *Ahvenanmaan itsehallinnon kehittäminen: Ahvenanmaa-komitean 2013 välimietintö*, Justitieministeriets publikation 6/2015, p. 98. On the work of the committees, cf. S. Simolin, The Aims of Åland and Finland Regarding a New Act on the Autonomy of Åland: An analysis of three parliamentary committee reports (2010–2017), *Journal of Autonomy and Security Studies* 2 (2018), pp. 16, 21.

11 Cf. in more detail Modeen, *supra* note 1, pp. 611–4; Hannikainen, *supra* note 5, pp. 61 et seq.; Harck, *supra* note 1, para. 8; Suksi, *supra* note 5, p. 150.

12 E.g. Hannikainen, *supra* note 5, p. 66.

13 For a more detailed account on the opinions expressed by state organs, cf. Modeen, *supra* note 1, p. 611; Hannikainen, *supra* note 5, pp. 63–4.

14 UN Economic and Social Council, *Study on the Legal Validity of the Undertakings Concerning Minorities*, 7 April 1950, E/CN.4/367, p. 69.

15 *Supra* note 14.

16 E.g. Y. Dinstein, Autonomy regimes and international law, *Villanova Law Review* 56 (2011), p. 448; T. Modeen, International Protection of the National Identity of the Aland Islands, *The Scandinavian Studies in Law* 17 (1973), p. 195; Modeen, *supra* note 1, pp. 612 et seq.

of these issues has become to some extent[17] obsolete, it does not seem unreasonable to assume, firstly, that Finland did not give its commitments a purely extra-legal effect (as this might ultimately have jeopardised the settlement of the dispute over Åland) and, secondly, that – irrespective of the nature of the agreement between Finland and Sweden – the League of Nations assumed the function of enforcing the results of the settlement reached under its auspices.[18] The latter is evident from the Council Decision of 24 June 1921, which, while leaving it to Finland and Sweden to draw up the individual guarantees, stated that "[...] in any case, the Council of the League of Nations will see to the enforcement of these guarantees."[19]

3 Legislative Developments in Finland

Following the 1921 Council decision, Finland transposed the above-mentioned guarantees into domestic law[20] by adopting both the 1922 Guarantees Act,[21] which complemented the 1920 Self-Government Act, and later the 1938 Redemption Act.[22] The complaint mechanism described above has been codified in section 6 of the Guarantee Act,[23] which corresponds verbatim to para. 7 of the Agreement of 27 June 1921.[24] Having lasted for more than two decades, this legal situation soon began to erode with the collapse of the League of Nations and the reorganisation of the political and legal landscape following World War II. The relevant developments in Finnish legislation were summarised in

17 This would appear to be the case at least to the extent that the autonomous regime has grown into customary law (*supra* note 8).

18 Cf. Modeen, *supra* note 16, p. 201, who describes the Council's role as a "supervisor of the observation of the Agreement" (id.).

19 Para. 4 sentence 3 of Resolution is reprinted in Hannikainen and Horn, *supra* note 1, p. 297.

20 For a detailed account of the implementation of the Council Decision, see Suksi, *supra* note 5, pp. 152 et seq.; Simolin, *supra* note 10, pp. 16 et seq.; and the work of the following parliamentary committees: *Betänkande från parlamentariska kommittén om förslag till reformering av självstyrelse systemet och självstyrelselagen för Åland*, Åländsk Utredning Serie 2010:2, pp. 36 et seq.; *Ahvenanmaa-komitean 2013 välimietintö, supra* note 10, pp. 34 et seq., 95 et seq.

21 Act containing Special Provisions concerning the Population of the Åland Islands (SoF 189/1922).

22 Act on the Exercise of the Right of Redemption at Sale of Real Property in the Åland Islands (SoF 140/1938).

23 Reprinted in *Ahvenanmaa-komitean 2013 välimietintö, supra* note 10, p. 95.

24 Modeen, *supra* note 16, pp. 189 et seq., Suksi, *supra* note 5, p. 152; *Ahvenanmaa-komitean 2013 välimietintö, supra* note 10, p. 95.

detail in a parliamentary committee report[25] from 2017.[26] According to this report, the Parliament of Åland (*Landsting*) requested the Finnish government to raise the issue of international guarantees during peace negotiations. In 1946 the Government proposed a bill to the Finnish Parliament (*Riksdag*) for a new Autonomy Act (RP 1946:100), which would have obliged the Finnish Government (section 46) to obtain such guarantees for Åland as soon as possible. However, the Soviet Union objected to these plans with a démarche that delayed the legislative process until in 1948 the *Riksdag* was dissolved. After the failure of this bill, the proposal submitted by a newly appointed committee (RP 1948:38) omitted any such obligation, but instead introduced an entry into force provision that left room for the application of section 6 of the 1922 Guarantees Act, i.e. the special complaints mechanism. However, this proposal was again met with criticism from the Soviet Union, which saw section 6 of the Guarantees Act as a violation of the 1944 Armistice Agreement and the 1947 Peace Treaty,[27] or rather, as one contemporary observer[28] noted, feared losing influence in Finland. The bill that eventually passed the *Riksdag* lacked any reference to such an international mechanism. Thus, the right of the Åland *Landsting* to lodge petitions or claims disappeared from domestic law with the 1951 Autonomy Act (1951/760).[29] Since then, the demand for the restoration of international guarantees and a corresponding complaints procedure has been repeatedly raised by Åland, including in the committees set up in 2010 and 2013 to make proposals on the revision of the Autonomy Act.[30] The 2010 Committee, for example, proposed

25 *Ahvenanmaan itsehallinnon kehittäminen. Ahvenanmaa-komitean 2013 loppumietintö*, Oikeusministeriön julkaisu 33/2017, pp. 108–10.

26 See also Modeen, *supra* note 16, pp. 188 et seq.; Hannikainen, *supra* note 5, p. 62; Suksi, *supra* note 5, p. 153.

27 On these developments, *Ahvenanmaa-komitean 2013 loppumietintö, supra* note 25, p. 109.

28 With regard to the proposal of an obligation to obtain international guarantees, Modeen, *supra* note 16, p. 189 noted, "This provision was considered to be a limitation of Russia's controlling power over Finland."

29 Cf. Modeen, *supra* note 1, pp. 610–1; Hannikainen, *supra* note 5, p. 60; Suksi, *supra* note 5, p. 153. On the domestic legal situation, under the Act on the Autonomy of Åland (16 August 1991/1144), cf. S. Palmgren, The Autonomy of the Åland Islands in the Constitutional Law of Finland, in L. Hannikainen and F. Horn (eds), *Autonomy and Demilitarisation in International Law: The Åland Islands in a Changing Europe* (Kluwer, The Hague et al., 1997), pp. 85–97. See furthermore Sections 75 and 120 of the Constitution of Finland, which entered into force on 1 March 2000. Cf. Suksi, *supra* note 5, pp. 156 et seq.

30 *Ahvenanmaa-komitean 2013 välimietintö, supra* note 10, pp. 97–98; *Ahvenanmaa-komitean 2013 loppumietintö, supra* note 25, pp. 109–10; Simolin, *supra* note 10, pp. 16, 21.

> that the guarantee of the right of appeal for the Parliament be restored in accordance with the 1921 Åland Agreement regarding the application of the guarantees and that the Parliament instruct the Government to negotiate a sustainable, functioning system.[31]

In principle, the 2010 Committee saw "no obstacles"[32] under international law to restore the original guarantees of 1921, including the *klagorätten* (right of appeal), although, it recognised the need to start negotiations with a view to entrusting the task to a competent body.[33] In this regard, the interim report of the 2013 Åland committee was somewhat more sceptical, considering it "problematic"[34] to reintroduce the former international guarantees for the autonomy of Åland in accordance with the dispute settlement of 1921, as it would require the participation of the states that initially agreed on the international status of the islands.

> However, the [2013 Åland] committee supports the implementation of an *international instrument to secure the status of Swedish as the official language of Åland*, as provided in Chapter 6 of the current Act on the Autonomy of Åland, and intends to examine which international body could be entrusted with this assignment.[35]

In the final report of the 2013 Åland committee, the collective complaint mechanism for language issues was only included among the "Specific issues on which there are no proposals",[36] indicating that the claim has been moderated to some extent in the course of the committee's work. As the final report further noted, existing international organisations that monitor human and minority rights "do not have a monitoring and complaints mechanism for collective language rights such as the one in question here."[37] Indeed this raises the question of the extent to which an international complaints mechanism could be restored after the collapse of the League of Nations.

---

31 *Betänkande från parlamentariska kommittén om förslag till reformering av självstyrelse systemet och självstyrelselagen för Åland*, Äländsk Utredningsserie 2010:2, p. 37, translation by the authors.

32 *Ibid*, p. 37, translation by the authors.

33 Cf. *ibid*, p. 37.

34 *Ahvenanmaa-komitean 2013 välimietintö, supra* note 10, para. 6 of the abstract of proposals, translation by the authors.

35 *Ibid*, translation by the authors.

36 *Ahvenanmaa-komitean 2013 loppumietintö, supra* note 25, p. 108, translation by the authors.

37 *Ahvenanmaa-komitean 2013 loppumietintö, supra* note 25, p. 110, translation by the authors.

4 International Guarantees after the Dissolution of the League of Nations

After the broader system of minority protection established under the League of Nations collapsed, the United Nations did not *ipso iure* succeed the League in these functions.[38] However, according to the Secretary General's 1950 study on the legal validity of the undertakings concerning minorities,[39] there are some peculiarities regarding Åland.[40] Contrary to the vast majority of cited cases, on the situation of the Åland Islands, the study concluded, inter alia:

> The obligation undertaken by Finland towards the Council of the League of Nations as representative of the international community is *suspended* until such time as an express decision has been taken by the United Nations to put it back into force.[41]

As the sections' introductory paragraph makes clear, the mentioned "obligation undertaken by Finland towards the Council" refers to the "obligation [that] was entered into by Finland in this matter before the Council of the League of Nations on 27 June 1921".[42] In this sense, on 27 June 1921, irrespective of the nature of the agreement between Finland and Sweden, Finland undertook before the Council (inter alia) to "forward to the Council of the League of Nations, with its observations, any petitions or claims of the Landsting of Aaland".[43] On the study's assumption that such an obligation was made towards the Council "as representative of the international community",[44] it

38 Hannikainen, *supra* note 5, p. 60; K. Henrard, Minorities, International Protection, in A. Peters (ed.), *Max Planck Encyclopedia of Public International Law* (online edn., OUP, February 2013), para. 34 et seq.; R. Hofmann et al., Introduction, in R. Hofmann et al. (eds.), *The Framework Convention for the Protection of National Minorities* (Brill, Nijhoff, Leiden, Boston, 2018), pp. 5 et seq.

39 E/CN.4/367, *supra* note 14, p. 69.

40 Cf. Hannikainen, *supra* note 5, pp. 60 et seq. See on the study in general, K. Doehring, Das Gutachten des Generalsekretärs der Vereinten Nationen über die Fortgeltung der nach dem ersten Weltkrieg eingegangenen Minderheitenschutz Verpflichtungen, *Zeitschrift für ausländisches öffentliches Recht und Völkerrecht 15* (1954), pp. 521–540; Scheu, *supra* note 6, p. 364.

41 E/CN.4/367, *supra* note 14, p. 69, emphasis added.

42 E/CN.4/367, *supra* note 14, p. 69.

43 *Supra* note 2.

44 E/CN.4/367, *supra* note 14, p. 69. See also the general part of the study at p. 15. The assumption that corresponding obligations have been made to the international community as such is not unassailable, but it does have merit. Cf. Doehring, *supra* note 40, p. 527. One might also consider the parallel that Doehring (*supra* note 40, p. 528) draws with the

would seem justified to conclude that the demise of the League did not *ipso iure* lead to the termination of this obligation, as the international community was re-organised under the UN Charter with the General Assembly as its representative organ (Article 9 para. 1 of the UN Charter).[45] However, an "express decision" would be required by the UN General Assembly to put the mentioned obligation "back into force".[46] Such a decision is still pending. In this context, it should be recalled that the General Assembly once took an explicit decision on the transfer of certain functions, activities and assets of the League of Nations, in its Resolution 24 (I) of 12 February 1946.[47] It is apparent from the systematics of this resolution that the UN would only be willing to assume certain enumerated functions, including, for example, functions pertaining to a Secretariat, while reserving the right not to assume other specific functions of the League. However, this resolution lacks any reference to the League's system for the protection of minorities.[48]

5 International Procedural Safeguards for Åland's Autonomy

5.1 *De lege lata*

In the absence of an explicit decision by the General Assembly, it is worth considering the conditions under which certain aspects of the autonomous status of the Åland Islands and their specific linguistic and cultural character could be subject to international review. In this context, human rights treaties that provide for an individual complaint or monitoring procedures deserve special attention. To begin with, there is no general right to autonomy; in particular, such a right cannot be derived from the peoples' right to self-determination, as codified in Article 1 of the International Covenant on Civil and Political Rights[49] (ICCPR).[50] However, it is held that self-determination may "protect

---

ICJ's advisory opinion on the *International status of South-West Africa*, I.C.J. Reports 1950, pp. 132 et seq.

45 Cf. E/CN.4/367, *supra* note 14, p. 16.

46 E/CN.4/367, *supra* note 14, p. 69.

47 UN General Assembly, *Transfer of Certain Functions, Activities and Assets of the League of Nations*, 12 February 1946, A/RES/24. Cf. K. Schmalenbach, International Organizations or Institutions, Succession, in A. Peters (ed.), *Max Planck Encyclopedia of Public International Law* (Online edn., OUP, September 2017), para. 15.

48 Cf. E/CN.4/367, *supra* note 14, p. 10–17.

49 United Nations, Treaty Series, vol. 999, p. 171 and vol. 1057, p. 407. Finland ratified the ICCPR on 19 August 1975.

50 D. Thürer, T. Burri, Self-Determination, in A. Peters (ed.), *Max Planck Encyclopedia of Public International Law* (Online edn., OUP, December 2008), para. 38; Suksi, *supra* note 9, para. 23.

such existing autonomy arrangements where the beneficiary can be regarded as a people".[51] The extent to which this could become relevant in relation to the Ålanders would require detailed consideration. In a procedural context, it should be noted that Article 1 ICCPR, unlike the other rights in the Covenant, cannot be subject of an individual communication due to its collective nature.[52] Only an inter-State communication (Article 41–43 ICCPR) would seem permissible.[53] The Human Rights Committee has made several observations under the said principle, also with regards to the Åland Islands,[54] however not in a systematic manner that would allow for further conclusions.[55] Under minority rights law, autonomy issues may be captured within the framework of the standards on effective participation, e.g. under Article 15 of the Framework Convention for the Protection of National Minorities[56] (FCNM) or, with some limitations,[57] under Article 2 para. 2 and 3 of the UN Declaration on Minorities[58] (UNDM).[59] The Advisory Committee on the FCNM has been dealing with certain aspects of Åland's autonomy in its country-specific opinions.[60] However, the mentioned practice is rather limited and the monitoring system provided for in Articles 24–26 of the FCNM is not specifically designed to examine the implementation of a particular form of autonomy arrangement, nor does the Advisory Committee accept individual or collective complaints to that effect.

51 Suksi, *supra* note 9, para. 23.

52 P.M. Taylor, *A Commentary on the International Covenant on Civil and Political Rights* (Cambridge, Cambridge University Press, 2020), pp. 47–8.

53 W.A. Schabas, *Nowak's ICCPR Commentary* (3rd edn, Kehl, Engel, 2019), p. 24.

54 E.g., Report of the Human Rights Committee (A/46/40), para. 111–2.

55 Taylor, *supra* note 52, p. 55.

56 European Treaty Series No. 157. Finland ratified the FCNM on 3 October 1997. See on autonomy-related issues under Article 15 of the FCNM, T. Malloy, Commentary of Article 15, in R. Hofmann et al. (eds.), *The Framework Convention for the Protection of National Minorities* (Brill, Nijhoff, Leiden, Boston, 2018), pp. 282 et seq.

57 First, the UNDM is a non-binding text. Secondly, the draft materials (E/CN.4/1992/48, para. 27) for the UNDM document a rather cautious position towards the explicit inclusion of the concept of autonomy. Cf. A. Phillips, Historical Background on the Declaration, in U. Caruso, R. Hofmann (eds.), *The United Nations Declaration on Minorities* (Brill, Nijhoff, Leiden, Boston, 2015), p. 11 (at note 34).

58 Declaration on the Rights of Persons Belonging to National or Ethnic, Religious and Linguistic Minorities of 18 December 1992, A/RES/47/135.

59 In general, Suksi, *supra* note 9, para. 23, 29.

60 ACFC/INF/OP/I(2001)2, para. 17, 46, 47; ACFC/OP/II(2006)003, para. 107; ACFC/OP/III(2010)007, para. 117; ACFC/OP/IV(2016)002, para. 13; ACFC/OP/V(2019)001, para. 88 (at note 82).

As far as linguistic and cultural aspects are concerned, Article 27 of the ICCPR[61] (and Articles 2 para. 1, 4 para. 2 and 4 of the UNDM) as well as Articles 10 and 14 of the FCNM[62] could be invoked should Finland seek to restrict the use of Swedish in the Åland Islands, particularly in education. From a procedural point of view, the fact that the Ålanders are considered to be a numerical majority on the islands does not render individual complaints under the International Covenant inadmissible.[63] On the merits, the question would arise as to the extent to which the 'common' minority standards should be applied in the light of the special linguistic and cultural character of the Åland Islands to the extent that it is reflected in customary international law.[64] This question could be addressed by the systematic interpretation of Article 31 para. 3 lit. c of the Vienna Convention on the Law of Treaties (CVLT). The said provision on the general rule of interpretation stipulates:

> There shall be taken into account, together with the context:
>
> any relevant rules of international law applicable in the relations between the parties.

The reference to "any relevant rules of international law" is understood to encompass all sources of international law (Article 38 para. 1 ICJ Statute), including customary international law.[65] There are prominent examples including the ICJ[66] or the European Court of Human Rights[67] (ECtHR) applying this method of interpretation.[68] By adopting this method of interpretation,

---

61 On this provision in general, Schabas, *supra* note 53, pp. 795–837; Taylor, *supra* note 52, pp. 787–823.

62 On these provisions in general, R. Hofmann, Commentary on Article 10, in R. Hofmann et al. (eds.), *The Framework Convention for the Protection of National Minorities* (Brill, Nijhoff, Leiden, Boston, 2018), pp. 205–233; B. Busch, Commentary of Article 14, in R. Hofmann et al. (eds.), *The Framework Convention for the Protection of National Minorities* (Brill, Nijhoff, Leiden, Boston, 2018), pp. 254–288.

63 Cf. CCPR/C/47/D/359/1989 and 385/1989/Rev.1 (1993), para. 11.2; Schabas, *supra* note 53, pp. 803–4; Taylor, *supra* note 52, p. 796.

64 *Supra* note 8.

65 O. Dörr, General rule of interpretation, in O. Dörr, K. Schmalenbach (eds.), *Vienna Convention on the Law of Treaties* (2nd edn., Springer, Berlin, 2018), pp. 604–7.

66 *Oil Platforms (Islamic Republic of Iran v. United States of America)*, Judgment, I.C.J. Reports 2003, p. 161 (para. 40–1).

67 *Marguš v. Croatia*, Application no. 4455/10, Judgment (Grand Chamber), 27 May 2014, para. 129–141.

68 On these examples, cf. Dörr, *supra* note 66, pp. 606–7.

certain linguistic and cultural aspects of the special status of the Åland Islands, insofar as they have become customary law, could be the subject of an individual complaint.

However, as noted in the final report of the 2013 Åland committee, the procedural avenues in the above cases are limited to individual complaints and do not provide for a "complaints mechanism for collective language rights".[69] Therefore, the option that comes closest to the original 1921 guarantees, although it is likely to face certain political hurdles, would be to refer specific issues relating to the status of the Åland Islands to the ICJ. As mentioned above,[70] Åland itself could not initiate such proceedings. Moreover, it does not seem feasible to initiate adversarial proceedings in which two parties would have to accept the jurisdiction of the ICJ (Article 36 paras 1 or 2 of the Statute of the ICJ[71]), especially since the subject matter of such a dispute would be unclear.[72] On the other hand, it seems possible, under certain conditions, to request the ICJ to render an advisory opinion (Article 65 para. 1 of the ICJ Statute) on certain international aspects of the islands' status. Article 96 of the UN Charter enables the General Assembly to make such a request on any legal question by majority of the members present and voting (Article 18 para. 3 UN Charter).[73] Such a request could be referred to the Legal Committee (Sixth Committee) for consultation on the legal aspects and the preparation of a draft.[74] This request could involve abstract questions, which do not relate to a dispute between two states.[75] A corresponding proposal would have to be submitted by a UN member in the General Assembly.

69 *Ahvenanmaa-komitean 2013 loppumietintö, supra* note 25, p. 110, translation by the authors.

70 *Supra* note 9.

71 On the conditions, cf. J. Crawford, *Brownlie's Principles of Public International Law* (9th edn., Oxford University Press, 2019), p. 700; C. Tomuschat, Article 36, in A. Zimmermann, C.J. Tams (eds.), *The Statute of the International Court of Justice* (Oxford: Oxford University Press, 2019), p. 1790.

72 For the same reasons, any option that would require two parties to refer the matter to a competent body (e.g. the OSCE Court of Conciliation and Arbitration or the Permanent Court of Arbitration), does not seem feasible. The same could be said of the European Convention for the Peaceful Settlement of Disputes (European Treaty Series 23).

73 Cf. H. Thirlway, Advisory Opinions, in A. Peters (ed.), *Max Planck Encyclopedia of Public International Law* (Online edn., OUP, April 2006), para. 10; Crawford, *supra* note 72, pp. 704–6; P. d'Argent, Article 65, in A. Zimmermann et al. (eds.), *supra* note 72, pp. 1789–80, 1795–98.

74 A/520/Rev.17, Annex II. Cf. H. Llewellyn, T. Bektas, United Nations, Sixth Committee, in A. Peters (ed.), *Max Planck Encyclopedia of Public International Law* (Online edn., OUP, May 2019), para. 22.

75 Crawford, *supra* note 72, p. 704.

5.2 *De lege ferenda*

As the 1950 study stated, Finland's obligations are *suspended* until such time as an express decision has been taken by the UN to put it back into force. However, the study did not indicate under what conditions the UN would take such an explicit decision. The common use of the word 'suspension' in the law of treaties[76] does not provide any information on these conditions either. However, if Finland decided to change its domestic law in order to enable the Finnish Government to accept corresponding complaints regarding Åland and forward them to the UN, there would in principle be no legal obstacles for the UN to consider international aspects of Åland's status in the General Assembly (Article 10 UN Charter). The appropriate body to deal with this issue would be the Legal Committee (Sixth Committee) of the General Assembly.[77] A corresponding proposal could be made, for example, by Finland and/or Sweden (respectively any member state to the UN). It could include proposals on how the status of the Åland Islands, which has grown into customary law, could be procedurally safeguarded and, in particular, which body could be entrusted with the task of settling disputes in this context. The Committee's decision would require a majority of the members present and voting.[78]

6 Concluding Remarks

The special procedural mechanism for Åland established under the League of Nations was suspended after the dissolution of the League. Such a mechanism could be reactivated, but only by an explicit decision within the UN framework. Although the conditions of the Swedish-speaking Ålanders in Finland are certainly more favourable than those of most other minority groups in Europe, such a procedural mechanism could resolve certain disputes on the basis of principles of international law and thus contribute to clarifying the scope of the customary status of the self-governing islands.

76 E.g., Art. 42, 57, 72 VCLT. Cf. I. Cameron, Suspension, Treaties, Suspension, in A. Peters (ed.), *Max Planck Encyclopedia of Public International Law* (online edn., OUP, December 2020).

77 Rule 98 lit. f of the Rules of Procedure, *supra* note 75. In general on the Committee's functions, cf. H. Llewellyn, T. Bektas, *supra* note 75, para. 8 et seq.

78 Rule 125 of the Rules of Procedure, *supra* note 75.

CHAPTER 7

On the Expression "The Special Status of Åland under International Law": a Formula with Potential

Ove Bring

1 EU Membership and Åland's Special Status

Finland, Sweden and Austria joined the European Union in 1995 in accordance with the Treaty of Accession of 1994. The need for separate negotiations between Finland and its European counterparts on how to deal with the special status of the Åland Islands was foreseen already in March 1992, when Finland applied for membership in what was then the European Communities (EC). Negotiations started in October 1993 and led to a specific protocol in the Act of Accession of Austria, Finland and Sweden. This was Protocol No. 2 on the Åland Islands, which entered into force at the beginning of 1995. Its *raison d'être* was to permit certain derogations from the EU instruments in favour of Åland. The opening words of the protocol run as follows:

> Taking into account *the special status that the Åland Islands enjoy under international law* [my italics], the Treaties on which the European Union is founded shall apply to the Åland Islands with the following derogations:

Thereafter follow three articles specifying the content of the derogations. They concern the right of domicile (regional citizenship), tax legislation, and equal treatment of natural and legal persons.

The "special status" is not defined, but one would expect it to include the two main features of the Åland diplomatic solution of 1921: (1) the autonomy with its language guarantees, and (2) the demilitarisation and neutralisation of the islands.

The autonomy regime of regional self-determination, or 'home rule' to borrow the expression from British history with regard to Ireland, was not controversial, and was obviously seen as a matter of mutual concern for the Union and its new member state in the north. Autonomy and language were regarded as having a privileged position under international law.

DOI:10.1163/9789004691117_009

On the other hand, during the negotiations the parties did not want to stress or even mention the demilitarisation issue; in fact they were prone to exclude it as a factor of relevance. This was especially true for the Finnish side, which felt that the demilitarisation issue definitely did not belong to the EU context.[1] However, this was a misapprehension. The Maastricht Treaty had entered into force on 1 November 1993 and, through it, the Common Foreign and Security Policy (CFSP) in Section V of the treaty. Section V consisted of one article only, Article J, which was divided into 11 paragraphs, most of them in turn divided into subparagraphs. According to Article J 1.2 the CFSP aims at, *inter alia*, strengthening the security of the Union and its member states, maintaining the peace and promoting international cooperation. Attainment of these goals clearly requires respect for arms control treaties, including multilateral agreements on regional demilitarisation and neutralisation.

2 The Holistic Character of the Åland Solution

The dimension of international security was an integral part of the Resolution of 24 June 1921, adopted by the Council of the League of Nations. On 27 June, the agreement between Finland and Sweden on "Guarantees for the Autonomy and Swedish Character of the Åland Islands" ('*Ålandsöverenskommelsen*') was approved by the League Council and annexed to its resolution of 24 June. But that resolution started out by expressing "the desirability of a solution involving a maximum of security both for the population of the Islands and the parties concerned".

Thereafter, in paragraph 1, the Council recognized that the sovereignty of the Åland Islands belonged to Finland. Paragraph 2 was given the following wording:

> Nevertheless, the interests of the world, the future of cordial relations between Finland and Sweden, the prosperity and happiness of the Islands themselves cannot be ensured unless (a) certain further guarantees are given for the protection of the Islanders; and unless (b) arrangements are concluded for the non-fortification and neutralisation of the Archipelago.

1 Information from Niilo Jääskinen, member of the Finnish negotiation team, in a conversation 10 June 2002.

In other words, the issue of different guarantees, later to be specified in the bilateral agreement, went hand in hand with an international security dimension of "non-fortification and neutralisation".

This security dimension was disregarded by the Finnish Government when, during the negotiations in 1994, it submitted the following declaration, a cumbersome text that only referred to the autonomy:

> The Government of Finland recalls that the autonomy of the Åland Islands is constitutionally guaranteed to its inhabitants in the Constitution of Finland and Finnish legislation on the autonomy on the basis of International Law in pursuance of the resolutions of 24 and 27 June 1921 on the Åland Islands of the Council of the League of Nations and that the Åland Islands are the subject of an established status under International Law.[2]

Thus, the autonomy issue was isolated through an interpretation that downgraded the holistic character of the Åland solution. The unwillingness to mention the disarmament/neutralisation issue may have mirrored an uneasiness in military circles in Finland, harbouring a negative attitude towards the restrictions flowing from the demilitarisation.

The Finnish Government's declaration of 1994 is characterised by its awkward and lengthy construction. Its purpose may have been to give the impression that the autonomy is above all grounded in Finnish legislation and sovereignty, and to a lesser extent in international law. The reference to "Finnish legislation on the autonomy", meaning the 1991 Åland Autonomy Act, is partly misleading. The central government in Helsinki seemingly wanted to conceal the major part the regional Åland authorities play in the legislative process. The official Swedish name of the act in question is '*självstyrelselagen*', indicating that the matter of home rule is seen from the perspective of the Åland Government in Mariehamn, not Helsinki.

Although the dimensions of autonomy and international security should be looked upon as an integrated whole, the international law status of the Åland Islands was blurred already in 1947, at the Paris Peace Conference after World War II. The Peace Treaty between Finland and its counterparts, the Soviet Union, the United Kingdom, and some other countries, states in Article 5: "The

2 The Finnish Declaration is included in a Protocol of a meeting with the Council of Ministers 22 February 1994.

Åland Islands shall remain demilitarised in accordance with the situation as at present existing."[3]

In a peace treaty it is not surprising that an autonomy regime of one contracting party is not referred to, but it is ominous that an existing arms control regime is not confirmed in its entirety. Article 5 confirms the Åland demilitarisation but says nothing about the neutralisation (the non-fighting requirement). It is unclear whether the text should be interpreted to include the follow-up to the League's resolution of 24 June, namely the 1921 multilateral Geneva Convention on the demilitarisation and neutralisation of the Åland Islands (although not confirming the neutralisation part of it), and the bilateral Soviet-Finnish Treaty of 1940 (limited to demilitarisation); or whether the text should be interpreted to refer exclusively to the bilateral treaty. The Soviet Union never became a party to the 1921 Geneva Convention and did not seem to recognize it in 1947 (nor does Russia today). If the latter, bilateral interpretation is correct, it implies a possible erosion of the multilateral regional regime (ten states are parties to the 1921 Convention).

In an official British commentary to the peace Treaty of 1947 the following was noted:

> The Aaland Islands were demilitarised under an International Convention concluded in 1921, to which the Soviet Government, however, was not a party. In 1940, the Soviet Government concluded an agreement with Finland which provided equally for the demilitarisation of these islands. This demilitarisation has now been confirmed in the Present Treaty.[4]

Nothing was said about neutralisation. It seems that the Western parties to the Peace Treaty (UK, Australia, Canada and New Zealand), together with two non-Western parties (Czechoslovakia and India), did in 1947 recognize the fundamental importance of the bilateral treaty in accordance with the Soviet view. However, one could argue that this ill-boding development has since been counteracted by at least Finland and Sweden, and by the Ålanders themselves, by emphasising the full ambit of the Geneva solution of 1921.

So far, the formula of the international law status of the Åland Islands has, in state practice, been characterised by a selective approach, confirming *that* part of the international regime that has concretely been dealt with, and not referring to the broader international scope. A more holistic description, beneficial to a correct understanding of the regime, is recommended for the future.

---

3 *International Treaties and Documents Concerning Åland Islands 1856–1992*, Ålands kulturstiftelse, Mariehamn 1993, p. 48.

4 Quoted by G. Lindholm in *Nordisk Tidsskrift for International Ret* 1982, p. 99*f.*

The most relevant aspect of the issue in question (be it autonomy, language, demilitarisation or neutralisation) should primarily be lifted forward, but also in some appropriate way be integrated with the other aspects of the regime. A full and integrated presentation in international fora would make the international status of Åland more well-known and understood in broader circles.

It is thus a matter of strengthening the awareness of the Åland regime, but besides that, and above all, it is a matter of establishing the strength of the regime itself. How strong is it today in legal terms, taking into account the changes that have taken place in the international community since 1921?

3 From the League of Nations to the United Nations

The final decision of the League Council on 27 June 1921 meant that the agreement between Sweden and Finland (*'Ålandsöverenskommelsen'*) was approved by the Council and annexed to its resolution of 24 June. The resolution encompassed the different elements of what was now emerging as a special international status of the Åland Islands: Autonomy in the form of regional self-determination, the Swedish language character of the islands, and the demilitarisation and neutralisation of the archipelago. It was a package deal, addressed to all members of the organisation. It was an opportune start for a customary law development among the then members of the international community.

The Council undertook to control the implementation of the guarantees linked to autonomy and language. As it was expressed in the resolution: "In any case, the Council of the League of Nations will see to the enforcement of these guarantees".

When the Convention on Demilitarisation and Neutralisation was adopted in October 1921, a more extensive formula for the role of the Council was adopted in Article 7. The text elaborated different measures in order to stop any violations of the provisions of the Convention. Article 9 prescribed that the Council should inform the members of the League of the text of the Convention, "in order that the legal status of the Aaland Islands", may, "in the interests of general peace, be respected by all as part of the actual rules of conduct among Governments". In the autumn of 1921, it was quite clear that a comprehensive, international legal status of the Åland Islands was established, comprising also the League decisions of 24 and 27 June (this will be elaborated further below).

With regard to the Swedish-Finnish agreement of 27 June, it is possible to suggest that the international community had a legal interest in Finland's compliance with its obligations concerning the Åland autonomy. However, the contracting parties themselves (Finland and Sweden) did not at the time recognise any binding effect of their agreement. This was due to certain political reasons (explained by Lauri Hannikainen[5]), and the agreement was not, in either of the two capitals, registered in the national treaty series. However, Sweden reversed its position in 1945 and took the view that the agreement had a legal status, which implied international obligations for Finland.[6] This has, never been disputed by the Finnish Government, which also has changed its position.

Irrespective of how one looks at the original bilateral agreement of 1921, as a political understanding or as a legal text, it is clear that over time Sweden and Finland have recognized the agreement as a legally binding treaty. Sweden recognised Finnish sovereignty over the islands as a confirmation of the earlier Swedish recognition with regard to the League's resolution of 24 June, where the Council had in point 1 decided that "[t]he sovereignty of the Aaland Islands is recognised to belong to Finland". At the same time, Finland recognised an obligation to Sweden (and the Åland population) to respect Åland's autonomy and Swedish character. Sweden now had a legal interest in verifying Finnish implementation of the agreement, and a right to react, but not a duty to guarantee. Today, taking into account the extremely cordial relations between the two Nordic countries, it is unthinkable that Sweden would put forward specific complaints in what could be seen as an internal Finnish affair.

Already in 1921 the Åland question was, beyond the bilateral dimension, an international affair. Since the Council resolution was communicated to the members of the organisation, they were expected to support the Åland autonomy solution as a political and legal fact. It is possible to argue that the multilateral context gave rise to an *opinio juris* among member states that there was a customary law development in the offing. First, this *opinio* accepted and welcomed such a development; later it confirmed it as a fact. Although this *opinio juris* was not explicitly articulated at the time, it nevertheless could be presumed to exist in late October 1921, when the updating of the demilitarisation, announced by the Council, was completed. At this point in time, the different parts of the Åland solution formed a whole. The autonomy regime gained the status of regional (particular) customary law, not only between Finland and Sweden, but for all states being active in the Baltic Sea region. The duty to respect Åland's autonomy and Swedish character is at least obligatory

---

5 Lauri Hannikainen and Frank Horn (eds.), *Autonomy and Demilitarisation in International Law: The Åland Islands in Changing Europe* (Kluwer Law International, The Hague, 1997) p. 61.

6 Love Kellberg, 'Ålandsöarnas internationellrättsliga ställning', 59 *Svensk Juristtidning* (1974) p. 190.

for the parties to the 1921 October Convention, states which are identified as having an interest in any legal regime of the Baltic Sea region.

The same conclusion of customary law can be drawn separately with regard to the demilitarisation and neutralisation; in fact, it can be drawn much more easily than is the case with the autonomy. The adoption in Geneva of the multilateral convention on 'Non-Fortification, etc.' meant in effect that a corresponding *opinio juris*, corresponding to the content of the convention, was explicitly articulated through that adoption. This was underpinned by the fact that the convention was foreseen and decided upon in the 5th point of the Council resolution of 24 June. Moreover, the convention as such was built on the past. It confirmed, developed and strengthened the 1856 Åland non-fortification regime of Paris. Due to these intersecting factors, it is possible to argue that the adoption in Geneva created instant customary law.

In sum, with regard to the situation in a broad sense, it can safely be said that after 1921 the international legal status of the Åland Islands had won general recognition within the international community, and that all states and international organisations had to act accordingly.

At the same time, it has to be admitted that this international legal status was somewhat reduced when the League of Nations collapsed. The organisation lost its ability to function already before the outbreak of World War II. It was finally dissolved in 1946, after the establishment of the UN. For the Åland Islands' regime this meant that the supporting, supervising and controlling function of the League Council vanished into thin air.

It also became evident that the entire minorities protection system of the League had collapsed and was not taken up by the UN. This was confirmed by a UN Secretariat Report of 1950, where it was said that the minorities protection system had ceased to exist in accordance with the doctrine of *clausula rebus sic stantibus*, a reference to the presumed existence of an implicit clause in every agreement that a change of fundamental circumstances makes the agreement in question void. However, the 1950 UN Report concluded specifically on the Åland question, that there was no fundamental change of circumstances:

> No change of circumstances has occurred. The special regime for the Aaland Islands concerns particularly Sweden, Finland and the population of the Aaland Islands. Sweden and Finland have not been at war.

3.1 *Conclusion*

Finland's obligation towards Sweden still exists. On the other hand, according to the UN Report, the obligation undertaken by Finland towards the Council of the League of Nations as representative of the international community is suspended until such time as an express decision has been taken by the United Nations to put it back into force.[7]

This statement was limited to the potential role of the UN Security Council, "as representative of the international community", or some other UN organ, to assume the League's supervisory functions. The report did not exclude that Finland owed its obligations concerning Åland's autonomy and Swedish character to the international community of states, irrespective of the role of the UN. The authors of the report did not seem to be aware of the potential of international customary law. The customary law factor with regard to the Åland Islands is nowadays not centred around organisational headquarters in Geneva or New York, but around the Baltic Sea and the surrounding geographical region. The autonomy and the demilitarisation/neutralisation regimes are interconnected. The Åland Government and population, in the implementation of their autonomous right to self-determination, have, at least since 1938,[8] supported the international security regime of their islands. The role of the League Council under the 1921 Convention has not been replaced by the UN, but in view of the customary law situation this presents no problem. In general, the two pillars of the international legal status of the Åland Islands, political autonomy and military security, adequately support one another in a joint customary law phenomenon.

4 Identification of International Customary Law

Assertions on the existence of customary law have already been made, but there is a need to offer some comments on the two constituent elements of international customary law. The Council of the League of Nations presented a solution which involved the international community as such. This was done in a diplomatic process with legal connotations.

The first step in the process of June 1921 was the Resolution of 24 June, where the Council decided, in five points, on the future of the islands. The text of the resolution noted that "the two parties interested in the fate of the Aaland Islands" had agreed upon the content of the resolution. Third states, the other members of the League, were aware that the agreed points – basically Finnish sovereignty, Åland autonomy and updated demilitarisation – constituted a

7 UN Doc. E/CN.4/367 (1950) p. 69.

8 On 31 October 1938, thousands of people joined in a protest march in Mariehamn against the on-going Finnish-Swedish talks on a partial remilitarisation of the islands. This plan, later called the Stockholm Plan, proved to be abortive. The Soviet Union did not accept it.

legal regime for the future. The diplomats in Geneva joined, on behalf of their governments, in a silent consensus that expressed an emerging *opinio juris*. Governments accepted and welcomed the legal outcome, but perhaps not knowing whether the solution could be equated with a treaty or whether it meant incipient customary law. The notion of instant customary law was not known (it belongs to the UN era), but for such a thing to occur one would have expected a manifest consensus on the text of a formal treaty.

Anyhow, the process was not complete. The resolution of 24 June was to a certain extent held in abeyance. It awaited, in accordance with point 4 of the resolution, an agreement between Finland and Sweden on guarantees. When that agreement was a fact, it was presented at the Council meeting of 27 June and its seven points were read out. Thereafter, according to the records of the meeting, "[t]he Council unanimously approved the terms of this agreement and decided that it should be annexed to its resolution of June 24th." The package deal of resolution and follow-up agreement was thereby completed and the minutes of the Council meeting were published in the *League of Nations Official Journal*. The member states of the League took note and their opinio juris now expressed acceptance of a legal fact. A customary law development had started.

To determine the existence of a norm of international customary law it is necessary to ascertain whether its two constituent elements are in place; the objective one and the subjective one. Is there a general practice of states (*usus*) and is this practice accepted as law (*opinio juris*)? In assessing evidence for this, regard must, in accordance with the legal doctrine on customary law, be taken to the overall context and the particular circumstances. Let us relate this to the League's autonomy solution.

This author has so far offered a number of references to opinio juris, but none to usus as a general practice of states. It has only been indicated that Finland and Sweden, in their bilateral practice over time, have upheld their agreement of 1921 ('*Ålandsöverenskommelsen*').

In the doctrine of international law it has often been stressed that each "of the two constituent elements is to be separately ascertained. This requires an assessment of evidence for each element".[9] In our case, with regard to the *usus* element, third states have been indirectly involved through the League Council, "as representative of the international community", to quote from the 1950 UN Report. No state took an issue with the normative leadership of the

9 Sir Michael Wood, Special Rapporteur of the International Law Commission on the identification of customary international law, in *Yearbook of the International Law Commission* (2018), Volume II, Part Two, p. 90.

Council at the time. This behaviour of passive acceptance, manifested over time, is also a form of general state practice. In fact, this is what has characterised the situation before and after the Second World War.

Moreover, there are situations in which the two constituent elements melt together into one. If an *opinio juris* can be ascertained amongst a large group of states, there is no need for a series of repeated acts. It will be sufficient with a general acceptance demonstrated in an international forum at one point in time. Conversely, it is possible to argue that a clear *opinio juris* may be difficult to ascertain, but that it can be inferred from a number of state acts. Michael Akehurst has pointed out that "[a] practice followed by a very small number of states can create a rule of customary law if there is no practice which conflicts with the rule".[10] Charles de Visscher has argued that the subjective element "may perfectly well be inferred from the external qualities of the precedents invoked".[11] Thus, legal doctrine offers examples of a flexible approach to the objective and subjective elements; one element can obviate the need for the other. Moreover, Anthony D'Amato has replaced the subjective element with the empirical state practice of *articulation* of a new norm.[12]

In our case, it is difficult to argue that a number of repeated acts have taken place. Rather, we have an *opinio juris* articulated by the Council, in the sense that its resolution is topped by a legally binding convention, implying that the whole package should be of a binding nature. This articulation by the Council is being confirmed by member states of the League through their quiet acceptance. A legal development has emerged creating almost instant customary law.

A final comment under this heading is called for. I have not used the *opinio juris* element with the only understanding that it refers to a view of existing law. I have also covered the situation where a state supports a certain law coming into being. This wider *de lege ferenda* oriented conception of *opinio juris* helps to explain how a legal development can start and come about.

5 Lessons Learned for the Future

As has already been argued, the legal status of the Åland Islands should not be referred to in bits and pieces, but as a whole. The expression "the special

---

10 M. Akehurst, 'Custom as a Source of International Law', 47 *British Yearbook of International Law* (1974–1975), p. 18.

11 Ch. de Visscher, *Theory and Reality in Public International Law* (Princeton University Press, Princeton, 1968), p. 442.

12 A. D'Amato, *The Concept of Custom in International Law* (Cornell University Press, Ithaca and London, 1971), pp. 264–271.

status of Åland under international law", or variations thereof, should in the future be used as an overarching formula, thereby maximising its potential to reach out in the international community. In concrete cases the most relevant aspect of the regime must be stressed, but, at the same time, the full scope of the special status should be lifted forward. One should avoid fragmentation *exclusively* stressing only one aspect – be it autonomy, language protection, demilitarisation or neutralisation, whatever the case may be in the specific circumstances. Åland's status in the international arena should thus be marketed with the full panoply of legal elements. The landscape's brand image will then be strengthened and this will serve the efforts for increased self-determination and home rule.

Åland delegates should be present in as many international fora as possible – in formal negotiations, in diplomatic seminars, in non-governmental gatherings, and in meetings with other autonomies, like the Faroe Islands, Gibraltar, the Isle of Man and others. Åland has the potential to transform itself from an object to a subject of international law, to become an actor in the international arena, to increase its international agency in line with what the 2007 UN Declaration on the Rights of Indigenous Peoples recognised for these peoples.

CHAPTER 8

The Demilitarisation and Neutralisation of the Åland Islands: Customary Law Aspects

Allan Rosas

1 Introduction

The demilitarisation and neutralisation of the Åland Islands constitutes a special regime under public international law, the first bricks of which were laid already more than 160 years ago. While a Convention of 1856 between France, Russia and the United Kingdom was limited to *demilitarisation,* with a focus on a ban on permanent military installations and forces, the treaty regime was in 1921 broadened to include *neutralisation*, which implies an obligation, in principle, to keep the territory outside military operations in times of armed conflict.[1] The multilateral Convention of 1921 relating to both demilitarisation and neutralisation was concluded as part of a broader framework sponsored by the League of Nations, which included recognition of Finnish sovereignty over the Åland Islands coupled with regional autonomy and guarantees for Swedish language and culture.

Especially the demilitarisation leg of the regime has been reaffirmed in two subsequent international agreements, a bilateral agreement between Finland and the Soviet Union of 1940, the continuation in force of which has been confirmed in a Protocol concluded in 1992 between Finland and the Russian Federation as the successor State to the Soviet Union, and the Paris Peace Treaty of 1947, concluded by Finland with several third States. That said, also the multilateral 1921 Convention, which is much more detailed than the other agreements referred to, is generally considered to remain in force today. Moreover, Protocol No. 2 to the Finnish Accession Treaty to the EU refers in

1 As will be elaborated in subchapter 4 below, the distinction between demilitarisation and neutralisation is not clear-cut. On the two concepts, *see*, e.g., M. Björkholm and A. Rosas, *Ålandsöarnas demilitarisering och neutralisering* (Åbo Akademi Press, Turku/Åbo, 1990) pp. 16–17, 56 *et seq*., 93 *et seq*.; A. Rosas, 'The Åland Islands as a Demilitarised and Neutralised Zone', in L. Hannikainen and F. Horn (eds.), *Autonomy and Demilitarisation in International Law: The Åland Islands in a Changing Europe* (Kluwer Law International, The Hague, 1997) p. 23 at pp. 23–24.

DOI:10.1163/9789004691117_010

its Preamble more generally to "the special status that the Åland Islands enjoy under international law".

The Åland demilitarisation and neutralisation regime is thus firmly anchored in international treaty law. It could accordingly be surmised that unwritten customary international law, that is, to quote Article 38(1) of the Statute of the International Court of Justice, "international custom, as evidence of a general practice accepted as law", would play a minor, if any, role in discussions about the legal status and relevance of the regime.

Yet, several factors contribute to a continued interest in the customary law aspects of the regime as well. Especially in the context of a Finnish security policy debate, there have from time to time been voices questioning the relevance or usefulness of demilitarisation and neutralisation or even proposing Finnish withdrawal from the 1921 Convention and/or the bilateral agreement concluded with the Soviet Union (now the Russian Federation) in 1940. Clearly, withdrawal from, or suspension of, the 1921 Convention and/or the 1940 agreement would raise the question as to the existence and scope of obligations which could remain in force as customary law, withdrawal or suspension notwithstanding. According to Article 43 of the Vienna Convention on the Law of Treaties of 1969, the non-continuance in force of a treaty "shall not in any way impair the duty of any State to fulfil any obligations embodied in the treaty to which it would be subject under international law independently of the treaty".[2]

In the context of the Russian war of aggression against Ukraine (which took a dramatic turn with the armed attack against Ukraine launched on 24 February 2022), and the ensuing Finnish NATO membership, renewed proposals have been made to withdraw from, or suspend the operation of, the 1940 bilateral treaty or at least to terminate the presence of a Russian Consulate in Mariehamn, which according to the 1940 bilateral agreement has the task of verifying respect for the demilitarisation regime. In view of this discussion, the Legal Service of the Finnish Ministry for Foreign Affairs has, on 14 November 2023, published a study on the international legal status of Åland and public international law questions concerning the Russian Consulate, which includes observations on the relevance of customary international law for the demilitarisation and neutralisation regime. Before its publication, the study was considered by the President of the Republic together with the

2 See also Article 38 of the Vienna Convention, according to which its provisions relating to the effects of treaties on third States do not preclude rules set forth in a treaty "from becoming binding upon a third State as a customary rule of international law, recognized as such".

Committee on Foreign- and Security Policy of the Finnish Government.[3] At the time of writing, it appears that the Government will not initiate withdrawal from, or suspension of the 1940 agreement or parts of it.

The following discussion will focus on the customary law aspects of the demilitarisation and neutralisation regime. It will not, within the confines of this short exposé, be possible to analyse in detail the provisions of the relevant international treaties and the 1921 Convention in particular, which is the most detailed instrument as compared to the 1856, 1940 and 1947 treaties.[4] Nor will it be possible to analyse the international legal status of the regional autonomy of Åland, including guarantees relating to Swedish language and culture, which dates back to decisions of the League of Nations in June 1921 and Finnish autonomy legislation of 1920 and 1922.[5] Suffice it to note here that there are arguments speaking in favour of the thesis that the autonomy and language regime, too, implies international legal obligations for Finland, be it in the form of regional or bilateral customary law,[6] unilateral commitments or treaty law.

3 Press Release of the Finnish Government of 14 November 2023. The study was published in Finnish and Swedish on 14 November, Ulkoasiainministeriö, *Kansainvälisoikeudellinen selvitys Ahvenanmaan kansainvälisestä erityisasemasta ja Venäjän Maarianhaminan konsulinvirastoon liittyvistä oikeudellisista kysymyksistä* <www.urn.fi/URN:ISBN:978-952-281-385-5>, visited on 16 November 2023.

4 There is an abundance of publications relating to the demilitarisation and neutralisations regime, including studies on the scope and content of the 1921 Convention. E.g., J.O. Söderhjelm, *Demilitarisation et neutralisation des Iles d'Aland en 1856 et 1921* (Söderström, Helsinki, 1928); H. Rotkirch, 'The Demilitarization and Neutralization of the Åland Islands: A Regime "in European Interests" Withstanding Changing Circumstances', 23 *Journal of Peace Research* (1986) p. 357; Björkholm and Rosas, *supra* note 1; L. Hannikainen, 'The Continued Validity of the Demilitarised and Neutralised Status of the Åland Islands', 54 *Zeitschrift für ausländisches öffentliches Recht und Völkerrecht* (1994) p. 614; Rosas, *supra* note 1; S Spiliopoulou Åkermark, 'Ålands Demilitarisation and Neutralisation: Continuity and Change', in S. Spiliopoulou Åkermark (ed.), *The Åland Example and Its Components: Relevance for International Conflict Resolution* (The Åland Islands Peace Institute, Mariehamn, 2011) p. 50; S. Åkermark, S. Heinikoski and P. Kleemola-Juntunen, *Demilitarization and International Law in Context: The Åland Islands* (Routledge, New York, 2018). *See also* the study by the Finnish Ministry for Foreign Affairs of 14 November 2023, *supra* note 3.

5 The most comprehensive and thorough study of the international law aspects of the autonomous status of Aaland is provided by T. Modeen, *De folkrättsliga garantierna för bevarandet av Ålandsöarnas nationella karaktär* (Skrifter utgivna av Ålands Kulturstiftelse VII, Mariehamn, 1973). *See also* L. Hannikainen, 'The International Legal Basis of the Autonomy and Swedish Character of the Åland Islands', in Hannikainen and Horn, *supra* note 4, p. 57.

6 According to Conclusion 16(1) of the Conclusions on Identification of Customary International Law, adopted by the International Law Commission (ILC) at its 3412th meeting, held on 25 May 2018 (ILC Report, UN doc. A/73/10, 2018 p. 117), and taken note of by the UN General Assembly in Resolution 73/203 of 20 December 2018, "[a] rule of particular

It should be recalled that the concept of customary international law is a difficult one, and one should be aware, inter alia, of the "complexity of assessing the existence of a rule of customary international law".[7] It goes without saying that it is not possible in this short contribution to delve into all the intricacies and doctrinal debates about the formation, evidence and development of customary law and, even after a rule of customary law has been identified, the difficulties which can be inherent in determining its precise scope and content.[8] The European Court of Justice, in settling for a limited judicial review of EU legal acts alleged to be in contravention of customary international law, has observed that "a principle of customary international law does not have the same degree of precision as a provision of an international agreement".[9] The ensuing discussion will be based on the assumption that the Conclusions on Identification of Customary International Law, adopted by the UN International Law Commission (ILC) in 2018,[10] constitute an authoritative guideline for the assessment of various issues relating to the formation, application and development of customary international law.

2 The 1856 Convention, the Peace Treaties of 1918 and the 1921 Convention

In the following, particular attention will be paid to the circumstances surrounding the birth of the demilitarisation regime in 1856, its reaffirmation in

---

customary international law, whether regional, local or other, is a rule of customary law that applies only among a limited number of States".

7 First report on formation and evidence of customary international law, by Sir Michael Wood, Special Rapporteur of the ILC, 17 May 2013, UN doc. A/CN.4/663, para. 2, referring to observations made on the agenda item related to the processes of formation and evidence of customary international law (later to be entitled Identification of Customary International Law, *supra* note 6) in the Sixth Committee of the UN General Assembly in 2012.

8 There is an abundance of literature on the theory and practice of customary international law, *see* the list of writings contained in the ILC report by Sir Michael Wood, Special Rapporteur, referred to *supra*, note 7. For but two examples, *see* A. Rosas, 'Customary Law: From "Universal" in a European System to "Regional" in a World System', in A. Grahl-Madsen and Jiri Toman (eds.), *The Spirit of Uppsala: Proceedings of the Joint UNITAR-Uppsala University Seminar on International Law and Organization for a New World Order* (Walter de Gruyter, Berlin, 1984) p. 222; J. Wouters *et al.*, *International Law: A European Perspective* (Hart Publishing, Oxford, 2019) pp. 134–156.

9 Case C-366/10 *Air Transport Association of America* EU:C:2011:864, para. 110. *See also* Case C-161/96 *Racke* EU:C:1998:203, para. 52.

10 *See supra*, note 6.

Peace Treaties concluded in March 1918 by Soviet Russia and Finland and the discussions and decisions at the League of Nations in 1920–21, leading to the adoption of the 1921 multilateral Convention. A separate subchapter will look at subsequent treaties and State practice, to explore whether these developments confirm or rather contradict the demilitarisation and neutralisation regime as established during the period from 1856 to 1921. It can be assumed that if a treaty rule has been in force for a long time and has been reaffirmed in a number of treaties and unilateral declarations or statements, its status as customary law becomes all the more plausible and perhaps probable.[11]

The demilitarisation of the Åland Islands has its origins in the Convention of Paris of 30 March 1856 respecting the Åland Islands, concluded by France, Russia and the United Kingdom. This Convention was annexed to the Peace Treaty of the same day,[12] which ended the Crimean War and provided, inter alia, for the neutralisation of the Black Sea, including a ban on warships.[13] These treaties were concluded at a time when Finland was an autonomous Grand Duchy within the Russian Empire and thus did not appear as a Contracting Party. At the insistence of France and the United Kingdom, the Russian Emperor agreed in the trilateral Convention relating to the Åland Islands to declare that "the islands of Åland shall not be fortified and that no military or naval base shall be maintained or created there". As this Convention was annexed to the Peace Treaty, it is arguable that it became binding on all

11 See Conclusion 11 of the ILC Conclusions on Identification of International Customary Law, *supra* note 6, which concerns the significance of treaties for the identification of customary international law. It is stated, inter alia, that "[t]he fact that a rule is set forth in a number of treaties may, but does not necessarily, indicate that the treaty rule reflects a rule of customary international law" (Conclusion 11(2)). See also the judgment of the International Court of Justice in *Continental Shelf* (*Libyan Arab Jamahiriya* v. *Malta*), Judgments, I.C.J. Reports 1985, para. 27.

12 The general Peace Treaty of Paris, signed on 30 March 1856, was concluded between Russia, on the one hand, and Austria, France, the Ottoman Empire, Prussia, Sardinia and the United Kingdom, on the other. According to its Article XXXIII, the Convention relating to the Aaland Islands "is and remains annexed to the present Treaty, and shall have the same force and validity as if it formed a part thereof".

13 According to Article XI of the Treaty of Paris, "[t]he Black Sea is Neutralised; its Waters and its Ports, thrown to the Mercantile Marine of every Nation, are formally and in perpetuity interdicted to the Flag of War, either of the Powers possessing its Coasts, or of any other Power, with the exceptions mentioned in Articles XIV and XIX of the present Treaty". The English version is here based on a text published by the Economic Cooperation Foundation, www.content.ecf.org.il, visited on 16 November 2023.

Parties to the latter Treaty, including Austria, the Ottoman Empire, Prussia and Sardinia.[14]

During the First World War, Russia, fearing that Germany would send troops and establish a naval base on the islands, built fortifications on the islands. This took place with British, French and Swedish acquiescence.[15] After the Finnish Declaration of Independence on 6 December 1917, there were Russian, and for shorter periods, Finnish, Swedish and German troops on the Islands. The Treaty of Peace of Brest-Litovsk between Germany, Austria-Hungary, Bulgaria and Turkey, for the one part, and Soviet Russia, for the other part, of 3 March 1918, provided (Article VI) that "Finland and the Åland Islands will immediately be cleared of Russian troops and the Russian Red Guard" and that "[t]he fortresses built on the Åland Islands are to be removed as soon as possible." The same provision also referred to a "special agreement" concerning the "permanent non-fortification" of the islands as well as "their future treatment in respect to military and technical matters" which was to be concluded between Germany, Finland, Russia and Sweden.[16]

At German insistence, a similar provision was included in the Treaty of Peace between Finland and Germany, signed in Berlin on 7 March 1918.[17] According to Article 30, the Contracting Parties agree that the fortifications built on the islands "are to be removed as soon as possible". Reference is also made to a future "special agreement between Germany, Finland, Russia and Sweden" to regulate "a permanent non-fortification of these islands as well as their further treatment in respect of military and technical navigation

14 Söderhjelm, *supra* note 4, p. 100; Spiliopoulous Äkermark, Heinikoski and Kleemola-Juntunen, *supra* note 4, pp. 22–23.

15 Björkholm and Rosas, *supra* note 1, p. 20. *See also* N.J. Padelford and K.G.A. Andersson, 'The Aaland Islands Question', 33 *American Journal of International Law* (1939) p. 465 at p. 467, mentions that Russia construed the terms of the 1856 Convention to mean, inter alia, that she could have 'temporary' fortifications on the Islands, that she could have war vessels stationed in adjacent waters and that the non-fortification obligations was only binding in peace time. According to the same authors, Russia in 1906 sent warships and 750 men to the Islands but after Swedish and British protests, the troops were withdrawn. See also Spiliopoulou Åkermark, *supra* note 4, p. 55.

16 English was not an official language of the Brest-Litovsk Treaty. The quotations are from an unofficial translation by Judah Leon Magnes published by Wikisource, www.en.m.wikisource.org, visited on 16 November 2023.

17 The official Finnish text was published in the Finnish Treaty Series (*Finlands överenskommelser med främmande makter*) No. 3–5/1918–20. For the German and unofficial English texts see www.histdoc.net, visited on 16 November 2023. There were no comparable provisions in the Peace Treaties concluded by Finland in 1918 with Austria-Hungary (Finnish Treaty Series No. 7/1918–1920). Bulgaria (No. 6/1918–20) and Turkey (No. 11/1918–1920).

matters". "Upon Germany's desire", other countries bordering upon the Baltic Sea were to be invited to join this special agreement. A more technical agreement between Finland, Germany and Sweden relating to the demolition of fortifications and other military installations was concluded in December 1918.[18] In this context it can also be mentioned that the Dorpat Peace Treaty between Finland and Soviet Russia of 14 October 1920 came to include a clause in which the Contracting Parties committed themselves to work towards the "neutralisation" of the Finnish Gulf and the Baltic Sea.[19]

In a memorandum to the Finnish Senate (as the government was still called in 1918) one of the negotiators of the 1918 Peace Treaty with Germany, Professor Rafael Erich, mentioned that "[i]t did not pass unnoticed for the Finnish negotiators that annulling the non-fortification pact relative to Åland, which formed part of Finland, might bring some favours to Finland". He added, however, that lifting the demilitarisation "can hardly find support" as Germany had made it clear "that in principle the non-fortification still holds and will form the basis for all future arrangements" and that it could be expected "that Sweden would in all circumstances do all she can to fight against fortification" and would regard a fortified Åland as a constant threat against her. Lifting the demilitarisation regime would accordingly result in a "serious quarrel" between Finland and Sweden with harmful effects on political relations in the Nordic area.[20]

These references to the political realities involved, including the position of Sweden, which was not a party to the 1856 Convention or the Peace Treaties of 1918, proved to be accurate forecasts for what was to be forthcoming in the discussions at the League of Nations. After the Peace Conference of Paris had declined to heed a Swedish proposal to take up the Åland Islands question, it was referred to the Council of the League of Nations, which put it on its agenda on 11 July 2020.[21] The Council appointed a Committee of Jurists to give an advisory opinion as to whether the dispute between Finland and Sweden was of such an international nature that it could be dealt with by the Council, and

18 Signed in Stockholm on 30 December 1918, Finnish Treaty Series No. 12/1918–1920. *See also* Padelford and Andersson, *supra* note 15, p. 471.

19 See Articles 12 and 16(2) of the Peace Treaty, Finnish Treaty Series No. 1/1921. As can be seen from Articles 13 and 14, which concerned the neutralisation of some islands in the Finnish Gulf, the term "neutralisation" seems to have referred to a prohibition of military installations and armed forces, that is, what generally is conceived as demilitarisation (*see supra*, at note 1).

20 Unofficial translation by Pauli Kruhse. The typewritten promemoria by Professor Erich, in Finnish, can be found in Dr. Edvard Hjelt's private archives in the National Archives of Finland. The Finnish text and English translation published by histdoc.net., visited on 18 November 2023.

21 Modeen, *supra* note 5, pp. 20, 25–26.

on the "present position with regard to international obligations concerning the demilitarisation of the Åland Islands".[22] The Commission came to the conclusion that the dispute was indeed of an international nature and that the Council was competent to make any recommendations which it deemed just and proper.[23]

As to the question of demilitarisation under the 1856 Convention, the Committee noted certain Russian unsuccessful efforts during the years 1907 and 1908 with a view to obtaining the abolition of the obligations under the Convention. In discussing the relevance of the Russian military works erected on the Islands in wartime, the Committee observed that the object of the Convention "was not to neutralise or make the Åland Islands inviolable" and that "it would appear impossible to draw legal conclusions, affecting the continuance in force of the said Treaty, from these works undertaken in time of war". The Committee also referred to the fact that Russia had given assurances to the British, French and Swedish Governments that the construction of the fortifications was only for the duration of the war and that Russia later agreed, under the terms of the Treaty of Brest-Litovsk, to demolish the military works (see above). Accordingly, the provisions of the 1856 Convention with reference to the non-fortification of the Islands were still in force.[24]

In analysing the legal effects of the 1856 Convention for third States, including Finland and Sweden, the Committee of Jurists first rejected the Swedish thesis that the Convention had created a "'real servitude' attaching to the territory of the Åland Islands".[25] This did not imply, however, that the Convention was binding on France, Russia and the United Kingdom only. An examination of the "political conditions under which the agreement was entered into" showed that it had "in reality a much wider bearing". There was not only a Swedish but a "general European interest arising out of the strategic importance of the Åland archipelago". The Committee referred, inter alia, to the wording of the Preamble to the Convention and to the fact that it had been annexed to the Treaty of Peace and was to have the same effect as if it formed part of this Treaty.[26] The intention had thus been "to make the Convention …

22 Report of the International Committee of Jurists entrusted by the Council of the League of Nations with the task of giving an advisory opinion upon the legal aspects of the Aaland Islands question, League of Nations – Official Journal, Special supplement No. 3 (October 1920), p. 3. The text of the Report has been published on-line by the Aaland regional parliament, www.lagtinget.ax, visited on 18 November 2023.

23 *Ibid.* p. 14.

24 *Ibid.* p. 16.

25 *Ibid.* pp. 16–17.

26 *Ibid.* p. 17.

'European law'. It was possible to create "true objective law, a real political status the effects of which are felt outside the immediate circle of contracting parties".[27] The provisions of the Convention had "the character of a settlement regulating European interests", which could not be abolished or modified by the Contracting Parties.[28] The conclusion was that the provisions of the Convention and of the Treaty of Peace "were laid down in European interests" and "constituted a special international status relating to military considerations, for the Åland Islands". "[E]very State interested" had the right to insist on compliance and any State in possession of the Islands had to conform to the obligations arising out of the system of demilitarisation.[29]

Another Committee (Commission of Rapporteurs) appointed by the Council took a more pragmatic view in the sense that while it recognised that the 1856 Convention was still in force, it recommended that it be replaced by a new broader agreement, which would involve all interested Powers and would cover neutralisation as well.[30] This approach was accepted by the League Council, which in its decision of 24 June 1921, providing for an overall settlement of the dispute between Finland and Sweden, not only combined recognition of Finnish sovereignty with guarantees for the autonomy and protection of Swedish language and culture but also recommended (in paragraph 5) that, in order to provide assurances to the Swedish people and all interested States that the Åland Islands would never constitute a danger from a military point of view, the 1856 Convention should be replaced by a broader convention under the guarantee of all interested Powers, including Sweden, and that the new treaty should, in broad terms, follow a Swedish draft convention for the neutralisation of the Islands.[31]

A Conference with a view to adopting such a convention accordingly met at Geneva from 10 to 20 October 1921, with representatives from Denmark, Estonia, Finland, France, Germany, Italy, Latvia, Poland, Sweden and the United Kingdom. There was thus participation of all riparian States, except Lithuania and Soviet Russia. The latter State, which was not at the time a Member of the League of Nations, was not invited, even if the two 1918 Peace Treaties referred to above mentioned also Russia as a party to a future convention. Soviet Russia

27 *Ibid.*
28 *Ibid.* p. 18.
29 *Ibid.* p. 19.
30 Council doc. B 7.21/68/106. *See also* Padelford and Andersson, *supra* note 15, pp. 475–476; Modeen, *supra* note 5, p. 38; Björkholm and Rosas, *supra* note 1, p. 22.
31 League of Nations, Official Journal, Sept. 1921, pp. 694–695, 699–700.

subsequently refused to recognise the 1921 Convention.[32] The Convention relating to the Non-fortification and Neutralisation of the Åland Islands was signed on 20 October.[33] The Preamble borrowed from the League of Nations Council decision of 24 June 1921 in stating that the Convention was concluded in order that the Åland Islands "may never become a source of danger from the military point of view". By contrast to the Council decision, however, the new Convention was not declared to 'replace' the 1856 Convention but to "supplement without prejudice thereto, the obligations assumed by Russia in the Convention of March 30, 1856". In the same vein, Finland agreed in Article 1 of the 1921 Convention not to fortify the Åland Islands, "confirming for her part, as far as necessary, the declaration made by Russia" in the 1856 Convention.

And according to Article 8 of the 1921 Convention, it was meant to remain in force "in spite of any changes that may take place in the present *status quo* in the Baltic Sea". Moreover, in Article 9 the Council of the League of Nations was requested to inform all Members of the text of the Convention, "in order that the legal status of the Åland Islands (…) as defined by the provisions of this Convention, may, in the interests of general peace, be respected by all as part of the actual rules of conduct among Governments".

The developments recalled above, starting with the 1856 Treaty of Peace and its annex, the 1856 demilitarisation Convention, and ending with the conclusion of the demilitarisation and neutralisation Convention of 1921, suggest that the Åland Islands had been endowed with a demilitarised status which had obtained the force of customary law. True, there were some attempts by Russia, and later to a lesser extent Finland, to question or even abandon this regime but the opposition from other interested States rendered these efforts largely ineffectual. While Soviet Russia was not invited to the 1921 Conference it committed itself in the Peace Treaty of Brest Litovsk of 3 March 1918 to the removal of Russian troops and fortifications. The opinion of the League of Nations Committee of Jurists referred, inter alia, to the 1856 rules as having been laid down "in European interests" and as constituting "a special international status relating to military considerations, for the Åland Islands" that "every State interested" had the right to invoke and that "any State in possession of the Islands" had to respect. The provisions of the 1921 Convention, and its Articles 1, 8 and 9 in particular, suggest a willingness to provide for continuity with the 1856 regime and to consider the 1921 Convention as reflecting, to cite Article 9, a "legal status" that should "be respected by all as part of the actual

32 Padelford and Andersson, *supra* note 115, pp. 477–478.

33 The Convention was published e.g., in the Finnish Treaty Series, No. 1/1922.

rules of conduct among Governments", a formula which seems to come close to saying that this status should be respected as customary international law.

3 Subsequent Developments

The above considerations relating to the Åland regime as part of customary law have been focused on demilitarisation, which is the common denominator of the 1856, 1918 and 1921 agreements. The League of Nations Committee of Jurists held explicitly that the 1856 Convention, unlike what the general Peace Treaty of Paris did for the Black Sea, did not provide for neutralisation and the Committee did not claim that demilitarisation was fully applicable in wartime as well. Neutralisation is, on the other hand, clearly regulated in the 1921 Convention and its Articles 8 and 9 can be seen as an invitation to consider neutralisation, too, as part of an emerging customary law.

Article 7 of the 1921 Convention provided for a role for the Council of the League of Nations in guaranteeing the observance of the Convention and putting a stop to any violations. As these guarantee provisions were cumbersome, and in any case the League of Nations was rapidly suffering a decline in prestige and relevance, Finland in 1937 entered into negotiations with Sweden on a plan to take military measures, partly in cooperation between the two countries, with a view to the defence of neutralisation. The so-called Stockholm Plan was in 1939 notified to the Contracting Parties and the Soviet Union but failed to obtain approval from the Council of the League. After the Soviet attack on Finland on 30 November 1939, Finland first invited Sweden to station troops on the Islands and after Sweden had declined, stationed forces on the Islands, laid mines in their territorial waters and installed temporary fortifications and coastal artillery thereon.[34] These measures were again notified to the Contracting Parties to the 1921 Convention, which do not seem to have made objections.[35]

It should be noted that according to Article 6(2) of the 1921 Convention, "in the event of a war affecting the Baltic Sea", Finland shall have the right, in order to ensure respect for the neutrality of the Åland Islands, temporarily to lay mines in the territorial waters of the Islands. Moreover, according to Article 7(2), if the neutrality of the zone "should be imperilled by a sudden attack either against the Islands or across them against the Finnish mainland",

34 Björkholm and Rosas, *supra* note 1, pp. 24–25; Spiliopoulou Åkermark, Heinikoski and Kleemola-Juntunen, *supra* note 4, pp. 36–38.

35 Rotkirch, *supra* note 4, p. 371.

Finland shall take the necessary measures in the zone to check and repulse the aggressor, until such time as the Contracting Parties are in a position to intervene to enforce respect for the neutrality of the Islands. While the Finnish military measures referred to above do not seem to have been entirely within the confines of Articles 6 and 7, if interpreted strictly,[36] a more flexible interpretation was probably called for, taking into account the precariousness, not to say disappearance, of the League of Nations-focused guarantee system and the absence of opposition from the other Contracting Parties.

Be that as it may, when after the Winter War the Soviet Union, which still did not recognise the 1921 Convention, insisted on a bilateral treaty, to replace the 1921 Convention, Finland proposed instead to confirm the relevance of the 1921 Convention.[37] While the bilateral treaty as agreed by the two Parties is silent on this point,[38] the Finnish Government Bill to Parliament did say that the bilateral treaty was without prejudice to the Convention.[39] According to Article 1(1) of the bilateral treaty, signed on 11 October 1940, Finland pledges "to demilitarise the Åland Islands, not to fortify them, and not to put them at the disposal of the armed forces of foreign states". It is further specified, in Article 1(2), that demilitarisation implies that neither Finland nor other States may keep or establish any "installations for military purposes" and that the artillery platforms present on the Islands were to be demolished. The Treaty does not contain any provision on its eventual applicability in wartime.

At the outbreak of the so-called Continuation War, in June 1941, the Åland Islands were again fortified but in the Armistice Treaty between Finland, the Soviet Union and the United Kingdom of 19 September 1944[40] and in a common understanding of 1948,[41] the 1940 Treaty was declared to be in force. Likewise, in a Protocol concluded in 1992 between Finland and Russia establishing an inventory of treaties concluded by the Soviet Union declared to remain in force, the 1940 Treaty is included.[42] More importantly from the point of view

36 For instance, the Finnish measures do not seem to have been preceded by a Russian armed attack "against the Islands or across them against the Finnish mainland".

37 The study undertaken in 2023 by the Legal Service of the Finnish Ministry for Foreign Affairs, *supra* note 3, p. 15.

38 Finnish Treaty Series No. 24/1940.

39 Government Bill HE No. 105/1940 vp.

40 According to Article 9 of the Armistice Treaty, "[t]he effect of the Agreement concerning the Aaland Islands, concluded between the Soviet Union and Finland on the 11th October 1940, is completely restored", Finnish Treaty Series No. 4/1944. *See also* the study undertaken in 2023 by the Legal Service of the Finnish Ministry for Foreign Affairs, *supra* note 3, p. 18.

41 Finnish Treaty Series No. 9/1948.

42 Finnish Treaty Series No. 102/1992.

of customary international law, according to Article 5 of the Peace Treaty of 1947, "[t]he Aaland Islands shall remain demilitarised in accordance with the situation as at present existing".[43] This provision calls for the following observations. *First*, the Peace Treaty is a multilateral treaty concluded by Finland with ten States, most of which are not Baltic Sea riparian States.[44] *Second*, the wording suggests that it is not limited to the 1940 bilateral agreement but refers at least to the demilitarisation part of the 1921 Convention[45] and could, because of its general nature, arguably cover the customary law aspects at least of demilitarisation as well. *Third*, when Finland, in 1990, declared some provisions relating to Germany and the limitations on armaments contained in the Peace Treaty to be obsolete, no reference was made to Article 5.[46]

The above developments suggest continuity rather than rupture or change in the treaty relations and State practice relating to demilitarisation in particular. True, both the First and Second World Wars saw fortifications and other military measures undertaken on the Åland Islands but these can be considered at most as 'glitches' to the regime as it had developed since 1856. This is because of the temporary nature of the measures and the possibility to consider them *either* lawful because, at least as far as the situation predating the 1921 Convention was concerned, demilitarisation did not apply in wartime *or*, as far as the Second World War was concerned, the military measures undertaken by Finland did not contravene a flexible interpretation of the 1921 Convention and was at least implicitly accepted by the other Contracting Parties. At any rate, the reaffirmation and development of the demilitarisation regime in 1918 and 1921, and later in 1944, 1947 and 1992, reinforce the idea of a solution intended to be permanent.

It is not necessary here to explore in any greater detail all the subsequent developments consisting of legal instruments or unilateral statements of relevance for the question of the legal status of the demilitarisation and neutralisation regime. The arguably most important instrument is the Åland Protocol to the EU Accession Treaty of 1994, which according to its Preamble was enacted "[t]aking into account the special status that the Åland islands enjoy

43 Finnish Treaty Series No. 20/1947.

44 Australia, Byelorussia, Canada, Czechoslovakia, India, New Zealand, South Africa, Soviet Union, Ukraine and the United Kingdom.

45 In various statements relating to the demilitarisation and neutralisation regime, the Finnish Government has not made any clear distinction between the 1921 Convention and the 1940 Treaty, *see* the study undertaken in 2023 by the Legal Service of the Finnish Ministry for Foreign Affairs, *supra* note 3, p. 18.

46 Study undertaken in 2023 by the Legal Service of the Finnish Ministry for Foreign Affairs, *supra* note 3, pp. 15 and 16.

under international law".[47] True, the substantive provisions of the Protocol relate to issues which are important from the point of view of the autonomous status of the region of Åland and the protection of Swedish language and culture rather than issues of relevance for demilitarisation and neutralisation. Yet, the wording of the Preamble is very general. A Finnish declaration accompanying the Protocol is somewhat ambiguous on the scope of the preamble reference.[48] However, with regard to the Treaty of Lisbon (2007), which amended certain provisions of the Treaty on European Union relating to the EU Common Foreign and Security Policy (CFSP), Finland made a statement at a meeting of the EU Permanent Representatives Committee (Coreper), recalling the 1921 Convention and the Preamble of the Protocol on the Åland Islands and stating that the entry into force of the Lisbon Treaty "will not affect" the applicability of the Convention and that the Protocol on the Åland Islands "will remain in force".[49] Thus, the latter Finnish statement suggests that Finland considered that the preamble reference to "the special status that the Åland islands enjoy under international law" encompasses both the autonomy leg and the demilitarisation and neutralisation regime of the Islands.

To name some other examples from treaty practice, according to the Preamble to an Agreement between Finland and Estonia, Latvia and Norway on the Establishment of the North European Functional Airspace Block of 2012,[50] the Contracting Parties took into account the 1921 Convention. Over the years, Finland has made numerous notifications relating to the application and interpretation of this Convention,[51] including a declaration deposited by Finland and Sweden upon the ratification of the UN Law of the Sea Convention (UNCLOS), according to which in accordance with an exception provided for in Article 35(c) of the Convention, the passage in the strait between the Åland Islands and Sweden "is regulated in part by a long-standing international convention in force", and thus the legal regime of innocent passage (rather than the Convention regime of transit passage) in the strait has remained unchanged

---

47 Protocol No. 2 on the Åland Islands, [1994] OJ L 29.8.1994. For a more thorough discussion on Protocol 2 and its relevance for Aaland Islands demilitarisation and neutralisation *see* N. Fagerlund, 'The Special Status of the Åland Islands in the European Union' in Hannikainen and Horn, *supra* note 4, p. 189 at pp. 227–231.

48 Compare Fagerlund, *supra* note 47, pp. 227–229 and the Study undertaken in 2023 by the Legal Service of the Finnish Ministry for Foreign Affairs, *supra* note 3, p. 10.

49 Summary record from the 2298th meeting of the Permanent Representatives Committee held in Brussels on 2–4 and 7 December 2009. *See also* the Finnish Government Bill relating to the Lisbon Treaty, HE No. 23/2008 vp, p. 101.

50 Finnish Treaty Series No. 94/2012.

51 Study undertaken in 2023 by the Legal Service of the Finnish Ministry for Foreign Affairs, *supra* note 3, p. 11. Reference is here made to notifications of 1969, 1984, 2012 and 2022.

after the entry into force of UNCLOS.[52] Finally, the Government Bill relating to Finnish adherence to the North Atlantic Treaty Organization (NATO) in 2022 states that Finnish accession will not affect the status of the Åland Islands under international law.[53] Reference is made not only to the League of Nations decisions of June 2021 but also to the treaties relating to demilitarisation and neutralisation (1854, 1921, 1940 (reaffirmed 1992) and 1947 and Protocol No. 2 annexed to the EU Accession Treaty (1994). It is added that the demilitarisation and neutralisation of the Åland Islands "has also been considered to be endowed with a status under regional, European customary law".[54] Taking also into account the study made by the Finnish Ministry for Foreign Affairs in 2023, the customary law status of demilitarisation and neutralisation seems to be official Government policy.[55] Many learned authors have espoused the view that at least demilitarisation is part and parcel of customary law.[56]

4 Scope and Content of the Customary Law Rule

While, as was noted above,[57] it is often challenging to determine the existence, scope and precise content of a rule of customary international law, it is obvious, taking also into account the ILC Conclusions on Identification of Customary International Law of 2018,[58] and the various manifestations of treaty and state practice and the opinions of authors referred to in subchapters 2 and 3 above, that there is a rule of customary international law requiring that the Åland Islands be demilitarised. Does the ban, under customary law, on fortifications and other military installations and the presence of armed forces continue unabated in wartime? The Russian military works during the First World War

52 *See*, e.g., *Note verbale* of 22 August 1997 to the UN Secretary-General, Oceans and the Law of the Sea, Deposition of Charts, Finland, Submission in Reference to Due Publicity Pursuant to UNCLOS. *See also* the Study undertaken in 2023 by the Legal Service of the Finnish Ministry for Foreign Affairs, *supra* note 3, pp. 10–11 and Spiliopoulou Åkermark, Heinikoski and Kleemola-Juntunen, *supra* note 4, pp. 62–63.

53 HE No. 315/2022 pp. 73–74.

54 *Ibid.*, p. 74 (translation by the present author).

55 Study undertaken in 2023 by the Legal Service of the Finnish Ministry for Foreign Affairs, *supra* note 3, pp. 11–13.

56 E.g., Rotkirch, *supra* note 4, p. 373; O. Bring, *Nedrustningens folkrätt* (Norstedts, Stockholm, 1987) p. 325; Björkholm and Rosas, *supra* note 1, pp. 112–115 (with references to literature); Hannikainen, *supra* note 4, pp. 624–626 (with references to literature); Rosas, *supra* note 1, pp. 28–29, 35.

57 *See supra*, at notes 7–10.

58 *See supra*, at notes 6, 7 and 10.

and the observations of the League of Nations Committee of Jurists[59] were perhaps factors speaking at the time in favour of a negative answer. But the question today is, has the extension, by the 1921 Convention, of the regime to neutralisation and subsequent developments contributed to broadening the scope of the customary law rule as well?

It should be recalled that the Preamble to the 1921 Convention refers to the goal that the Åland Islands "may never become a cause of danger from the military point of view". Article 8 provides that the provisions of the Convention "shall remain in force in spite of any changes that may take place in the present *status quo* in the Baltic Sea". Article 9 of the Convention refers to "the legal status of the Åland Islands" as defined by the provisions of the Convention, which should, "in the interests of general peace, be respected by all as part of the actual rules of conduct among Governments". Taken together, these formulations can be seen as an endeavour to contribute to the formation of a broadened regime of customary international law. In subsequent treaty and State practice, apart from the 1940 bilateral treaty and the 1947 Peace Treaty, references have been made to the special status of the Åland Islands in a way which seems to cover both demilitarisation and neutralisation.[60] The above-mentioned Finnish Government Bill of 2022 and the Foreign Ministry study of 2023 speak explicitly of not only demilitarisation but also neutralisation as part of regional customary law.

In this context, it should also be noted that the distinction between demilitarisation and neutralisation is not clear-cut. In the 1920 Peace Treaty of Dorpat between Finland and Soviet Russia, the demilitarisation of some islands in the Gulf of Finland is referred to as 'neutralisation'.[61] While Article 15 of the Fourth Geneva Convention relative to the Protection of Civilian Persons in Time of War of 1949 regulates the establishment, in regions where fighting is taking place, of "neutralized zones" intended to shelter wounded, sick and civilian persons from the effects of war, Article 60 of Protocol I additional to the 1949 Geneva Conventions of 1977, which entails partly corresponding but more detailed provisions, uses the term "demilitarised zones" for areas not to be used for military purposes in times of war or other armed conflict.[62] Although it is not clear to what extent, if any, such 'demilitarised' zones could become relevant in an armed conflict affecting the Åland Islands, the use of term seems to

59 *See supra*, at notes 22–29.

60 See also Björkholm and Rosas, *supra* note 1, p. 113; Rosas, *supra* note 1, p. 29.

61 *See supra*, at note 19.

62 On the customary law nature of these provisions see J.-M. Henckaerts and L. Doswald-Beck, *Customary International Humanitarian Law, Volume I: Rules* (Cambridge University Press/International Committee of the Red Cross, Cambridge, 2005) pp. 119–121.

point to a tendency to view demilitarisation as potentially relevant during war as well.[63]

Assuming that neutralisation, including 'wartime demilitarisation', has become part of the Aaland regime, the consequence would be not only that both demilitarisation and neutralisation could continue to be relevant after a possible demise of the 1921 Convention but also that States such as Lithuania, Norway and the United States which are not Contracting Parties to this Convention would be bound by corresponding applicable customary law rules. As to Russia, the Soviet Union, which was not invited to the 1921 Conference, did later resist becoming bound by the Convention and insisted on the 1940 bilateral treaty instead. That said, the present author is not aware of any subsequent consistent Russian opposition to the principle of neutralisation as such[64] and Russia thus does not seem to qualify as a "persistent objector", which could prevent the relevant rule of customary law from becoming applicable to it.[65]

It is in fact arguable that all States that have a capability of taking measures affecting the demilitarisation and neutralisation regime are bound by the relevant customary law rules in force. If that is so (which would mean that all States are potentially affected by the regime), it is questionable if the relevant customary law rules should be considered as 'regional' law in the strict sense of the word.[66] Be that as it may, put in the perspective of UN law, which prohibits any acts of aggression but allows, pursuant to Article 51 of the UN Charter, self-defence, also a State that wages a legitimate war of self-defence would, at least as long as she is not the object of military action emanating from the Åland Islands be prevented from extending military action to the neutralised zone. Finland is an exception, since as the territorial State, she is, as recognised in Articles 6(2) and 7(II) of the Convention, responsible for the defence of the neutrality of the Islands.

63 Björkholm and Rosas, *supra* note 1, pp. 17, 94–96.

64 See also the Study undertaken in 2023 by the Legal Service of the Finnish Ministry for Foreign Affairs, *supra* note 3, p. 12, which refers to the fact that Russia did not react to the Finnish and Swedish declarations relating to the 1921 Convention and UNCLOS of 1982 and 1996 (*see supra*, at note 52).

65 According to Conclusion 15(1) of the ILC Conclusions on Identification of Customary International Law, *supra* notes 6 and 10, "[w]here a State has objected to a rule of customary international law while that rule was in the process of formation, the rule is opposable to the State concerned for as long as it maintains its objection". According to Conclusion 15(2), "[t]he objection must be clearly expressed, made known to other States, and maintained persistently".

66 Conclusion 16(1) of the ILC Conclusions on Identification of Customary International Law, *supra* notes 6 and 10, refers to particular customary international law, "whether regional, local or other" as a rule "that applies only among a limited number of States".

That said, as the 1921 Convention is quite detailed, it is plausible to consider that not all its provisions have become part of customary law. Arguably, the essential principle of neutrality should be respected.[67] As far as Finland is concerned, this could mean that, at least under customary law, she would not be bound by all the details embedded in the relevant provisions of the 1921 Convention limiting her right and obligation to defend neutrality as well as the territory of the Islands as part of Finnish territory. In any case, a literal interpretation of those provisions is no longer called for, since they appear in the Convention in the context of a League of Nations guarantee system, which has ceased to exist.[68] On the other hand, both under treaty and customary international law, Finnish military measures should be geared towards repulsing the aggressor and enforcing respect for the neutrality of the zone.

---

67 Rosas, *supra* note 1, p. 29; Study undertaken in 2023 by the Legal Service of the Finnish Ministry for Foreign Affairs, *supra* note 3, p. 12.

68 *See* Article 7 of the Convention and Björkholm and Rosas, *supra* note 1, p. 97. *See also* supra, at note 36.

CHAPTER 9

The Right of Self-Determination of Peoples in the Light of the Åland Islands Agreement

The Jurisprudence of the Human Rights Committee and Other Bodies

Alfred de Zayas

The success story of the Åland Islands arrangement between Finland and Sweden is a living example that the model of autonomy as a form of internal self-determination works when there is good will and common sense among the parties concerned. More than a hundred years since its adoption, the Åland precedent demonstrates that conflict can be prevented through dialogue and the rule of law. Pertinent judgments and advisory opinions of the Permanent Court of International Justice (PCIJ) and International Court of Justice (ICJ) as well as judgments of regional human rights courts and expert committees, like the UN Human Rights Committee, confirm that human rights are juridical, justiciable and enforceable.

The centennial of the Åland model justifies a degree of optimism that local, regional and international peace and security can be achieved through law. In the case of peoples and minorities, it is important to recognise that self-determination is a fundamental human right, a combination of the rights to freedom and democratic choice, the rights to culture and identity. It is also important to acknowledge empirical evidence showing that addressing the right of self-determination in a timely fashion constitutes an effective conflict-prevention strategy.

The tension between the principle of territorial integrity and the right of self-determination can be resolved, and has been solved in many parts of the world. However, it is crucial to rise above intransigence and inflexible ideologies that pretend that the principle of territorial integrity or the right of self-determination are absolute.[1] Both international law norms are valid and must coexist. With a modicum of good will, the norms can be made to function side by side as required by the UN Charter. History teaches us that it is not the

1 See criteria for the exercising of the right of self-determination in the Report of the Independent Expert on International Order to the General Assembly A/69/272 (2014). "Self-Determination", Chapter 5 in A. de Zayas, *Building a Just World Order*, Clarity Press, 2021.

right of self-determination that leads to conflict and war, but the unjust denial thereof, as documented by countless wars that have occurred since 1945.

The UN Charter is akin to a world constitution, whose main purpose is to maintain international peace and security through joint action, particularly preventive measures, such as organising and monitoring plebiscites on self-determination. Alas, the UN has failed in its preventive functions and has only conducted self-determination referenda, e.g. in Ethiopia/Eritrea, Timor-Leste and Sudan, after tens of thousands of people had been killed. Better "early warning" by United Nations (UN) agencies and enhanced international solidarity might have avoided the violence.

Following the end of the First World War, the League of Nations conducted several plebiscites, including those in Schleswig, Upper Silesia, East Prussia, Marienwerder and the Saarland. The self-determination referendum in the Åland Islands was homegrown, and in June 1919 ninety-five percent of the Åland islanders voted for reunification with Sweden. Finland, however, wanted to keep the islands under its jurisdiction, relying on some valid historical links. In order to settle the dispute, Great Britain referred the issue to the League of Nations (LoN), which declared itself competent to deal with the dispute, while recognising that sovereignty belonged to Finland. The League of Nations rapporteurs were of the opinion that the wish of the Swedish islanders to join Sweden was driven principally by their desire to preserve their cultural identity, and less by their intention to become part of Sweden.

While this opinion may be challenged, the rapporteurs went on to claim that the issue was not one of self-determination but rather a question of minority rights, thus creating a normative confusion that unfortunately has had its impact all the way down to the jurisprudence of the UN Human Rights Committee, which still treats the rights of the US and Canadian[2] indigenous peoples not as peoples under Article 1 of the International Covenant on Civil and Political Rights (ICCPR, 173 States parties), but rather as minorities under Article 27 ICCPR, although they are clearly peoples, the original peoples of the continent. The same applies to the treatment of other indigenous peoples in the Americas, like the Mapuches of Argentina and Chile, and the Aymara people of Peru,[3] whose claims are treated as minority rights issues and not as peoples' entitlements, although the authors of petitions to the Human Rights Committee invariably invoke Article 1 ICCPR and come out mostly empty-handed.

2 https://www.refworld.org/cases,HRC,4721c5b42.html.

3 http://www.bayefsky.com/pdf/peru_t5_iccpr_1457_2006.pdf.

At this point it is useful to recall that international law is dynamic, and that the progressive development of international law has advanced the concept of self-determination far beyond the League of Nations' approach and far beyond the decolonisation process under the auspices of the UN. The language of Common Article 1 of the International Covenant on Civil and Political Rights (ICCPR) and the International Covenant on Economic Social and Cultural Rights (ICESCR) constitutes a quantum step forward and establishes self-determination as a *jus cogens* human right, which is also solidly anchored in Articles 1 and 55, and Chapters XI and XII of the UN Charter. The text of Common Article 1 stipulates:

1. All peoples have the right of self-determination. By virtue of that right they freely determine their political status and freely pursue their economic, social and cultural development.
2. All peoples may, for their own ends, freely dispose of their natural wealth and resources without prejudice to any obligations arising out of international economic co-operation, based upon the principle of mutual benefit, and international law. In no case may a people be deprived of its own means of subsistence.
3. The States Parties to the present Covenant, including those having responsibility for the administration of Non-Self-Governing and Trust Territories, shall promote the realisation of the right of self-determination, and shall respect that right, in conformity with the provisions of the Charter of the United Nations.

The bottom line is that the right-holders of self-determination are all "peoples", and the duty bearers are all states parties to the ICCPR and ICESCR. Clearly, the drafters did not intend to limit the right to the colonies and as the progressive development of international law has shown, the territorial integrity of a given state does not prohibit the exercise of self-determination by its constitutive peoples. We have the precedent of the dismantlement of the territorial integrity of the Soviet Union and of Yugoslavia since 1991, and the voluntary separation of Czechoslovakia into the Czech and Slovak Republics in 1993. Moreover, it bears repeating that the principle of territorial integrity is only applicable externally and cannot be invoked to nullify the self-determination of peoples living under a state's jurisdiction. In paragraph 80 of its Kosovo Advisory Opinion of 22 July 2010, the International Court of Justice stated, "the scope of the principle of territorial integrity is confined to the sphere of relations between States."[4]

4 https://icj-cij.org/sites/default/files/case-related/141/141-20100722-ADV-01-00-EN.pdf "80. Several participants in the proceedings before the Court have contended that a prohibition of unilateral declarations of independence is implicit in the principle of territorial

Furthermore, it should be noted that the concept of "peoples" has been gradually consolidating, partly thanks to several UNESCO conferences in Budapest[5] and Barcelona, where the 'Kirby definition' was discussed. Justice Kirby defined peoples as:

> a group of persons with a common historical tradition, racial or ethnic identity, cultural homogeneity, linguistic unity, religious or ideological affinity, territorial connection, or common economic life. To this should be added a subjective element: the will to be identified as a people and the consciousness of being a people. A people must be numerically greater than just "a mere association of individuals within the State.[6]

Their claim becomes more compelling if they have established institutions or other means of expressing their common characteristics and identity. In plain language, the concept of "peoples" embraces ethnic, linguistic and religious minorities, in addition to identifiable groups living under alien domination, or under military occupation, and indigenous groups who are deprived of autonomy or sovereignty over their natural resources.

In principle, the right of self-determination should be justiciable. Certainly, all parties to the ICCPR and ICESCR are bound to respect it. And while the Human Rights Committee wants to focus only on "individual" human rights, the Committee on Economic, Social and Cultural Rights (171 states parties) can

---

integrity. The Court recalls that the principle of territorial integrity is an important part of the international legal order and is enshrined in the Charter of the United Nations, in particular in Article 2, paragraph 4, which provides that: 'All Members shall refrain in their international relations from the threat or use of force against the territorial integrity or political independence of any State, or in any other manner inconsistent with the Purposes of the United Nations.' In General Assembly resolution 2625 (XXV), entitled 'Declaration on Principles of International Law concerning Friendly Relations and Co-operation among States in Accordance with the Charter of the United Nations', which reflects customary international law (Military and Paramilitary Activities in and against Nicaragua (Nicaragua v. United States of America), Merits, Judgment, I.C.J. Reports 1986, pp. 101–103, paras. 191–193), the General Assembly reiterated '[t]he principle that States shall refrain in their international relations from the threat or use of force against the territorial integrity or political independence of any State'. This resolution then enumerated various obligations incumbent upon States to refrain from violating the territorial integrity of other sovereign States. In the same vein, the Final Act of the Helsinki Conference on Security and Co-operation in Europe of 1 August 1975 (the Helsinki Conference) stipulated that '[t]he participating States will respect the territorial integrity of each of the participating States' (Art. IV). Thus, the scope of the principle of territorial integrity is confined to the sphere of relations between States."

5 https://www.michaelkirby.com.au/images/stories/speeches/1990s/vol24/906-Peoples%27_Rights_and_Self_Determination_-_UNESCO_Mtg_of_Experts.pdf.

6 https://searchlibrary.ohchr.org/record/1284.
https://unpo.org/article/446.

certainly entertain collective rights petitions under its Optional Protocol (only 26 states parties). In this author's opinion, the Human Rights Committee has taken an unduly restrictive approach when interpreting its jurisdiction under the Optional Protocol. For instance, in its Views in the *Lubicon Lake Band v. Canada* case,[7] it essentially auto-restrained itself by refusing to consider "collective" rights and limiting its competence to examining only those cases that allege violations of the ICCPR provisions contained in Part III ICCPR (articles 6 to 27). It held:

> While all peoples have the right of self-determination and the right freely to determine their political status, pursue their economic, social and cultural development and dispose of their natural wealth and resources, as stipulated in Article 1 of the Covenant, the question whether the Lubicon Lake Band constitutes a "people" is not an issue for the Committee to address under the Optional Protocol to the Covenant. The Optional Protocol provides a procedure under which individuals can claim that their individual rights have been violated. These rights are set out in part III of the Covenant, articles 6 to 27, inclusive.

Although the same Human Rights Committee had declared the petition by the Lubicon Lake Band admissible under Article 1 ICCPR, the ultra-conservatives in the Committee succeeded in reversing its prior decision by excluding Parts I and II of the ICCPR from the Committee's mandate under the Optional Protocol, notwithstanding the fact that this is nowhere required in the text of the Optional Protocol, or for that matter in the *travaux preparatoires*. It is sad that the only "remedy" the Lubicon people eventually got from the Committee was the mild statement that "Historical inequities, to which the State party refers, and certain more recent developments threaten the way of life and culture of the Lubicon Lake Band, and constitute a violation of Article 27 so long as they continue."[8] Alas, to this day, the fate of the Lubicon has not improved. It has become much worse.

It is worth noting that the drafters of the ICCPR and ICESCR deliberately chose the terminology 'right of' rather than 'right to' self-determination. I interpret that as an affirmation that the right is inherent to the persons and

7 https://www.refworld.org/cases,HRC,4721c5b42.html.

8 *Chief Bernard Ominayak and Lubicon Lake Band v. Canada*, para 33. See also Jakob Möller/Alfred de Zayas, The United Nations Human Rights Committee Caselaw, N.P.Engel 2009, pp. 447f, 534f. See also https://archive.org/details/laststandoflubic0000godd.

groups concerned and is not something to be contemplated sometime in the distant future. The right exists today.

In the second edition of Manfred Nowak's *CCPR Commentary* (adopted before the 2010 ICJ Advisory Opinion on Kosovo,[9] Nowak deals with the scope of the right of self-determination rather generously. The third edition of the *CCPR Commentary*, edited by William Schabas,[10] suggests that there is a right to 'remedial secession' outside the colonial or foreign occupation context.[11] Undoubtedly, all states parties to the ICCPR and ICESCR are bound by the unambiguous text of Article 1, which does not restrict its application to the colonial context. Moreover, Article 1(3) ICCPR imposes an affirmative obligation on states parties to proactively 'promote' the realisation of the right of self-determination. This is of enormous importance for peoples aspiring to self-governance, including the Palestinians, the Kurds, the Tamils, the Sahraouis, the Luchuans of the Ryukyu Islands (Okinawa), the Bubis of the Island of Bioko (Equatorial Guinea), the West Papuans, the Rapa Nuis, the Catalans, the Corsicans, the Southern Tyrolians, the Scots, the Québécois and many others.[12]

It is also worth noting that several Human Rights Committee members have stated that Article 1 should be justiciable under the Optional Protocol, since self-determination is not only a collective right, but has an individual rights dimension. With regard to the *Lubicon Lake Band v. Canada* case, Schabas regrets that "the Committee reduced the original claim of this Cree Indian Band to internal economic self-determination into a mere right of its members to enjoy their own culture".[13] Schabas also reminds us that the Human Rights Committee in its General Comment on reservations clearly stated that "reservations to Article 1 denying peoples the right to determine their own political status and to pursue their economic, social and cultural development would be incompatible with the object and purpose of the Covenant".[14]

9 *Accordance with International Law of the Unilateral Declaration of Independence in Respect of Kosovo*, Advisory Opinion, *ICJ Reports* 2010, p. 403, https://www.icj-cij.org/files/case-related/141/141-20100722-ADV-01-00-EN.pdf.

10 See my review of Schabas' Commentary in the Netherlands International Law Review, 2020 https://link.springer.com/article/10.1007/s40802-020-00179-y.

11 William Schabas, CCPR Commentary, N.P. Engel, Kehl and Strasbourg, 2019, p. 25.

12 See the report to the General Assembly of the Independent Expert on the promotion of a democratic and equitable international order, A/69/272.

13 Schabas, op. cit., p. 28.

14 Human Rights Committee General Comment 24, § 9. https://www.refworld.org/docid/453883fc11.html. See also General Comment 12 on the right of self-determination https://www.refworld.org/docid/453883f822.html.

Meanwhile the Human Rights Committee's restrictive attitude concerning its competence under the Optional Protocol is being softened, since there have been numerous cases where the Committee has found violations of articles outside Part III ICCPR, for instance of Article 2, which is contained in Part II of the ICCPR. In the landmark case *L.P. v. Czech Republic*, the Committee found a violation of Article 2 in conjunction with Article 17 of the Covenant.[15] This precedent was also followed in *Lalith Rajapakese v. Sri Lanka*, where the Committee found a violation of Article 9 in conjunction with Article 2.[16] It is only a matter of time until a new, more progressive membership of the Committee will see fit to assert and promote the right of self-determination under the Optional Protocol procedure.

Of course, the Committee on Economic, Social and Cultural Rights and the Committee on the Elimination of All Forms of Racial Discrimination could also entertain petitions demanding self-determination. Thus far they have not done so, although a case has recently been submitted on behalf of the Catalan people living in Spain, which is one of the 26 countries that has ratified the Optional Protocol to ICESCR. Another possible avenue of redress would be through the ICCPR and ICERD inter-state complaints procedure (Article 41 ICCPR, Article 11 ICERD), which, of course, has considerable political ramifications.

An aspect of the right of self-determination that has not been sufficiently examined by the Human Rights Committee is the right to hold referenda on self-determination issues. This right has been recognised by many academics, including Professors Nicolas Levrat of the University of Geneva and Paul Williams of American University in Washington DC,[17] and myself in my function as Independent Expert on International Order.[18]

On 12 July 2022 the Human Rights Committee found that Spain had violated multiple rights of Catalan independentists.[19] The case had been filed by

15 http://www.bayefsky.com/pdf/czechrepublic_t5_iccpr_946_2000.pdf. Möller/de Zayas, op. cit. pp. 334, 388.

16 Möller/de Zayas, op. cit. pp. 127 f. https://www.omct.org/en/resources/urgent-interventions/the-united-nations-human-rights-committee-rules-against-sri-lanka-in-torture-case.

17 https://papers.ssrn.com/sol3/papers.cfm?abstract_id=3078292.

18 https://www.ohchr.org/en/special-procedures/ie-international-order/mr-alfred-maurice-de-zayas-former-independent-expert-2012-2018. https://www.catalannews.com/politics/item/independent-expert-proposes-un-hold-catalan-referendum.

19 https://www.euronews.com/2022/08/31/spain-violated-political-rights-of-former-catalan-leaders-says-un-committee. https://www.elnacional.cat/en/politics/reactions-puigdemont-aragones-junqueras-spain-blow-democracy_876273_102.html.

Oriol Junqueras i Vies, former Vice-President of Catalonia, and three former ministers, Raül Romeva i Rueda, Josep Rull i Andreu and Jordi Turull i Negre. They had been prosecuted and sentenced for their participation in the independence referendum and later events that led to the Parliament of Catalonia declaring independence in October 2017.

The Office of the United Nations High Commissioner for Human Rights (OHCHR) press release states in part:

> In September 2017, the Parliament of Catalonia passed a law authorising a referendum on Catalonia's independence. Despite the Constitutional Court's suspension order and police intervention, the referendum was held on 1 October. In mid-October, the Constitutional Court ruled that both the law and the referendum were unconstitutional, null and void. Nevertheless, the Catalonian Parliament declared independence and was thus immediately dissolved by the Government of Spain. Junqueras and the three ministers were prosecuted, together with other officials, for the crime of rebellion, which entails a call for a violent uprising against the constitutional order. In July 2018, they were suspended from their functions as Members of Parliament in accordance with the Criminal Procedure Act, which only allows the suspension of officials when they are charged with rebellion.
>
> During their pretrial detention, the four former Parliament members brought their case to the Committee, alleging that their suspension from public duties, prior to any conviction violated their political rights under Article 25 of the ICCPR. In October 2019, the four of them were convicted of sedition, a crime that does not include the element of violence, as opposed to rebellion, and their suspensions were lifted.

Human Rights Committee member Hélène Tigroudja commented: "The Committee took an important step in affirming that the safeguards against the restrictions of political rights must be applied more rigorously if these restrictions occur prior to, rather than after, a conviction for an offence". The Committee had taken due note that the four complainants had urged the public to remain strictly peaceful, and thus considered that the decision to charge them with the crime of rebellion, which led to their automatic suspension prior to a conviction, was not foreseeable and therefore not based

---

https://www.catalannews.com/politics/item/puigdemont-v-spain-catalan-president-takes-case-to-un-human-rights-committee.

on reasonable and objective grounds provided for by law. Committee member Tigroudja added: "The decision to suspend elected officials should rely on clear and foreseeable laws which establish reasonable and objective grounds for the restriction of the political rights, and must be applied based on an individualised assessment. Such an approach and safeguards are the best way to ensure respect for institutions and to promote the rule of law in a democratic society."[20] The Committee, however, did not address the right of the Catalans to self-determination. Still a very hot potato.

The issue of self-determination is not likely to go away anytime soon. There are many aspirants in Latin America, Africa, Asia and even in Europe, who have a legitimate claim to self-government. Among the many territories in the world that still have not achieved self-determination are the French overseas territories. The Human Rights Committee has had the opportunity of examining the validity of the criteria used in self-determination referenda in the context of the examination of State party reports, and in rare cases under the Optional Protocol. In its Views in case No. 932/2000 (*Gillot v. France*), the Committee found that the exclusion of new settlers from participation in a self-determination referendum in New Caledonia was reasonable and compatible with France's obligations under Article 1 of the International Covenant on Civil and Political Rights. The Committee observed:

> The Committee notes that the 21 authors were excluded from the 1998 referendum because they did not meet the 10 years' continuous residence requirement. It also notes that one author will not be able to participate in the next referendum because of the 20 years' continuous residence requirement, whereas the other 20 authors do, as things stand, have the right to vote in that referendum – 18 authors on the basis of the residence criterion and 2 others on the strength of having been born in New Caledonia, their ethnic origin and national extraction being of no consequence in this respect.
>
> The Committee considers, first, that the cut-off points adopted do not have a disproportionate effect, given the nature and purpose of the referendums in question, on the authors' situation, particularly since their non-participation in the first referendum manifestly has no consequences for nearly all of them as regards the final referendum.

20 https://www.ohchr.org/en/press-releases/2022/08/spain-violated-former-catalan-parliament-leaders-political-rights-un-human.

> The Committee further considers that each cut-off point should provide a means of evaluating the strength of the link to the territory, in order that those residents able to prove a sufficiently strong tie are able to participate in each referendum. The Committee considers that, in the present case, the difference in the cut-off points for each ballot is linked to the issue being decided in each vote: the 20-year cut-off point – rather than 10 years as for the first ballot – is justified by the time frame for self-determination, it being made clear that other ties are also taken into account for the final referendum.
>
> Noting that the length of residence criterion is not discriminatory, the Committee considers that, in the present case, the cut-off points set for the referendum of 1998 and referendums from 2014 onwards are not excessive inasmuch as they are in keeping with the nature and purpose of these ballots, namely a self-determination process involving the participation of persons able to prove sufficiently strong ties to the territory whose future is being decided. This being the case, these cut-off points do not appear to be disproportionate with respect to a decolonization process involving the participation of residents who, over and above their ethnic origin or political affiliation, have helped, and continue to help, build New Caledonia through their sufficiently strong ties to the territory.[21]

It is to be expected that the UN will have to conduct numerous self-determination referenda in the future. The language of the *Guillot* decision provides a reasonable guideline. Only persons who have a genuine link to a territory should be allowed to vote. It would be a travesty of justice if the settlers coming from a former colonial power would frustrate the historical rights of native populations to their own indigenous self-government and self-determination.

Historical Considerations

Self-determination is not the "flavour of the month", nor an invention of 20th century thinkers. Indeed, Francisco de Vitoria formulated the noble concept already in the 16th century in connection with the indigenous populations of the Americas, and this ethical norm gradually gained acceptance among

---

21 Report of the Human Rights Committee to the General Assembly, Fifty-seventh Session, Supplement No. 40 (A/57/40), Volume II, Annex IX, Section GG, paras. 14.4-14-7 and 15.

theologians, philosophers and international lawyers. The eminent Salamanca professor had formulated this simple human rights concept: "Every nation has the right to govern itself and can accept the political regime it wants, even if it is not the best."[22]

It is sad that notwithstanding de Vitoria, Antonio de Montesinos, Bartolomé de las Casas and others, there was no effective mechanism for the protection of the self-determination of the indigenous peoples of Cuba, Mexico, Colombia, etc., as the natives were subjugated, exploited and colonised. Worse, the indigenous peoples of North and South America were subjected to large-scale massacres, what today would be considered "genocide".[23]

European imperialism and colonialism had no room for the concept of self-determination, and it was not until the establishment of the League of Nations and the United Nations that this fundamental, human rights concept started making its gradual ascent toward *jus cogens*. The principle gained a degree of popularity with Wilson's 14 Points, issued in 1918, and the Atlantic Charter of 1941, signed by President Franklin D. Roosevelt and Prime Minister Winston Churchill. But it was at the League of Nations that the first concrete successes were achieved, notably through the minority rights treaties and the League's minority protection system.

While the Åland Islands agreement proves to be a success story, in other cases the League of Nations' intervention was not entirely consistent with the results of certain plebiscites conducted following the First World War, among others the plebiscite in Upper Silesia[24] of 1921, which accorded the most valuable parts of Upper Silesia to Poland, although the general vote had been 60 per cent for remaining with Germany, and the towns of Königshütte and Kattowitz had voted 75 and 85 per cent respectively in favour of staying in Germany. Another denial of self-determination occurred with regard to the Austrians of the Southern Tyrol, who were simply given to Italy without any plebiscite.[25]

22 Toda nación tiene derecho a gobernarse a sí misma y puede aceptar el régimen político que quiera, aún cuando no sea el mejor. https://solidaridad.net/los-derechos-humanos-por-francisco-de-vitoria-794/.

23 David Stannard, *American Holocaust*, Oxford 1992. Marcel Grondin et Moema Viezzer, *Le Génocide des Amériques*, Ecosociété, Quebec, 2022. Martin Luther King Jr., *Why we can't wait*, Beacon Books, Boston, (1963, 2010 especially p. 141).

24 Alfred de Zayas, *Anmerkungen zur Vertreibung*, Kohlhammer, Stuttgart, 1993, p. 37f. *Nemesis at Potsdam*, Routledge 1977.

25 T.H. Herford, *The Case of German South Tyrol against Italy*, London 1927.

Conclusion

The Office of the UN High Commissioner for Human Rights and the UN Human Rights Council should consider making self-determination a permanent item in the agenda of the Council, as indeed it had been a permanent item in the Commission's agenda until 2006. Moreover, it would be appropriate to establish the function of a Special Rapporteur on Self-determination. Similarly, the UN General Assembly should establish the function of a Special Advisor to the Secretary General on "Self-Determination and Early Warning". The General Assembly would be well advised to adopt a resolution under Article 96 of the UN Charter asking the International Court of Justice to elaborate on the concrete implications of the right of self-determination as defined in Article 1 of the ICCPR and ICESCR, and the continuing obligation of former colonial powers for the well-being of their former colonies,[26] taking due account of Human Rights Council Resolution 48/7 of 8 October 2021.[27]

The Åland Islands precedent proves that internal self-determination in the form of genuine autonomy is a win-win proposition that deserves being followed. On the other hand, the necessity of external self-determination in numerous cases must also be taken seriously, because there are many situations in which it makes no sense to force two peoples to stay together when they do not wish to do so, merely for the sake of vindicating the formerly sacrosanct principle of territorial integrity. It is far more important for international peace and security to ensure stability by organising UN-monitored referenda that would facilitate a "no fault" divorce without violence and bloodshed. *Pax optima rerum.*

26 My 2014 report to the General Assembly (A/69/272) is devoted to the theory and practice of self-determination, and formulates criteria for its application. My 2013 GA report proposed expanding the list of "non-self-governing territories" and allowing petitions to be sent to the Committee of 24 (A/68/284, paragraph 69n), possibly through the CERD procedures. I expanded on this subject in chapter 5 of my book *Building a Just World Order*, Clarity Press, Atlanta 2021.

27 https://documents-dds-ny.un.org/doc/UNDOC/GEN/G21/286/52/PDF/G2128652.pdf?OpenElement.

CHAPTER 10

International Standards on Minority Autonomy

Gudmundur Alfredsson

1 Introduction

International human rights law stipulates that we are all equal in rights, in law and in fact. Discrimination on national, ethnic, linguistic and religious grounds is prohibited, including discrimination as a result of minority membership. Special measures and special rights have been introduced in order to combat discrimination and to speed up the achievement of the equal exercise of human rights. The political rights of minorities are included, and autonomy is one of the special measures intended to overcome discrimination and to bring about equal rights in minority representation and participation in public life at local, national and even international levels.

Notwithstanding the prohibition, minority persons and groups are often the victims of discrimination that is based on objective characteristics like appearances, cultures, identities, languages and/or religions that differ from those of the majority population. The effects extend across the spectrum of human rights, but discrimination in the political sphere is particularly harmful, with a negative impact on the ability of minorities to influence multiple issues, such as education, social services and the local economy. The benefits of fair, just and inclusive societies are obvious for both group and State, but multiple obstacles still line the road to that goal.

Autonomies exist around the world, created for the prevention of violent conflicts and/or the protection of human rights, not least for overcoming discrimination. By the author's rough estimate, counting arrangements for both minorities and indigenous peoples, more than 100 States have established hundreds of group autonomies. The extent of self-governance may be uneven, with different functions and institutions set up for different reasons, carrying various labels, and sometimes available for some groups and not others within the same State. Some of the autonomies are territorial (with internal boundaries) and others are non-territorial (cultural or personal and without geographical boundaries).[1]

1 There is plenty of literature on minority autonomies, see in particular Louis B. Sohn, "The Concept of Autonomy in International Law and the Practice of the United Nations" in

DOI:10.1163/9789004691117_012

The worldwide exercise of autonomy has shown the value of delegating certain legislative and executive functions from the central to the group level. Many of these arrangements have contributed to the respect for human rights and to keeping the peace. Where such autonomy arrangements have not been successful, one is more often than not looking at collectivities and territories with unresolved international disputes involving historical grievances, gross rights violations or other justified demands for separation.

Despite the potential usefulness to both States and groups, governments and intergovernmental organisations (IGOs) have been, and continue to be, slow in improving or adding to minority rights in general and autonomy standards in particular. The same is true for monitoring and assistance procedures for responding to minority rights violations and related threats to peace and security. Still, the scattering of available standards and procedures in multiple instruments can and should be employed for gainful purposes.

Even States which call themselves human rights friendly are often reluctant partners when it comes to the acceptance of minority rights. Minority rights are part and parcel of human rights, but group recognition, group rights and group access to power cause States to stay on the defensive. The possibility of separatism is undoubtedly a major reason behind this reluctance, not least when the autonomy comes with internal borders and serious functions delegated to significant institutions. Other likely reasons for this attitude of reluctance are ignorance resulting from inadequate information and education, and arrogance resulting from the supposed superiority of the majority group.

This chapter is intended to provide an overview of the international standards on autonomy, both those serving the prevention of violent conflicts and human rights in general, and those serving minority rights in particular. References will also be made to available monitoring procedures and case law. International standards concerning the rule of law, good governance and democracy inevitably play a role in the realisation of autonomy.

Israel Law Review, vol. 15, 1980, pp. 180–190; Hurst Hannum, Documents on Autonomy and Minority Rights, Martinus Nijhoff, 1993; John Packer, "On the Content of Minority Rights" in Juha Raikka (editor), Do We Need Minority Rights? Conceptual Issues, Leiden: Brill, 1997, pp. 121–178; Markku Suksi (editor), Autonomy: Applications and Implications, The Hague: Kluwer Law International, 1998; Gudmundur Alfredsson, "Minority Rights: Norms and Institutions" in Kevin Boyle (editor), New Institutions for Human Rights Protection, Oxford: Oxford University Press, 2009, pp. 175–206; Peter Hilpold (editor), Autonomy and Self-Determination. Between Legal Assertions and Utopian Aspirations, Edward Elgar Publishing, 2018; and Olgun Akbulut and Elçin Aktoprak (editors), Minority Self-Government in Europe and the Middle East: From Theory to Practice, Leiden: Brill, 2019.

The autonomy of the Åland Islands rests on international arrangements made under the auspices of the League of Nations, soon after WWI, in order to settle a dispute over the Åland archipelago involving Finland, Sweden and the national/ethnic/linguistic minority inhabiting the Islands.[2] This autonomy is often referred to as a model for other minority situations, but unfulfilled demands of the Åland Islanders and disagreements between Åland and Finland have appeared from time to time. Interesting questions do arise as a result. Does Åland have something to gain from the international standards and the monitoring of State compliance; do the international law-makers have something to learn from the Åland arrangements, including a century of practice; and can other States make use of the model for their own group situations?

2 Autonomy, General Observations

Various terms are used to designate autonomy, such as devolution, home rule, self-administration, self-government, self-management, self-rule or traditional or tribal government. The delegation of functions to municipal or other local authorities can serve the same purpose, and so can federal systems. The labels do not matter as long as the delegation of functions is meaningful, with significant issues coming under the legislative and executive control of the institutions of a minority group. Autonomous institutions generally involve an elected assembly and an executive, occasionally accompanied by a judicial component, and these should have adequate financial resources to enable them to carry out their functions.

The motivation for introducing autonomy is mainly twofold; it can be based on the desire to prevent violent conflicts and maintain peace and security by keeping minority groups happy within the State borders, or the arrangements are expressly or implicitly grounded in human rights considerations. The two scenarios are often linked, as situations involving marginalisation, exclusion and other human rights problems are often the basis for threats to or breaches of internal stability and may even cause external interference, while respect for human rights is likely to prevent or reduce tensions and ease the management and resolution of violent conflicts.

In the context of human rights, autonomy can be seen as a special measure or a separate right for the facilitation of equal enjoyment of political rights.

2 Markku Suksi, Sub-State Governance through Territorial Autonomy, Heidelberg: Springer, 2011, p. 150, and generally pp. 146–152.

Minority persons, individually or in community with other members of the group, have the right to be represented and to participate in public affairs, and to actively engage in the discussion of issues affecting them on equal footing with everyone else. Autonomies are ideal tools to this end and, while delegated issues differ widely, they should as a minimum include the management of issues that concern identities, languages, education and other mainly cultural, social and economic affairs that affect the groups' dignity, way of life and destiny.

Furthermore, international standards concerning good governance and democracy, including accountability, transparency and non-corruption, as well as free, fair, periodic and genuine elections, apply to both national governments and the autonomies.[3] So does article 21 of the Universal Declaration of Human Rights: "The will of the people shall be the basis of the authority of government." Decentralisation and the principle of subsidiarity should also be seen as benefiting minority participation and as a justification for autonomy; the European Charter of Local Self-Government thus states that public responsibilities shall generally be exercised by the authorities closest to the citizen (article 4.3). In addition, reserved seats or observer status in national bodies also benefit minority participation.

Autonomies can be either territorial or non-territorial. Also referred to as 'personal' or 'cultural', non-territorial autonomy is typically employed when a minority group is geographically dispersed. Non-territorial autonomies are designed to be useful for the maintenance and development of minority identities and cultures, but they usually have less powers than the more frequently employed territorial ones. Substantive issues often delegated under the non-territorial arrangements include culture, education, use of the minority language, religion and social affairs.

Keeping in mind the fears of governments concerning separatism, it is surprising that non-territorial autonomies are not more common. After all, they come without internal borders, which some governments may see as red lines. The non-territorial arrangements ought to, or at least could, be seen as attractive options by both governments and groups, as their jurisdiction and activities extend to group members living outside traditional areas.

Finally, the international standards on minority rights and autonomy exclude activities contrary to the purposes and principles of the United Nations

3 For elaboration, see Asbjörn Eide, "Good Governance, Human Rights, and the Rights of Minorities and Indigenous Peoples" in Hans-Otto Sano, Gudmundur Alfredsson and Robin Clapp (editors), Human Rights and Good Governance. Building Bridges, The Hague: Martinus Nijhoff Publishers, 2002, pp. 47–71.

and those of other IGOs, such as the sovereignty, territorial integrity and political independence of States. Provisions of this kind have come about as many governments feel that autonomy, let alone self-determination, involves the threat of separatism.[4] In academic literature the process leading to autonomy is sometimes referred to as internal self-determination, as opposed to the right of peoples to external self-determination where independence and statehood count among the options. Even in its internal version, international instruments devoted to minority rights usually avoid the term 'self-determination'.

3 Autonomy in the International Instruments

While country practices are the common source of what can and is being done, two international instruments contain important express provisions on autonomy. One builds on conflict prevention, the other on human rights. The two instruments are the OSCE Lund Recommendations on the Effective Participation of National Minorities in Public Life,[5] and the UN Declaration on the Rights of Indigenous Peoples (UNDRIP).[6] Other instruments, like the ILO Convention No. 169 concerning Indigenous and Tribal Peoples,[7] indirectly address autonomy by foreseeing group management of land and resources.

The Lund text builds on the 1990 Copenhagen Document, a key OSCE security instrument, in particular paragraph 35. Relating to minority participation in public affairs and the protection and promotion of identity, it draws attention to "establishing, as one of the possible means to achieve these aims, appropriate local or autonomous administrations corresponding to the specific

4 See, for example, article 8,4 of the 1992 UN Declaration on the Rights of Persons Belonging to National or Ethnic, Religious and Linguistic Minorities adopted by General Assembly resolution 47/135; article 46,1 of the 2007 UN Declaration on the Rights of Indigenous Peoples adopted by General Assembly resolution 61/295; the preamble and article 21 of the 1995 Framework Convention for the Protection of National Minorities of the Council of Europe; and paragraph 37 of the 1990 Copenhagen Document of the Conference on the Human Dimension of the Conference on Security and Co-operation in Europe (CSCE, now OSCE).

5 See "https://www.osce.org/hcnm/lund-recommendations". An accompanying Explanatory Note describes the drafting history and the reasoning behind each provision. The instrument was drafted by international experts under the auspices of the OSCE High Commissioner on National Minorities, then Max van der Stoel of the Netherlands, and named after the Swedish university city where the experts adopted the text in 1999.

6 The 2007 UN Declaration on the Rights of Indigenous Peoples, adopted by General Assembly resolution 61/295.

7 For the text of the Convention and a commentary, see "https://www.ilo.org/wcmsp5/groups/public/---ed_norm/---normes/documents/publication/wcms_205225.pdf".

historical and territorial circumstances of such minorities and in accordance with the policies of the State concerned."

Notwithstanding State reluctance, the importance of a human rights approach to minorities and minority rights has repeatedly been underlined. In 1948, the General Assembly resolved[8] that "the United Nations cannot remain indifferent to the fate of minorities" and a call was made for "a thorough study" so that the UN could take "effective measures for the protection of racial, national, religious or linguistic minorities."[9]

Several instruments with minority rights have been adopted and, while they are scattered and less than complete, they do provide for equal rights and non-discrimination. For realising minority representation and participation in policy- and decision-making in public affairs, some of the instruments require States to take action to effectively introduce such political rights. States may have a choice between a variety of special measures, but the expectation is equal and effective enjoyment of the rights involved. Autonomy is one of the tools likely to accomplish exactly that but, as already stated, it is rarely spelled out.

To the degree that autonomy constitutes a human right, it combines individual and group rights. The group has the right to autonomy, but autonomous authorities in turn must respect the rights of all individuals who come under their jurisdiction, also minorities within the minority (paragraph 21 of the Lund Recommendations).[10] Whether an individual belongs to a minority rests with that individual and "shall not be imposed upon her or him". Self-identification is an element in the definition (paragraph 4 of the Lund Recommendations), but one must also keep in mind stipulations in other instruments. Obviously,

8 General Assembly resolution 217C (III) entitled Fate of Minorities, adopted on 10 December 1948 along with the Universal Declaration of Human Rights (UDHR) in resolution 217A (III).

9 Several UN studies on minority rights have been undertaken by Special Rapporteurs and/or experts of the Sub-Commission on Prevention of Discrimination and Protection of Minorities (later renamed Sub-Commission for the Promotion and Protection of Human Rights, before it was abolished in 2006): Study on the Rights of Persons belonging to Ethnic, Religious and Linguistic Minorities by Francesco Capotorti, first issued in 1977, UN publication with sales number E.91.XIV.2; Working Paper on Possible Ways and Means to Facilitate the Peaceful and Constructive Resolution of Situations involving Racial, National, Religious and Linguistic Minorities by Claire Palley, in document E/CN.4/Sub.2/1989/43; and Study on Constructive National Arrangements for Minorities by Asbjorn Eide, with the final report contained in documents E/CN.4/Sub.2/1993/34 and Addenda 1–4.

10 Notwithstanding the views of the Human Rights Committee in a Quebec case, see Communications Nos. 359/1989 and 385/1989, submitted by John Ballantyne and Elizabeth Davidson, and Gordon McIntyre, vs Canada, available at "http://hrlibrary.umn.edu/undocs/html/v359385.htm", see in particular paragraph 11.2.

women enjoy these rights on equal footing with men. States should take the group interests into account, and States and groups should respect community approval and the harmony of domestic laws and international standards.

In addition to lending backup and legitimacy to autonomy, the ability to engage in political participation is crucial for minorities, not least because exercising political rights gives group members the opportunity to assert and even regulate many aspects of their lives, such as identity, culture, education, social affairs and employment. At the national level, they would often be short of votes and influence, but autonomies enable them to call the shots at the local level to the benefit of the group to the degree that functions have been delegated to them. Again, it's difficult to see other measures achieve what autonomy can accomplish.

The UN Charter does not expressly address minority rights, but it does list human rights and peace and security together among the very purposes of the organisation (article 1). Another early instrument, the UDHR, underlines the link: "Whereas it is essential, if man is not to be compelled to have recourse, as a last resort, to rebellion against tyranny and oppression, that human rights should be protected by the rule of law" (third preambular paragraph). Some of the above-mentioned human rights studies and instruments on minority and indigenous rights bring up the peace and security aspect. The idea is that respect for human rights, obviously including minority rights, will contribute to peace and stability within and between States.

Like the UN Charter, key instruments of the OSCE seek to strengthen peace and security through the respect for human rights, including minority rights. This link has been repeated in several OSCE documents and reports named after conferences in cities like Copenhagen, Geneva, Helsinki, Lisbon, Madrid, Paris and Vienna. In addition to encouraging minority participation in public life, the aim of the instruments is to alleviate and preferably overcome possible tensions involving minorities and thus contribute to the prevention of violent conflicts in line with the OSCE mandate.

Underlining the importance of the standards in the Copenhagen Document, in the Lund Recommendations and in other texts, the OSCE maintains a High Commissioner on National Minorities (HCNM), with a mandate for early warning and prevention of violent conflicts. Through expert reports and country advice, the HCNM has offered a broad range of recommendations on minority representation and participation; access to civil service, law enforcement and the judiciary, and advisory and consultative bodies and autonomy. Many of these expert instruments are named after cities like Bolzano, Graz, The Hague, Ljubljana, Lund, Oslo and Warsaw where texts have been adopted.[11]

11 For full texts, see "https://www.osce.org/hcnm".

With a total of 24 paragraphs, the headings of the four parts of the Lund Recommendations describe the contents: general principles, participation in policy- and decision-making, autonomy and delegated functions and institutions, extending to both territorial and non-territorial arrangements, and guarantees and remedies. The point of departure is that "Effective participation of national minorities in public life is an essential component of a peaceful and democratic society" (paragraph 1). It should be pursued in "an inclusive, transparent, and accountable process of consultation in order to maintain a climate of confidence" (paragraph 5).

The third part of the Lund Recommendations (paragraphs 14–21) is specifically devoted to self-governance, giving a minority and the persons belonging to the group a degree of control over local matters affecting them. In addition to legislative and administrative authority, it may even encompass judicial jurisdiction. States should devote adequate resources to such arrangements. Achieved through legislation or a constitutional setup, the autonomous institutions "must be based on democratic principles to ensure that they genuinely reflect the views of the affected population" (paragraphs 14–16).

Certain State-wide activities usually remain under central governments, such as "defence, foreign affairs, immigration and customs, macroeconomic policy, and monetary affairs". Other fields with national implications will likely be regulated at least to some degree by the central authorities, or the regulation in these fields may be shared (paragraph 15). These and other provisions, as is often the case with international human rights instruments, are minimum standards, which are often surpassed in practice.

As to activities shared by governments and autonomies, the UNESCO Convention against Discrimination in Education[12] spells out in some detail how to accomplish the sharing, be it in State-run schools or minority schools. Minorities may obtain the right to run their own schools and to determine the curricula and the language, but the culture and language of the State should also be taught, and the standard of education should not be lower than the general quality demands laid down by the competent national authorities. Although not mentioned by the Convention, in order to run minority schools, by the minority and for the minority, a degree of self-rule would seem to be required.

The Lund Recommendations state that "Effective participation of minorities in public life may call for non-territorial or territorial arrangements of

12 About the Convention, see "https://www.unesco.org/en/right-education/convention-against-discrimination#:~:text=The%20Convention%20reaffirms%20that%20education,promotes%20equality%20of%20educational%20opportunity.".

self-governance or a combination thereof" (paragraphs 17–21).[13] Ideally, internal borders should be determined by an independent and impartial body; a comparison can be made with electoral districts, with proportionality taken into account and preceded by prior consultation of the local communities (paragraph 19 of the Lund text and article 5 of the European Charter of Local Self-Government).

Starting with the non-territorial arrangements, the Lund Recommendations spell out the functions of autonomies: "The issues most susceptible to regulation" by non-territorial autonomies include "education, culture, use of minority language, religion, and other matters crucial" to minority identity and way of life (paragraph 18). The more extensive functions of territorial autonomies encompass "primary or significant authority" over "education, culture, use of minority language, environment, local planning, natural resources, economic development, local policing functions, and housing, health, and other social services". Functions shared by central and regional authorities can include "taxation, administration of justice, tourism, and transport" (paragraph 20).

4 The Åland Islands and Finland

In the following sections, the following issues will be examined: 1) the Åland autonomy in light of existing international standards, 2) the applicability and possible application of these standards to other Swedish speakers on the Finnish mainland, 3) a comparison of the Åland and Sami autonomies in Finland, and 4) the relevance of these standards for Finnish minorities abroad.

4.1 *The Åland Autonomy and the International Standards*

The Åland legislative and administrative bodies, responsible for a wide range of functions, enjoy at the national level a number of measures for ensuring that the autonomy status of the islands is respected and taken into account in policy- and decision-making. The Lund Recommendations are clearly applicable to the Åland Islands, and perhaps some of the recommendations as well as relevant human rights standards can be applied to the occasional hiccups in the Åland-Finland relationship.

The Lund Recommendations call for constitutional and legislative safeguards in order to provide stability and security for all, not least the minority persons. "Self-governance arrangements should be established by law and generally not be subject to change in the same manner as ordinary legislation." It

13 Tove H. Malloy and Francesco Palermo (editors), Minority Accommodation through Territorial and Non-Territorial Autonomy, Oxford University Press, 2015.

is common that changes require "approval by a qualified majority of the legislature, autonomous bodies or bodies representing national minorities, or both" (paragraph 22).

As to remedies for shortcomings or other problems, regular, alternative or ad hoc mechanisms of consultation for both the prevention and resolution of conflicts should be available for giving effect to minority participation. Minority questions "can only be satisfactorily resolved in a democratic political framework based on the rule of law, with a functioning independent judiciary" (paragraph 30 of the Copenhagen Document) and/or independent national human rights/minority rights institutions (in line with the 1993 Paris Principles). Methods like negotiation, fact-finding, mediation or arbitration can be employed to resolve grievances (paragraph 24 of the Lund text), and international human rights monitoring bodies could also play a role (see paragraph 27 of the Copenhagen Document, and article 14,2 of the International Convention on the Elimination of All Forms of Racial Discrimination). Are any of these avenues or methods actively used for dealing with ongoing grievances in the Åland-Finland relationship?

Finally, looking at the relationship with Finland, should the Åland Islanders prepare a constitution of their own? Would there be good political reasons to go ahead with the drafting of an Åland constitution, as is being done in the Faroe Islands and in Greenland, although their history and international and constitutional law status is quite different?

4.2 *The Swedish Minority on the Mainland*

About 30,000 Swedish speakers live in the Åland Islands and another 250–350,000 on the Finnish mainland. The Åland autonomy is territorial and covers only the archipelago. The Swedish speakers on the mainland enjoy minority rights, in particular linguistic rights and political representation and participation in political life, but they do not have an autonomy, neither territorial nor non-territorial. Should they? Why not?

If the answer is negative, are we looking at autonomy solely in a conflict-prevention context? In other words, as long as the Swedish minority on the mainland does not threaten the sovereignty and territorial integrity of Finland, are there no reasons to try to keep them happy? If the autonomy were about human rights, what necessary and objective reasons justify discrimination against the mainland Swedes as compared with the Åland Islanders? What about justice and equal opportunities throughout the State (paragraphs 2 and 3 of the Lund Recommendations)?

Autonomy for the mainland Swedes would likely have to take a non-territorial form, as they are spread over large areas, but it could be done in two or more ways: separately, with arrangements limited to the mainland, or in combination with the Åland autonomy. In the latter case, one option would be an expanded Åland Parliament with two chambers, one for the islanders, where they could continue to control and manage their wide-ranging functions, and another (lower) chamber for the Swedish speakers on the mainland.

With the knowledge and use of the Swedish language on the mainland on the decline, an Åland parliament accommodating both population groups in two chambers would seem to make sense from the points of view of both human rights and conflict prevention, and serving both majority and minority. For the majority it would mean continued diversity and enhanced stability, and for the minority it would mean a significant increase in political and economic weight with a ten-fold population and better rights protection.

Avenues for pursuing options of this kind appear in the Lund Recommendations where it is suggested that periodic reviews of self-governance arrangements could be useful for determining whether these should be amended or new ones added in light of experience and changed circumstances (paragraph 22). Likewise, "provisional or step-by-step arrangements" of testing and developing new forms of participation can be considered (paragraph 23). Could approaches of this kind be employed to accommodate the idea of a joint or separate autonomy for the Swedish speakers on the mainland?

4.3 *The Sami Autonomy*

As pointed out above, even within one and the same country, group participation in public life at the autonomy level is not always consistent. The Lund Recommendations (paragraph 15) state that different functions can be allocated to different groups within the same country, and one would expect that the variations are necessary, objective and reasonable for autonomies motivated by both human rights and conflict prevention. State practices as to issues covered, institutions allowed and consultations held vary widely and may not allow groups to effectively contribute to policies and decisions that affect them directly, let alone indirectly. Of course, in-country democracy and availability of human rights protection in general will also affect the extent and effectiveness of the autonomies, but often the differences seem haphazard and without much substantive reasoning.

International human rights instruments today offer indigenous peoples stronger and more comprehensive protection than what is available to minorities. This coverage includes autonomy stipulations. UNDRIP and ILO Convention No. 169 are the key instruments, both motivated by human rights considerations.[14] Notwithstanding certain differences, as they have been

14 Key UN studies on indigenous peoples' rights by Sub-Commission Rapporteurs are: José Martínez Cobo, Study of the Problem of Discrimination Against Indigenous Populations,

formulated, minority and indigenous rights have many things in common across the board as to form, content and consequences.

Under UNDRIP, "Indigenous peoples have the right of self-determination. By virtue of that right they freely determine their political status and freely pursue their economic, social and cultural development" (article 3). This formulation suggests external self-determination, but law and justice do not always go hand in hand. Other provisions of UNDRIP narrow the scope to an internal version (article 4): "Indigenous peoples, in exercising their right to self-determination, have the right to autonomy or self-government in matters relating to their internal and local affairs, as well as ways and means for financing their autonomous functions." The limitation concerning the non-threat to sovereignty and territorial integrity has already been quoted (article 46).

ILO Convention No. 169 does not use the term autonomy, but an indigenous role in the administration of lands and natural resources is clearly foreseen. Reference is thus made to the groups' right to control their own economic, social and cultural development and to participate in the use, management and conservation of the resources, while governments should consult the peoples concerned through representative institutions before undertaking or permitting programs for exploring or exploiting such resources (preamble and articles 5–8 and 14–17). It is difficult to see how indigenous peoples could carry out the functions listed in the ILO Convention, in a democratic manner, without meaningful autonomous institutions.

Rooted in human rights considerations, the Sami are self-governing as stipulated in the Constitution of Finland, with an elected Sami Parliament responsible, throughout the country, for the Sami culture, traditions, language and social life, as well as the status of the Sami as an indigenous people. The Sami Parliament may submit initiatives and proposals, issue statements in matters coming under its purview, and allocate funds intended for joint use of the Sami people.[15]

---

with the final part in document E/CN.4/Sub.2/1983/21; and Miguel Alfonso Martinez, Study on treaties, agreements and other constructive arrangements between States and indigenous populations, with the final report in document E/CN.4/Sub.2/1999/20.

15 See "https://www.suomi.fi/citizen/rights-and-obligations/digital-support-and-administrative-services/guide/how-finlands-public-administration-works/self-governance". For additional literature, see James Anaya, The situation of the Sami people in the Sápmi region of Norway, Sweden and Finland, report of the UN Special Rapporteur on the rights of indigenous peoples, UN document A/HRC/18/35/Add.2 (2011); and Adam Stępień, Anna Petrétei and Timo Koivurova, "Sámi Parliaments in Finland, Norway, and Sweden" in Tove H. Malloy, Alexander Osipov and Balázs Vizi (editors), Managing Diversity through Non-Territorial Autonomy: Assessing Advantages, Deficiencies, and Risks, Oxford University Press, 2015, pp. 117–138.

The description of the Åland autonomy inevitably brings up questions concerning the Sami autonomy. If anything, indigenous groups are more vulnerable and in greater need of protection than minorities so, from a human rights point of view, the Sami should have no less and perhaps more autonomy than the Åland Islanders. Historical circumstances may help explain the different arrangements, and the Lund Recommendations do acknowledge the allocation of different functions to different groups in the same country (paragraph 15), but why do the Åland Islanders have much stronger institutions and more delegated functions than what has been made available to the Sami? Does the need for conflict prevention override the human rights considerations? Or is it the presence of a kin-State?[16] Or is it about chronology, where the more recent Sami autonomy has not had the time and opportunity to fully develop and mature?

Furthermore, considering the tendency to narrowly define who is a Sami in Finland, restricting the application of indigenous rights to those with Sami as the first language and with traditional livelihoods, maybe the Sami Parliament also needs two chambers as was suggested above in the context of the Åland Islands? In that scenario, the traditional Sami would have one chamber for themselves for policy- and decision-making on the traditional indigenous issues, while all Sami in Finland would be represented in another (lower) chamber for policy- and decision-making on joint interests.

4.4 *Finnish Minorities Abroad*

As a kin-State, Finland should keep a respectful distance from interfering in situations affecting Finnic minorities in Norway and Sweden, such as the Kveni and the Tornedalians. These are recognised as minorities in the two countries, but minority rights, let alone autonomous arrangements for the two groups, have not received much attention. The situations of all these groups underline the striking inconsistencies and minimalistic approaches to minority and indigenous rights in Scandinavia.

Some of the groups concerned are small and may not have the necessary numbers to be able to run an effective autonomy or uphold national representation, but solutions also exist when the numbers are insufficient for obtaining a seat in the plenary of political fora at national or local levels. The solutions could involve observer status or committee seats with the right to speak and table proposals, with or without the right to vote.

---

16 On the role and place of kin-States, see the 2008 Recommendations on National Minorities in Inter-State Relations, adopted under the auspices of the OSCE High Commissioner on National Minorities, at "https://www.osce.org/hcnm/bolzano-bozen-recommendations".

5 Conclusions: Minimum Standards and Other Questions

Several questions inevitably arise in connection with the issues raised in this chapter. These questions concern both the international standards and Finnish State practices. Some of the answers may not be clear, and some of them may not even be the subject of current discussion. As far as the human rights approach is concerned, there are good reasons to expect minimum standards that could and should apply across the board to basic minority and indigenous rights, like identity, language and other aspects of culture and politics, as well as land and resources for the indigenous peoples.

Do minorities and indigenous peoples have a human right to autonomy? Do different standards apply to minority and indigenous autonomies? If autonomy indeed constitutes a human right, as stipulated for example in article 4 of UNDRIP, do minimum standards exist for autonomies in terms of institutions and functions? Are the minimum standards being met by Finland? Are different standards applicable to autonomies depending on whether they are established for human rights or for peace and security purposes?

The drawing of parallels and cross-references are inevitable when discussing autonomy established for the two purposes, that is conflict prevention and/or human rights, in order to avoid dissatisfaction and tensions as a result of different treatment of groups for less than obvious reasons. Does the threat of violence justify more advanced autonomy? All the questions are significant, in terms of both international instruments and State practices, when answering the question to what degree there are international law rules on the autonomy processes and the results.

In light of the many existing national arrangements by some 100 States practising autonomy, and with the backup of a scattering of international standards, have these led to the emergence of international customary law? Maybe there is an obligation of having autonomy of some sorts, but it is going to be difficult to draw lines across the board concerning the shape of the institutions, their powers, and the delegated functions.

Finally, with reference to the overall topic of the present book, it would be interesting and worthwhile to see these questions debated at the intergovernmental level. International standards could be improved or new ones added so that autonomies would be clearly based on the rule of law, democracy, good governance, human rights and conflict prevention. Minimum functions should be introduced, with the necessary institutions for implementation. The various existing autonomies should be carefully studied and compared in order to identify best practices, in particular arrangements that do not entertain separatist aspirations.

There may indeed be instances where the existing international standards may be useful for the claims of the Åland Islanders. At the same time, the international community has many lessons to learn from the Åland arrangements. The governments of both the Åland Islands and Finland have an opportunity to maintain well-functioning autonomy arrangements, even improve upon them to the benefit of both parties, and to actively present and promote them to the surrounding world.

CHAPTER 11

Minorities and Group Rights

Human Rights Complaints at Regional Organisations by Individuals, Groups and or Other States: the Council of Europe

Fredrik Sundberg

1 The Origins

The main complaints-based human rights system in Europe is that set up by the Council of Europe, as part of its efforts to guarantee human rights, rule of law and democracy on the continent. The system set up was that of the 1950 European Convention on Human Rights "the Convention" below. The aim was to provide the foundations for cooperation and unification, as well as economic and social progress based on the values of the United Nations.[1]

The new Convention system – deemed revolutionary by many at the time – aimed at providing a collective European guarantee for some of the rights protected by the 1948 Universal Declaration on Human Rights, in fact what are traditionally called civil and political rights. The Council of Europe did not forget other more cultural and social rights and work quickly started to adopt other instruments, notably a Cultural Convention in 1955[2] and a Charter of Social Rights, completed in 1961.[3]

To no surprise, the Convention said little about group or minority protection. The abuse, especially by Germany, of the special minority protection systems set up after World War I had largely removed the issue from the international agenda and renewed special international protection for such rights did not receive much political support in either the United Nations or in the European context for a long time. The basic idea, once again, was that the general protection of civil and political rights for all without discrimination was the better solution. Many states also had developed, pragmatic arrangements that eased tensions between groups or vis à vis minorities to ensure a peaceful "living together", as was for example the situation in the frontier regions between

1 See the preambles to the Statute of the organisation from 1949 and to the European Convention on Human Rights from 1950.

2 European Treaties Series (ETS) n° 18 of 19 December 1954.

3 ETS n° 35 of 18 October 1961.

DOI:10.1163/9789004691117_013

Denmark and Germany or with respect to the Finnish speaking minorities in Sweden. As to the special Åland question, the 1921 solution had been confirmed in 1947.

Nevertheless the Convention contained numerous rights of considerable interest also for groups and minorities. Indeed, a democratic state can hardly exist if not civil society is able to group and organise itself and manifest its dissatisfaction, opinions and desires. Among relevant rights one may cite the right to create associations with legal personality or the right of individuals and groups to assemble peacefully, to enjoy religious freedom and the general right to education and the concomitant right of parents to have their convictions respected in the education of children.

2 The Convention's Complaint System

The only compulsory complaint system immediately set up by the Convention, the possibility of inter state complaints, was interesting, but not revolutionary. Revolutionary was, however, the optional possibility of also accepting individuals' complaints.[4] Also, other aspects of the new collective guarantee had revolutionary traits.

The right of "individual petition" immediately received support from a number of states and has been crucial for the development of a European public order and legal space which have also been largely integrated into the European Union.[5] The interstate complaints were too rare to fine tune protection, and mainly allowed Europe to respond to gross and major violations, notably those

4 It was a revolution in international law and thus just an option until the end of the 1980's. By 1955, 2 years after the entry into force of the Convention, it had, however, already been accepted by 7 states. Its acceptance increased steadily, and it was accepted by all member states, Turkey being last, just before the big events of 1989. Shortly afterwards it was also made a condition for membership for all new member states. The evolution is well described in Hans Winkler "Democracy and Human Rights in Europe. A survey of the Admission Practice of the Council of Europe" in Austrian Journal of Public and International Law, Springer, 1995, pp. 147–172.

5 The integration of the Convention into the then Communities legal order was essential for the trust required for major progress in the development of the supremacy of Community law – see for example the judgement of the European Court of Justice in the Rutili case, case 36–25 of 28 October 1975, a development strongly politically supported in a joint declaration of 27 April 1977 by the European Parliament, the Council and the Commission concerning the protection of fundamental rights and the European Convention for the protection of Human Rights and Fundamental Freedoms (OJ C 103). See also the Charter of Fundamental Rights of 18 2000 OJ C 364/13.

which challenged democratic government in Europe.[6] There were also some attempts to secure protection for certain groups and minorities.[7] The consequences of the new surge of interstate complaints, mainly in the wake of Russian actions, starting with the expulsion of Georgians from Russia in 2006 and culminating with the present war against Ukraine, remain, however, to be assessed.

A further, also in many respects revolutionary, feature of the system was that it was binding.

It was thus the first European system after World War II that allowed for supranational binding majority decision making. Under Article 32, as it then was, all Contracting states accepted that the Committee of Ministers of the Council of Europe was entitled to decide by 2/3 majorities whether one of them had violated the Convention. The Committee also supervised that findings of violations were respected. States were expected to implement the findings in good faith. However, had the State concerned not of itself taken adequate remedial action, the Committee could with the same majority decide what effect its decision should have. Article 32 expressly indicated that all Contracting states accepted that also these decisions were binding. Those who wanted, and in the beginning, they were few, could also accept the binding jurisdiction of the European Court.[8] This option is today, after Protocol N° 11 of 1998, compulsory, and the Committee of Ministers can concentrate on the supervision of execution.

The importance of the Convention for Europe led from the outset (indeed already from the very first individual cases in the 1960's) to a Committee of Ministers' requirement also in individual cases that reparation and redress should not only be offered to applicants, whether individuals or groups, but to all in similar situations – the necessity of general measures.[9] Respondent states thus had to change their legislations, even constitutions, court or administrative practices or other, to ensure that the national situation aligned with the Convention standards and that new violations were prevented. An

6 Most notably in Greece after the military coup in 1967 and in Turkey after the military coup in 1980, both leading eventually to successful interstate complaints to uphold European public order around the values of the Council of Europe and the Convention.

7 See notably Austria v. Italy, application 7.78/60, Committee of Ministers resolution 23 October 1963 (re German speakers in Ost Tirol) and Ireland v. United Kingdom, application 5310/71, judgement 18 January 1978 (re the handling of IRA suspects).

8 At the time of its entry into force on 3/9/1953 only 2 states had accepted the Court's compulsory jurisdiction, Ireland and Denmark. However, 6 others followed rather quickly, and the Court was set up on 3/9/1958 following Austria's acceptance of its jurisdiction.

9 See Pataki and Dunshirn, applications 596/59 and 789/60, Committee of Ministers resolution of 16 September 1963.

individual/group winning a case in Strasbourg thus provided relief for the whole group of persons exposed to the general problem revealed.

The efforts in the Committee of Ministers to define, in dialogue with the respondent state, the scope of the problems to be addressed after a finding of violation often requires considerable fact finding and is one of the most important and sensitive elements of the supervision process. In principle, the aim is to address all foreseeable problems on the basis of the Court's judgement and the Court's general case law in the area concerned.[10] On occasion, the Court will itself provide assistance, notably by adopting the so-called pilot judgement procedure, to help the State concerned and the Committee by also assessing itself the scope of possible problems to address.

In particular the requirement of general measures has allowed the system to make a major contribution to the more general integration of the Convention values into law and practice in the different member States and to the creation of a common pan-European legal space/area. Over the years some 5.000 more general reforms have been adopted, be it in the form of changes to legislation or constitutions, in the form of changes of judicial and administrative practice or practical measures such as reinforcing the resources of courts, police, prison administration and regulatory agencies or even of schools and hospitals.

In view of the importance of the system, notably for European unity and integration, the Committee of Ministers has repeatedly stressed that the obligation to respect the Convention and the judgements of the Court is unconditional and a condition for membership in the organisation.[11]

The efforts to render the supervision process more effective has led to a number of reforms to improve its sensitivity. As from 2000, there has thus been an opening of the process to the public, integrating over time not only individual and group applicants to allow these to contribute to securing full

10 See for example the description adopted by the Committee of Ministers in its annual reports on its supervision of the execution of the Court's judgements up to 2018, e.g. the 2017 report, pp. 249–250. In 2018 the budgetary crisis caused by Russia's nonpayment of its dues to the organisation, resulted in a radically shortened report and the mainly descriptive parts, as the presentation of the supervision process and its more detailed results in different cases, were cut out.

11 Acceptance of the Convention and the right of individual petition and the compulsory jurisdiction of the Court have over time become conditions for membership of the Council of Europe and the Committee of Ministers has added that also respect for the judgements of the Court is unconditional and a condition for remaining a member of the organisation – see e.g. Committee of Ministers Interim Resolution ResDH(2001)80 concerning the judgement of the European Court of Human Rights of 28 July 1998 in the case of Loizidou against Turkey and Interim Resolution ResDH(2006)26 in the case of Ilascu v. Russia and the Republic of Moldova.

redress for themselves,[12] but also others to better secure the larger effects of judgements. The Committee has thus since 2006 enlarged the right to submit observations to NGO's, national human rights institutions ("NHRIS") and bar associations, and also to a number of international bodies and institutions.[13] These observations are often crucial whether to assess the scope of problems, necessary execution measures or their implementation.[14]

In order to ensure the alignment of national standards with the Convention more generally there are also other instruments and activities, e.g., intergovernmental cooperation to develop and adopt treaties, recommendation, guidelines[15], political monitoring and dialogue in the Committee of Ministers, the Parliamentary Assembly and the Congress of Local and Regional authorities and also numerous cooperation activities with individual or groups of states.

The more general implementation of the Convention is supported by a number of additional and/or more detailed human rights protection mechanisms set up over the years, many with their own monitoring systems. Most have, however, been based on state reports coupled with country visits and have not contained new complaints mechanisms.

Much of this development took place shortly after the fateful events of 1989 and the "immense hopes"[16] they engendered with the accession of more than 20 new states to the organisation, pledging allegiance to its values and norms, in particular to the Convention. The situation led not only to a big number of new control mechanisms, it also intensified the cooperation with other organisations, notably the EU and the OSCE, and encompassed the opening

12 Comprising above the mere payment of just satisfaction ordered, also the reopening of unfair proceedings, the reinstatement of a residence permit unjustly revoked or the cancellation of an expulsion order implying excessive risks of persecution in the receiving country, release from unwarranted detention, access to children unjustly denied, acceleration of excessively lengthy proceedings etc. …

13 This development can be traced when looking at the Committee's Rules for the supervision of the execution of judgements of the terms of friendly settlements – available notably on the web site of the Department for the execution of judgements of the Court www.coe.int/execution.

14 The procedure has been described in more detail in the Committee of Ministers Annual reports and on the web site of the Department for the execution of judgements.

15 See e.g. "Guidelines of the Committee of Ministers on the prevention and remedying of violations of the Convention for the protection of human rights and fundamental freedoms," from 28 September 2022.

16 See the Vienna Declaration made at the Council of Europe summit on 9 October 1993: "This [new] Europe is a source of immense hope which must in no event be destroyed by territorial ambitions, the resurgence of aggressive nationalism, the perpetuation of spheres of influence, intolerance or totalitarian ideologies".

of special political dialogues, not only with states concerned, but also with the new High Commissioner for National Minorities set up by the CSCE in 1992.

As regards the new mechanisms, the most important of these are, in order of adoption, the Charter for Regional or Minority languages of 1992, the European Commission against Racism and Intolerance (ECRI) founded in 1993, the Convention for the protection of national minorities of 1995 (eventually found to be a better solution than the rival idea of a Protocol on minority rights to the European Convention on Human Rights[17]), the revised Social Charter of 1996 which added belonging to a national minority to the grounds for discrimination. In addition, the Council of Europe Commissioner for Human Rights, set up in 1999, received a mandate allowing the coverage of many minority issues.

However, only one new complaints procedure saw the light: the collective complaints procedure set up in 1995 under the Social Charter (and the revised Social Charter). This absence of other formal complaints procedures does not usually prevent groups and minorities from having access to all the Council of Europe bodies responsible for the above instruments in order to provide information and solicit assistance or interventions, but without any legal obligation for the bodies approached to react (even if they often do in one form or another). The latter procedures will thus not be further developed in this contribution.

Group and minority interests are often multifaceted. It is therefore not uninteresting to stress the close links between civil and political and social and economic rights, links which have been continuously stressed in the post war human rights discussions. The division between the different rights is certainly not clear-cut. Indeed, many social, economic and cultural rights affect or overlap civil and political rights such as private life or the right of property.

Some social and economic rights have indeed been expressly integrated in the text of the Convention, as e.g. the protection against inhuman treatment and forced labour, the right to education or the right of property (Articles 3 and 4 of the Convention and 1 of Protocol N° 1).

In addition, the Convention develops in symbiosis with the Social Charter, and vice versa. Social rights developed under the Charter will frequently be considered "civil rights" for the purpose of Article 6 and trigger judicial protection. They will, not infrequently, also relate to "private" or "family life" and

17 See for example the relation of these developments in "Economic, Social and Cultural Rights" by Matti Pellonpää or "The Convention and the Protection of Minorities under International Law" by Andrés B. Baka, both in "The European System for the Protection of Human Rights", ed. R. St. J. Macdonald, F. Matscher, H. Petzold, Martinus Nijhof 1993, pp. 855–874 and 875–888, respectively.

attract the protection of Article 8 or that of Article 1 in Protocol 1, and thereby also the right to an effective remedy under Article 13 and the wider protection against all forms of discrimination inherent in Article 14, and not only as under the Charter, against discrimination of national minorities. In addition, for states that have accepted Protocol 12, the guarantee against discrimination is not limited to the exercise of the rights and freedoms protected but extends to all kinds of discrimination. It goes without saying that the requirements developed under the Convention may in turn, inspire the development of Social Charter practice.

Notwithstanding the absence of more specific group or minority rights in the Convention, the case law of the Court has thus integrated elements of such rights in other rights, the mix leading to a considerable measure of protection for group or minority interests.

The lifestyle of a minority has for example been considered included in the protection offered under Article 8 as being part of the group members' "private" or "family life" leading to the necessity of always justifying interferences therewith.[18] The criminalisation of certain other groups for example homosexuals[19] or of the members of religious creeds, such as the Jehovah's' witnesses,[20] has been found clearly unacceptable under the Convention.

The Court's case law has also demonstrated aversity to anything engendering hatred or violence, be it in the exercise of freedom of expression, freedom of demonstration or freedom of religion or otherwise.

For example, the use of freedom of expression under Article 10 in order to incite to violence or hatred against certain persons, groups or minorities has been considered a factor allowing/requiring harsher sanctions, even imprisonment.[21] The Court has also considered that any negative stereotype of a group may, when it reaches a certain level, affect that group's sense of identity and its members' feelings of self-esteem and self-confidence, so when exercising freedom of expression this has to be taken into account.[22]

---

18 See for example G. and E. v. Norway, application 9278/81, Commission decision 3 October 1983, and Noack v. Germany, application 46346/99, Court decision 25 May 2000.

19 An evolution starting with Dudgeon v. United Kingdom, application 7525/76, judgement of 22 October 1981, §§ 61–62.

20 See e.g. Jehovah's witnesses of Moscow and Others v. Russia, application 302/02, judgement 10 June 2010, cf also the de facto situation in Members of the Gldani Congregation of Jehovah's witnesses and Others v. Georgia, application 71158/01, judgement of 3 May 2007, §§ 97, 122–125; 133–135; 140–142.

21 See e.g. Arslan v. Turkey, application 23462/94, judgement of 8 July 1999, § 48.

22 See e.g. Aksu v. Turkey, application 41449/04, judgement of 15 March 2012, § 58.

Similarly, criminal investigations have to examine if racial, ethnic or discriminatory motives may lie behind criminal activity or the state action underlying the violations[23] so as to allow for remedial actions to be taken. Concrete measures must also be taken if a group or minority is facing physical assaults and effective remedies secured.[24]

As regards the promotion of group or minority interests, the right to form political parties[25] or associations[26] and to demonstrate[27] have also often been invoked before the Court, and successfully so. So have a number of schooling and language questions.[28] Excluding certain groups/minorities from full participation in political life evidently raises serious questions under the Convention and is in general not permitted.[29]

The same evidently holds true for the right to religious freedom, including the right proselytise,[30] to open places of worship,[31] to object to military service,[32] not to be compelled to pay taxes destined to finance another state supported religion.[33]

To all these cases you must add all those where the alleged violation has been caused by the victim's membership of a certain group or minority so as to triggere the protection of Article 14.[34]

---

23 See e.g. Antayev and Others v. Russia, application 966/07, judgement of 3 July 2014, § 110.

24 See e.g. Members of the Gldani Congregation of Jehovah's witnesses and Others v. Georgia, application 71158/01, judgement of 3 May 2007, §§ 97, 122–125; 133–135; 140–142 or Moldovan and Others v. Romania n° 1, application 41138/98, judgement of 5 July 2005, Friendly settlement, and Moldovan and Others n° 2, application 41138/98, judgement of 12 July 2005.

25 See e.g. UMO Ilinden and Pirin, application 59489/99, judgement of 20 October 2005, §§ 59–63.

26 See e.g. Bekir Ousta and Others v. Greece, application 35151/05, judgement of 11 November 2007.

27 See e.g. Barankevich v. Russia, application 10519/03, judgement of 26 July 2007, § 31.

28 See e.g. Cyprus v. Turkey, application 27781/94, judgement 10 May 2001, §§ 273-280, Egitim ve Bilim Emekcileri Sendikasi v. Turkey, application 20641/05, judgement of 25 September 2012, Catan v. Russia and the Republic of Moldova, application 43370/04, judgement of 19 October 2012.

29 Sejdic and Finci v. Bosnia and Herzegovina, application 27996/06, judgement of 22 December 2009.

30 See Kokkinakis v. Greece, application 14307/88, judgement of 25 May 1993.

31 See Manousakis v. Greece, application 18748/91, judgement of 0 October 1994.

32 See e.g. Ülke v. Turkey, application 39437/98, judgement of 24 January 2006.

33 See e.g. Darby v. Sweden, application 11581/85, judgement of 11 April 1988.

34 See e.g. also Antayev and Others, cited above §§ 126–129, Stoica v. Romania, application 42722/02, judgement of 4 March 2008 or Lakatosova v. Slovakia, application 655/16, judgement 11 December 2018.

Group rights may also be seen as relevant for the protection not only of small, but also big vulnerable groups such as women and children. It would go too far for present purposes to also cover this multifaceted area in any detail. Suffice it perhaps to indicate here the protection due to women under the Convention against domestic violence,[35] discrimination in the enjoyment of pension rights[36] (even if the same has been true vis à vis men[37]) or at the workplace.[38] With respect to children, the major right is that of education, but there is also the obligation to constantly work for the best of the child in access or custody disputes or in cases of public care.[39] In addition, the physical integrity of the child is protected and corporal punishment is not accepted.[40]

3 Collective Complaints under the Social Charter

Collective complaints under the Social Charter are handled by the European Committee of Social Rights. So far some 196 complaints have been received. Evidently, this poses some problems in order to identify the full potential of this procedure and all possible issues that might be dealt with. The examples below are thus more illustrative.

Also this procedure is open to outside scrutiny and comment, including at the execution stage. Therefore, besides other governments, international trade unions and employer organisations may also submit comments. Upon invitation from the President of the Committee any organisation, institution or person may be invited to submit observations. The findings of the Committee are binding on the states as a matter of international law, but the respect of the Committee's conclusions is basically followed up through the regular examination of the conclusions by the Committee of Ministers in order to adopt relevant recommendations to the contracting states, including, as the case may be, compensation to victims.

Among matters dealt with so far figure the right to a home (confiscation of caravans), especially relevant for Roma,[41] the right to participate in collective

35 See e.g. Z.B. v. Croatia, application 47666/13, judgement of 11 July 2017, §§ 52–63.
36 See e.g. Wessels-Begervoet v. the Netherlands, application 34462/97, judgement of 4 June 2002, §§ 47–55.
37 See e.g. Willis v. the United Kingdom, application 36042/97, judgement of 11 June 2002, §§ 39–43.
38 See e.g. Jurci v. Croatia, application 54711/15, judgement of 4 February 2021, §§ 68–69, 76–85.
39 See Z. v. United Kingdom, application 29392/95, judgement 10 May 2001.
40 See e.g. A. v. United Kingdom, application 35373/97, judgement of 17 December 2002.
41 See European Roma Rights Centre (ERRC) v. Belgium, complaint 197/2020, decision 8 December 2022.

bargaining,[42] the handling of children, whether migrant children,[43] underage children in pre-trial investigations[44] or children with intellectual disabilities with respect to their schooling,[45] continuing pay gaps between men and women and absence of gender equality requirements regarding decisions making positions in companies,[46] reductions of unemployment benefits for elderly,[47] the requirement of sterilisation of transgender persons in order to obtain official documents reflecting their gender identity[48] and the absence of any right for gendarmerie non-commissioned officers to join a trade union.[49]

In the above areas, the requirements in the Convention and the Social Charter often overlap to quite some degree. This is also so as regards "negative" and "positive" protection. Not only is there under both instruments "negative" protection against undue state interference with the rights and freedoms protected, but also "positive obligations" to put in place the necessary framework for the exercise of the right in question so that it can be effectively enjoyed.[50]

4 The Victim Problem

Before moving further, it should be noted that, under the Convention, complex practical problems may arise in the vindication of group and minority rights before the Court. The reason is the limitation of the right of individual petition to "victims".

Under the Court's case law, "victims" have been limited to those directly affected and their personal interests, not necessarily wide enough to cover

42 See Confederazione General Sindicale 5CGS) and Federazione dei Lavoratori e Funzione pubbliche FLP) v. Italy, complaint 161/2018, decision 19 October 2022.

43 See International Commission of Jurists (ICJ) and European Council for Refugees and Exiles (ECRE) v. Greece, complaint 173/2018, decision 16 January 2021.

44 See International Commission of Jurists (ICJ) v. Czech Republic, complaint 148/2017.

45 International Federation for Human Rights (FIDH) and Inclusion Europe, complaint 141/2017.

46 University Women of Europe (UWE) v. Bulgaria, complaint 125/2016, decision 6 December 2019 – NB a complaint lodged against a big number of states.

47 Finnish Society of Social Rights v. Finland, complaint 108/2014? Decision 8 December 2016.

48 Transgender Europe and ILGA-Europe v. the Czech Republic, complaint 117/2015, decision 15 May 2018.

49 European Council of Police Trade Unions (CESP), v. France, complaint 101/2013, decisions 27 January 2016.

50 See for example as regards the Convention the "Belgian linguistic" judgement (merits) 23 July 1968, §3; Marckx v. Belgium, application 6873/74, judgement of 13 June 1979. Re Social Charter see for example Conclusions XV-1 Portugal, Article 12 § 4 of 31 March 2000.

those of the group/association they belong to. Certain violations have, however, demonstrated close links between the two, allowing applications lodged by a few to cover, at least through the execution process, the violations suffered by the whole group, or their associations (and vice versa), and numerous groups and minorities have successfully complained to the Court.[51] It would appear that the Court's jurisprudence has developed a greater sensitivity to group rights over time and the matter is very much at the centre of present climate litigation cases.[52]

Guidance in the matter prepared by the UN Office of the High Commissioner for Human Rights has the pragmatic recommendation that applications be submitted both by the organisations and the individuals concerned.[53] This advice is, in many cases, also followed.

This procedural hurdle does not exist under the Social Charter's collective complaints' procedure. Here social partners and authorised associations[54] may complain about anything falling under the Charter even if they are not victims themselves.

As we have seen, the execution process under the Convention can often help overcome these "victim" problems as it will "automatically" ensure that execution will also cover the remedying of the general problem revealed by the Court's judgement and thus the provision of redress to all affected.

---

51 Numerous associations and sometimes minority groups (frequently also complaining through a representative group of members, see e.g. Catan and others against the Republic of Moldova and Russia, application 43370/04, judgement 19 October 2012.

52 Verein KlimaSeniorinnen Schweiz and Others v. Switzerland, application 53600/20, pending before the Court and brought by the association and certain of its members; Duarte Agostinho and Others v. Portugal, application 39371/20, pending before the Court and brought by a number of young persons claiming to be direct victims of climate change.

53 See e.g. the Pamphlet N° 7 of the United Nations' guide for minorities: "Minority rights under the European Convention on Human Rights" (2000).

54 The following organisations are entitled to lodge collective complaints: the European social partners (European Trade Union Confederation (ETUC), Business Europe and International Organisation of Employers (OIE)); international non-governmental organisations (INGOs) holding participatory status with the Council of Europe and included at their request on the list drawn up by the Governmental Committee of the European Social Charter and the European Code of Social Security (61 such INGO's were included in the list as of 1 July 2023); representative trade unions and employers' organisations in the country concerned. Furthermore, any State may grant representative national non-governmental organisations (NGOs) within its jurisdiction the right to lodge complaints against it. So far only Finland has done so.

5 Note on Interstate Cases

Even if interstate complaints, due to their rarity, are not at the centre of this overview, some interstate cases merit attention as they illustrate the hopes regarding the Convention's relevance also for minority issues, especially trans frontier ones, which existed already at an early stage.

Already the two first interstate cases before the Convention organs, (the European Commission of Human Rights and the Committee of Ministers – at the time only a minority had accepted the compulsory jurisdiction of the European Court) hinted at the Convention's potential for minority issues, even if both led to timid results.

The case of Greece v. United Kingdom, lodged in 1956, was launched by Greece because of the British handling of the situation in Cyprus, allegedly denying the population most of the rights protected by the Convention in its attempts to keep peace and uphold its authority in the conflict between the Turkish (22%) and Greek (78%) communities on the Island. In view of the political settlement of the Cyprus question and the creation of a new and independent republic through the Zurich and London agreements of 1959, the Committee of Ministers found no reason to take further action in response to the complaints.[55] Similarly, the case of Austria v. Italy was engaged by Austria in 1960 in the context of the major crisis caused by the forcible efforts to bring the mainly German speaking region of the Upper Adige under fuller Italian control. Austria challenged the fairness of a high-profile criminal case brought against a group of young men from the German speaking part accused of having killed an Italian border guard during a fight. Even if the case was largely declared admissible by the Commission, it eventually led the Commission to find no-violations of the Convention, findings upheld by the Committee of Ministers.[56] A further interstate case, lodged by Ireland against the United Kingdom in 1971 concerned notably the United Kingdom's handling, through the Northern Ireland authorities, of the violent "Troubles" and suspected IRA terrorists and sympathisers and was more successful. The Court here found that the treatment amounted to inhuman and degrading treatment in violation of Article 3 of the Convention. The United Kingdom had, however, already stopped the impugned practices at the time of the Court's judgement.[57]

55 See the resolution adopted by the Committee of Ministers on 20 April 1959 re application 176/56.

56 See the resolution adopted by the Committee of Ministers on 23 October 1963 re application 778/60.

57 It can be noted that the Irish Government subsequently got hold of documents allegedly proving that the hardships suffered had in fact amounted to torture and sought a

A series of cases were also engaged by Cyprus against Turkey with respect to human rights violations which took place in the context of, and after, the Turkish military intervention in 1974 and the situation of the Greek Cypriots' in the northern part of the island, which came under Turkish jurisdiction for Convention purposes after the intervention.

The last of these Cyprus cases, lodged in 1994, highlighted numerous hardships suffered by the Greek Cypriots under the self-proclaimed local authorities, notably as regards the Greek Cypriot's right to ensure an education for their children corresponding to their convictions and meeting the needs of their children – a violation of Article 2 of Protocol N° 1. As a result, the faltering Greek speaking school was reinvigorated under the Committee of Ministers' supervision. It may be noted that individual complaints lodged against Moldova and Russia with respect to the plight of Latin script schools in Transnistria, led to similar violations by Russia because of its control over the self-proclaimed local authorities and Russia's inaction in face of their harassment of the schools. Since Russia's responsibilities under the Convention were engaged before Russia was excluded from the Council of Europe and since the harassment continues, the matter is still on the agenda of the Committee of Ministers.[58]

6 Final Comments

This brief overview of the complaints systems set up under the auspices of the Council of Europe demonstrate the unique character of these systems and their important contribution towards ensuring that European integration and unification take place with due respect for individual and certain minority human rights, the rule of law and the requirements of democracy. It is from this encouraging perspective that the Convention organs have found, notably because of the EU's early integration of the Convention into its legal system, that they can trust the EU to provide equivalent protection. It is sad that this is not the case with the Social Charter, where it has been impossible to express the same level of trust in the EU. Nevertheless the two Council of Europe

revision of the 1978 judgement. Revision was, however, denied by the Court in 2018 as it had doubts whether the documents submitted contained sufficient prima facie evidence of the alleged new facts and that in any event these would not have changed the conclusions in the first judgement – application 5310/71, judgement of 20 March 2018.

58 Moldova for its part, was found by the Court to have lived up to its limited obligations resulting from its unchallenged sovereignty rights over the territory, but absence of territorial control (reduced to diplomatic or "domestic" actions).

systems are both essential and overlap to quite some extent. Moves have also been engaged to ensure EU adhesion also to the Charter.

These questions aside, a major conclusion from this overview is that the two Council of Europe complaint systems provide considerable protection also for group and minority rights. As highlighted already in the introduction, the capacity of civil society to organise and manifest its positions and beliefs is crucial for a democratic society to function. This stresses the importance of the Convention is the right of individual petition to ensure respect for all persons, groups and minorities. The existence of a good social conscience is important to be able to live together peacefully and respectfully and an important element also for peaceful and productive relations between groups on the labour market, and thereby for the long-term efficiency of the economy.

The handling of the special needs of different kinds of minorities may, however, create problems. It is for example positive that the lifestyle of a minority enjoys the protection of Article 8, but when you look at the results, namely that under the Convention's proportionality test the importance of preserving that lifestyle has often to cede to the interests of economic development, you become more sceptical regarding the real value of the protection. The fact that several important European states have still done little to ratify the Convention for the Protection of National Minorities is another concern, even if much has been achieved under the reporting procedure used under that treaty (Finland was among the first to ratify). Still, minority rights are back on the agenda, not least as regards the Åland islands, and constitute a very relevant resource to ensure a peaceful and respectful "living together" within our culturally diverse societies.[59]

A final remark relates to one of the Council of Europe's complaint procedures' big advantages for the outside world as compared to many other, especially reporting, procedures. The procedures are binding and public from the outset. The results of the subsequent phases are immediately published until the problems revealed are solved. This provides a unique opportunity, notably for groups and minorities, to usefully intervene, both domestically and in Strasbourg, to ensure that the success they may be able to obtain before the Court or the Social Charter Committee also leads to required redress and reforms.

59 See also the 2016 Council of Europe guidelines "Human Rights in culturally diverse societies" and the judgement of the European Court in S.A.S. v. France, application 43835/11, judgement, grand chamber, 1 July 2014.

CHAPTER 12

A Short Exploration of the Nexus of Autonomy, Culture and Security

Sia Spiliopoulou Åkermark

1 Introduction

The inception of this article dates to 2014 when the illegal occupation of Crimea made me realise how little academia and much of the international community knew about the complex status of that region, and how little interest had been shown for a long time. That situation made me also realise how little we knew and understood about the complex, both similar and different, status of the Åland Islands. The present article focuses on the interplay between the three core components of the Åland regime, or arrangement, as it was negotiated and legally entrenched in 1921 and as it has evolved thereafter. By regime, I mean a system of legal rules which gives the basic framework for the position and governance of the region. The Åland Islands are a Swedish speaking autonomous, demilitarised and neutralised archipelago in the Republic of Finland. The population of the islands is today 30,359 persons.[1]

Territorial autonomy refers to the legislation, institutions and practices of and about the Åland Islands ensuring an exclusive legislative competence, a regional parliament (*Ålands lagting*), and a regional government (*Ålands landskapsregering*) guaranteed in the international decisions within the League of Nations, in the quasi-constitutional *Act on Autonomy* and the Constitution of Finland.[2] The official language of the Åland Islands is Swedish, following the international decisions of 1921 and the Autonomy Act. The language used in state administration, Åland administration, municipal administration, and the so-called Åland Delegation is Swedish. This arrangement operates against

1 Åland in Figures, Åland Statistics 2023. https://www.asub.ax/en/publications/aland-figures (as of 15.09.2023). On population trends see R. Palmer, "Lönar sig självstyrelse? De nordiska autonomiernas utveckling under efterkrigstiden", in S. Spiliopoulou Åkermark and G. Herolf (eds), *Självstyrelser i Norden i ett fredsperspektiv*, (Mariehamn: Nordiska rådet & Ålands fredsinstitut, 2015), 27–50 https://peace.ax/wp-content/uploads/2021/02/Sjalvstyrelser_i_norden_webbversion.pdf (as of 15.09.2023).

2 Autonomy Act for Åland 1144/1991. An English translation is found here: https://www.finlex.fi/en/laki/kaannokset/1991/en19911144.pdf.

the backdrop of the constitutionally entrenched bilingualism in Finland with Finnish and Swedish as official languages. The right of everyone to use his or her own language, either Finnish or Swedish, before courts and other authorities, is further guaranteed by law.[3] These cultural guarantees regarding language are, in the Åland regime, escorted by various other guarantees in the field of education, the right of domicile etc.

Demilitarisation and neutralisation refer to the multiple treaties concerning the islands, ever since 1856, limiting military presence and activities. In short, *demilitarisation* prohibits military presence or installations, while *neutralisation* prescribes that the islands should not be drawn into military confrontations and war while Finland has the right to self-defence as regulated in the 1921 Convention. Security arrangements on Åland include, however, not only the demilitarisation and neutralisation, but also special solutions as regards the conditions for the right of domicile, ownership of real property, conscription, the border guard, (regional) police, rescue services as well as rules and practices about emergency situations. In this regard there is complementarity between international and domestic rules and practices in the field of security.

The basic argument in the present text is that the three core components, i.e. *autonomy, culture* (especially in the form of the Swedish language), and *security* (especially, but not exclusively, in the form of demilitarisation and neutralisation), are intimately interlinked and can thus be disentangled legally and politically only with difficulty and involving great complexity and risks. It is also argued that these sets of rules and core components of the regime are often triggered and activated in political and legal debates in tandem. Nevertheless, there is no determinism in this statement. I simply argue that the security solutions, the political power distribution and the cultural guarantees are understood and function as intimately linked in practice, and that they have been developed in parallel historically, in spite of the fact that their legal entrenchment and foundations are partly separate in (domestic and international) law and they have multiple justificatory grounds.[4] To discuss these linkages between the internal and international security dimensions of the Åland regime and, on the other hand, of the autonomy of Åland is by no means an uncontroversial or simple enterprise. The issues are not only complex and multifaceted; they are also tainted by the layers of historical experiences understood and interpreted in different ways by different actors on Åland, in Finland and internationally. The entanglement of components in the Åland regime

---

3 Language Act 423/2003, https://www.finlex.fi/en/laki/kaannokset/2003/en20030423.pdf.

4 A. Spiliopoulou Åkermark, *Justifications of Minority Protection in International Law* (Kluwer Law, 1997); & "Shifts in the multiple justifications of minority protection", *European Yearbook of Minority Issues*, Vol. 7 (2007/2008), 5–18.

has been highlighted by several commentators. The Finnish ambassador, René Nyberg, who served for decades as a diplomat and was highly involved in the multiple processes of reorientation in the 1980s and early 1990s, has described the Åland regime as a "wooden block puzzle".[5] Similarly, the interplay of domestic and international dimensions has been described by Markku Suksi as "a peculiar blend of international law and constitutional law as well as of international and domestic politics".[6]

2 Nuanced Views

The official Finnish stand has often been to emphasise the separate legal basis and goals of these parts of the regime pertaining to Åland. As recently put by Sten Palmgren, the demilitarisation and neutralisation of the islands "are sometimes seen as a guarantee for the self-government, since the goal is to keep Åland outside international conflict". But, he adds, "there is no direct connection between the self-government and the demilitarisation".[7] Other commentators seem to understand the components of the Åland regime rather as a "trinity". This term has been used by Peter Lindbäck, head of the Åland Government administration (1987–1999) and until recently as governor of Åland.[8] According to Lindbäck, this trinity encompasses the demilitarisation-neutralisation, the

5 R. Nyberg, "Åland är som en träknut – lätt att plocka isär, men svår att sätta ihop" (my informal translation: Åland is like a wooden blockpuzzle; easy to disentangle but difficult to put together), *Hufvudstadsbladet*, November 24, 2015. See also R. Nyberg, "Finlands säkerhetspolitik och Ålands status," *Hufvudstadsbladet*, September 26, 1990. It is interesting that Nyberg interprets the rejection by the inhabitants of the Åland Islands of a military presence on Åland, as being an expression not of a 'defence nihilism' (*försvarsnihilism*) but of concern for the uniqueness of the islands (*Ålands särart*). On the wider debates at the time see Y. Poullie, "Åland's Demilitarisation and Neutralisation at the End of the Cold War – Parliamentary Discussions in Åland and Finland 1988–1995," *International Journal on Minority and Group Rights* 23 (2016): 179–210.

6 M. Suksi, 'The Constitutional Setting of the Åland Islands Compared', in Frank Horn & Lauri Hannikainen, *Autonomy and Demilitarisation in International Law: the Åland Islands in a Changing Europe*, Brill 1997, 99–129.

7 S. Palmgren, *Ålands självstyrelse. En introduktion för statsrådets tjänstemän*, Justitieministeriet 2023:11. Sten Palmgren worked for very many years at the Ministry of Justice with matters concerning the Åland autonomy.

8 Act on Autonomy of Åland, Section 4–5, S. Stephan, "The Autonomy of the Åland Islands" in S. Spiliopoulou Åkermark (ed.), *The Åland Example and Its Components: Relevance for International Conflict Resolution*, (Mariehamn: The Åland Islands Peace Institute, 2011), 28–49. Alessi, N.P. (2021) "Joint Bodies – a Key Factor for Successful Autonomous Systems? The Cases of the Italian Special Regions and the Åland Islands". *Journal of Autonomy and Security Studies*, 5(1), 8–25. Retrieved from https://jass.ax/index.php/jass/article/view/51 (07.10.2023).

autonomous status, including guarantees for the Swedish language and local culture, and the confirmation of Finnish sovereignty.[9] The link between the three components is also understood as a crucial reference point for Gunnar Jansson, who asserts that the Ålanders regard demilitarisation and neutralisation "as part of their autonomous arrangement".[10] According to Niklas Fagerlund, during the process of Finland's EU accession negotiations, the overall conclusion was that "the international legal rules relating to the autonomous, demilitarised and neutralised status of Åland comprised a single regime under regional customary law".[11] Christer Ahlström found that the Ålanders seem to view "the autonomous status and the restrictions on military uses of the Islands as an indivisible whole", and adds "the actual linkage between the two is not as strong as was the case with some of the other examples of demilitarised and neutralised zones in which the population had autonomy".[12] This refers presumably to the cases of Saarland and the Free City of Danzig discussed briefly by Ahlström.[13] This assertion shows that *at the time of the inception of the Åland settlement, a close linkage between on the one hand autonomy and on the other hand demilitarisation security solutions was not uncommon.*

Even though the present argument about the interconnections of self-government and demilitarisation/neutralisation is then not an entirely new argument and discussion, I shall try to show how this has worked in law and in practice during three important periods, i.e. the formative years around 1921; the turbulent years 1938–1951 during the Second World War and the first major revision of the Autonomy Act; and, finally, after the end of the Cold War, i.e. after 1990, with the second major revision of the Autonomy Act (1991) and up until Finland's membership of the North Atlantic Treaty Organisation (NATO) in 2023.

9 Interview with Peter Lindbäck by Sarah Stephan for the Åland Islands Peace Institute, 18.3.2014; C. Scarpulla, *The Constitutional Framework for the Autonomy of the Åland Islands: A survey of the status of an autonomous region in the throes of European integration*, Meddelanden från Ålands högskola Nr 14, 2nd ed., 2002, at 23–24.

10 G. Jansson, 'Introduction', in: L. Hannikainen and F. Horn (eds.), *Autonomy and Demilitarisation in International Law: The Åland Islands in a Changing Europe* (Kluwer Law International, The Hague, 1997), 6.

11 N. Fagerlund N., 'The Special Status of the Åland Islands in the European Union', in Hannikainen & Horn (supra note 6), 189–256, at 194.

12 C. Ahlström, 'Demilitarised and Neutralised Zones in a European Perspective', in Hannikainen & Horn (1997, supra note 6) 41–56, at 53.

13 See also C. Ahlström, *Demilitarised and Neutralised Territories in Europe* (Mariehamn: Ålands fredsinstitut, 2004). Ahlström's comparative assertion deserves future scientific attention.

3 Early 20th Century: the Åland Regime Shaped

Like many other border regions, the history of the Åland Islands is marked by shifts between long eras of peaceful trade, fishing, agriculture, tourism, hard work and societal and cultural development, interrupted by the effects of failures of crops, harsh climate, human mobility, conquest and war.[14] For almost 700 years, Åland, together with most of present-day Finland, formed the eastern part of the Swedish Kingdom (hereinafter "Sweden"). In 1809, Sweden was defeated by the Russian Empire (hereinafter "Russia") and Åland, as a part of the Grand Duchy of Finland, was ceded to the victor.[15] By becoming the western-most part of the empire, Åland grew in significance while Tsar Alexander also wanted to boost progressive policies and contacts with Europe.[16] The Grand Duchy of Finland, including Åland, held an autonomous position within the Russian empire. In August 1854, the Baltic Sea became the theatre of a stage of the Crimean War (1853–1856) which raged mainly in the Black Sea, when the joint British and French forces attacked and destroyed the fortress of Bomarsund. Sweden declined an offer to gain sovereignty over Åland, maintaining its policy of neutrality while also fearing possible retaliation from Russia. In March 1856, Great Britain, France and the Russian Empire signed in Paris the Convention on the Demilitarisation of the Åland Islands (1856 Convention).[17] This convention was annexed to the Paris Peace Treaty terminating the Crimean War, thus linking the settlement to the broader arrangement at the end of the war. A new international status of the Åland Islands was anchored in international law. The autonomy of the Grand Duchy of Finland was enhanced when in 1881 new conscription rules in Russia allowed for the creation of a Finnish army, underlining the pattern of connections between security and autonomy.[18]

World War I broke out in 1914 with France, Great Britain and Russia on the same side of the Allied Powers, joined later by Italy and the United States. In

14 I. Hughes Tidlund. *Autonomous Åland: a hundred years of borderwork in the Baltic Sea.* (Diss. Stockholm: Stockholm university, 2021).

15 S. Spiliopoulou Åkermark, *The Multiple Paths to Territorial Autonomy – Examples and Conceptual Underpinnings*, in O. Akbulut & E. Aktoprak (eds.), *Minority Self-Government in Europe and the Middle East*, Brill (2019), 62–82.

16 H. Yllikangas, "Finlands administrativa ställning inom det ryska riket," *Historisk Tidskrift För Finland* 80, no. 3 (1995): 289–308.

17 S. Spiliopoulou Åkermark et al., *Demilitarisation and International Law in Context – The Åland Islands*, Routledge, 2018.

18 Yllikangas (supra note 16) argued that one of the reasons why the Senate was not convened until 1863 was that the Russian Empire wanted to avoid a discussion on a possible Finnish army.

January 1915, Russia resorted to fortifications on Åland to prevent a German presence on the islands and following communication between Russia, Sweden and the allies.[19] In December 1917, Finland took "its fate into its own hands" and declared independence.[20] In January 1918, civil war erupted in Finland between Red Guards and White Guards. Sweden decided to send ships to Åland and, in March 1918, there was a simultaneous presence of Finnish, Swedish, Russian and German troops on Åland.[21] The civil war, also referred to as the war of independence, ended only in May 1918 with the victory of the White Guards.[22] It had a death toll of more than 36,000 victims.[23]

The Ålanders did not remain a passive object in all these events; they too wanted to take their fate into their own hands. Realising the importance of institutionalising their own polity and voice, and of self-governing institutions, they established the Legislative Assembly in June 1918 and addressed the Allied Powers to raise the issue of Åland in the forthcoming peace negotiations. Sweden expressed the view that Finland should allow the Ålanders to decide their fate by plebiscite, a first diplomatic note in the Swedish-Finnish dispute over the islands.[24] From January 1919 onward, Paris hosted the peace conference, which was to decide what a post-WWI world would look like. The representatives of Åland departed for Paris, the place to which all eyes, ears and hopes were turned.[25] Sweden wanted the Åland Question to be resolved quickly, and mobilised its diplomatic resources. Finland employed, successfully, the strategy of delaying the issue. Finland replied to the above-mentioned Swedish note only in June 1919 and refused the plebiscite, but assured Sweden

19 The "Central Powers" consisted mainly of Germany, Austria, Hungary, the Ottoman Empire and Bulgaria. J.O. Söderhjelm, *Démilitarisation et neutralisation des Iles d'Aland en 1856 et 1921*, Helsingfors 1928, 126–127. Martin Isaksson, *Ryska positionen Alandskaja*, Söderströms, 1983, 47–49.

20 "*har Finlands folk tagit sitt öde i egna händer* [...]" from the Finnish Declaration of Independence.

21 A. Bondestam, *Åland vintern 1918*, Schildts förlag, 1972.

22 A little earlier the Peace Treaty of Brest-Litovsk (3 March 1918) had Germany, Austria-Hungary, Bulgaria and the Ottoman Empire on the one side and Russia on the other.

23 Figures gathered in the research project 'War victims in Finland, 1914–1922' at the State Archives of Finland, See: https://sotasurmat.narc.fi/en (visited 16.09.2023).

24 A brief overview of the Åland dispute in the League of Nations is found in S. Spiliopoulou Åkermark, "The Åland Islands Question In The League Of Nations: The Ideal Minority Case?", *Redescriptions: Yearbook of Political Thought, Conceptual History and Feminist Theory* 13 (2009): 195–205. An extensive analysis of the political and diplomatic intricacies is found in James Barros. *The Aland Islands Question: Its settlement by the League of Nations*. New Haven: Yale University (1968).

25 T. Modeen, *De folkrättsliga garantierna för bevarandet av Ålandsöarnas nationella karaktär*, Mariehamn (1973).

of proposed constitutional guarantees. First to come was the 1919 Finnish Constitution, including the provisions on the two national languages.[26] Finland realised that strong diplomatic efforts alone might not suffice and, fearing to lose Åland, began to work on legislative changes to grant Åland a degree of autonomy. The Åland Question was discussed only sporadically in 1919 and the issue lingered unresolved. Meanwhile, a solution to another issue was found through the Svalbard/Spitsbergen agreement.[27]

In May 1920, Finland enacted the first Act on the Self-Government of the Aland Islands ("1920 Autonomy Act").[28] It provided for a list of the competences of the state leaving the residual powers to the Åland Parliament. *Police* matters were not mentioned among the powers of the state (in contrast e.g. to defence, customs, courts and penal law), so policiary issues were under the jurisdiction of the Åland authorities from the outset. In para. 27 of the same Act is found the *exemption from military service* and the possibility of doing alternative civilian service in the piloting and lighthouse service "as provided in special legislation". The Act was nonetheless rejected by the Ålanders. In June 1920, Great Britain submitted the Åland Question to the newly established Council of the League of Nations. The Council of the League of Nations appointed first a Commission of Jurists, which submitted its report in September 1920, and soon thereafter a Commission of Rapporteurs, which presented its Report in April 1921.[29] In the meeting of 24 June 1921, the Council first reminded that Sweden and Finland "have agreed to abide by its decision" and continued with what became the Resolution of 24 June 1921, which reads:

26 Constitution Act, adopted on 19 July 1919.

27 Treaty concerning the Archipelago of Spitsbergen (signed 9 February 1920, in force 14 August 1925) 2 LNTS 7 Available here: http://library.arcticportal.org/1909/1/The_Svalbard_Treaty_9ssFy.pdf (visited 29.09.2023).

28 Act on the Self-Government of the Aland Islands FFS 124/1920 of 7 May 1920 provided i.a. for a legislative assembly, a local government and various language rights, and was followed by the Implementation Act FFS 125/1920 and the so-called Guarantee Act FFS 189/1922. It was only after the League of Nations decisions of 1921 and the Guarantee Act of 1922 that the Ålanders endorsed the settlement. Preparatory works in the Finnish Parliament, Bill 73/1919. For an overview of the early legislation and legal documents on Åland see A. Tollet & J. Uggla, *Lagstiftningen angående självstyrelse för Åland*, Helsingsfors, 1930, p. 11. Early versions of the Autonomy Act and preparatory works are found at the website of the Åland Parliament https://www.lagtinget.ax/sjalvstyrelsen/sjalvstyrelselagen (visited 29.09.2023. In Swedish).

29 J. Barros, *The Aland Islands Question: Its settlement by the League of Nations*. New Haven: Yale University (1968) p. 304.

> 1. The sovereignty of the Aaland Islands is recognized to belong to Finland; 2. Nevertheless, the interests of the world, the future of cordial relations between Finland and Sweden, the prosperity and happiness of the Islands themselves cannot be ensured unless (a) certain further guarantees are given to the protection of the Islanders; and unless (b) arrangements are concluded for the non-fortification and neutralisation of the Archipelago.[30]

The *culture-oriented guarantees* were, according to the Council, to be included in and expand the *Autonomy Act* which was in place but had been rejected by the Ålanders. The Council met three days later and approved these guarantees in what is referred to as "the Åland Agreement" settled between Sweden and Finland, annexing it to the above-mentioned resolution.[31] Finland emphasised the constitutional and legislative guarantees offered to Swedish speakers in Finland in general and in the Åland Islands in particular.[32] This is a crucial point in the history and conceptualisation of the Åland regime and for understanding the nexus between autonomy, cultural guarantees and security arrangements. On 24 and 27 June 1921, the Council of the League of Nations outlined the basic framework to be applied. The framework included both domestic and international legal entrenchment and institutions in the fields of governance (autonomy), cultural guarantees and security. For Finland, a newly proclaimed republic, the Åland issue was to be understood as one of a domestic character, where the Council of the League of Nations had no jurisdiction.[33] At that point, the Statute of the Permanent Court of International Justice had not yet been opened for ratification.[34] While the claims of the Ålanders relied heavily on the salience of the Swedish language and culture, the settlement meant a strengthened autonomous arrangement accompanied by cultural and security guarantees for all involved actors. The demilitarisation expectations of Sweden as supported by the United Kingdom took the form of the

30 The minutes of the Fourteenth Meeting of the Council, June 24th 1921, League of Nations Official Journal. September 1921, pp. 697–700.

31 The minutes of the Seventeenth Meeting of the Council, June 27th 1921, p. 701.

32 Notes of the Government of Finland of 5 June 1919, 3 June 1920 and 12 June 1920, in *Ålandsfrågan Inför Nationernas Förbund: La Question Des Îles d'Aland*, Aktstycken, (Stockholm: Utrikesdepartementet), Vol. 1 (1920).

33 O. Korhonen, "International Law Situated: An Analysis of the Lawyer's Stance towards Culture, History and Community" (Hague: Kluwer, 2000).

34 LNOJ and Special Supplements (1921). The minutes and decisions of the League of Nations in the Åland Question, are accessible at: https://kulturstiftelsen.ax/internationella-avtal/ (Ålands kulturstiftelse, visited 07.09.2023).

convention relating to the non-fortification and neutralisation of the Åland Islands adopted in October 1921.[35]

The issue of the jurisdiction of the League of Nations was dealt with by the Commission of Jurists. The lawyers asserted that a question does not become international simply because a state refers it to an international institution. A question belongs to the international domain, on the basis of the issue's *intrinsic characteristics*.[36] They concluded that the transitional character of the situation, in combination with the implications of the principle of self-determination, had as an effect that the Åland Question could not be deemed to fall exclusively under the domestic competence of Finland, and the League Council had thus jurisdiction.[37] The Commission of Jurists noted that the 1856 Paris Convention goes further than meeting Swedish interests and establishes rather a European regime to meet the needs of European interests. The parties thus created an "objective legal regime and true political rules".[38] The League of Nations convened soon thereafter an international conference where the Convention on Demilitarisation and Neutralisation of Åland[39] (the 1921 Convention) was adopted in October. A link between domestic/regional and international aspects of security is found in Article 4a of the Convention. It provides:

> In addition to the regular police force necessary to maintain public order and security in the zone, in conformity with the general provisions in force in the Finnish Republic, Finland may, if exceptional circumstances demand, send into the zone and keep there temporarily such other armed forces as shall be strictly necessary for the maintenance of order.

---

35 LNTS 1922, p. 213. S. Spiliopoulou Åkermark, "Åland's Demilitarisation and Neutralisation: Continuity and Change," in *The Åland Example and Its Components – Relevance for International Conflict Resolution* (Mariehamn: The Åland Islands Peace Institute, 2011), 50–71.

36 *Ålandsfrågan Inför Nationernas Förbund : La Question Des Îles d'Aland*, Aktstycken, (Stockholm: Utrikesdepartementet), Vol. 1 (1920), 234–279.

37 Ibid., p. 264.

38 In the original *"un veritable droit objectif, vrais statuts politiques"*. Ibid., pp. 272–275.

39 As the number of riparian states in 1921 in the Baltic more than doubled compared to 1856, there was a need for a comprehensive treatment of the status of the Åland Islands. The 1921 Convention signed on 20 October 1921 was ratified by all ten states who attended the Conference, i.e. Finland, Sweden, Britain, Germany, France, Denmark, Poland, Italy, Estonia and Latvia, and entered into force in April 1922.

This has been interpreted as referring mainly to situations of armed insurrection on the islands.[40] Less attention, however, has been directed towards the recognition in this provision of the complementarity of the security components in the Åland regime. Regional public order and security is to be maintained with the least possible level of violence through the local police. This has been the idea ever since 1921 when the Commission of Rapporteurs concluded: the less military presence, the more security (*moins il y aura d'appareil militaire à Aland, plus la tranquillité y sera assurée*).[41]

As regards the guarantees for Åland's culture and autonomy, they were incorporated in 1922 into domestic legislation through the so-called Guarantee Act,[42] after which the first elections for an autonomous regional parliament were held and Åland's Legislative Assembly (*landsting*, later renamed *lagting*) convened for the first time in June 1922.[43] In the first law on autonomy adopted by the Finnish Parliament in 1920 and the Guarantee Act of 1922 there was an explicit provision on matters pertaining to *conscription*. This provision was thus originally introduced prior to the dispute settlement in June 1921 and prior to the October 1921 Convention on the Demilitarisation and Neutralisation.[44] Section 27 of the 1920 Law on Autonomy provided for alternative, civilian forms of service, namely in the lighthouse authority or the pilotage service in the islands. Tollet and Uggla note in their commentary on the early legislation for Åland that there was at the time wide public opinion seeking to justify a full exemption from all such service based on the demilitarised status of the islands.[45] The length of alternative service, the place of service, but also the language to be used, had been among the other reasons for the rejection of proposals for alternative service.[46] In the interwar period there was often a

40 J.O. Söderhjelm, *Démilitarisation et neutralisation des Iles d'Aland en 1856 et 1921*, Helsingfors, 1928. Björkholm M. & Rosas A., *Ålandsöarnas demilitarisering och neutralisering*, Åbo: Åbo Akademis förlag, 1990.

41 S. Spiliopoulou Åkermark, "The 1921 Convention on the Non-Fortification and Neutralisation of the Åland Islands as an integral part of the Åland Solution". *Journal of Autonomy and Security Studies*, 2022, *6*(1), 20–27. Retrieved from https://jass.ax/index.php/jass/article/view/71 (visited 29.09.2023).

42 Act Embracing Certain Provisions Regarding the Population of the Province of Åland No. 189/1922.

43 The Autonomy Act of 1920 remained thus ineffective between 1920 and 1922.

44 A. Tollet and J. Uggla, *Lagstiftningen Angående Självstyrelse För Åland: Jämte Tillhörandeförfattningar*, (Helsingfors, Holger Schildts förlag, 1930), 119.

45 Ibid, 119.

46 Ibid.

polarised debate in the Finnish press concerning the exemption of Ålanders from conscription.[47]

4 The Turbulent Years 1938–1951 and a Revised Autonomy Act

Already before World War II the autonomous islands started developing the institutions and legislation of the autonomy. However, the militarisation of Germany and several crises coupled to a weakening of loyalty to the League of Nations, presented serious threats to a delicate peace. Military circles in Sweden and Finland argued for a partial geographical limitation of the demilitarised and neutralised zone of the Åland islands. A joint Finnish-Swedish defence plan for Åland ("The Stockholm Plan") was presented in 1938. Without abrogating the entire 1921 Convention it proposed military installations in the southernmost areas of the zone, causing political controversy in both countries.[48] On 31 October 1938, a large demonstration was held in Mariehamn to protest. Without going into details of the plan as such, we are interested here in the perceptions prevailing with regard to the plan, and in the simultaneous proposals in Finland to introduce a conscription in Åland.[49] The Åland Parliament had made proposals for the deletion of Section 27 from the 1920 Act on Autonomy on alternative service, but those had been rejected in the Finnish Parliament.[50] In 1938 a legislative proposal was made by the Finnish Government concerning a partial military service for Ålanders, but since it required the approval of the autonomous parliament, something which was rejected, the provision remained.[51] As we shall see below, the provision on alternative service was retained also in the Autonomy Act of 1991.[52] The 1938 demonstration, referred to as the Farmers' March (*Bondetåg*) – which alludes to the 1808–1809 resistance to the Russian rule on Åland – revolved around the conscription provisions in the Autonomy Act, the role of the autonomous authorities in security matters, and the demilitarisation and neutralisation of the islands. Nearly 4,000 people demonstrated against the multifaceted risk of war, military conscription, and of a modification to the demilitarisation and

47 E. Tudeer, *Ålands hemvärn 1939–1940*, Krigshistorisk tidskrift no 9 (1990), concerning the "home guard" (*hemvärn*) of Åland during the early stages of World War II.

48 K. Wahlbäck, *Finlandsfrågan i svensk politik 1937–1940*. Stockholm: P.A. Norstedt (1964).

49 K. Gustavsson, *Ålandsöarna – En Säkerhetsrisk? Spelet Om Den Demilitariserade Zonen 1919–1939* (Mariehamn: PQR-kultur, 2012), 221.

50 Wahlbäck (1964) supra note 48, 137–170.

51 RP 73/1990, s. 41.

52 Ibid.

neutralisation of the islands. In speeches made, including by the speaker of the Åland Parliament, Julius Sundblom, and several others, the issues of conscription and that of the demilitarisation and neutralisation regime of the islands were understood as linked.[53] The Åland parliamentarians called to negotiate with the Finnish Government in November 1938 were in effect discussing as much the Autonomy Act as Finnish foreign and defence policy, i.e. they were discussing the linkages between self-government and the security regime. The interconnection of issues and their domestic and international aspects remained strong in perceptions as well as in practice. This connection is, thus, not a particularly recent phenomenon.[54] Perhaps one could go as far as saying that the 1938 demonstration was the moment when the significance of the demilitarisation and neutralisation regime became internalised for the first time on Åland.

The Second World War broke out on 1 September 1939 and on 30 November came the start of the Winter War when the Soviet Union attacked the Eastern border of Finland. A Treaty between Finland and the Soviet Union concerning the Åland Islands was concluded in October 1940 after Finland's defeat.[55] The treaty was registered by notification to the Treaty Office of the United Nations and was published in the United Nations Treaty Series in 1950.[56] It was confirmed in 1948 and in 1992 (see below). In the so-called Continuation War, which broke out in June 1941 and lasted until an armistice was signed in 1944, Finland found itself in a precarious position siding with Germany. Unlike the situation on the mainland, where the war had a heavy toll, Åland's neutralisation was largely upheld.[57] The 1944 Moscow Armistice reactivated the 1940 Treaty and restored the demilitarised status of Åland.[58] It was not until later, in 1947, that a separate peace treaty was signed between Finland and the Allies, which also reconfirmed the demilitarised status of Åland.[59] The post-war relations of Finland were further entangled in 1948 when Finland

53 *Ålandstidningen* 1.11.1938 and 3.11.1938 and interview with author Johannes Salminen in *Ålandstidningen* 20.8.2010 on his recollections as one of the youngest participants in the 1938 demonstration.

54 P. Joenniemi (2014). "The Åland Islands: Neither local nor fully sovereign", *Cooperation and Conflict*, *49*(1), 80–97.

55 FTS 24/1940.

56 67 UNTS (1950), No. 872, 139–51.

57 H. Rotkirch (1986) The Demilitarization and Neutralization of the Åland Islands, *Journal of Peace Research* 23 (4): 357–375.

58 L. Hannikainen, 'The Continued Validity of the Demilitarised and Neutralised Status of the Åland Islands', 54: 3 *Zeitschrift für ausländisches öffentliches Recht und Völkerrecht* (1994), 622–623.

59 Rotkirch, supra note 57, 372.

and the Soviet Union signed the Treaty on Friendship, Cooperation and Mutual Assistance.[60]

The postwar period resulted in a new Autonomy Act for Åland after three committee enquiries and lengthy negotiations.[61] It reinforced the autonomy by transferring further powers to Åland.[62] Already in 1936, a motion had been presented in the Åland Parliament for a revision of provisions concerning the financial system and the right of Åland to dispose of tax incomes.[63] Carl Björkman, head of the Åland Government, informed in June 1938 the Åland Parliament that the Finnish Parliament had rejected a proposal to review these provisions.[64] In 1938, the Government of Finland appointed a first parliamentary enquiry, under Urho Castrén, to examine a possible revision of the Autonomy Act.[65] During the war, the issue of a revision was left latent, but at the end of 1945, a new committee was appointed under Albert von Hellens. The draft bill presented by the von Hellens Committee identified that among the core concerns were the issue of access to land in the islands and the dissolution of the League of Nations.[66] The draft proposed a revision of former Section 27 according to which the reference to alternative service in piloting or lighthouses should be replaced by a reference to alternative service in "civil administration" (*civilförvaltningen*). The bill revised the main logic in the way the distribution of powers was understood, by presenting first the list of exclusive competences of the autonomous region, followed by the areas in which

60 FTS 17/1948.

61 Act on the Self-Government of the Aland Islands No. 670/1951.

62 K. Myntti, "The Åland Model – Its Background and Special Characteristics". In: H. Jansson and J. Salminen (eds.), *The second Åland Islands question. Autonomy or independence?* (the Julius Sundblom Memorial Foundation, Mariehamn, 2002) 107–124. Myntti concludes that the demilitarisation and neutralisation is not a 'component of the autonomy of Åland as such' but part of the special status of Åland under international law.

63 Motion No. 22/1936 available at: https://www.lagtinget.ax/sites/www.lagtinget.ax/files/torsten_rothbergs_motion_om_ss21_sjalvstyrelselagen.pdf (In Swedish ; accessed 15.09.2023).

64 Landskapsstyrelsens skrivelse om ändring av självstyrelselagen (15.06.1938). https://www.lagtinget.ax/sites/www.lagtinget.ax/files/landskapsstyrelsens_skrivelse_ang_ss21_sjalvstyrelselagen.pdf (accessed 16.09.2023).

65 The Report of the Castrén Committee and draft Bill, was presented in February 1939. Available at https://www.lagtinget.ax/sites/www.lagtinget.ax/files/castrenkommittens_bet_1939.pdf (accessed 14.09.2023).

66 Report of the von Hellens Committee, 12 April 1946. Available at: https://www.lagtinget.ax/sites/www.lagtinget.ax/files/vonhellenskommittens_bet_1946.pdf (accessed 14.09.2023). On land issues, see Concluding Comments by Gunnar Jansson in Sia Spiliopoulou Åkermark (ed.), *The Right of Domicile on Åland* (Mariehamn: The Åland Islands Peace Institute, 2009), 137–138.

the Finnish Parliament had power. Most importantly, the committee proposed the introduction of the concept of a "right of domicile", something that had earlier been rejected. Parliamentary debates continued in 1946–1947 without concluding the work for new legislation.[67] Yet another committee was appointed in 1948, this time under Tauno Suontausta.[68] One of its core concerns was that of the international guarantees. The Åland Parliament was of the view that the strengthening of such guarantees after the replacement of the League of Nations by the United Nations was a priority based on the "recognised neutral position of the region" (*landskapets erkända neutrala ställning*).[69] The ensuing bill put focus on the issue of a right to domicile, while the proposed provision on exemption from military conscription followed the wording used already by the 1946 committee. The issue of international guarantees was put aside.[70] The 1951 Autonomy Act recognised explicitly the policiary competences of the Åland authorities. It provided that Åland had jurisdiction concerning "the establishment of *public order and safety and the prevention and suppression of crime*, with the exception of the activities of the police force to safeguard national security, as well as police duties in those areas in which national legislation also applies in the Åland Islands".[71] This Act gave Åland the right to have its own flag and regional coat of arms. It provided once more for the exemption from military service of Ålanders and guaranteed that the Åland Parliament would be heard should any state legislation concerning alternative ways of doing service be introduced. In 1985, the Act was amended by referring (Section 1) to the 1982, technically adjusted delimitation of borders between Finland and Sweden, thus introducing a direct reference to the constant international dimensions of the Åland regime.[72] Meanwhile, the Åland Parliament established in 1972 the Self-Government Committee (*Självstyrelsepolitiska nämnden*), which has since addressed both the wider international aspects of the autonomy, originally focusing on the standing of the Åland Islands in

67 RP 100/1946. See further: Justitieministeriet, *Ålands självstyrelse i utveckling, Ålandskommitténs 2013 delbetänkande*, Betänkande 6/2015, p. 96.

68 Suontausta Committee Report on the revision of the Åland Autonomy Act (Bill 38/1948) https://www.lagtinget.ax/sites/www.lagtinget.ax/files/suontaustakommittens_bet_1948.pdf (accessed 17.09 2023).

69 Ibid., p. 476. Finland had applied for UN membership in 1947, after the signing of the Peace Treaty, but such membership was possible only in 1955.

70 A. Häggblom, *Ålands internationella garantier*, Åländska perspektiv 2011:1.

71 An example of such national legislation is penal law. Penal Code of Finland (FFS 39/1889).

72 On the delimitation concerning the islet of Märket see I. Hughes Tidlund. *Autonomous Åland: a hundred years of borderwork in the Baltic Sea*. Diss. Stockholm: Stockholm university, 2021.

Nordic cooperation,[73] as well as the regime of demilitarisation and neutralisation, in particular through its annual review of the functioning and respect of the demilitarised zone on the basis of Åland Government annual reports.[74]

5 End of the Cold War and the Second Revision of the Autonomy Act

The last period we focus on is characterised by broad political and societal changes in Europe and beyond, in what in sum is called the end of the Cold War. Finland and Sweden joined the European Union in 1995. For the Åland Islands these complex processes meant the adoption of a revised Autonomy Act, still valid today, reconfirmations of the international status and a decision to join the European Union together with Finland, following double referenda.[75]

As already mentioned, the Åland Parliament had established a Self-Government Committee and Åland started taking a more proactive interest in the demilitarisation regime.[76] Voices, mainly from some military circles in Finland, argued about the risks of the demilitarisation and neutralisation, while lawyers wrote about the effects of the transitions, concluding that the international legal obligations concerning Åland remained valid.[77] An increased presence of Finnish military vessels and aircraft in the archipelago prompted

73 K. Creutz & S. Spiliopoulou Åkermark, *The Faroe Islands, Greenland and the Åland Islands in Nordic Cooperation*, FIIA report No 69, December 2021 https://www.fiia.fi/en/publication/the-faroe-islands-greenland-and-the-aland-islands-in-nordic-cooperation.

74 Landstingsordning för landskapet Åland, ÅFS 11:1972, paras. 29–33. The first regular discussion on issues of demilitarisation and neutralisation by the Åland Parliament took place in spring 1987. Självstyrelsepolitiska nämndens yttrande 1986–87 L t – Ls redogörelse 1985–86 – SjpN.

75 P. Joenniemi, "The Åland Islands Issue". In: *The Nordic Peace* (ed. Clive Archer, Pertti Joenniemi Ashgate, 2003) p. 92. See also Protocol No. 2 to Finland's accession to the EU, found in EU Doc.CONF-SF 20/94, 21 February 1994. Hasan Akintug, *The EU referendums on Åland: An overview of the EU debates in the Åland Parliament during autumn 1994*, Report from the Åland Islands Peace Institute No. 2–2020.

76 Barbro Sundback, MP in the Åland Parliament and later the parliament's speaker (2005–2007) and key figure in the local peace movement, has described this period in "A Success Story" in Eriksson S. et al., *Islands of Peace – Åland's autonomy, demilitarisation and neutralisation*, The Åland Islands Peace Institute, 2006, 77–125, at 107–115. Janne Holmén, "Åland – navigating between possible identities, 1852–2012", in Edquist, S. & Holmén, J. (2015). *Islands of identity: history-writing and identity formation in five island regions in the Baltic Sea*. Huddinge: Södertörns högskola (2015), 143–241.

77 Björkholm & Rosas (1990) supra note 40; Hannikainen L. (1994) supra note 58; Poullie (2016) supra note 5.

sharp reactions both from the Åland public and politicians.[78] A new bilateral agreement between Finland and the Russian Federation (1992) replaced the 1948 so-called Friendship Treaty.[79] Nyberg has described this process with the words "diplomacy is not law, but law can be diplomacy".[80] This period has been described as one of cautious internationalisation for Åland, one of the core events of which was the adoption of a new Autonomy Act in 1991.[81] The exclusive legislative competence of the Åland Parliament is defined in Section 18 of the Autonomy Act. Among others we find reference to security issues as "public order and security [...]; the firefighting and rescue service". So, the *local dimensions of security* under autonomous powers became more prevalent. The legislative competence of Finland includes firearms and ammunition, explosive substances, the armed forces and the border guards, the security of the state and rules on state of emergency. The Autonomy Act regulates the role of the Åland authorities in matters of an international character (Sections 58–59).[82] The provisions regarding exemption from conscription remain (Section 12).[83] This rule does not prohibit, however, Ålanders who want to do military service in the Finnish army from doing so.[84] In 2015, the Åland Government approved

78 Mauno Koivisto, *Witness to History: The Memoirs of Mauno Koivisto, President of Finland 1982–1994* (1997).

79 FTS 63/1992, *Överenskommelse med Ryska Federationen om grunderna för relationen mellan länderna*. The new Russian-Finnish agreement had been negotiated in January 1992 and was thereafter approved by the Finnish Parliament. Entered into force through Regulation 648/1992.

80 Nyberg R., "Ni har vidrört VSB-avtalet" in Bergquist, Mats & Johansson, Alf W. (eds.). *Säkerhetspolitik och historia: essäer om stormaktspolitiken och Norden under sjuttio år: vänbok till Krister Wahlbäck*. Stockholm: Hjalmarson & Högberg (2007), 285–299.

81 Act on the Autonomy of Åland No. 1144/1991, hereinafter 'the 1991 Autonomy Act' adopted on 16 August 1991. Important amendments were made through Law 68/2004 concerning the effect of EU membership and international matters on the autonomy. See Poullie (2016) supra note 5.

82 S. Silverström, "The Competence of Autonomous Entities in the International Arena – With Special Reference to the Åland Islands in the European Union", *International Journal on Minority and Group Rights* 15(2–3) (2008) 259–271. For an account of discussions in Finland and in Åland on demilitarisation within the EU accession process see Poullie (2016) supra note 5.

83 Finnish Law on Conscription 1438/2007. Section 3 provides: "Section 12 of the Autonomy Act for Åland (1144/1991) contains provisions on alternative service. The fulfilment of military service is also subject to the provisions of international agreements that are binding upon Finland".

84 "Älänningar kan kallas in till finska militären", Nya Åland, 06.11.2009.

a *Policy for the Demilitarisation and Neutralisation of Åland* with the subtitle "A handbook for the officials of the Åland Government".[85]

The intersection between autonomy provisions and demilitarisation and neutralisation came to the forefront during the process of Finnish membership in NATO following the Russian invasion of Ukraine in February 2022. In April 2022, the Government of Finland presented its "Report on Changes in the Security Environment".[86] The report included the following passage about the islands:

> The autonomous province of Åland has a recognised status under international law. This does not prevent Finland from deepening military cooperation with various actors. Finland is obliged to take necessary measures to ensure the neutrality of the Åland Islands. The Defence Forces is prepared to defend Åland. As a civilian authority, the Border Guard has continuous presence in Åland and is prepared for different contingencies. The Border Guard is able to increase its presence in the area quickly, if necessary.

In Annex 2 of the same document on the steps for a possible accession of Finland in NATO, it is noted that the status of Åland under international law should be taken into consideration, that the Government of the Åland Islands should be notified about the negotiations, and that the states parties to the 1921 and 1940 conventions are to be notified of Finland's intention to accede to the alliance. Finland and Sweden applied for membership in May 2022.[87] The Finnish President appointed a delegation for negotiations with NATO and its member states. Åland had the opportunity to have a representative present in the negotiations. Russia maintained the view that Åland's demilitarised status should be respected.[88] Minister for Foreign Affairs Pekka Haavisto, represented Finland in Brussels in July 2022 when NATO ambassadors signed

85 Government of Åland, *Policy för Ålands demilitarisering och neutralisering – Handbok för landskapets myndigheter* https://www.lagtinget.ax/sites/www.lagtinget.ax/files/policy2c_demilitarisering_och_neutralisering_0.pdf (accessed 15.09.2023).

86 Finnish Government Report on Changes in the Security Environment 2022:20.

87 Ministry for Foreign Affairs of Finland website: Finland's membership in NATO – Ministry for Foreign Affairs (um.fi) (accessed 29.09.2023). See also Spiliopoulou Åkermark S., *New Contexts for Old Questions – The Centenary of the Åland Islands Solution in a Troubled World*, 10 August 2022, available at https://portal.vifanord.de/blog/new-contexts-for-old-questions-the-centenary-of-the-aland-islands-solution-in-a-troubled-world/ (visited 6 October 2023).

88 "Moscow Raises Two Territorial Issues After Helsinki Requests to Join NATO", Eurasia Daily Monitor Vol. 19, Issue 79, 31.05.2022.

Finland's Protocol of Accession. Minister Haavisto presented then the Åland case and noted the presence of the Åland representative. There were no objections raised by NATO and its members as explained by Haavisto in his letter to the Åland Premier, Veronica Thörnroos.[89] The Åland Parliament has discussed NATO matters as part of the examination of the Åland Government reports on international affairs.[90] Finland became a full member of NATO in April 2023.

6 The Nexus of Autonomy, Culture and Security

While territorial autonomy arrangements around the world have their distinct historical, political backgrounds and legal foundations, there is a wider logic discernible. In autonomy regimes and their institutional solutions, matters of security and defence are generally considered to be reserved for the state.[91] As argued, however, by Wolfgang Danspeckgruber, autonomy arrangements need often address three core aspects to prove viable, namely *military-strategic, socio-economic and humanitarian*.[92] So, such arrangements need to consider the interests of the state, the autonomous region as well as of significant other actors. The Åland regime addresses, from the outset and as it has evolved, the *political dimension* through the establishment of territorial autonomy, the *security dimension* internationally through the demilitarisation and neutralisation, and domestically i.a. through rules on the border guard, police, firefighters and rescue services. The needs for *cultural protection* are attended to for instance through rules on language, education, the right to domicile, the acquisition of land as well as constitutional bilingualism.[93] The system addresses in a pragmatic way the conditions for economic viability of solutions.

89 Exchange of letters between the Finnish Minister for Foreign Affairs Pekka Haavisto (letter of 5.7.2022) and the Premier of Åland Veronica Thörnroos (letter of 19.8.2022, ÅLR 2022/5820). Also report in *Tidningen Åland*, 06.07.2022.

90 Ålands landskapsregering, *Meddelande nr 3/2022–2023 om landskapsregeringens externpolitik*, 19.01.2023. Ålands lagting, Självstyrelsepolitiska nämnden, Betänkande nr 2/2022–2023, 20.09.2023.

91 For examples see: Hannum H. *Procedural Aspects of International Law: Autonomy, Sovereignty, and Self-Determination: The Accommodation of Conflicting Rights* (2nd ed). University of Pennsylvania Press, 1996.

92 W. Danspeckgruber "Self-governance plus regional integration – A possible solution to self-determination claims", in M. Weller and S. Wolff, *Autonomy, Self-Governance and Conflict Resolution: Innovative Approaches to Institutional Design in Divided Societies* (Routledge, 2005), 26–48.

93 Spiliopoulou Åkermark (ed.), 2009, supra note 66. R. Williams, "One Hundred Years of Solitude: The Significance of Land Rights for Cultural Protection in the Åland

There are important legal and political insights and effects encapsulated in this nexus of the core elements of the Åland regime. The regime is entrenched both internationally and domestically in law as well as in practice. The regime concerns not only the autonomous region and the state, but also other states and actors, holding rights and obligations. Major changes on one core aspect of the regime are bound to have, and historically have had, an impact on the other core aspects. So, authorities in Finland and on Åland need to cooperate beyond the formal division of competences. For Åland this is a challenge in terms of having adequate information from the state in Swedish and in finding the human resources to ensure such cooperation. For Finland the challenge is usually remembering and considering effectively the special conditions pertaining to the islands, having adequate understanding about the nexus of the regime, and, simply put, to be able to communicate in Swedish.

The second set of questions concerns the "voice", in other words the role of the Åland autonomous authorities in international matters and matters pertaining to security, as regards public order and safety on the islands according to the Åland Autonomy Act, as well as security matters, nationally and internationally, in a broader sense. This is one of the areas examined in the on-going revision of the legislation on state of emergency, appointed by the Ministry of Justice in Finland in March 2022 and expected to present its results in 2025.[94]

The regime creates a multilateral mode where no actor has too much power or can disregard the views and interests of others, especially those of the Ålanders. This entanglement of actors and of the overlapping normative webs infuses the idea of a system. Elements of power balance and *realpolitik* are thus combined with *normative commitments* and with principled reasons of justice, the rule of law and respect of diversity in the domestic and international legal orders.[95]

The regime includes *autonomy* plus *demilitarisation, neutralisation* plus *cultural guarantees* and fulfils several goals. Among other things it works to the effect that Åland is not to be instrumentalised in power plays affecting the Baltic Sea, while Finland retains the right to self-defence. Furthermore, the regime ensures that local security and safety issues can be handled by the Åland autonomous institutions through a local police and rescue service. The restrictively regulated right of presence of the Finnish military on Åland and the

---

Islands". *Journal of Autonomy and Security Studies*, 2(1) (2018) 50–81. Retrieved from https://jass.ax/index.php/jass/article/view/22 (20.09.2023).

94 Beredskapslag 1552/2011.

95 Saila Heinikoski, *The status of the Åland Islands is not only a defence policy issue*, https://peace.ax/en/the-status-of-the-aland-islands-is-not-only-a-defence-policy-issue-1/ (Blog 13 November 2016; accessed 07.10.2023).

special characteristics of a Swedish-speaking Border Guard, combined with the arrangements for the police, ensure that armed force is not used unduly to suppress local culture and political life on the islands. Since the regime is considered to have customary standing, it entails that all states, whether signatories or not, operating in the Baltic Sea have obligations to respect the status of the islands as well as the territorial integrity of Finland. One could say that in the case of Åland, *diplomacy and law are given priority ahead of armed force, without one disregarding or precluding the other*. This is a strong message to send at times when authoritarianism, nationalism and militarisation are often targeting minorities, regional cultures and "the others", whoever they may be, and when the use of violence against minorities is, once more, not so uncommon.

CHAPTER 13

Autonomy from an OSCE Perspective: Updating an Earlier Optimistic Picture

Lars-Erik Lundin

In this brief article, it is impossible to make a detailed analysis of all the conflicts in the OSCE area where autonomy has been an issue over the 25 years since the end of the Cold War. However, an effort will be made to paint a more overall picture, updating, in particular, one earlier contribution to this debate.

The former German ambassador to Belgrade and the OSCE, Hans Jörg Eiff, in 1998, described and analysed the various efforts to deal with demands for secession and independence in the OSCE.[1] His article is titled "Autonomy as a Method of Conflict Management and Protection of Minorities within the OSCE Framework". He detailed some of the specific questions involving Croatia and Kosovo, the latter issue still being negotiated. He also expressed hope that the mandate of institutions such as the High Commissioner on National Minorities (HCNM) and the Court of Conciliation and Arbitration would be more extensively used in the future. And he argued:

> Further development of the OSCE's set of norms in the politically binding fashion appropriate to the Organization could prove to be more practical than efforts to bolster the law on minorities with legally binding agreements within the framework of the Council of Europe or of the United Nations.

Eiff sought to portray a gradual, long-term effort to deal with the relics of the Cold War and to resolve the future status of former communist states, that had belonged to the Soviet Union and Yugoslavia:

> Autonomy arrangements have typically proven to be in demand for certain portions of the territory in the successor states to Yugoslavia and the

1 Eiff, H.J. (no date) *Autonomy as a method of conflict management and protection of …* Available at: https://ifsh.de/file-CORE/documents/yearbook/english/98/Eiff.pdf (Accessed: 06 June 2023). Eiff was a colleague of the current author during the end of the nineties in Vienna.

DOI:10.1163/9789004691117_015

> Soviet Union where national minorities constitute a regional majority – thus in parts of Croatia, Kosovo, Transnistria, South Ossetia, Abkhazia, Nagorno Karabakh, the Crimea, and Chechnya.
>
> As a practical matter, what is usually involved is the attempt to forestall efforts at secession by the granting of extensive rights of self-government. The idea is to satisfy the demands of minorities for self-determination in a way consistent with the territorial integrity of the country in question. In the cases mentioned above it is primarily a question of territorial autonomy, of introducing a special status into a particular area. Thus, the terms "special status" or "special status of autonomy" or "self-government" are in some cases used in place of "autonomy."
>
> Now that autonomy has been included in certain OSCE documents on minority matters as a possible form of settlement, it has become more difficult to reject international involvement with reference to the principle of non-intervention (as the Federal Republic of Yugoslavia is presently trying to do in connection with the Kosovo question), even though these texts cannot be regarded as a basis for autonomy claims under international law.

Eiff published his article the year before the war in Kosovo started, detailing some of the steps the OSCE had decided to prevent a conflict from breaking out. This included the mission to Belgrade by former Spanish Prime Minister Felipe Gonzalez, accompanied i.a. by the EU Troika from Vienna.[2] In hindsight, what seemed to be an issue relating to the situation in Kosovo was, to a large extent, also associated with the domestic political situation in Belgrade at a time when President Milošević experienced weakness and political conflict with several charismatic political opponents in the country. He then proceeded to seek to form a political unity on the issue of Kosovo, which in turn led to what now is history. This war was later used as a pretext by Russia for its aggression in Georgia and Ukraine.

1 The Current State of Affairs: a Bleak Picture of the Prospects for the OSCE

Looking at the status of *minority rights* in various regions across the OSCE area in 2023, *pessimism* now prevails among many, if not most, observers. Full

2 Including the current author representing the European Commission.

respect for the rights of national minorities is a distant and subordinate objective in the security policy of most European states. In some cases, the existence of national minorities is not recognised, whereas in others only some national minorities and not others are legally established. Even when national minorities are recognised, their rights are sometimes not a priority in internal politics. In addition, in an ever more tense international environment, the competition for political attention to multiple crises often relegates minority issues to a subordinate level of priority. From the perspective of some countries, minority issues even tend to become a political tool in the quest for international influence. In a number of these cases, the issue of autonomy has been an important part of the discourse.

The main argument of this article is that the OSCE, the Organisation for Security and Cooperation in Europe, which in 1994 succeeded the CSCE, (Conference for Security and Cooperation in Europe), is a mirror of this situation, or more correctly, perhaps, a mirror of this negative development from the end of the Cold War – from a very promising beginning. The organisation, for reasons that will be briefly outlined below, can be seen as more of an *arena* than an *actor* in this context. Hopes for a strong OSCE contribution to security and cooperation were, as noted above, much higher right after the end of the Cold War. But the OSCE was never equipped with the capabilities and the mandates required to make a major and sustained difference. A Russian commentator would most likely argue that this is due to the fact that the OSCE never received the *legal status* proposed by Russia during the period of Dimitry Medvedev as President of the Russian Federation. OSCE parliamentarians, for their part, have for many years argued that the *consensus* principle has crippled the capabilities of the organisation to take robust decisions. More specifically, as regards the institutional set up, it was intentionally *fragmented*, with different institutions in Vienna, Prague, Warsaw, and the Hague kept together by a Secretary General with a lower formal status in terms of protocol than his/her counterparts in the Council of Europe. This was the result of the fact that the political leadership of the organisation was entrusted to a chairpersonship on the level of foreign ministers, effectively subordinating the Secretary-General to a level below that.

To make things even more complicated, the mandate of the HCNM in the Hague was limited to the protection not of national minorities but *persons* belonging to national minorities. Several participating states, including notably Turkey, insisted on this since they do not recognise certain types of national minorities within their borders, notably in the Turkish case the existence of a Kurdish minority, referring to language in the treaty of Lausanne from 1923, which only recognises non-Muslim minorities. The HCNM mandate was agreed in 1992 after extensive negotiations.[3] In the OSCE documents, an early decision was thus taken not to link the issue of autonomy and potential secession to minorities but rather to *persons* belonging to national minorities. In this way, on the other hand, the mandate remained relevant to include situations inside countries such as Latvia and Estonia, with significant Russian-speaking parts of the population distributed across the entire country.

Over the years, several intervening factors in a deteriorating international climate have tended to reduce the role of the organisation in this domain. Already in 2008, the integrity of Georgia was compromised by an invasion of South Ossetia through the Roki Tunnel, connecting this part of Georgia with Russian parts of North Caucasus. Before that, Abkhazia as a part of Georgia was separated from Georgia through Russian subversive action. And in 2014, Crimea was annexed to the Russian Federation alongside significant parts of eastern Ukraine.

At the time of writing, the *very existence of the OSCE is threatened* and so is the notion of an all-European security order that includes the Russian Federation. This stands in strong contrast to a strengthened European Union as well as a revitalised and enlarged NATO. In addition, in parallel to the OSCE, a renewed format for informal political cooperation involving almost 50 countries as proposed by France, the *European Political Community* has already held several summits, excluding Russia and Belarus.[4]

There is still hope, of course, for a renewed dialogue reminiscent of the dramatic developments in the mid-1980s. At the end of the tunnel some sort of settlement may come about as, after all, happened after the First and Second World Wars. But hope is ever more distant as the popular support for President Putin is maintained on a level difficult to understand, given the impact of the war in Ukraine.

2 The Fundamental Role of the Human Dimension

The limited, positive attention to minority rights issues, however, must not hide the fact that issues relating to *democracy, human rights and the rule of law* continue to play a fundamental role in international relations and in domestic developments in the OSCE region, and have done since the end of the Cold

3 *Mandate OSCE*. Available at: https://www.osce.org/hcnm/107878 (Accessed: 6 June 2023).

4 *Meeting of the European political community – consilium*. Available at: https://www.consilium.europa.eu/en/meetings/international-summit/2023/06/01/ (Accessed: 6 June 2023).

War. But the role of minorities in this context, as a part of civil society, is often seen either as a vain hope or – by state actors – as an *existential threat*, depending on the perspective. The notion that the entire human dimension of the OSCE is a factor of promoting *peace* is problematic in several respects, since the quest for democracy often is perceived as requiring *regime change* in countries such as Belarus. The legacy of the policies of President George W. Bush is very much alive among many civil society groups.

Developments in Ukraine play a central role in this picture. The *Maidan Uprising* of February 2014 introduced remarkable changes in the security environment of Europe after the fall of the Berlin Wall. That Russia in one blow lost political control over a major part of the former Soviet Union without a major military battle, led to violent conflict and war in the eastern part of Ukraine in 2014. From 2022 onwards, Russia invaded the entire Ukraine.

The significance of this development can be seen more clearly from the perspective of a Russian threat, which has been thoroughly analysed in the academic literature in recent years. The notion of *Colour revolutions,* which has played an important role in several countries inside and outside Europe, including the so-called Arab Spring, has long since emerged as a perceived threat to Russian national security.[5] On top of this, an ideology outlining a struggle to return to Tsarist days of greatness has made it possible for the Russian leadership to subject its population to increased suffering over a longer period.

Against this background it is only natural that in a number of these cases the nexus *nationalism-autonomy-secession* has become a more important part of the discourse concerning international peace and security than the non-violent path towards greater respect for minority rights outlined in early OSCE documents after the Cold War, here represented by an extract from the CSCE Copenhagen document from 1990:

> (35) The participating States will respect the right of persons belonging to national minorities to effective participation in public affairs, including participation in the affairs relating to the protection and promotion of the identity of such minorities. The participating States note the efforts undertaken to protect and create conditions for the promotion of the ethnic, cultural, linguistic and religious identity of certain national minorities by establishing, as one of the possible means to achieve these aims, appropriate local or autonomous administrations corresponding to the

5 Jonsson, O. (2019) *The Russian understanding of war: Blurring the lines between war and peace, Amazon.* Available at: https://www.amazon.com/Russian-Understanding-War-Blurring-between/dp/1626167346 (Accessed: 6 June 2023).

> specific historical and territorial circumstances of such minorities and in accordance with the policies of the state concerned.
>
> (36) The participating States recognize the particular importance of increasing constructive co-operation among themselves on questions relating to national minorities. Such co-operation seeks to promote mutual understanding and confidence, friendly and good-neighbourly relations, international peace, security and justice. Every participating State will promote a climate of mutual respect, understanding, co-operation and solidarity among all persons living on its territory, without distinction as to ethnic or national origin or religion, and will encourage the solution of problems through dialogue based on the principles of the rule of law.[6]

The resolution of the *Åland question* thus remains a shining exception rather than, as sometimes hoped for after the Cold War, a formula for success also in other contexts.

3 The Role of the OSCE in Hindsight

The fact that the Åland question forms the exception rather than the rule has not always been the case. It is worth remembering that the then EU, the European Community, through the so-called *Carrington Plan* in 1991, proposed a solution to the future status of different minorities in the former Socialist Federal Republic of Yugoslavia, which arguably "represents the most ambitious project so far to introduce autonomy as a method of conflict settlement into multinational states that were once communist."[7] As we now know, this approach failed.

Indeed, a number of conflicts led to the establishment of several independent states, partly following historical precedents, rather than simply adapting to the notion of a region divided into territories, each dominated by one ethnic group (for instance the sometimes-discussed division of territory between Serbia-Albania-Croatia). Several serious problems of stability remain to be resolved in this context, both in Bosnia, between its three constituent peoples,

6 *Document of the Copenhagen meeting of the conference on the human dimension of the CSCE* (no date) *OSCE*. Available at: https://www.osce.org/odihr/elections/14304#:~:text=The%20 1990%20CSCE%2FOSCE%20Copenhagen,the%20rights%20of%20the%20child. (Accessed: 6 June 2023).

7 See Eiff, *supra* note 1.

Bosniaks, Croats and Serbs, and in Kosovo as regards the Serbian minority and the recognition of Kosovo by all European states. A number of OSCE participating states have not yet recognised Kosovo as an independent state, including not only Russia and Serbia but also notably several members of the European Union, Spain, Greece, Slovakia, Cyprus, and Romania as well as Moldova.[8]

Hopes were as noted high for peace and development towards democracy, human rights, and the rule of law in the entire OSCE area after the Cold War. The initial wars in the Balkans were widely perceived as an exception to prove the rule. And several countries, not least in Central Asia, were invited into the OSCE with the hope that they would develop in a democratic direction, although they never had experienced such a development before. Historically difficult internal and international conflicts in the region of the former Soviet Union were of course identified, but many thought that there was a way to deal with them, at least to contain them, and if possible, to promote sustainable solutions. The OSCE emerged as a potential organisation with the flexibility required to introduce the possibility of dialogue with non-state entities in such regions.

Several OSCE institutions were set up and assigned to serve that purpose. This included the Office for Democratic Institutions and Human Rights in Warsaw with a focus on elections and the promotion of democracy, and the High Commissioner on (notably not *of*) National Minorities in The Hague, which was set up in a way closely aligning with the vision of its first incumbent, the former foreign minister of the Netherlands, Max van Der Stoel. He promoted a methodology of carefully developing one dossier after the other in which to primarily pursue silent diplomacy, initially notably in the southern part of the Balkans region, such as between Albania-Greece and inside what is now North Macedonia. The High Commissioner, however, was in several countries never mandated to deal with the overall situation. In Turkey the HCNM was not authorised to engage in the protection of national and minority groups, since the OSCE does not address issues of minorities but rather *persons belonging to national minorities*. And Kurds are not, as previously noted, recognised by the Turkish Constitution as persons belonging to a Kurdish minority. In Ukraine the HCNM was invited by the government from 1994 and in some ways engaged on issues related to the status of Crimean Tatars and on the relationship between the Ukrainian majority and Russian-speaking minority. But there were major difficulties for the HCNM to come up with solutions on overall issues that would be seriously discussed between the parties concerned.

---

8 *International recognition of Kosovo* (2023) *Wikipedia*. Available at: https://en.wikipedia.org/wiki/International_recognition_of_Kosovo (Accessed: 6 June 2023).

In cooperation with the Council of Europe and European Commission, the HCNM, however, played an important role in helping to define solutions as regards Russian-speaking inhabitants in the Baltic countries ahead of their EU membership. The HCNM was also active in several other regions and conflicts.

But there are also other formats in which the OSCE played a visible role. One such specific format that consistently played a role since 1991 has been the Conference on Nagorno Karabakh under the auspices of the OSCE (Minsk Conference) led by a group of countries typically co-chaired by Russia, the United States and France but also in the mid-nineties with a prominent role for Sweden and Finland in succession. This format is interesting not least since it, at the initiative of the Finnish co-chairmanship, tried to inform the parties about the *Åland solution*.[9] Even if the then Finnish co-chairmanship of the Minsk Group on Nagorno-Karabakh made a valiant effort to promote reconciliation between Armenia and Azerbaijan using the Åland example, what counted in the end was the relative military capabilities of the two countries to gain and regain territory.[10] The OSCE Minsk Group is, however, an example of a flexible solution accommodating the possibilities for informal arrangements allowing dialogue with non-state entities and international organisations that might be helpful in financing costs related to a peace settlement, such as the European Commission. It was also an important point of reference during a negotiation of formats for so-called *third-party peacekeeping* in the former Soviet space, unsuccessfully under negotiation during the OSCE Rome ministerial in 1993.[11]

One of the most innovative proposals during the Paris summit of 1990 was the Canadian idea to set up a Conflict Prevention Centre (CPC) inside the OSCE. As an example, this part of the Secretariat played a role as a partner to the United Nations and its small observer mission to Abkhazia (UNOMIG), sometimes supported by the OSCE mission to Georgia. CPC also in a more general sense played a role in managing and coordinating a growing number of OSCE field missions led by nationals, often senior diplomats, from participating states. Sometimes these missions were led by senior diplomats from one OSCE participating State in succession, as has been the case in Bosnia and Moldova where consistently the Head of Mission has been a US diplomat, which has tended to increase OSCE leverage in the country concerned.

9 Admin (2018) *Aland Islands Model: Pro Et Contra, Caucasus Edition*. Available at: https://caucasusedition.net/aland-islands-model-pro-et-contra/ (Accessed: 6 June 2023).

10 Admin (2018) *Aland Islands Model: Pro Et Contra, Caucasus Edition*. Available at: https://caucasusedition.net/aland-islands-model-pro-et-contra/ (Accessed: 6 June 2023).

11 (No date a) *A role for OSCE peacekeeping? – IFSH*. Available at: https://ifsh.de/file-CORE/documents/Working_Papers/CORE_WP27.pdf (Accessed: 6 June 2023). The current author participated in these negotiations as a Swedish representative.

Sometimes the heads of missions have also enjoyed a considerable freedom of action, for instance when introducing cooperation between the mission and NATO and the EU Commission as was the case in Kosovo.

Some of these missions have been large, amounting to 500 people in countries such as Bosnia and in Kosovo. Their role in preparing countries, such as the Baltic states and Croatia, for EU membership was not insignificant. Many mission members, for instance in Croatia, observed judicial proceedings involving settlement of property claims on a scale not possible for the local EU delegation to follow. The long-term mission in Croatia notably had the mandate to:

> monitor implementation of Croatian legislation and agreements and commitments entered into by the Croatian government on – the return of all refugees and displaced persons and on protection of their rights, and – the protection of persons belonging to national minorities.[12]

Also, the mandate of the OSCE's long-term mission in Moldova expressly makes an agreement on a "special status" for Transnistria one of its goals. In Georgia, the OSCE mission sought a solution of territorial autonomy within the framework of the federal state.

However, the possibilities for the OSCE and the OSCE missions to play an important role inside the Russian Federation, as was the case when dealing with the Chechnya conflict between 1995 and 1998, were soon dramatically circumscribed. Russia did not hesitate at an early stage to establish parallel diplomatic formats for dealing with the situation in the Caucasus region, notably by appointing plenipotentiary diplomatic envoys and mediating formats – while at the same time forming an alliance with one of the parties to the conflict, Armenia.

Following the International Criminal Court (ICC) indictment of the President of the Russian Federation and the official deemed responsible for forcibly removing children from their homes in parts of Ukraine in order to change the ethnic composition of contested regions now annexed into the Russian Federation, a new dimension of complexity has been introduced into the picture.[13]

---

12 *OSCE Mission to Croatia / OSCE Office in Zagreb (closed)* (no date) *OSCE*. Available at: https://www.osce.org/croatia-closed (Accessed: 6 June 2023).

13 *Situation in Ukraine: ICC judges issue arrest warrants against Vladimir Vladimirovich Putin and Maria Alekseyevna Lvova-Belova* (no date) *International Criminal Court*. Available at: https://www.icc-cpi.int/news/situation-ukraine-icc-judges-issue-arrest-warrants-against-vladimir-vladimirovich-putin-and (Accessed: 6 June 2023).

The OSCE has paid very limited attention to autonomy issues inside the European Union despite repeated requests from the Russian Federation for the OSCE to do so. One of the reasons for this has been the existence of a European Monitoring Centre on Racism and Xenophobia in Vienna.[14] There are a couple of exceptions, for instance, when the Office for Democratic Institutions and Human Rights (ODIHR) as directed called for increased attention to the right for peaceful assembly after the referendum in Catalonia. The OSCE has also welcomed the *Good Friday* agreement. Regarding developments of relevance to the rule of law inside the European Union and countries such as Hungary and Poland, the OSCE contribution has been weak compared with that of the Council of Europe, something partly to be explained by the consensus principle of the OSCE.

From the perspective of several OSCE secretary-generals, the competition for a clear mandate and sufficient *resources* to promote conflict prevention, conflict management and resolution was closely related also to the role of the United Nations and the European Union in the various conflict areas. The division of labour in the beginning of the period after the Cold War between different international organisations was not obvious and led to wide-ranging discussions both on the level of the United Nations (Agenda for Peace), the European Union, the Council of Europe, NATO with its Partnership for Peace, the OSCE, as well as a number of sub-regional formats for cooperation, including the Council of the Baltic Sea States in the Nordic region.

The United Nations after some hesitation took the overall coordinating role through UNMIK in Kosovo, whereas the European Union was a particularly attractive partner to countries seeking membership in the Union. As a result, it was sometimes felt that EU missions, for example in Georgia after the 2008 war, undermined OSCE presence in the area. This example is of interest given the active involvement of the President of France, in the capacity of President of the EU, in the settlement of the war at the same time as Finland, holding the chair of the OSCE with a Finnish ambassador heading up the OSCE mission to Georgia, sought to maintain its earlier OSCE presence in South Ossetia after the war, which did not turn out to be possible.[15]

---

14 *Fundamental rights agency* (2023) *Wikipedia*. Available at: https://en.wikipedia.org/wiki/Fundamental_Rights_Agency (Accessed: 6 June 2023).

15 Deutsche Welle (2009) *EU in Georgia – DW – 08/07/2009, dw.com*. Available at: https://www.dw.com/en/praise-for-eu-mission-in-georgia-but-questions-over-us-role-remain/a-4547031 (Accessed: 06 June 2023). The importance of the OSCE presence in South Ossetia before the war was clearly seen during av visit of OSCE ambassadors, including the current author, just a few weeks before the war.

At an early stage, competition also arose between the OSCE and the Council of Europe with its legally based foundations and well-established Parliamentary Assembly. From the perspective of the Council of Europe, the new institutions of the OSCE should have been much more closely coordinated with the Council, which was counteracted by the United States. The US, in the person of President George H.W. Bush, took a leading role in configuring the new OSCE at the Paris summit, together with French President Mitterrand, with Russian President Gorbachev taking a more passive part.[16]

4 What Is a Chairman-in-Office to Do?

The political leadership of the OSCE as an organisation was at the end of the Cold War entrusted to the Chair-in-Office in yearly succession, starting with Hans Dietrich Genscher and followed, after a couple of years, by the Swedish Foreign Minister in 1992, with Sweden returning to the position once more in 2021 on the eve of the full-scale Russian invasion of Ukraine. Finland took up the position in 2008 before and during the Russian aggression against Georgia, and is again scheduled to be Chair-in-Office during the year of the 50th anniversary of the Helsinki final act in 2025. It goes without saying that this is an ominous challenge, not least for the President of the Republic of Finland after the presidential election in 2024. The possibilities to reaffirm and improve upon the Helsinki final act from 1975 are, of course, minuscule. As regards the Swedish presidency in 2021, it had to scale down expectations for substantial progress and focus on an issue not planned to be of central importance, namely the role of the OSCE on environment and climate change. However, efforts were made, despite remaining difficulties to interact due to the COVID-19 pandemic, and some progress was made on Moldova at the Stockholm ministerial.

Some twenty frozen conflicts in the OSCE region added to the difficulties of keeping the organisation operational, including the decisions enabling the organisation to work with approved budget. When the Polish Chair took over on 1 January 2022, it did not do so as an actor seeking compromises with the Russian Federation but rather as a country effectively aligned with Ukraine, not hesitating to use its position as Chairman-in-office to promote the Ukrainian case's visibility.

16 As observed by the current author as a Swedish delegate.

CHAPTER 14

The Åland Islands and European Union Law: Current Issues and Perspectives

Rainer Hofmann, Alexander Heger and Moritz Malkmus

1 Introduction

The very special status of the Åland Islands under international law comprises two central features: their demilitarised and neutralised status, and their autonomy which implies the guarantee of the 'Swedish character' of the Islands.[1] Both statuses are based on a set of international treaties:[2] whereas this situation applies also to the international status of Spitsbergen (Svalbard)[3]

1 This article is partly based on a study commissioned by the Åland Islands Government. The study was submitted on 2 November 2023: R. Hofmann, M. Malkmus, A. Heger, The Åland Islands in International and European Union Law: Present Situation and (Potential) Problems, *Research Paper of the Faculty of Law of Goethe University Frankfurt/M. No. 1/2024*, https://publikationen.ub.uni-frankfurt.de/frontdoor/index/index/docId/67050, para. 69 et seq.

2 Convention between France and Great Britain and Russia respecting the Aaland Islands of 30 March 1856, which was confirmed by the 1856 Paris Peace Treaty; Council of the League of Nations Resolution on the Aaland (Åland) Islands of 24 June 1921 and the Agreement of 27 June 1921 (annexed to the prior resolution); Convention Relating to the Non-Fortification and Neutralisation of the Aaland Islands of 20 October 1921; Treaty between Finland and the Union of Soviet Socialist Republics concerning the Åland Islands of 11 October 1940; Protocol between the Government of the Russian Federation and the Government of the Republic of Finland concerning Inventory of the Judicial Basis for the Bilateral Relations between Finland and Russia of 11 July 1992; Treaty of Peace with Finland of 10 February 1947. This collection of documents is (partly) reprinted in L. Hannikainen and F. Horn (eds), *Autonomy and Demilitarisation in International Law: The Åland Islands in a Changing Europe* (Kluwer, The Hague et al., 1997), pp. 297 et seq.

For a detailed account on the Åland Islands' special status, see A. Rosas, The Åland Islands as a Demilitarised and Neutrallsed Zone, in L. Hannikainen and F. Horn (eds), *Autonomy and Demilitarisation in International Law: The Åland Islands in a Changing Europe* (Kluwer International Law, The Hague 1997), pp. 23–40; L. Hannikainen, The International Legal Basis of the Autonomy and Swedish character of the Åland Islands (ibid), pp. 57–84; S. Palmgren, The Autonomy of the Åland islands in the Constitutional Law of Finland (ibid), pp. 85–97; M. Suksi, *Sub-State Governance through Territorial Autonomy* (Springer, Heidelberg, 2011), pp. 142 et seq.; Hofmann, Malkmus and Heger, para. 12 et seq.

3 Cf. G. Ulfstein, Spitsbergen/Svalbard, in A. Peters (ed), *Max Planck Encyclopedia of Public International Law* (online edn., OUP, September 2019); Hofmann, Malkmus and Heger, *supra* note 1, para. 43–4.

DOI:10.1163/9789004691117_016

as another demilitarised area, the autonomy of the Åland Islands is the only such structure which is not solely based on domestic (constitutional) law[4] but also benefits from an international law protection of such status.[5] The very specific feature of this situation is that this status is – as has convincingly been shown[6] – not only based on these treaties but that this originally treaty-based status has grown into (regional) customary international law. This means, on the one hand, that Finland is, from an international law point of view, not in a position to unilaterally alter this status in such a way that would threaten the 'Swedish character' of the Islands, let alone to adopt measures resulting in the termination of this status, and, on the other hand, that Finland is under an international legal obligation to ensure in all her foreign policy activities that this status is fully maintained. Furthermore, it also means that all other actors, States and international organisations, have an international law right – and even a duty – to request from Finland respect for her international law obligations with regard to the status of the Islands while they are, at the same time, under an international law duty to respect these obligations incumbent on Finland, i.e. they are prevented from demanding from Finland any action that would be incompatible with the protection and preservation of this specific status. Recently, the demilitarised and neutralised status of the Islands became an important political issue in the context of Finland's accession to NATO in 2023. Since this contribution focuses on issues concerning the Åland autonomy and European Union law, suffice here to stress that it has been convincingly shown[7] that Finland's membership of NATO does not result in any changes of the international treaty and customary law-based demilitarised and neutralised status of the Islands.

In contrast thereto, starting with Finland's membership in the European Economic Area (EEA) as a result of her membership in EFTA,[8] the first legal

4 See the following Finnish Acts: SoF 124/1920, 89/1922, 140/1938, 670/1951, 3/1975, 1144/1991. Cf. Suksi, *supra* note 2, p. 144 et seq.

5 It should be recalled, that the 1946 Gruber-De Gasperi Agreement is only a bilateral treaty and there was no involvement of the UN (as with the League of Nations in the Åland Islands case).

6 For the Islands' neutralised and demilitarised status, see Rosas, *supra* note 2, p. 35. For its autonomous status, see Hannikainen, *supra* note 2, p. 65, 67; Suksi, *supra* note 2, p. 153. Hofmann, Malkmus and Heger, *supra* note 1, para. 24 et seq., 62.

7 Hofmann, Malkmus and Heger, *supra* note 1, para. 43 et seq.

8 Finland became an associated member of EFTA in 1961 and a full member in 1986. In 1994, the 1992 Agreement on the European Economic Area entered into force between the EU and its Member States and five EFTA Member states including Finland which, however, left EFTA in 1995 to become a Member State of the EU.

issues arose relating to the protection of the autonomous status of the Islands.[9] Fully in line with all parties' obligation to protect this status as relates to the Islands' autonomy as a precondition to preserving their 'Swedish character', Finland's accession to the EU was accompanied by successful negotiations on the drafting of the 1994 'Åland Protocol'.[10] Whereas the first pillar of the 'Swedish character', i.e. the preservation of the linguistic situation of the Islands with Swedish as the only official language and far-reaching legislative competences of the Åland authorities in the fields of education (Swedish as the major language of instruction) and culture,[11] did and does not raise any issue with respect to EU law as it does not concern any EU competences and law, the situation is fundamentally different as concerns the second pillar, the right to domicile, a kind of regional citizenship (*hembygdsrätten*).[12] This right was first introduced by the 1951 Autonomy Act and further elaborated by the 1991 Autonomy Act. It is acquired upon birth by any person born on the Islands whose father or mother is a holder of the right.[13] Moreover, it may be granted by the Åland Government, on application, to any Finnish citizen who has taken up residence in Åland, and who has been legally domiciled without interruption in Åland for at least five years, and who is satisfactorily proficient in the Swedish language.[14] However, even giving a short presentation of its (possible) conflicts with EU law, let alone providing a detailed analysis thereof, would clearly exceed the frame of this contribution; therefore, only the following, very short indication of the major aspects will be given. The first component, i.e. the fact that holders of the right to domicile are exempt from military service,[15] does not raise any issue with EU law. The second component concerning the right to political participation, i.e. in particular the right to vote and to stand for election, does not raise any issues with applicable EU law

9 For an account see K. Myntti and M. Scheinin, The Right of Domicile in the Åland Islands in the Light of Human Rights Treaties and the European Integration Process, in L. Hannikainen and F. Horn (eds), *supra* note 2, pp. 131–149 (pp. 146–147).

10 Official Journal C 241, 29.8.1994, p. 352; for an extensive early account see N. Fagerlund, The Special Status of the Åland Islands in the European Union, in L. Hannikainen and F. Horn (eds), *supra* note 2, pp. 189–256; N. Jääskinen, The Application of Community law in Finland: 1995–1998, 36 *Common Market Law Review* (1999), pp. 407–441.

11 For a short account see R. Hofmann, Conclusions, in L. Hannikainen and F. Horn (eds), *supra* note 2, pp. 281–296 (289 et seq.); see also M. Ackrén, The Åland Islands: 100 years of stability, in B.C.H. Fong and A. Ichijo (eds), *The Routledge Handbook of Comparative Territorial Autonomies* (London, Routledge, 2022), pp. 107–118 (111–2).

12 For an overview see Myntti and Scheinin, *supra* note 9, pp. 131–149.

13 See Section 6 Autonomy Act (*Självstyrelselagen*).

14 See Section 7 Autonomy Act (*Självstyrelselagen*).

15 See Section 12 Autonomy Act (*Självstyrelselagen*).

as every person who has been settled on the Islands for one year, is entitled to vote and to be elected in the Ålandic municipal elections,[16] which means that this situation is fully in line with Article 20 para. 2 subpara. 1 lit. b) TFEU; the limitation of the right to vote and to be elected as regards elections of the Åland Parliament (*Lagting*) which is reserved for persons holding the right to domicile[17] does not raise any issue with EU law as Article 20 para. 2 subpara. 1 lit. b) TFEU does not apply to elections for regional legislative organs; finally, it might be added that all EU citizens who have been settled for more than one year on the Islands are entitled to vote and to stand for election in elections to the European Parliament. The third component relates to the fact that persons who are not holders of the right to domicile may not, without permission from the Åland Government, acquire ownership or, through land lease or other contract, possess real property on the Islands.[18] Furthermore, pursuant to the fourth component only holders of the right to domicile enjoy an unqualified right to exercise a trade or to conduct business in Åland.[19] Obviously, these two restrictions raise considerable problems as to their compatibility with applicable EU law, in particular Article 18 TFEU, Article 49 TFEU and Article 56 TFEU; it was, therefore, imperative to include in the Åland Protocol to the Accession Treaty of Finland a provision according to which the existing above-mentioned restrictions on the right of EU citizens to acquire and hold real property, and on their rights to establishment and to provide services on the Islands would remain in force.[20] The exact determination of the implications of this clause raised and continues to raise some quite intricate legal issues, which will be discussed in this contribution. In addition thereto, some currently controversial consequences of the permanent exclusion of the Åland Islands from EU harmonisation legislation in the field of indirect taxes, as provided for in

16 See Section 2 Election Law (*Vallagen*) in conjunction with Section 30 Local Government Act (*Kommunallagen*).

17 See Section 2 Election Law (*Vallagen*) in conjunction with Section 9 Autonomy Act (*Självstyrelselagen*).

18 See Section 10 Autonomy Act (*Självstyrelselagen*).

19 See Section 11 Autonomy Act (*Självstyreslagen*).

20 Article 1 Åland Protocol: "The provisions of the EC Treaty shall not preclude the application of the existing provisions in force on 1 January 1994 on the AAland islands on: – restrictions, on a non-discriminatory basis, on the right of natural persons who do not enjoy hembygdsraett/kotiseutuoikeus (regional citizenship) in AAland, and for legal persons, to acquire and hold real property on the AAland islands without permission by the competent authorities of the AAland islands; – restrictions, on a non-discriminatory basis, on the right of establishment and the right to provide services by natural persons who do not enjoy hembygdsraett/kotiseutuoikeus (regional citizenship) in AAland, or by legal persons without permission by the competent authorities of the AAland islands."

Article 2 lit. a Åland Protocol will be presented. Finally, possible implications of the future development of an EU Common Defence and Security Policy (CDSP) for the status of the Islands will be dealt with.

2 Territorial Scope of EU Law and its Exemptions

The territorial scope of application of the EU Treaties is defined by Article 52 TEU, which follows a general principle of international law according to which international treaties are binding "upon each party in respect of its entire territory" (Article 29 VCLT).[21] Article 52 para. 1 TEU reiterates this in general terms for the territory of Finland, while its second paragraph refers to Article 355 TFEU, which sets out the details of the territorial scope.[22] According to Article 355 para. 4 TFEU, the provisions of the Treaties shall apply to the Åland Islands in accordance with the provisions set out in the 1994 Åland Protocol. As indicated above, this basically means that the domestic regulations on the right to domicile (*hembygdsrätten*), the right of establishment (Article 1 Åland Protocol) and VAT or excise duties (Article 2 Åland Protocol) remain in force on the Åland Islands.[23]

Therefore, the modified application of EU law to the Åland Islands is determined in principle by primary law, in contrast to the situations of the regions, for which certain 'specific measures' can be adopted under Article 349 TFEU. It goes without saying that this Treaty provision cannot be used as a basis for (further) special arrangements for the Åland Islands, since the Islands are neither explicitly listed nor situated as 'outermost regions' within the meaning of this provision, even though there may be certain similarities with the regions explicitly listed. Nevertheless, further derogations could indeed be negotiated

21 W. Heintschel von Heinegg, Art. 52 EUV, in C. Vedder and W. Heintschel von Heinegg (eds), *Europäisches Unionsrecht* (Munich, Beck, 2nd edn., 2018), para. 2.

22 It should be recalled that the scope of application of secondary legislation follows the territorial application of the Treaties. Cf. Court of Justice of the European Union (CJEU), C-132/14, ECLI:EU:C:2015:813, judgment of 15.12.2015, para. 77; D. Kochenov, Article 52 TEU, in M. Kellerbauer et al. (eds), *The EU Treaties and the Charter of Fundamental Rights: A Commentary* (Oxford, OUP, 2019), para. 1; L. Jaeckel, Art. 355 AEUV, in E. Grabitz et al. (eds), *Das Recht der Europäischen Union* (Munich, Beck, 79th edn., May 2023), para. 12.

23 See, in general, N. Fagerlund, The Special Status of the Åland Islands in the European Union, in L. Hannikainen and F. Horn (eds), *Autonomy and Demilitarisation in International Law: The Åland Islands in a Changing Europe* (Kluwer, The Hague et al., 1997), pp. 205–27.

under primary or secondary law.[24] Whether this is politically desirable and, if so, feasible, cannot be assessed here either; from the perspective of EU law, there would be no obstacles to the creation of such further special regulations/arrangements in secondary law.

Whereas the special conditions resulting from the primary law framework for the right to domicile and the right of establishment have already been outlined above and in other publications, one aspect that has sometimes remained underexposed is to be highlighted here: the tax exemptions for VAT and Excise Duty. The main legal acts in the field of indirect taxation are the VAT Directive (Directive 2006/112/EC)[25] and the Excise Duty Directive (Directive (EU) 2020/262).[26] Both Directives fall within the scope of the tax exemptions provided for in Article 2 Åland Protocol. The aim of these exemptions is to allow tax-free shopping, at least on ferry routes between Finland and Sweden.[27] According to its Article 6 para. 1 lit. d, the VAT Directive does not apply to the Åland Islands. It should be noted that provisions of the Customs Code of the European Union apply as compensation for the non-application of the VAT and Excise Directives (cf. Articles 275, 276, 279 and 280 VAT Directive).

According to its Article 4 para. 2, the Excise Duty Directive as well as Directives 92/83/EEC, 92/84/EEC, 2003/96/EC, and 2011/64/EU do not apply to the Åland Islands (lit. c). However, the formalities laid down in the Customs Code of the European Union (UCC) also apply *mutatis mutandis* to special excise duties. Article 1 para. 3 UCC confirms that certain customs provisions, including the simplifications for which it provides, shall apply to the trade in Union goods between parts of the customs territory of the Union to which the provisions of VAT-Directive or of Excise Duty Directive apply and parts of that territory where those provisions do not apply, or to trade between parts of that territory where those provisions do not apply. Article 2 UCC allows – as also suggested by Article 1 para. 3 – to lay down the rules for this as well as simplifications compared to the general customs regulations in a delegated act. Different formalities apply to trade in Union goods between a special tax territory and the rest of the customs territory of the European Union.[28]

24 D. Kochenov, Article 355 TFEU, in M. Kellerbauer et al. (eds), *supra* note 22, para. 22.

25 Council Directive 2006/112/EC of 28 November 2006 on the common system of value added tax OJ L 347, 11 December 2006, pp. 1–118.

26 Council Directive (EU) 2020/262 of 19 December 2019 establishing the general arrangements for excise duty (recast) OJ L 58, 27 February 2020, pp. 4–42.

27 Fagerlund, *supra* note 23, pp. 214–5; Ackrén, *supra* note 11, p. 115.

28 See in detail: Hofmann, Malkmus and Heger, *supra* note 1, para. 101 et seq.

3 Accommodating National Interests within the Structures of Union Law

While the legal consequences described above follow directly from those provisions of primary law which explicitly address the special status of the Åland Islands, the question remains whether there might be other policy areas in which the special circumstances of Åland could be appropriately taken into account, directly or indirectly, by recourse to general principles of Union law. It will therefore first be considered to what extent certain regional interests can be accommodated within the framework of Union law.

3.1 *Respect for National Identities, Article 4 para. 2 TEU*

The EU as such is based on the premise of the continued existing statehood of its members.[29] There are several provisions in the Treaties protecting the plurality and diversity.[30] However, the EU can only act within the limits of the competences conferred upon it by the Member States. All competences not conferred on the Union remain with the Member States (Article 5 para. 2 TEU). In order to ensure the effectiveness of Union law, the EU must rely on the cooperation of its Member States in the application of Union law.[31]

Article 4 para. 2 TEU is particularly important in this respect. The purpose of this provision is often described as a safeguard clause for national interests.[32] Its functions are manifold;[33] some see in Article 4 para. 2 TEU a limitation on the exercise of EU competences to the benefit of certain (core) competences of the Member States, although it should be noted that the Court of Justice of the EU (CJEU) has not yet – as far as can be seen – taken an explicit position on this.[34] However, it is clear that Article 4 para. 2 TEU can be invoked to jus-

29 F. Bieber and R. Bieber, *Negotiating Unity and Diversity in the European Union* (Palgrave Macmillan, 2021), p. 84.

30 Cf. Bieber and Bieber, *ibid*, p. 86 set seq.

31 B. De Witte, Article 4(2) TEU as a Protection of the Institutional Diversity of the Member States, 27 *European Public Law* (2021), pp. 560 et seq.

32 On this interpretation, see H.-P. Folz, Die Kompetenzverteilung zwischen der Europäischen Union und ihren Mitgliedstaaten nach föderalen Maßstäben, in A. Gamper et al. (eds), *Föderale Kompetenzverteilung in Europa* (Baden-Baden, Nomos, 2016), p. 652.

33 C. Calliess, Art. 4 EUV, in C. Calliess and M. Ruffert (eds), *EUV/AEUV* (Munich, Beck, 6th edn., 2022), para. 54 et seq.; M. Dobbs, Sovereignty, Article 4(2) TEU and the Respect of National Identities: Swinging the Balance of Power in Favour of the Member States?, 33 *Yearbook of European Law* (2014), pp. 298 et seq.

34 W. Obwexer, *Föderale Kompetenzverteilung in Europa* (Baden-Baden, Nomos, 2018), p. 715; S. Schill and C. Krenn, Art. 4 EUV, in E. Grabitz et al. (eds), *Das Recht der Europäischen Union* (Munich, Beck, 79th edn., May 2023), para. 45.

tify a national measure restricting fundamental freedoms.[35] This function has indeed been confirmed by the CJEU.[36] Another central function is attributed to Article 4 para. 2 TEU in cases before the CJEU concerning the interpretation of secondary law in accordance with the protection of national constitutional identity.[37] Moreover, the concept enshrined in Article 4 para. 2 TEU constitutes a genuine concept of Union law and is therefore, in principle, independent of the legal systems of the Member States.[38] However, it is a vague concept.[39] The decisive factor is whether the provision or the matter which the Member State considers to be covered by Article 4 para. 2 TEU is fundamental to its constitutional and political identity.[40] Article 4 para. 2 TEU is addressed first and foremost to the Union and all its institutions and bodies, including the CJEU.[41] According to its wording, Article 4 para. 2 TEU is not directly addressed to the Member States themselves.

3.2 *Subsidiarity Principle, Article 5 para. 3 TEU*

The principle of subsidiarity also protects national interests. According to Article 5 para. 3 TEU the Union may take action in areas which do not fall within its exclusive competence, i.e. shared competences (Article 4 TFEU) as well as supporting, coordinating and complementary measures (Article 6 TFEU), only if and insofar as the objectives of the proposed action cannot be sufficiently

---

35 B. Guastaferro, Beyond the Exceptionalism of Constitutional Conflicts: The Ordinary Functions of the Identity Clause, 31 *Yearbook of European Law* (2012), pp. 290 et seq.; A. Schnettger, Article 4(2) TEU as a vehicle for national constitutional identity in the shared European legal system, in C. Calliess and G. v.d. Schyff (eds), *Constitutional Identity in a Europe of Multilevel Constitutionalism* (Cambridge, CUP, 2019), pp. 34 et seq; Schill and Krenn, *supra* note 34, para. 21; M. Klamert, Article 4 TEU, in M. Kellerbauer et al. (eds), *supra* note 22, para. 21.

36 Cf. CJEU, C-36/02, ECLI:EU:C:2004:614, judgment, 14.10.2004, para. 33 et seq. – Omega; CJEU, C-112/00, ECLI:EU:C:2003:333, judgment, 12.06.2003, para. 71 et seq. – Schmidberger; CJEU, C-208/09, ECLI:EU:C:2010:806, judgment, 22.12.2010 – Sayn-Wittgenstein; CJEU, C-391/20, ECLI:EU:C:2022:638, judgment, 7.09.2022 – Boriss Cilevics u.a.

37 Schnettger, *supra* note 35, p. 30.

38 Schill and Krenn, *supra* note 34, para. 15; M. Polzin, Constitutional Identity as a Constructed Reality and a Restless Soul, 18 *German Law Journal* (2017), pp. 1596 et seq.

39 P. Faraguna, Constitutional Identity in the EU – A Shield or a Sword?, 18 *German Law Journal* (2017), pp. 1622 et seq.; A. Kaczorowska-Ireland, What Is the European Union required to Respect under Art 4(2) TEU?: The Uniqueness Approach, 25 *European Public Law* (2019), pp. 57 et seq.

40 Kaczorowska-Ireland, *supra* note 39, pp. 70 et seq.; A. von Bogdandy and S. Schill, Overcoming absolute primacy: Respect for national identity under the Lisbon Treaty, 48 *Common Market Law Review* (2011), pp. 1432 et seq.

41 Calliess, *supra* note 33, para. 62; T. Weber, *Bundesstaatliche Identitäten und ihre Achtung im Unionsrecht* (Baden-Baden, Nomos, 2022), pp. 135 et seq.

achieved by the Member States (negative criterion) but can rather, by reason of the scale or effects of the proposed action, be better achieved at Union level (positive criterion).[42] Article 5 of the Protocol on the application of the principles of subsidiarity and proportionality provides guidance for determining whether these conditions are met.[43] Special attention should be paid to self-governing bodies, as the negative criterion must be explicitly based on the fact that the objectives cannot be sufficiently achieved at central, regional or local level.

4 Relevance of Article 4 para. 2 TEU Concerning the Åland Islands

The following section identifies two key areas where Article 4 para. 2 TEU may have a particular impact, and which may also be relevant to the Åland Islands. The section concludes with a discussion of one policy area where national interests could be better addressed in the future.

4.1 *State Aid and Tax*

A particular aspect of the application of Article 4 para. 2 TEU is the selectivity principle in State aid law, in particular with regard to corresponding tax autonomies. For example, the Åland Protocol does not provide that Articles 107 et seq. TFEU are not applicable in the territory of the Åland Islands. Aid granted regionally could therefore constitute illegal aid and be prohibited. Article 107 para. 1 TFEU prohibits the selective granting of economic advantages to undertakings. The selectivity criterion aims at distinguishing general economic policy measures from those that only benefit certain enterprises or branches of production.[44] A favourable measure may be either territorially selective (i.e., only applying to a part of the reference area) or materially selective (i.e., only

---

42 CJEU, C-508/13, ECLI:EU:C:2015:403, judgment, 18.06.2015, para. 44 – Estonia v. Parliament and Council; Obwexer, *supra* note 34, p. 703; C. Calliess, Art. 5 EUV, in C. Calliess and M. Ruffert (eds), *supra* note 33, para. 28 et seq.; M. Klamert, Article 5 TEU, in Kellerbauer et al. (eds), *supra* note 22, para. 23 et seq.; P. Craig, Subsidiarity: A Political and Legal Analysis, 50 *Journal of Common Market Studies* (2012), pp. 72–87.

43 CJEU, C-508/13, ECLI:EU:C:2015:403, judgment, 18.06.2015, para. 44 – Estonia v. Parliament and Council; CJEU, C-176/09, ECLI:EU:C:2011:290, judgment, 12.05.2011, para. 76 – Luxembourg v Parliament and Council.

44 C. Arhold, Part I, 107 TFEU, in F. J. Säcker and F. Montag (eds), *European State Aid Law* (Munich, C.H. Beck, 2016), para. 362; A. Bartosch, *EU-Beihilfenrecht* (Munich, C.H. Beck, 3rd edn., 2020), Art. 107(1) TFEU, para. 135; T. Rusche, Article 107 TFEU, in M. Kellerbauer et al. (eds), *supra* note 22, para. 57.

bringing benefits for a certain sector of the economy or certain enterprises).[45] Territorial selectivity is evident when the economic advantages do not apply to an entire Member State but are limited to a region. This is particularly relevant as the Åland Islands have a certain degree of fiscal autonomy in relation to Finland under the Autonomy Act (*Självstyreselag*). Furthermore, they are considered to be a special tax zone. As mentioned above, the Åland Islands are exempt from the EU's VAT and excise duty regulations. The extent to which the exercise of fiscal autonomy correlates with selectivity is therefore of particular importance.

4.1.1 Main Elements of Selectivity in Article 107 para. 1 TFEU

Selectivity is often established by means of a three-step test,[46] starting with the determination of the frame of reference to be applied in the specific case. In the case of taxes, the frame of reference is based on elements such as the tax base, the taxpayers, the taxable event, and the tax rates.[47] In addition, it must be established that undertakings in a comparable legal and factual situation benefit from this advantage to a different extent,[48] i.e. that the measure in question constitutes a deviation from the reference system which leads to undertakings which are in a comparable legal and factual situation being treated differently.[49] A deviation from 'normal market conditions' or an exception to a general frame of reference do not constitute a selective advantage if the measure in question is in principle accessible to any undertaking and is thus not intended to favour a particular group of undertakings but a group of economic transactions.[50] Thirdly, it must be determined whether such a derogation is justified by the nature or general scheme of the reference system. If

---

45 C. Panayi, *Advanced Issues in International and European Tax Law* (Oxford, Hart, 2015), p. 254; E. Traversa, Implementation of regional taxing powers and EU law: recent cases and future challenges, in V. Simonart, *Fiscal federalism in the European Union*, 2011, p. 57 (71).

46 M.-A. Kronthaler and Y. Tzubery, The State Aid Provisions of the TFEU in Tax Matters, in M. Lang et al. (eds), *Introduction to European Tax Law on Direct Taxation* (Vienna, Linde-Verlag, 5th edn., 2015), para. 387 et seq.

47 C. Cipollini, *Special Tax Zones and EU Law* (Alphen aan den Rijn, Wolters Kluwer, 2019), p. 56.

48 CJEU, C-15/14 P, ECLI:EU:C:2015:362, judgment, 04.06.2015, para. 59 – MOL; CJEU, C-524/14 P, ECLI:EU:C:2016:971, judgment, 21.12.2016, para. 58 – Commission/Hansestadt Lübeck; CJEU, C-374/17, ECLI:EU:C:2018:1024, judgment, 19.12.2018, para. 22 – Finanzamt B/A Brauerei; H. Schweitzer and E.-J. Mestmäcker, Art. 107 Abs. 1 AEUV, in U. Immenga and E.-J. Mestmäcker (eds), *Wettbewerbsrecht* (Munich, C.H. Beck, 6th edn. 2022), para. 168.

49 Cipollini, *supra* note 47, p. 56; Rusche, Article 107 TFEU, in M. Kellerbauer et al. (eds), *supra* note 44, para. 63; Panayi, *supra* note 45, p. 254.

50 Schweitzer and Mestmäcker, *supra* note 48, para. 168.

the derogation is justified by the nature or general scheme of the system, it is not considered selective and will therefore fall outside the scope of Article 107 para. 1 TFEU.[51]

4.1.2 Territorial Selectivity

In particular, as far as tax aspects are concerned, the frame of reference is the selective advantage in relation to the 'normal taxation' applicable in the geographical area.[52] The relevant principles for resolving this conflict with autonomous regions were established by the CJEU in its so-called *Azores* ruling.[53] Several cases must be distinguished: if a central government unilaterally decides to apply a low tax rate in a certain geographical area, this is territorially selective.[54] If, on the other hand, the legislative competence does not lie with the central government, but rather with public bodies of this Member State, which are on a lower hierarchical level (for example, local or regional authorities), the fact that a more favourable regulation (for example, a lower tax rate) is applied to one area of competence than to another cannot be considered as a selective advantage, since no uniform frame of reference can be established.[55] If, however, a regulation defining the frame of reference exists at the central level, but the central government has left autonomous powers to a specific region, then the tax regulation adopted by the autonomous region can exclude territorial selectivity on the basis of the relevance of this regulation to the frame of reference, if the legislative competence that the region has is also autonomous in a qualified sense.[56] This case law has now been incorporated into the guidelines of the European Commission.[57] This presupposes that the relevant regional or local body has been constitutionally granted its own political and administrative status vis-à-vis the central government (institutional autonomy); that the regulation was adopted without the central government having the possibility of directly influencing its content (procedural autonomy); and that the regulating region bears the political and

51 Bartosch, *supra* note 44, para. 137; Cipollini, *supra* note 47, p. 56; Panayi, *supra* note 45, pp. 254 et seq; Kronthaler and Tzubery, *supra* note 46, para. 388 et seq.

52 CJEU, C-88/03, ECLI:EU:C:2006:511, judgment, 06.09.2006, para. 56 – Portugal v Commission.

53 CJEU, C-88/03, ECLI:EU:C:2006:511, judgment, 06.09.2006 – Portugal v Commission. Bartosch, *supra* note 44, para. 156; Panayi, *supra* note 45, pp. 256 et seq.

54 Cipollini, *supra* note 47, p. 56; Panayi, *supra* note 45, p. 257.

55 CJEU, C-88/03, ECLI:EU:C:2006:511, judgment, 06.09.2006, para. 64 – Portugal v. Commission; Bartosch, *supra* note 44, para. 157.

56 See Bartosch, *supra* note 44, para. 15; Panayi, *supra* note 45, p. 257.

57 Commission Notice on the concept of State aid within the meaning of Article 107(1) of the Treaty on the Functioning of the European Union (2016/C 262/01), para. 142 et seq.

financial consequences of the measure adopted, in particular that the financial effects of the reduction of the national tax rate for companies in the region are not offset by grants or subsidies from the other regions or from the central government (political, economic and financial autonomy).[58] With regard to the situation in the Azores, the CJEU rejected the qualified autonomy of the Azores for lack of sufficient financial autonomy on the basis of a principle of national solidarity.[59] The criteria for qualified autonomy were confirmed and further developed by the CJEU in the *UGT Rioja* case concerning the autonomous Basque Country.[60] It can be assumed that the mere reference to financial regulations for the implementation of a national principle of solidarity can no longer exclude the corresponding financial autonomy.[61] However, the causal link between the relevant fiscal regime and the financial allocations by the central government must be examined on a case-by-case basis and for each region individually. The extent to which qualified autonomy exists with regard to the Åland Islands requires further investigation, but it is likely to be the case concerning Section 18 para. 5 Autonomy Act. The existence of such financial autonomy is assumed by Suksi,[62] for example.

4.1.3 Material Selectivity Despite Qualified Autonomy?

Even if territorial selectivity can be ruled out, the tax regime can still be considered selective from a material point of view.[63] Therefore, even in the case of sufficiently qualified autonomy, tax measures must always be designed for meeting the situation of all companies in a legally and factually comparable

58 CJEU, C-88/03, ECLI:EU:C:2006:511, judgment, 06.09.2006, para. 67 – Portugal v. Commission; Schweitzer and Mestmäcker, *supra* note 48, para. 203; Bartosch, *supra* note 44, para. 157; Rusche, Article 107 TFEU, in M. Kellerbauer et al. (eds), *supra* note 22, para. 69; Panayi, *supra* note 45, p. 257.

59 Cf. CJEU, C-88/03, ECLI:EU:C:2006:511, judgment, 06.09.2006, para. 71 et seq. – Portugal v. Commission.

60 CJEU, C-428/06 and C-434/06, ECLI:EU:C:2008:488, judgment, 11.09.2008 – Unión General de Trabajadores de la Rioja; see also Bartosch, *supra* note 44, para. 161, 162; Panayi, *supra* note 45, pp. 257 et seq.

61 Bartosch, *supra* note 44, para. 162.

62 M. Suksi, Funding of and Public Spending in the Autonomous Aland Islands, 17 *Academia Puertorriqueña De Jurisprudencia Y Legislación* (2020), p. 98.

63 General Court, T-95/21, ECLI:EU:T:2022:567, judgment, 21.09.2022, para. 56 et seq. – Portugal v. Commission; Court of Justice, Commission v. Gibraltar, para. 100–102; Traversa, *supra* note 45, p. 73; Schweitzer and Mestmäcker, *supra* note 48, para. 203; Panayi, *supra* note 45, pp. 259–260.

situation that are established in the territory of a special tax zone, in order not to be considered as (harmful) material selectivity.[64]

4.2 *Further Relevance for the Application of Union Law*

Moreover, Article 4 para. 2 TEU can also constitute a justification for a selective non-application of secondary law.[65] Indeed, the CJEU has consistently held that a Member State may not invoke provisions, practices, or situations of its internal legal order to justify non-compliance with its obligations under EU law.[66] On the other hand, Article 4 para. 2 TEU requires as an obligation under Union law to take into account the national identity with which the application of secondary law may conflict. It is therefore possible in individual cases, via Article 4 para. 2 TEU, to develop national identity with regard to individual secondary law or even primary law in appropriate constellations and to take national identities into account.[67] The individual deviation follows normatively from Union law and not from Member State concepts of identity.[68] However, the decisive factor in each individual case is a substantive balancing of the various interests resulting from the non-application of a Union law provision with the interests of protection resulting from the respective national identity.[69] Such a legal consequence, however, is not an exception to the primacy of application of Union law, but merely limits the unity of the EU legal order in the specific case.[70] It is not a blanket provision for derogation from Union law obligations.[71]

Article 4 para. 2 TEU has a special significance in the case law of the CJEU regarding in-house procurement. The case concerned the award procedure in the city of Pori, in which public transport services for health services were awarded in-house to a private company, wholly owned by the city of Pori. This award was challenged by a competitor and several questions concerning the

64 General Court, T-95/21, ECLI:EU:T:2022:567, judgment, 21.09.2022, para. 57 et seq. – Portugal v. Commission; Cipollini, *supra* note 47, p. 71.

65 Schill and Krenn, *supra* note 34, para. 44, 47.

66 CJEU, C-423/00, ECLI:EU:C:2002:32, judgment, 17.01.2002, para. 16 – Commission v. Belgium; CJEU, C-205/96, ECLI:EU:C:1997:63, judgment, 06.02.1997, para. 10 – Commission v. Belgium; CJEU, C-473/13 and C-514/13 ECLI:EU:C:2014:2095, judgment, 17.07.2014, para. 30, 31 – Bero; cf. T. Weber, *Bundesstaatliche Identitäten und ihre Achtung im Unionsrecht* (Baden-Baden, Nomos, 2022), p. 65; M. Klamert, Article 4 TEU, in Kellerbauer et al. (eds), *supra* note 22, para. 20.

67 Schnettger, *supra* note 35, pp. 26 et seq.

68 Schnettger, *supra* note 35, p. 33.

69 Schnettger, *supra* note 35, p. 34.

70 Schnettger, *supra* note 35, p. 34; Calliess, *supra* note 33, para. 8.

71 I. Gillich, *Die integrierte Staatlichkeit der Länder* (Tübingen, Mohr Siebeck, 2022), p. 428.

award modalities were referred to the CJEU. It is important to know whether the situation in question is really a public contract falling under secondary public procurement law or whether it is rather a transfer of (public) competences that is secured by Article 4 para. 2 TEU (sometimes also referred to in the literature as self-execution in the narrower sense).[72,73] The allocation of competences to a Member State is thus part of the national identity. In this context, the CJEU has already ruled in several cases that Article 4 para. 2 TEU also refers to the national reorganisation of competences, which excludes the application of public procurement law – and thus also secondary procurement law.[74] However, the assumption of such a transfer of competences is not without preconditions. According to the case law of the CJEU, it is necessary:

> that the public body to which a competence is delegated has the power to organise the performance of the tasks deriving from that competence and to establish the legal framework relating to those tasks. Furthermore, it must have a financial independence that allows it to ensure the financing of these tasks. This is not the case, on the other hand, if the body originally responsible retains primary responsibility for these tasks, reserves financial control over them or has to agree in advance to the decisions that the body it calls in wants to take.[75]

The importance of Article 4 para. 2 TEU is also illustrated by the *Digibet* case, which dealt with the regulation of betting and gambling in Germany. The Maltese gambling company *Digibet* argued before the CJEU that German legislation infringed EU law on the free movement of services because the restrictions on gambling varied from one *Land* to another. This inconsistency arose from the fact that the regulation of gambling falls within the competence of the *Länder*, which means that they can take different measures in this area and impose different restrictions on the provision of gambling services by operators from other EU countries. The Court argued that "the division of competences between the Länder cannot be called into question, since it

72 N. Eisentraut, Der Grundsatz der Ausschreibungsfreiheit der Eigenerledigung, 33 *Europäische Zeitschrift für Wirtschaftsrecht* (2022), p. 981.

73 CJEU, C-51/15, ECLI:EU:C:2016:985, judgment, 21.12.2016, para. 40, 41 – Remondis; CJEU, C-328/19, ECLI:EU:C:2020:483, judgment, 18.06.2020, para. 45 – Porin kaupunki.

74 CJEU, C-51/15, ECLI:EU:C:2016:985, judgment, 21.12.2016, para. 41 – Remondis; CJEU, C-328/19, ECLI:EU:C:2020:483, judgment, 18.06.2020, para. 46 – Porin kaupunki.

75 CJEU, C-51/15, ECLI:EU:C:2016:985, judgment, 21.12.2016, para. 49 – Remondis; CJEU, C-328/19, ECLI:EU:C:2020:483, judgment, 18.06.2020, para. 48 – Porin kaupunki.

benefits from the protection conferred by Article 4(2) TEU".[76] Furthermore, the CJEU ruled that the existence of such divergences was not in itself contrary to EU law.[77]

In another case concerning the implementation of an obligation to establish special detention facilities for detainees awaiting deportation, the CJEU ruled that in federal states the obligation does not go so far as to require the establishment of special detention facilities in each federal subdivision if no such facilities exist there.[78] This application also shows that there needs to be leeway in implementing secondary legislation in federal states.[79] Although the EU's prohibition on encroaching on Germany's autonomy does not release Germany from its obligations under Union law, it remains free to find a solution that respects its internal division of competences in fulfilling these obligations.[80]

In this system, Article 4 para. 2 TEU fulfils its function of optimising the interplay between EU law and national law[81] by providing an effective solution to the relevant conflict of laws. Numerous cases of application are also conceivable with regard to the Åland Islands. If, for example, opt-out rights exist (cf. most recently, for example, in Article 4 para. 6 or Article 5 para. 5 Regulation (EU) 2020/698), the distribution of competences between Åland and Finland must be taken into account. Thus, if the Åland Islands have competence for road traffic and the corresponding licenses, it must be considered whether the decision is within the competence of the Åland Islands. Other cases may concern the organisation of authority structures, for example in the case of independent authorities such as the data protection officer (see Article 51 et seq. Regulation (EU) 2016/679) or the planned independent media authorities (Article 7 et seq. of the Proposal for a European Media Freedom Act).[82]

---

76 CJEU, C-156/13, ECLI:EU:C:2014:1756, judgment, 12.06.2014, para. 34 – Digibet.

77 CJEU, C-156/13, ECLI:EU:C:2014:1756, judgment, 12.06.2014, para. 36 et seq. – Digibet.

78 CJEU, C-473/13 and C-514/13, ECLI:EU:C:2014:2095, judgment, 17.07.2014, para. 30 et seq. – Bero and Bouzalmate.

79 D. Fromage, National Constitutional Identity and Its Regional Dimension Post-Lisbon as Part of a General Trend Towards Multilevel Governance Within the EU, 27 *European Public Law* (2021), p. 511.

80 Fromage, *supra* note 79, p. 511.

81 C. Calliess and A. Schnettger, The Protection of Constitutional Identity in a Europe of Multilevel Constitutionalism, in C. Calliess and G. van der Schyff (eds), *Constitutional Identity in a Europe of Multilevel Constitutionalism* (Cambridge, CUP, 2019), p. 354.

82 European Commission, Proposal for a Regulation of the European Parliament and of the Council establishing a common framework for media services in the internal market (European Media Freedom Act) and amending Directive 2010/13/EUCOM(2022) 457 final.

4.3 *Media Services*

Media services also play a central role in the protection of minorities.[83] This concerns the availability of media in the minority languages in the respective states, but also the cross-border access to media services in a language that is spoken in the region, such as (potentially) the consumption of Swedish media services on the Åland Islands. The digital single market faces a number of conflicting interests. The key issue for "free" availability is geo-blocking. Geo-blocking refers to the practice of restricting access to certain content or services on the internet based on the geographical location of the user.[84] Media services in particular are closely linked to territorially limited copyrights.[85] Geo-blocking is intended to protect existing copyrights by protecting the copyright owner's contractual power/freedom to geographically divide, by contract, the markets for the work, to set different prices for different territories and to maximise the profits deriving from the exploitation of the work.[86]

There is a geo-blocking Regulation in order to improve access to goods and services and to remove barriers to the internal market (see Article 1 para. 1 Regulation (EU) 2018/302). However, audiovisual services and access to copyrighted works are excluded from the scope of Regulation (EU) 2018/302 (see Article 1 para. 3, 5 and recital 8 of Regulation (EU) 2018/302), which means that geo-blocking remains possible there.[87] With regard to the planned evaluation of the Regulation (Article 9 Regulation (EU) 2018/302), the European Parliament has adopted a resolution according to which the inclusion of audiovisual services should be examined.[88] The Parliament acknowledges the particularly negative impact of geo-blocking practices on citizens living

83 Cf. S. Oeter, Minderheitenmedien zwischen medienökonomischen Effizienzanforderungen, Gerechtigkeitspostulaten und Spracherhalt, in P. Donath et al. (eds), *Der Schutz des Individuums und das Recht – Festschrift für Rainer Hofmann* (Berlin, Heidelberg, Springer, 2023), pp. 517 et seq. On certain proposals of the Minority SafePack Initiative, see M. Malkmus, On the dismissal of the MSPI action by the General Court of the EU (case T-158/21), *European Yearbook of Minority Issues* (2024, forthcoming). For an overview of EU law and minorities, see R. Hofmann and M. Malkmus, The Treaties and Minority Rights, in T. Malloy and B. Vizi (eds), *Research Handbook on Minority Politics in the European Union* (Edward Elgar, Cheltenham and Northampton 2022), pp. 16–37.

84 T. Synodinou, Geoblocking in EU Copyright Law: Challenges and Perspectives, *Gewerblicher Rechtsschutz und Urheberrecht Internationaler Teil* (2020), p. 137.

85 Synodinou, *ibid*, p. 136.

86 *Ibid*, p. 137.

87 For a critical overall view, see *ibid*, p. 136.

88 European Parliament, Implementation of the 2018 Geo-blocking Regulation in the Digital Single Market: Parliament resolution on the introduction of rules for licenses for border regions and minorities, P9_TA(2023)473, para. 19, 25.

in cross-border regions or belonging to linguistic minorities.[89] The evaluation of the relevant regulation provides an opportunity to identify new ways which will ultimately respect the minority rights dimension of Finland's national identity and its relations with the Åland Islands and other regions in the EU.[90] However, no direct obligations can be derived from Article 4 para. 2 TFEU in a corresponding context; a reference to Article 4 para. 2 TFEU remains merely political.

5 Strengthening the Role of the Åland Islands in the Institutional System of the EU

In the following, some possible starting points for strengthening the role of the Åland Islands in the EU institutional system are presented and accompanied by brief *de lege ferenda* remarks.[91]

5.1 *Committee of the Regions*

The Åland Islands are represented by one member in the Committee of the Regions (CoR). The CoR is set up by primary law to ensure that regional and local identities are better taken into account.[92] However, Article 300 para. 1 TFEU and Article 13 para. 4 TEU give the CoR a predominantly advisory/consultative role. In addition, the CoR has an important task in monitoring the principle of subsidiarity. According to Article 8 para. 2 of the above-mentioned Subsidiarity Protocol, the CoR can bring an action before the CJEU against legislative acts that violate the principle of subsidiarity, provided that the legislative act was subject to a consultation obligation under the TFEU. However, the Treaties do not provide the CoR with a full mandate.[93] In terms of the CoR's development prospects, the heterogeneity of the regions and the non-binding nature of its opinions pose structural challenges.[94]

---

89 *Ibid.*

90 Cf. Grenzecho, declaration by DG and Åland: In favour of minorities and against geoblocking, available at: https://www.grenzecho.net/96964/artikel/2023-10-12/erklarung-von-dg-und-aland-fur-minderheiten-und-gegen-geoblockin.

91 On the Autonomy representation in the European Parliament, Council and Commission see the chapter by Julia Lindholm and Elisabeth F. Rasmussen in the present volume.

92 M. Kotzur, Art. 300 TFEU, in R. Geiger et al. (eds), *EUV/AEUV* (Munich, Beck, 7th edn., 2023), para. 5.

93 M. Klamert, Article 307 TFEU, in M. Kellerbauer et al. (eds), *supra* note 22, p. 1965 (para. 1–2).

94 O. Suhr, Art. 300 TFEU, in C. Calliess and M. Ruffert (eds), *EUV/AEUV. Das Verfassungsrecht der Europäischen Union mit Europäischer Grundrechtecharta* (6th edn., C.H. Beck, Munich, 2022), para. 43.

5.2 *Conference of European Regional Legislative Assemblies (CALRE)*

The Parliament of Åland is a member of the Conference of European Regional Legislative Assemblies. This is a network of regional parliaments with legislative powers in the European Union, consisting of 72 presidents of such European regional legislative assemblies. The founding declaration in 1997 already states:

> Whereas, in order to strengthen the democratic principle, the regions of the Member States with assemblies with legislative competence must be more involved in the process of European integration.[95]

With regard to the objectives, it states:

> The procedures for parliamentary monitoring and evaluation of European affairs should be strengthened in each region. This should be done both in a bottom-up phase when formulating the State's demands and in the top-down phase when implementing Community policy. To this end, and in order to make it possible to control the European action of the respective Executives, it would be indispensable to provide the Regional Parliaments with an information service that would allow them to regularly follow all issues that could affect their competences.[96]

The CALRE Plenary Assembly is held annually. By focusing on the parliaments with legislative powers, a more specific pursuit of interests is also to be ensured than in the CoR (mainly local, regional, and municipal representatives), although there is also cooperation between the two institutions.

5.3 *Participation in the Council*

One of the central EU institutions is the Council. It is part of the democratic legitimacy of the EU (cf. Article 10 para. 2 TEU). Representatives of the regional governments can in principle be regarded as representatives of the respective Member State. Whether a power of representation exists for the entire Member State in federal states depends on national law.[97] According to Article 12 para. 3 Council Decision of 1 December 2009 adopting the Council's Rules of Procedure, the members of the Council and the Commission are

95 Oviedo Document on Regional Legislative Assemblies in the European Union 1997, available at: https://www.calrenet.eu/wp-content/uploads/2022/01/Documents_Declarations_Oviedo_1997_EN.pdf.

96 *Ibid.*

97 C. Ziegenhorn, Art. 16 TEU, in E. Grabitz et al. (eds), *Das Recht der Europäischen Union* (Munich, Beck, 79th edn., May 2023), para. 33.

to be assisted by officials. Further participation may take place through the Committee of the Permanent Representatives of the Governments of the Member States to the European Union (Coreper), which is established by Article 240 para. 1 TFEU. Pursuant to Article 19 para. 3 of the Council's Rules of Procedure, committees or working groups can be set up by Coreper or with the approval of Coreper to carry out certain preparatory work or studies defined in advance. However, these committees or working groups tend to be organised on a topic-specific basis.[98]

Article 19 para. 7 lit. h) of the Council's Rules of Procedure authorises Coreper to consult an institution or body wherever such consultation is not required by the Treaties. However, these possibilities are at the discretion of Coreper and the persons concerned and are not institutionalised. CALRE demands that the legislative institutions of the EU (Council and European Parliament) invite representatives of local and regional authorities to meetings of their committees and working groups and to hearings if this is relevant and appropriate in the case of the respective proposal.[99] In the view of the authors, there have been specific opportunities in this respect so far, but these are not binding rights for the regions. Overall, with regard to active work in the Council, it should be noted that the heterogeneity of the Member States can have an impact on political decision-making. In the political science literature, it is assumed that larger states have much more power than smaller states.[100] This may hamper the current system.

5.4 *Importance of the Election to the European Parliament*

The elections to the European Parliament are also of central importance to the democratic legitimacy of the European Union (cf. Article 10 para. 2 TEU). The Members of the European Parliament are elected in direct elections, but the lists are prepared by the Member States (see Article 1 para. 1 Direct Elections

98 For an overview, see: https://data.consilium.europa.eu/doc/document/ST-11597-2023-INIT/en/pdf.

99 Final Resolution of the CALRE Working Group on Subsidiarity (2018), available at: https://www.calrenet.eu/wp-content/uploads/2015/05/resolution_CALRE_WG_Subsidiarity_en.pdf. For the practice regarding the Åland Islands, see the chapter by Julia Lindholm and Elisabeth F. Rasmussen in the present volume.

100 Cf. in detail: D. Panke, Small states in the European Union: structural disadvantages in EU policy-making and counter-strategies, 17 *Journal of European Public Policy* (2010), pp. 799–817, see also W. Wessels and J. Wolters, The European Council, in P. Becker, B. Lippert (eds), *Handbook European Union* (Springer VS, Wiesbaden, 2019).

Act).[101] There are therefore 27 different electoral systems.[102] The long-standing debate on the allocation of one seat of the Finnish contingent of MEPs in the European Parliament to the Åland Islands[103] is, according to the current concept, a purely domestic decision of Finnish electoral law. However, changes to the electoral system for the European Parliament are being discussed not only in academia but also in political circles. One aspect are the so-called transnational lists.[104] However, the Parliament's current proposal only provides for 28 seats to be allocated via such a transnational list. According to the current proposal, any 'European electoral entity', including a European coalition of national political parties and/or associations of voters, a European political party, a European association of voters, a European electoral coalition or a political alliance, would be authorised to draw up a transnational list (cf. Article 15 para. 3). The broad scope would not exclude the extension of the cooperation of regional bodies with legislative functions to transnational lists. However, given the small number of seats allocated by these lists and possible electoral thresholds, it seems unlikely that every region would be represented by an MEP. Nevertheless, transnational lists seem to improve the possibility of bringing specific interests into the parliamentary process. Irrespective of this, greater cooperation among the European political parties would also be a conceivable way of incorporating these interests.[105]

In the current system, the European Parliament can conclude interinstitutional agreements with other institutions to improve and clarify procedures (see Article 148 RP EP). Overall, however, it would also seem sensible to adapt the legal basis so that it is possible to invite representatives of local and

---

101 See also A. Heger, Europäische politische Parteien und die Stärkung der europäischen Demokratie, in A. Heger, M. Malkmus and S. Gourdet (Hrsg.), *Zur Zukunft der Demokratie in der Europäischen Union* (Nomos, Baden-Baden, 2023), 159–198.

102 Cf. also Heger, *supra* note 101, p. 190; M. Bogaards, The European Union: Consociational Past, Centripetal Future?, 58 *Journal of Representative Democracy* (2022), p. 445.

103 Cf. Nordic Labour Journal, available at http://www.nordiclabourjournal.org/nyheter/news-2023/article.2023-11-20.5094261510.

104 European Parliament, European Parliament legislative resolution of 3 May 2022 on the proposal for a Council Regulation on the election of the members of the European Parliament by direct universal suffrage, repealing Council Decision (76/787/ECSC, EEC, Euratom) and the Act concerning the election of the members of the European Parliament by direct universal suffrage annexed to that Decision, P9_TA(2022)0129; for views from the literature see K. Hoffmeister, Transnational Lists in European Parliamentary Elections – European Democracy, 23 *Zeitschrift für europarechtliche Studien* (2020), p. 129; Bogaards, *supra* note 102, p. 448 et seq.; and Heger, *supra* note 101, p. 190 et seq.

105 Cf. Heger, *supra* note 101.

regional authorities to meetings of EP committees and working groups and to hearings where this is relevant and appropriate.[106] In both parliamentary and extra-parliamentary spheres, the institutional aspects of greater involvement of regions with legislative powers need to be further examined from the perspective of multi-level governance.[107]

5.5 *Access to the CJEU*

Compared to the Member States, sub-national entities such as the regions have only limited access to the CJEU: In the context of an action for annulment, the regions – in contrast to the Member States – are not regarded as privileged applicants under Article 263 para. 2 TFEU,[108] but can only bring an action under the additional conditions of Article 263 para. 4 TFEU.[109] They are also not entitled to bring infringement proceedings (Articles 258, 259 TFEU). In the context of the preliminary ruling procedure under Article 267 TFEU, it goes without saying that the courts of the autonomous regions can, under the usual conditions, refer a matter to the CJEU.

However, the situation of the Parliament of Åland as a sub-state legislative body raises specific issues under the current system of European legal remedies with regard to the legal control, i.e. the special procedure provided for in Section 19 of the Autonomy Act (1991/1144),[110] which enables the President of the Republic to annul "in full or in part" an Act of the Parliament if "he considers that the Åland Parliament has exceeded its legislative powers or that the Act of Åland relates to the internal or external security of the State". The actual review is carried out by the Åland delegation and the Supreme Court of Finland (*Högsta Domstolen*, HD), which will issue a legal opinion[111]

106 Final Resolution of the CALRE Working Group on Subsidiarity (2018), available at: https://www.calrenet.eu/wp-content/uploads/2015/05/resolution_CALRE_WG_Subsidiarity_en.pdf.

107 See also R. Trobbiani, European regions in Brussels: towards functional interest representation?, *Bruges Political Research Papers* 53/2016, https://www.coleurope.eu/sites/default/files/research-paper/wp53_trobbiani_0.pdf.

108 CJEU, C-180/97, ECLI:EU:C:1997:451, judgment, 1 October 1997 – Regione Toscana v Commission; CJEU, C-95/97, ECLI:EU:C:1997:184, judgment, 21 March 1997 – Walloon Region v Commission, [1997] ECR I-1787.

109 CJEU, C-142/00 P, ECLI:EU:C:2001:623, judgment, 21 November 2001, para. 51 – Nederlandse Antillen v Council; CJEU, C-417/04 P, ECLI:EU:C:2006:282, judgment, 2 May 2006, para. 24 – Regione Siciliana v Commission; cf. C. Perathoner, Die Regionen der Europäischen Union. Ist-Zustand und Ausblick, in P. Hilpold et al. (eds), *Europa der Regionen* (Heidelberg/Berlin, Springer, 2016), pp. 78–9.

110 An English version is available at https://peacemaker.un.org/sites/peacemaker.un.org/files/FI%20SE_930101_Act%20on%20the%20Autonomy%20of%20Aland.pdf.

111 See e.g. Högsta Domstolen, Utlåtande KKO-HD/1377/2023, of 11 January 2024 on the Ålandic Act on conduct of businesses (näringsliv); Högsta Domstolen, Utlåtande

on the matter. Echoing the CJEU's case law concerning 'actes claires' and 'actes éclairés', the HD, inter alia, examines whether the Åland legislator has exceeded its legislative powers by passing an Act that is 'clearly' or 'evidently' (*uppenbar*) incompatible with EU law. The opinions of the HD are not legally binding on the President but are followed and implemented in consistent state practice. Neither the President's decision to annul an Act of Åland nor the preceding opinion of the HD is subject to appeal under the Autonomy Act, and Finland – fully in line with other Nordic countries and in contrast to most of the Continental European countries – does not have a constitutional court (*Staatsgerichtshof*) before which such a decision could be challenged on legal grounds.

While it is correct that it is the sole competence of the CJEU to decide whether a legislative act of a Member State or of a constituent part (sub-state entity) of a Member State is compatible with EU law, and while it is equally correct that it is up to the competent national (judicial) body to decide whether the legislative act of a sub-state entity remains within the legislative powers vested with that sub-entity (*intra vires*), it is by no means clear that the undisputed general competence of a national organ to decide whether a legislative act of a sub-state entity such as the Åland Islands remains within the legislative powers vested with the Åland legislature under Finnish constitutional law including the Autonomy Act necessarily includes the power to decide on the compliance of such an Åland legislative act with EU law as this conflicts with the general principle, explicitly recognized by HD, that it is the CJEU only which decides on the compatibility of national law with EU law.

The problem in such a case is that the (final) interpretation of Union law, as expressed in the opinion of the HD, has a direct impact on the decision of the President of the Republic regarding the validity of a legislative Act by the autonomous sub-state parliament, without such issues being referred to the CJEU. Irrespective of whether the HD would even consider requesting a preliminary ruling, it is also doubtful whether such a request would even be admissible under Article 267 TFEU in the context of the legislative procedure described above. Although admissibility does not necessarily require *inter partes* proceedings, the court would still have to exercise compulsory jurisdiction in such a way that its decision would be binding,[112] which is not the case

KKO-HD/10192022, of 25 April 2023 on a previous version of the Ålandic Act on the Conduct of Businesses; or Högsta Domstolen, OH 2018/197, of 27 September 2018, on the Ålandic Hunting Act.

112 B. Schima, Article 267 TFEU, in M. Kellerbauer et al. (eds), *supra* note 22, pp. 1822–1840 (para. 24, 25).

in the legal control under Section 19 of the Autonomy Act where the HD gives 'only' an opinion to the President of the Republic.

Given the procedural autonomy of the Member States, the CJEU remains very reluctant to create new domestic legal remedies.[113] Whether in such a constellation, in which the CJEU is not involved in reviewing the legality of a national law, infringement proceedings under Article 257 TFEU by the European Commission would be promising, is not examined here, but should be seen with scepticism.

De lege ferenda, it seems worth considering the extent to which the Finnish legal control could be modified, either to subject the President's decision to (judicial) review, to change how the law is enacted or otherwise to strengthen the involvement of the CJEU. The added value might be illustrated by the following considerations: Once an Åland law has entered into force, requests for preliminary rulings on its compatibility with Union law under Article 267 TFEU would undoubtedly be admissible in the context of national court proceedings concerning such a law. However, by repealing a law before it enters into force, the President deprives the competent authorities of the possibility of referring the matter to the CJEU and obtaining a final binding decision. It is therefore suggested to change the state practice in such a way that the President would, notwithstanding serious doubts as to the compatibility of the Åland law in question with EU law, not prevent the law from entering into force which would eventually open the way to the CJEU. The introduction of such an arrangement, whereby it would no longer be the national authorities that decide on the compatibility of Åland law with EU law, but the CJEU, which is designated to do so, would certainly be conducive to respecting Åland's (legislative) autonomy.

5.6 *Strengthening the Principle of Subsidiarity*

As shown above, the principle of subsidiarity is of particular importance in primary law. In particular, the European Parliament's proposals to amend the Treaty in 2023 – following the Conference on the Future of the European Union – aim to clarify and strengthen the provisions on the principle of subsidiarity by amending the Treaty.[114] Firstly, the rules on subsidiarity would be incorporated into the TFEU. If a national parliament or parliamentary chamber considers a draft to be incompatible with the principle of subsidiarity, the deadline for a reasoned opinion will be extended from six to twelve weeks. The new text also requires the opinion of regional parliaments with legislative powers to be included in the reasoned opinion if regional exclusive competences

113 Cf. CJEU, C-432/05, ECLI:EU:C:2007:163, judgment, 13 March 2007 – Unibet.

114 European Parliament, Proposals of the European Parliament for the amendment of the Treaties, P9_TA(2023)0427.

could be affected (cf. Article 299f). Up to now, the national parliaments have been free to decide whether to consult the regional parliaments with legislative powers (cf. Article 6 para. 1 sentence 2 Subsidiarity Protocol). If the relevant quorum of opinions is reached and the Commission decides to maintain a proposal, it must provide a reasoned opinion, justifying why it considers the proposal to be in compliance with the principle of subsidiarity (see Article 299h para. 3 subpara. 1). According to Article 299b, the European Commission should also be obliged to conduct widely consultations before proposing a legislative act. According to the draft, "the regional and local dimension of the action envisaged" shall be taken into account where appropriate. In its amendments, the Parliament also proposes that the corresponding draft legislative acts of the various institutions should also be forwarded to the regional parliaments with legislative powers (see Article 299d). However, the Parliament's proposals do not provide for the right of regional parliaments with legislative powers to bring an action before the CJEU on grounds of infringement of the principle of subsidiarity (cf. Article 299i). Finally, Article 299j provides for the Commission to submit an annual report on the application of Article 5 TFEU to the regional parliaments with legislative powers. All these proposals can contribute to achieving the stronger institutional involvement in the political process, which is also called for in the CALRE resolutions.[115]

6 Åland's Special Status and the Common Security and Defence Policy of the EU

In the course of Finland's accession to NATO, issues relating to the special (demilitarised and neutralised) status of the Åland Islands have once again come to the fore. While these matters have already been discussed in detail in other publications,[116] including in the present volume,[117] it should be recalled that the current situation, in particular Russia's unprovoked and illegal invasion of Ukraine, raises certain questions for the security of the Baltic Sea Region, which may also become relevant within the institutional structures of the Union's Common Security and Defence Policy (CSDP), not least against the background of the mutual assistance clause in Article 42 para. 7 TEU[118] but also the other provisions of that chapter. Although the main focus in the

115 Oviedo Document on Regional Legislative Assemblies in the European Union (2022), available at: https://www.calrenet.eu/wp-content/uploads/2022/10/20221007_Document_of_Oviedo.pdf.

116 E.g. Hofmann, Malkmus and Heger, *supra* note 1, para. 41 et seq., including the cited works.

117 See the chapter on Military service and NATO membership by Gun-Mari Lindholm.

118 On this provision in detail, see T. Ramopoulos, Article 42 TEU, in M. Kellerbauer et al. (eds), *supra* note 22, pp. 281 et seq.

defence context remains on NATO and even if, strictly speaking, such issues do not affect the *autonomous* status of the Islands, some brief remarks on the specificities of CSDP should be made due to its current importance.[119]

First, it should be recalled that the Union's CSDP is characterized, to a large extent, by respect for "the specific character of the security and defence policy of certain Member States" (Article 42 para. 2 subpara. 2 TEU).[120] This provision, which is commonly referred to as the 'Irish clause', stipulates a principle of "non-encroachment"[121] and is considered to address the situation of Member States, which have traditionally remained neutral in these matters. With regard to the present issue, it should be noted that the legal literature, when discussing Finland, mainly refers to its (former) policy of non-alignment,[122] but there is no reason to assume that "the specific character of the security and defence policy of certain Member States" (Article 42 para. 2 subpara. 2 TEU) would not equally include Åland's well-established status under international law, which has shaped Finland's defence policies for more than 100 years. It could even be argued that this clause continues to fulfil an independent function after Finland's NATO accession, given the extent to which EU member states mandate autonomous missions,[123] but also given current considerations of increased integration in CSDP matters. In this context, the consequences for Åland's special status, which is based on international obligations[124] that predate the EU founding treaties (cf. Article 351 TFEU),[125] must be carefully considered. Since Article 351 TFEU also applies by analogy to norms of customary international law,[126] Åland's status enjoys additional protection, should there

119 Hofmann, Malkmus and Heger, *supra* note 1, para. 51 et seq.

120 Cf. Ramopoulos, *supra* note 118, para. 10. In general, on this policy field, see J. Wouters et al., *The Law of the EU External Relations* (Oxford, OUP, 3rd edn., 2021), pp. 382 et seq.

121 Ramopoulos, *supra* note 118, para. 10. On the previously mentioned clause in the context of the Maastricht Treaty, see L. Hannikainen, The Continued Validity of the Dernilitarised and Neutralised Status of the Åland Islands, 54 *Zeitschrift für ausländisches öffentliches Recht und Völkerrecht* (1994), p. 645.

122 E.g., Ramopoulos, *supra* note 118, para. 10; H.-J. Cremer, Art. 42 EUV, in C. Calliess and M. Ruffert (eds), *supra* note 33, para. 14; W. Kaufmann-Bühler, Art. 42 EUV, in E. Grabitz et al. (eds), *Das Recht der Europäischen Union* (C.H. Beck, Munich, supplement 79, Mai 2023), para. 29.

123 Cf. Council of the EU, Press Release, 19 February 2024, Security and freedom of navigation in the Red Sea: Council launches EUNAVFOR ASPIDES, https://www.consilium.europa.eu/en/press/press-releases/2024/02/19/security-and-freedom-of-navigation-in-the-red-sea-council-launches-new-eu-defensive-operation/.

124 *Supra* note 2.

125 On the predecessor provision in the present context, cf. Hannikainen, *supra* note 121, pp. 647–8. More generally on this provision, see M. Kellerbauer and M. Klamert, Article 351 TFEU, in M. Kellerbauer et al. (eds), *supra* note 22, pp. 2065 *et seq.*

126 K. Schmalenbach, Art. 351 AEUV, in C. Calliess and M. Ruffert (eds), *supra* note 33, para. 4.

be future considerations to conduct certain manoeuvres or operations in the Baltic Sea.

Second, it should be borne in mind that the decision-making process under the CSDP framework requires unanimity.[127] This means that in the relevant fora (i.e. the European Council) Finland would have to vote, also by virtue of its obligations under international law, in a way that respects the status of Åland. Moreover, like Finland, the other parties to the 1921 Åland Convention[128] that are also members of the EU, such as Estonia, France, Germany, Latvia, Poland, and Sweden, would be obliged under international law to exercise their voting rights in the Council on security and defence issues in a way that preserves the demilitarised and neutralised status of Åland.

7 Concluding Remarks

As the foregoing discussion has shown, there are a number of significant modifications within the framework of Union law that ensure the protection of the special legal status of the Åland Islands. The most important of these were explicitly codified in the course of Finland's accession to the EU through the Åland Protocol, which has primary law status, e.g. with regard to the right to domicile and freedom of establishment, but also with regard to certain tax concessions. Nevertheless, it has been argued that even under the more general principles of Union law, there is some room for accommodating Åland's autonomy, as it has developed into customary international law, within the Union's legal system. This concerns, among other things, the principles enshrined in Articles 4 para. 2 and 5 para. 3 TEU. In addition, a number of areas could be identified, such as State aid law or the regulation of cross-border audiovisual media, as well as the institutional involvement of the regions, in which more flexibility for Åland's autonomous affairs could be provided. All these matters require a careful balance between the special international status of the Islands and the legitimate concerns of Union policies.

127 Articles 31 para. 1, 42 para. 2 subpara. 1 and para. 4 TEU. Cf. Ramopoulos, *supra* note 118, para. 11–3; Wouters, *supra* note 120, p. 383. With reference to the norms applicable under the Maastricht Treaty, see Hannikainen, *supra* note 121, p. 645.

128 *Supra* note 2.

CHAPTER 15

Autonomy Representation in the European Parliament, Council and Commission

Julia Lindholm and Elisabeth F. Rasmussen

1 The Faroe Islands and the EU – an Overview

Located where the North Atlantic meets the Arctic, the Faroe Islands are one of the European Union's closest neighbours in Northern Europe. The Faroe Islands are a part of Europe, not only geographically, but also due to shared European history, linguistic, and cultural heritage and common European values of freedom, democracy, respect for human rights, and the rule of law.

The Faroe Islands lie at the centre of one of the world's most productive fisheries regions and govern a maritime area of 274,000 km^2 with a continental shelf area of 301,000 km^2.

The Faroe Islands are a self-governing country within the Danish Realm with exclusive competence to legislate and govern independently in a wide range of areas. These include taxation, conservation and management of living marine resources, protection of the environment, sub-surface resources, domestic and international trade, industry, energy, transport, communications, social security, culture, education and research.

Faroese autonomy in foreign relations is stipulated by a treaty between the Faroe Islands and Denmark. The Foreign Policy Act gives full powers to the Government of the Faroe Islands to negotiate and conclude agreements under international law on behalf of the Kingdom of Denmark where such agreements relate solely to matters which have been fully transferred to the Faroese Government.

1.1 *Formal Faroe Islands-EU Relations*

With extensive autonomy under the sovereignty of the Kingdom of Denmark, the Faroe Islands decided not to become a part of the European Communities when Denmark joined in 1973. As such, the Treaties do not apply to the Faroe Islands (TFEU Article 355, 5 (a)).

Consequently, the Faroe Islands are a third country in relation to the EU and EU legislation is therefore not directly applicable to the Faroe Islands.

However, Faroese legislation is highly influenced by legislation in Denmark, other Nordic countries and the EU. EU standards are applicable in several key areas in the Faroe Islands, e.g. banking, finance and company law, making business cooperation between the actors in the Faroe Islands and the EU effortless in most areas.

1.2 *Bilateral Agreements*

Formal relations between the Faroe Islands and the EU are currently based on three separate bilateral agreements dealing with trade in goods, fisheries and scientific and technological cooperation.

1.2.1 Trade

The EU is the Faroe Islands' largest trading partner by far. The Faroe Islands' trade relations with the EU are governed by the EU-Faroe Islands Free Trade Agreement. The current Agreement is a first-generation agreement which entered into force in 1997, focusing on tariff liberalisation for goods and was later supplemented with a Protocol on Veterinary Matters. The Joint Committee established by the Agreement is responsible for ensuring the proper implementation of the Agreement and meets regularly to consider relevant issues. Even though the provisions of the Trade Agreement stipulate that the Joint Committee meets annually, the activity varies.

The free trade agreement covers trade in goods and is the foundation for solid and long-standing bilateral trade relations. In 2022, around 45 per cent of Faroese exports went to the EU, and around 70% of the imports to the Faroe Islands originated from the EU.

1.2.2 Scientific and Technological Cooperation

The Faroe Islands have been associated to the EU's programme on Research and Innovation since 2010, and in recent years the Faroe Islands have had a high overall success rate.[1]

Negotiations for the association of the Faroe Islands to Horizon Europe were concluded in 2021 and on 24 May, 2022 the agreement of the participation of the Faroe Islands to EU programmes, with a specific protocol on its association

1 European Commission. "Faroe Islands Joins Horizon Europe Research and Innovation Programme – European Commission." < https://research-and-innovation.ec.europa.eu/news/all-research-and-innovation-news/faroe-islands-joins-horizon-europe-research-and-innovation-programme-2022-05-24_en-islands-joins-horizon-europe-research-and-innovation-programme-2022-05-24_en> Accessed 28 February. 2024.

to Horizon Europe, was signed and entered into application. This association brings value for the research community in the Faroe Islands and is a major pillar of the bilateral relations between the Faroe Islands and the EU.[2]

1.2.3 Fisheries

The Agreement on Fisheries between the EU and the Faroe Islands, which came into effect in 1980, provides a framework for annual consultations between the EU and the Faroe Islands on the exchange of fishing opportunities and reciprocal fishing access in each other's waters.

1.3 *Lack of Overall Framework for Faroe Islands-EU Relations*

Unlike the Faroe Islands' closest neighbours in the European Arctic region, Iceland and Norway, the Faroe Islands are not a part of the EEA Agreement, nor does it have the status of Overseas Countries and Territories, as Greenland.

As a result, the level of awareness and knowledge about the Faroe Islands in the EU system is limited. As an important step towards enhanced cooperation, the Faroe Islands and the EU have engaged in discussions on a non-binding overall framework for the cooperation.

1.4 *Future Relations and Enhanced Cooperation*

The Government of the Faroe Islands, supported by the Government of Denmark, is committed to enhance the relations between the Faroe Islands and the European Union. The aim is to develop a joint framework for the existing cooperation and a platform for the future enhancement of bilateral relations.

Additional steps towards closer bilateral relations will be to advance cooperation on education, people-to-people, culture and youth. Another important element will be to advance collaboration in new areas such as digitalisation, telecommunication, sustainable development, maritime services, tourism, and green energy.

1.5 *Inclusion of the Faroe Islands in EU Policies*

The Mission of the Faroe Islands to the EU has these past years facilitated enhanced cooperation and information sharing about the Faroe Islands in

2 European Commission. "International Cooperation with the Faroe Islands in Research and Innovation." <www.research-And-Innovation.ec.europa.eu, 29 Nov. 2023, research-and-innovation.ec.europa.eu/strategy/strategy-2020-2024/europe-world/international-cooperation/association-horizon-europe/faroe-islands_en> Accessed 28 February 2024.

the EU institutions. Relations between the Faroe Islands and the EU are mentioned in the EU Arctic Policy[3] and the Council Conclusions.[4]

1.6 *Mission of the Faroe Islands to the European Union*

The Faroe Islands have diplomatic representations in Brussels, Reykjavík, London, Moscow, Beijing and Tel Aviv, as well as a Representation in Copenhagen. The Representations in Brussels, London, Reykjavík, Moscow, Beijing and Tel Aviv are established in cooperation with the Danish Ministry of Foreign Affairs, thus granting diplomatic status to the Faroese Heads of Representations.

The Faroese heads of Representations are the formal representatives of the government in relation to the authorities of the host countries/international organisations and local institutions.

The Representations keep abreast of matters of interest to the Faroe Islands. A natural part of their activities is working to promote the Faroe Islands and to show what the country has to offer, both in terms of the main industries, as well as in other fields that make the Faroe Islands an interesting partner. This includes highlighting the talent and diversity of Faroese arts and culture – music, visual art, literature, design, cuisine and other aspects of Faroese creativity.

1.6.1 Main Tasks of the Mission

The role of the Mission in Brussels is to facilitate and enhance cooperation, contacts and the exchange of information between the Faroe Islands and the EU institutions and EU member states in all areas of mutual interest. These relate both to existing formal bilateral agreements in trade, fisheries and participation in EU programmes (currently, Horizon Europe), as well as to potential new areas of cooperation. An important task is to highlight what the Faroe Islands have to offer as one of the EU's closest northern European neighbours at the crossroads of the North Atlantic and Arctic regions.

---

3 European Commission. "Joint Communication To The European Parliament, The Council, The European Economic And Social Committee And The Committee Of The Regions". 13 October 2021.

4 European Council. "Council conclusions on a homogeneous extended single market and EU relations with Non-EU Western European countries and with the Faroe Islands", 21 June 2022. https://www.consilium.europa.eu/en/press/press-releases/2022/06/21/council-conclusions-on-a-homogeneous-extended-single-market-and-eu-relations-with-non-eu-western-european-countries-and-with-the-faroe-islands/. Accessed 28 February 2024.

The Mission provides general information and further contacts in all aspects of Faroese society, from government and business to research, education, culture and tourism, as well as assisting Faroe Islanders with advice, information and contacts in the EU system.

2 The Åland Islands: Background and Legal Framework

Åland joined the EU in 1994 together with Finland, Sweden and Austria. The Legislative Assembly's decision was preceded by two referendums, one in Finland and one in Åland. The result of the negotiations meant that the international guarantees for the preservation of the national identity, language, culture and local customs of the Åland population became part of the EU's primary law and are thus not affected by the Union's legal systems. In addition, Åland received third-country status in terms of the tax union in order to be able to maintain tax-free status on communications to and from Åland.[5]

The Autonomy Act, Åland's constitution, was changed so that a special EU chapter was introduced in order to guarantee that the Åland Parliament's legislative power is taken into account in the internal Finnish preparation of EU matters.[6] The Autonomy Act stipulates that the Åland Parliament must approve all international treaties that affect Åland's legislative jurisdiction, otherwise Åland will be outside the agreement's scope of application. With the Åland Parliament (sv. *Lagtinget*) delegating parts of its legislative power to EU institutions, like the Finnish Parliament, demands were raised from the Åland side to obtain a seat in the EU Parliament.

With regard to international affairs, the Åland Autonomy Act stipulates that foreign affairs are a competence of the Parliament of Finland. From the Åland side, it has been argued that relations with the EU are not foreign policy because the Åland Parliament has delegated legislative powers to the EU's institutions within domestic policy fields. This view has not been accepted in the constitutional control of Åland laws carried out by the Supreme Court in Finland. However, there are a few interesting exemptions in the Åland Autonomy Act.

Firstly, if Finland enters into an international agreement containing provisions that fall within the Åland area of competence, approval by the Parliament of Åland is required for the agreement to come into force and for Åland to be

5 The Åland Protocol, Fördrag om Finlands, Sveriges och Österrikes anslutning till EU 1994.

6 Autonomy Act, 9a Kap.

included in the scope of application. About twenty such requests for approval are annually submitted to the Parliament of Åland.

Secondly, Åland can hold membership in international organisations such as the Nordic Council, the Baltic Sea Parliamentary Conference, and the EU Committee of Regions.

Thirdly, even if the Åland Autonomy Act excludes foreign affairs from the region's competence, the chapter on national EU coordination stipulates that Åland shall always be consulted when Finland is drafting its national position, have the right of direct correspondence with the European Commission, and for the Government of Åland's position to be stated at the Council of Ministers if the matter falls within the region's legal competence or if it is of specific interest for the region. This last part allows the Government of Åland to take part in the national decision-making in almost all policy areas, but given the limited size of the Åland public administration, strict prioritisation must be made.

If Finland and Åland have different opinions, Åland's position must be included when the Finnish position is presented to the EU institutions. With regard to the Council, when the position is presented at the ambassadorial level this opposing position is normally presented orally, and at the ministerial level in written form.

The Åland Parliament can also give the Finnish Parliament a reasoned opinion on a legislative act from the EU if it is compatible with the principle of subsidiarity and if the matter falls under Åland's jurisdiction.

2.1 *Åland's Representative in Brussels*

In order to handle the practical application of Åland's membership in the EU, Åland has its own representative, a Minister Counsellor on Åland matters. The representative is placed at Finland's permanent EU representation in Brussels and formally employed by the Finnish Ministry of Foreign Affairs. The representative is also assisted by two trainees a year. These posts are financed by the Åland Government.

The counsellor's primary tasks are to convey knowledge and information about the work at the EU's institutions and to pursue the Åland Government's affairs and interests in accordance with given mandates.

In concrete terms, the counsellor monitors matters during the legislative process in Brussels that are of interest to the Åland Government and passes on the information to relevant parties. The counsellor also works actively to present Åland's positions to the EU's institutions already during the preparation period. The counsellor cooperates closely with other officials at the Finnish permanent representation who in their respective areas can monitor matters pertinent to Åland within the Commission and the Council. An intern also works at the Åland office thus strengthening the coverage of Åland issues.

The counsellor is expected to identify, together with the responsible official at the respective department of the Åland Government, legislative proposals that may be of interest to Åland. This is done according to selection methods based on legislative competence, present Åland legislation in the area, and any experience from previous initiatives in the area.

The counsellor's work can be divided into two main assignments: to passively monitor a case, and to conduct active advocacy work. Passive monitoring basically means monitoring the working group meetings held within the Council regarding a certain matter. After the meeting, a report is written and sent to the responsible minister and civil servants in the Åland administration. The objective is for the Åland Government to better prepare for upcoming legislative change.

Active advocacy work is key to enabling the Åland administration to identify the relevance of a policy proposal before the commission's proposal is published. When an EU proposal is still at the draft stage within the Commission services, the small scale of the Åland administration can mean swift positioning. The initial objective is to ensure that the Commission's proposal is in line with the priority of the Åland Government. After that, the Åland Government's position needs to be formally formulated and anchored in the Finnish national preparatory process. After the Commission's proposal for legislation has been adopted, the legislative process needs to be monitored very closely. Åland should ensure visibility in the negotiations and take an active role in the process in which the positions of the Council and the European Parliament are developed.

The first assignment, to passively monitor a case, can be largely carried out both by the counsellor and by the trainee. The latter assignment, to conduct active advocacy work, requires long-term networking and responsiveness to changes in the legislative drafting process, and should mainly be carried out by the counsellor. Active advocacy work requires resources with uncertain results but should be prioritised regarding matters of particular importance to Åland, and where the Åland position is not reflected in the Finnish national position. During the months when a legislative matter requires active lobbying, the workload is higher for the counsellor in Brussels and for the responsible official within the Åland Government. The priority is however to ensure that the Åland position is taken into account in the Finnish national position.

2.2 *The Practical Possibility for Åland to Participate in the Finnish National Process*

The Finnish Government's EU Affairs Department has a coordinating role in EU affairs and, as such, is central in ensuring that Åland's possibilities for participation and influence in EU affairs are met. It is essential that, when preparing national positions, the significance of a case for Åland is assessed and that Åland's viewpoint is clarified.

The Åland Government's external policy unit is responsible for ensuring that the system for coordinating EU affairs works and that the Åland Government's EU policy is consistent. The external policy unit prepares matters concerning amendments to the EU treaty and international agreements, as well as horizontal and institutional issues that are central to the autonomy. The relevant department in the Åland Government's general administration carries out ongoing processing of EU matters within their particular policy field.

Finland's permanent representation to the EU in Brussels participates in the preparation of EU matters based on directives from the national government. The close cooperation with the state administration in Helsinki enables a functional division of labour between the representation and the ministries in Helsinki.

It has been established that the coordination in the Finnish Government of matters prioritised by the Åland Government, and Åland's opportunities to influence EU issues, can be improved without legislative changes by improving routines and working methods.[7]

The fundamental step is that the Åland position and the importance of the case for Åland is included in the material submitted by the national government to the Finnish Parliament. The Åland position is a permanent headline in the material but whether the content is correctly and fully presented varies greatly. An easy solution would be to insert a responsibility to communicate with the Åland Government in the national instructions relating to the handling of EU matters.

The biggest practical obstacle to this is language. The knowledge of Swedish within the Finnish state administration is limited, even though the Autonomy Act stipulates that the official language is Swedish in all contacts between the governments of Finland and Åland. The Åland Government has formally both insight and inclusion in the national preparation of EU matters but given that the preparation takes place in Finnish and that the Åland Government's

7 Ålands Lagting, Meddelande 1/2018–2019, Landskapsregeringens externpolitik (Mariehamn, 2019) 3.1.7.

administration works exclusively in Swedish, the respective administrations cannot take in and understand each other's information and views. Informal structures need to be identified to bridge the administrative units' ability to fulfil the statutory requirement that Åland must be involved in the preparation of EU matters.

The unit for information management at the Prime Minister's Office's EU affairs department is responsible for the distribution of EU documents and the maintenance and development of the IT-system (EUTORI) that supports the national EU preparation. As the documents are not translated into Swedish, the Åland Government does not have the opportunity to utilise this information. The Åland Government should, to a greater extent than today, be offered the opportunity to access negotiation documents in English through the Council's internal information-sharing tool, Delegates Portal. Adopted EU proposals and later legal texts are distributed in all official EU languages. The documents distributed from the Council during negotiations are not public and normally only in English, which means that the Åland Government can make use of the information. However, Finnish positions or briefing material are distributed only in Finnish. Given the short deadlines, translations to Swedish are not done and the Åland Government's right to take part in the process and provide possible divergent positions is not respected.

The Åland Government has the right to be heard in the EU Committee of Ministers in the Finnish Government when a matter falls within the jurisdiction of the Åland Parliament or if it is of particular interest to Åland. The possibility for the Åland Government to raise its position in EU matters regarding other issues than those of a constitutional type should be ensured. As a suggestion, an informal routine could be established where the Åland Government is given access to the briefing material[8] that is distributed before the meetings of the EU Ministerial Committee of the Finnish Government. A similar, informal, proactive system can also be considered for the Finnish Parliament's Committee for EU Affairs.

Before the EU's Council of Ministers meetings, Finland compiles a document containing relevant information in the policy areas. This document does not currently come to the attention of the Åland Government. To distribute the document to Åland would be an efficient way to guarantee the Åland Government a possibility to attach its positions, when necessary, in an initial stage.

8 The greatest challenge is to get the material translated to Swedish or English. *Ibid.* 3.1.7.

Officials at the ministries, including the ministers' special advisers, have been perceived by the Åland Government to be uncertain about the right to share information regarding the preparation of the national position, and especially to share the national briefing documents with the Åland Government. A structural problem is that the Åland position is seen as a divergent element and not as an extra set of arguments when the two administrations have the same position.

The uncertainty to share information should be remedied by informing officials in Finland that the Åland administration must be informed about the preparation of EU matters according to the Autonomy Act. To identify already existing structures as efficient ways to assure the Åland Government's participation in the preparatory process is the key. Both administrations are, in the context of the EU, small, and especially the Åland administration will not benefit from a burdensome additional system. Both administrations have a legal obligation to cooperate, but the language barrier is a significant problem. Until a satisfactory solution is found, the identification of informal ways of sharing information is a good first step to both building trust and ensuring Åland's inclusion in the process.

2.3 *Right to Participate in the Meetings of the EU Institutions*

Åland has the right to participate in the meetings of the Council of Ministers as part of Finland's delegation. As a result of the COVID-19 pandemic, restrictions on meeting participation in the council were adopted. For physical working group meetings, national delegations were limited to one or two people, as well as for video conferencing at working group level. In the Committee of Permanent Representatives (Coreper), the rule was two people per member country, which meant the ambassador and an expert. This meant that Åland did not have access to meetings in the Council, neither at working group level nor Coreper.

The Åland Government and the Prime Minister's Office's EU Affairs Department must ensure that Åland's positions are anchored in the national preparation, as physical presence for Åland at meetings cannot be guaranteed at all times.

Today, all the pandemic restrictions are abolished and a minister from the Åland Government, if needed, and the Åland Minister Counsellor, can take part in Council meetings when matters affecting Åland are processed. Generally, the cooperation between the Finnish representation and the Minister Counsellor works very well and the Åland interests are considered when noted.

3 Conclusion and Recommendations

Åland's right to participate in the preparation of Finland's national positions on EU matters, in which Åland's position must also be included, seems to be legally satisfied in the Autonomy Act. However, in reality, the implementation leaves a lot to be desired, mainly due to the fact that current practice, the different preparatory languages, and the lack of informal structures for exchange of information mean that the Åland Government's positions are rarely taken into account as intended in the Autonomy Act. Many of the practical difficulties could be solved with mutual understanding between the administrations in Helsinki and in Mariehamn, and in the creation of a structure that would allow the Åland position be presented and considered in Brussels.

Small states can strengthen their status by prioritising international relations.[9] Diplomatic protocol is formalised, an aspect that can be beneficial for small jurisdictions since their status is the same regardless of size. The Åland administration should therefore prioritise international relations beyond the scope of the EU in other to strengthen the international perception of Åland as a counterpart to the Finnish administration.

Small administrations can organise themselves in such a way that they do not need to rely on formal structures and networks. To some extent, this is already the case in Finland's advisory system with regard to Åland. If the central organisational structure can be altered so that policy claims – in this case sensitivity for the autonomous administration and its legal framework – are institutionalised within the organisation, it could benefit the Government of Åland. Likewise, with better knowledge of how the Finnish central administration functions and informal networks of both political and non-political advisers, the Government of Åland can better utilise its right to take part in the EU decision-making process within the Finnish administration.

9 Lindholm, A qualitative study of political room for manoeuvre in sub-state governance system (2023), Hertie School of Governance.

CHAPTER 16

Access to and Relevant International Issues at the Council of Europe and the Organisation of Security and Co-operation in Europe

Krzysztof Drzewicki

1 Introduction

The question of strengthening the Åland Islands' autonomy is examined in the present section with regard to the Council of Europe (CoE) and Organisation of Security and Co-operation in Europe (OSCE). It will however be limited to certain selected instruments within both international organisations because their other arrangements are expected to be examined by other contributors to the present book. Importantly, the status and powers of both organisations are essentially different and need to be taken into consideration in the course of examining their potential for the Åland Islands.[1] Within the limits of the present paper it is discussed how contributions can be made to the longer-term strengthening of the Åland Islands' autonomy. Åland's present status and system of governance is taken as a point of departure for considering a number of possible options for achieving this objective.[2]

It should be kept in mind that the final decision of the Council of the League of Nations which declared in operative paragraph 1 that "The sovereignty of the Aaland Islands is recognised to belong to Finland" was followed by a number of guarantees for the protection of the islanders, aimed especially at the preservation of the Swedish language in schools, other establishments and

---

1 *See* more on those differences K. Drzewicki, 'European Systems for the Promotion and Protection of Human Rights', in C. Krause and M. Scheinin (eds.), *International Protection of Human Rights: A Textbook* (Åbo Akademi University, Institute for Human Rights, Turku/Åbo, 2009) pp. 365–388.

2 *See Decision of the Council of the League of Nations on the Åland Islands Including Sweden's Protest*, 1921, League of Nations Official Journal, September 1921, No. 697. IV. Minutes of the Fourteenth Meeting of the Council, June 24th. *See* also on the Autonomy Law of 7th May, 1920 with amendments, in: B. Lindström and G. Lindholm, *The Future Conditions for the Åland Autonomy. A Study of the Legal and Political Development of Åland's Self-Determination* (The Report Produced on Behalf of and Funded by Olof M. Jansson's Foundation for the Promotion of Historical Research on Åland, 2021) pp. 1–93.

DOI:10.1163/9789004691117_018

modalities (Paras. 2–3). The representative of Sweden (M. Branting) declared that his government was "ready loyally to recognise that the decision of the Council has the force given to it by the Covenant". Nevertheless, he made a statement whereby he expressed a "feeling of profound disappointment" about the resolution. He further explained that:

> Sweden was not influenced by the desire to increase her territory. She only wished to support noble and just aspirations and to defend the right of an absolutely homogenous island population to reunite itself to its mother-country, from which it had been detached by force, but to which it is still united by the ties of a common origin, a common history, and a common national spirit.[3]

The new guarantees for autonomy were included in the treaty between Finland and Sweden regarding the guarantees, and were to be amended to the Law of 7 May 1920 on the autonomy of the Åland Islands, and signed on 27 June 1921 with numerous amendments.[4] The status of the islands is also regulated by the Finnish Constitution of 2000. It is against the above legal background and its subsequent developments that specific arrangements can be suggested and examined.

2 The Council of Europe

The Council of Europe is a regional organisation for European co-operation set up in 1949 by ten democracies. Its aim is to achieve a greater unity between its members for safeguarding and realising the ideals and principles which are their common heritage and the true source of individual freedom, political liberty and the rule of law, principles which form the basis of all genuine democracy (fr. *démocratie véritable*).[5] The Council has become a 'club for democratic membership', thus its statute permits only the admission of countries

---

3 *Ibid.*

4 B. Arp, *International Norms and Standards for the Protection of National Minorities. Bilateral and Multilateral Texts with Commentary* (Martinus Nijhoff Publishers, Leiden-Boston, 2008) pp. 83–84. On the Åland Autonomy model see M. Suksi, 'What Can We Learn From the Åland Islands Case?' in D. Thürer and Z. Kędzia (eds.), *Managing Diversity. Protection of Minorities in International Law* (Zurich: Schultens, 2009) pp. 147–173.

5 *The Statute of the Council of Europe*, London, 5.V.1949 (*See* Para. 3 of the Preamble and Articles 1–2) in: <www.coe.int/en/web/conventions>, visited on 10 July 2023.

which constitute representative and pluralist democracies, accept the principles of the rule of law and of the enjoyment by all persons within their jurisdiction of human rights and fundamental freedoms.[6] The Council's organs are the Committee of Ministers, with its secretariat and two assemblies, the Parliamentary Assembly, and the Congress of Local and Regional Authorities (CLRA).

From amongst the numerous arrangements which may potentially exert a meaningful impact on the status of the Åland Islands' autonomy, only a couple of them are of interest when considering possible effective reforms. Other arrangements may formally be useful for pursuing different reform proposals but for a number of reasons they do not offer conducive prospects. This can be illustrated by considering examples from the Parliamentary Assembly and the Committee of Ministers. Access to both these bodies appears to be formalised, and without the consent of the Finnish parliament and government no successful actions of the Åland administration could be undertaken. There is yet another group of bodies which are more openly accessible and of which the following options are the most convenient for examination.

2.1 *The European Charter of Local Self-Government and the Congress of Local and Regional Authorities*

Issues of local self-government were absent at the beginning of the activities of the Council of Europe but in the course of time these gained ground. Considering local authorities as one of the main foundations of democratic systems, the Council adopted a treaty – the European Charter of Local Self-Government, on 15 October 1985, supplemented by the Additional Protocol to the European Charter of Local Self-Government on the right to participate in the affairs of a local authority (CETS No. 207).[7] For monitoring the application of the European Charter and its Additional Protocol, two bodies were made responsible: the Congress of Local and Regional Authorities (CLRA), and the Committee on the Honouring of Obligations and Commitments by Member States of the European Charter of Local Self-Government (Monitoring Committee).

6 *Ibid.* Articles 3 and 8 of the CoE's statute do not mention democracy as a membership requirement explicitly but it is construed implicitly in a presumptive way.

7 *European Treaty Series* No. 122. The Charter has been in force since 1988 and the Additional Protocol since 2012 (Council of Europe Treaty Series No. 207). The Charter is often described as "the only international treaty in the field of local self-government" – *see State of Democracy, Human Rights and the Rule of Law. Report of the Secretary General of the Council of Europe*, Strasbourg, 2023 p. 73.

The Congress was born out of the earlier committee of the Consultative (now Parliamentary) Assembly of the CoE, which subsequently became the Conference of Local and Regional Authorities. The first CoE's Summit of Heads of State and Government (Vienna 1994) decided "to approve the principle of creating a consultative organ genuinely representing both local and regional authorities in Europe".[8] In this way the CoE recognised local democracy as a cornerstone of the democratic system. Each member state of the Council has the right to the same number of representatives and substitutes in Congress as it has in the Parliamentary Assembly. Finland and Sweden have five seats each in both assemblies. They are appointed for a period of five years. The Congress is composed of two chambers: the Chamber of Local Authorities and the Chamber of Regions.[9]

The Monitoring Committee regularly undertakes, among other things, a general, country-by-country, monitoring mission to each member state approximately once every five years, examining specific issues related to local and regional democracy, organising fact-finding missions, and then drafts its reports and recommendations on the state of local and regional democracy. In addition, the Group of Independent Experts on the European Charter of Local Self-Government (GIE) was established by the Congress in 2017. It brings together competent experts in legal, political or financial fields, who are specialised in issues of local and regional democracy. The group helps the three statutory committees to carry out their responsibilities under the statute, particularly in drafting reports on the situation of local and regional democracy in the states which are subject to a follow-up to the application of the Charter, as well as the drafting general reports on the working themes of the three committees.[10] In this sense, the primary task of the group is to provide legal assistance to the Congress's political mission.

---

8 *Council of Europe Summit. Vienna Declaration* (Vienna, 9 October 1993).*The Third Summit of Heads of State and Government. Plan of Action*(Warsaw, 17 May 2005) decided in para. 4 to continue to promote localdemocracy and decentralisation.

9 *See* Art. 1–5 of the Appendix to *Statutory Resolution CM/Res(2020)1relating to the Congress Local and Regional Authorities of the Council ofEurope and the revised Charter appended thereto (Adopted by theCommittee of Ministers on 15 January 2020 at the 1364th meeting of theMinisters' Deputies)*.

10 *See* Art. 1–14 of *the Revised Statute of the Group of Independent Experts on the European Charter of Local self-Government* (2017). *Document adopted by the Bureau of the Congress on 17 October 2017, CG/GIE(2017)01final.* As expert members from Finland and Sweden the Secretary General of the Congress appointed, respectively, Professors Markku Suksi and Anders Lidström.

All these organisational and functional arrangements for local self-government probably create the most conducive environment for attempts at reforming the Åland Islands' autonomy. This has been demonstrated by the report concerning the third monitoring visit to Finland by the Monitoring Committee since the ratification of the European Charter.[11] Importantly, as well as describing the existing state of implementation of the Charter, the report also encouraged Finland within the on-going reforms to consider extending the scope of responsibilities, to opt, in the framework of regional reform, for the creation of effectively autonomous regions, to grant these new regions a legislative basis, and to create a special status for the capital city Helsinki and its metropolitan area.

This report devoted a separate subsection (3.4: Paras. 71–78) to the Government of Åland, noting the main features of its status based upon the decision of the Council of the League of Nations of June 1921, Articles 75 and 120 of the Finnish Constitution, and the Act on the Autonomy of the Åland Islands in its version of 1993. The report commented further on the structural and functional dimensions of the autonomy. Although there were concerns on the part of the Government of Åland about the impact of the then on-going revisions, the region had its own assurance, of internationally and constitutionally guaranteed, autonomous status. The report by GIE has admitted that the Government of Åland does "not view the current level of autonomy as a *status quo*, since the level of autonomy is constantly changing, which can be seen from the ongoing revision of the Autonomy Act".[12]

It may then be safely concluded that a number of further reform proposals concerning the Åland autonomy could be channelled through the accessible and promising mechanisms of consultation offered by the European Charter of Local Self-Government and the Congress of Local and Regional Authorities.

2.2 *Applicability of Various Other Instruments and Mechanisms*

We should examine moreover whether other available international instruments could be equally successful at reforming the Åland autonomy. Three such arrangements need to be mentioned. The first two are specific treaties adopted within the Council of Europe: The Framework Convention for the Protection of National Minorities (FCNM), and the European Charter for Regional or Minority Languages (ECRML). Both instruments, together with

11 *Congress of Local and Regional Authorities, 32nd Session, Local and regional democracy in Finland, Monitoring Committee, CG32(2017)08final*, 28 March 2017 pp. 20/45.

12 *Ibid.*, pp. 20–21 (Paras. 73–78).

expert committees established by them in areas of their respective competence, can address issues of national minorities and regional or minority languages. Their implementation mechanisms include the opportunity of submitting observations on the part of non-governmental entities. From the perspective of comprehensive reforms of the Åland autonomy, both arrangements appear thus overly focused and narrow. A possible resort to them may be of auxiliary character and scope.

A third option for possible resort is the Council of Europe Commissioner on Human Rights, a body established in 1999 by a resolution of the Committee of Ministers as a sort of international ombud-type of institution, like those set up and developed by the Nordic countries, and which are applied as a model in other countries under the general denomination of extra-judicial means for the protection of human rights. Both the mandate and its practical implementation demonstrate that the commissioner undertakes human rights either as individual country assessments or as thematic issues. The commissioner's reports, conclusions and recommendations regarding Finland did not concern specific aspects of the Åland autonomy.

3 The Organization for Security and Co-operation in Europe

The Organisation (initially Conference – CSCE) for Security and Co-operation in Europe (OSCE) was set up in 1975 as a diplomatic type of regular conference arrangement without treaty basis. Its constitutive document – the Helsinki Final Act – was adopted on 1 August 1975.[13] The OSCE was the very first European arrangement or organisation which built a bridge between East and West as an attempt at ending the Cold War. The Helsinki Final Act was a politically and not legally binding agreement. This practice of undertaking predominantly political commitments has been continued and constitutes a characteristic feature of the organisation. Members of the OSCE, called participating states, grew from the initial 35 participating states in 1975 to 56 in 2008.

The rationale of the OSCE has been firmly embedded in ensuring security and stability in Europe as a comprehensive approach to pan-European

13 For more on the evolution and mandate of the OSCE see A. Bloed (ed.), *The Conference on Security and Co-operation in Europe. Analysis and Basic Documents, 1972–1993* (Dordrecht/Boston/London: Kluwer Academic Publishers, 1993) pp. 92–95; and K. Drzewicki, 'Minority Protection within the OSCE', in D. Thürer and Z. Kędzia (eds.), *supra* note 4, pp. 108–131.

co-operation and security. The mandate of the OSCE has been organised in three main areas or 'baskets', called nowadays 'dimensions' of security: the politico-military dimension, the economic and environmental dimension, and the human dimension, which entails democratic governance, election monitoring, democratic policing, the rule of law, human rights and fundamental freedoms, and humanitarian issues. The fall of communist governance in Eastern and Central Europe saw the actual eruption of human dimension commitments in 1990–1991.

The most extensive and far-reaching catalogue of human dimension commitments ever agreed upon in the CSCE/OSCE was a contribution of the Document of the Copenhagen Meeting of the Conference on the Human Dimension of the CSCE in 1990. It constitutes a sort of charter, which brings together provisions on pluralist democracy, the rule of law and democracy. Its regulations are far broader than those of the European Convention on Human Rights (ECHR) and International Covenant on Civil and Political Rights (ICCPR). The Copenhagen Document is altogether the most extensive and far-reaching catalogue of human dimension commitments ever agreed upon in the OSCE.[14] They were moreover drafted in a clear, precise and detailed language with a relatively small number of limitation clauses (e.g. public order, national security, rights of others, etc.). The OSCE has pioneered a "holistic approach to human rights, which proceeds on the assumption that individual rights are best protected in states which adhere to the rule of law and democratic values and are so constituted as to permit these concepts to flourish".[15]

As far as local democracy is concerned, the Copenhagen Document, though impressive in itself, has been reflected in only a few references dealing with democratic institutions. In Paragraph 26 of the Copenhagen Document the participating states have recognised that:

> vigorous democracy depends on the existence as an integral part of national life of democratic values and practices as well as an extensive

---

14 For more comments on the Copenhagen Document see D. Gomien, 'Human Rights Standard-Setting and the CSCE Conference on the Human Dimension: The Contribution of the Copenhagen Document', in Z. Kędzia, A. Korula, M. Nowak (eds.), *Perspectives of an All-European System of Human Rights Protection. The Role of the Council of Europe, the CSCE, and the European Communities. Proceedings and Recommendations of an International Conference. Poznań, Poland, 8–11 October 1990* (Kehl-Strasbourg-Arlington: N.P. Engel, Publisher, 1991) pp. 93–102.

15 T. Buergental, *International Human Rights in a Nutshell*, Second Edition (St. Paul, Minn.: West Publishing Co., 1995) p. 167.

> range of democratic institutions. They will therefore encourage, facilitate and, where appropriate, support practical co-operative endeavours and the sharing of information, ideas and expertise among themselves and by direct contacts and co-operation between individuals, groups and organizations.

Among several areas in which such activities are expected to be developed the document mentions "local government and decentralization".[16] It is of importance that the establishment and improvement of democratic institutions is envisaged with a wider participation of individuals, groups and organisations.

Another instance of such a modest approach is the Report of the CSCE Meeting of Experts on National Minorities (Geneva, 1991). It is in the context of national minorities that the question of the Åland Islands can also be examined as a part of larger arrangements relating to the autonomy. The Geneva report admitted that the diversity and varying constitutional systems obtained positive results in an appropriate manner, *inter alia*, in such areas as "decentralized or local forms of government".[17]

Not only are these human dimension commitments modestly and cautiously formulated but they also need something more if they are to stimulate a possible initiation and application of the OSCE supervisory mechanisms. To resort to them would namely require local government issues becoming a concern from the perspective of security and maintenance of democratic governance in the OSCE area. One must fairly admit that such aspects are missing in the case of the Åland Islands. Their security situation may serve as a model of stability and as such does not provide any reason for the initiation and application of supervisory mechanisms. There is however an OSCE instrument or arrangement which may be instrumental in this regard.

4 The OSCE High Commissioner on National Minorities

The post of the High Commissioner on National Minorities (HCNM) was established by the 'CSCE Helsinki Document 1992: The Challenges of Change' as a highly autonomous and independent political body working in confidence as

16 See OSCE *Human Dimension Commitments*, 3rd Edition, Vol. 2. *Chronological Compilation*, (Warsaw: OSCE/ODIHR, 2011) pp. 67–68.

17 *Ibid.*, pp. 83–88.

"an instrument of conflict prevention at the earliest possible stage" (Paras. 1–2 and 4 of the mandate).[18] To achieve this end, the High Commissioner is required to provide "early warning" and, as appropriate, "early action" at the earliest possible stage "in regard to tensions involving national minority issues which have not yet developed beyond an early warning stage, but, in the judgement of the High Commissioner, have the potential to develop into a conflict within the OSCE area, affecting peace, stability or relations between participating States, requiring the attention of and action by the Council or the CSO" (Para. 3).[19]

Consequently, the High Commissioner's function is both to identify – and seek early resolution of – ethnic tensions, which may threaten peace and stability. In other words, the High Commissioner's mission is basically twofold: "first, to address and de-escalate tensions before they ignite and, second, to act as a 'tripwire', meaning that he is responsible for alerting the OSCE whenever such tensions threaten to develop to such a level that he cannot alleviate them with the means at his disposal."[20] In other words, the HCNM is expected to contribute to the de-escalation of emerging tensions. One may thus conclude that the position of HCNM was created as an instrument for international security; hence the Commissioner does not become engaged in all minority-related issues but only in those with security aspects or implications.

Within this unique evolution of the High Commissioner's mandate the office has developed a number of instruments which may be useful in specific situations. The most typical are country recommendations, which actually constitute suggestions by the HCNM addressed to a state concerned with the aim of changing its policy and legislation in regard to national minorities. The High Commissioner has also developed another type of instrument – general recommendations. Formally, the Commissioner has no explicit powers in standard-setting or interpretation of OSCE commitments in the field of the human dimension and democratic governance. There are at least two compelling reasons for the HCNM to undertake certain actions which could facilitate

18 *See Concluding Document of Helsinki – The Fourth Follow-up Meeting, 10 July 1992*, Chapter II.

19 These bodies were subsequently renamed, respectively, the Ministerial Council and the Permanent Council. For more on the content of the mandate *see* J. Packer, 'The OSCE High Commissioner on National Minorities', in G. Alfredsson *et al.* (eds.), *International Human Rights Monitoring Mechanisms. Essays in Honour of Jacob Th. Möller* (The Hague-Boston-London: Martinus Nijhoff Publishers, 2001) pp. 641–656.

20 *See Annual Report on OSCE Activities 2003. Security and Co-operation for Europe*, p. 138. More information on the HCNM's mandate may be found at: <www.osce.org/hcnm>.

the process of application and implementation of OSCE commitments in general and notably in regard to minority standards.[21]

Firstly, there are the practical demands for clarification of standards in the field of national minorities, particularly when the High Commissioner discusses with governments specific modalities and recommendations for their domestic regulations, policy-making and administrative decision-making. The need for clarification largely stems from the malaise of the deficit of minority standards. The Copenhagen and Geneva reports have, after some delay, finally arrived, but have also been insufficient to respond to detailed questions on the scope of minority rights. The HCNM construes and refers to the minority standards, their genuine content and gaps. Secondly, there are the practical demands for the effective application and implementation of minority standards. This is not a question of clarifying the content but rather one of determining which of the modes of effective implementation should be recommended.

Such practical and concrete considerations were at the root of the drawing up by the HCNM, with the help of independent experts, of nine sets of recommendations or guidelines in such areas as the education rights of national minorities (The Hague, 1996), linguistic rights of minorities (Oslo, 1998), the effective participation of minorities in public life (Lund, 1999), the use of minority languages in the broadcasting media (2003), policing in multi-ethnic societies (2006), national minorities in international relations (Bolzano, 2008), integration of diverse societies (Ljubljana, 2012), access to justice of national minorities (Graz, 2017) and national minorities and the media in the digital age (Tallin, 2019).[22]

All of these recommendations and guidelines do not set new standards, but they are expressions of good practice. They constitute a set of rules of both hard and soft law with a number of more detailed issues addressed and proposals recommended for domestic application. Their provisions are mere recommendations or guidelines aimed at facilitating the practical implementation of minority standards even if some of them seem to be formulated like a 'delegated legislation'. Although thematic recommendations do not set new

21 K. Drzewicki, 'The Lund Recommendations on the Effective Participation of National Minorities in Public Life – Five Years After and More Years Ahead', 12:2–3 *International Journal on Minority and Group Rights* (2005) pp. 123–131.

22 For the texts of all thematic recommendations of the HCNM together with explanatory notes see *National Minority Standards. A Compilation of OSCE and Council of Europe Texts* (Strasbourg: Council of Europe Publishing, 2007) pp. 45–152 and <www.osce.org/hcnm>.

standards, they are nonetheless an influential instrument in the hands of the High Commissioner.[23]

As far as the process of reforming the Åland Islands' model is concerned, it may be envisaged that the High Commissioner could be invited by the Åland local authorities and/or non-governmental organisations to examine the situation of minorities on the islands in a wider context of debates on the autonomy. It should help to identify why this model has generated the 'Åland paradox' whereby it delivers "less actual home rule than its legal arrangement indicates", and further, why "Åland's scope for action is considerably more limited than that of other autonomies with a constitutionally weaker position than Åland's."[24]

The question of whether the High Commissioner might be seen to have a mandate in the Åland case can tentatively be answered in the positive. The Commissioner's mandate does not appear to be confined to a narrow understanding of conflict prevention. The HCNM has never ignored the potential of the concept of "comprehensive security", which defines security and co-operation within a broader formula of all three baskets, including the human dimension (democratic governance, the rule of law, human rights and fundamental freedoms and humanitarian issues).[25] The assessment of the HCNM's activities demonstrates that the human-dimension approach has become an integral part of the 'tool-box' for conflict-prevention diplomacy, which in turn often brings with it indirect protective effects. Furthermore, under the umbrella of the OSCE's 'principles and commitments' it is also relevant what has been a contribution of the Charter of Paris for a New Europe of 1990, whereby it was commendably agreed that "questions related to national minorities can only be satisfactorily resolved in a democratic political framework" and that "the rights of persons belonging to national minorities must be fully respected as part of universal human rights".

The focus of the mandate on conflict prevention has neither deprived the High Commissioner of, nor prevented this body from being involved in, the

23 According to S.R. Ratner, 'Does International Law Matter in Preventing Ethnic Conflict?', 32:3 *New York University Journal of International Law and Politics* (2000) pp. 668–673, the HCNM is a 'normative intermediary' as he promotes observance of a norm and induces 'compliance through a hands-on process of communication and persuasion with relevant decision-makers' (at p. 668).

24 Lindstrom and Lindholm, *supra* note 2, p. 60.

25 For more details *see* T. Buergenthal, 'CSCE Human Dimension: The Birth of a System', in A. Clapham and F. Emmert (eds.) I-2: *Collected Courses of the Academy of European Law*, 1990 (Dordrecht- Boston-London: Martinus Nijhoff Publishers, 1992) pp. 160–209.

concomitant monitoring of human dimension commitments. This largely stems from the interpretation of Paragraph 6 of the Helsinki mandate, whereby the High Commissioner "will take fully into account the availability of democratic means and international instruments to respond to it, and their utilization by the parties involved". The potentials of Paragraph 6 can also be seen from the perspective of the achievements of nine sets of recommendations/guidelines in regard to the vast area of commitments on minority-majority relations. Furthermore, this new role of integrating conflict prevention with human dimension commitments was boldly demonstrated by the High Commissioner in his eventually successful diplomatic advocacy for introducing a clause on minority rights into the Draft European Constitution.[26] The High Commissioner has thus demonstrated the intrinsic potential of the concept of "comprehensive security".

All in all, it is submitted that the HCNM mandate has undergone a gradual transformation under the impact of a changing situation in Europe which desperately needs more of the High Commissioner's direct, conflict-prevention involvement. Initially, human dimension commitments constituted 'merely' a toolbox for the HCNM in the role of 'fireman', extinguishing the focal points of conflicts. In further decades, the HCNM will slowly shift the focal point from short-term conflict prevention to medium-term activity, which transforms human dimension commitments from a mere toolbox to a broader area of involvement as such. This is coupled with the increasing role of the HCNM in exerting influence on delegated standard-setting by the continuation of work on further sets of general recommendations.[27] Against this background, there are no strong obstacles against attracting the attention of the High Commissioner to examine national minority-majority issues in the Åland Islands in the context of prevailing regulations on the autonomy. This may be arranged by inviting the High Commissioner to attend a working seminar on the spot to present and discuss the situation of Åland with the aim of identifying problems and potential remedies.

26 For more on the successful intervention by the High Commissioner to have a minority rights provision included in the European Constitution in spite of strong initial resistance *see* K. Drzewicki 'A Constitution for Europe: Enshrining Minority Rights. Words Can Make Worlds of Difference', *OSCE Magazine* (March 2005) pp. 19–21.

27 *See* K. Drzewicki, 'The OSCE High Commissioner on National Minorities – Confronting Traditional and Emerging Challenges', in S. Parzymies (ed.) *OSCE and Minorities. Assessment and Prospects* (Warsaw: Wydawnictwo Scholar, 2007) pp. 14–16.

In conclusion, what may be inferred from the above overview of available instruments and mechanisms seems to suggest that probably the most successful arrangements for reforming the Åland Islands' autonomy are working mechanisms of consultation under the European Charter of Local Self-Government and the Congress of Local and Regional Authorities as well as a conflict-prevention involvement of the OSCE High Commissioner on National Minorities within that this body's modern approach to comprehensive security.

CHAPTER 17

The Right to Language in International Human Rights Law: Åland Islands and Other Finnish Minorities

Reetta Toivanen

> Language is the key to inclusion. Language is at the centre of human activity, self-expression and identity. Recognizing the primary importance that people place on their own language fosters the kind of true participation in development that achieves lasting results.[1]

1 Introduction

In a world where thousands of different languages and dialects are spoken and all of them are undergoing continuous change, is there a need to define a specific right for a specific language? When a baby is born to parents, should not the parents decide what language or languages they choose to speak, and not society at large?

When all languages are changing and all language variations are undergoing alterations, it may seem difficult if not even unnecessary to uphold a linguistic diversity consisting of stable languages and rights attached to them. However, the fact is that some languages are more in danger of disappearing than others. The majority of the world's 6000 languages are spoken by Indigenous peoples or other minorities, and their languages are at the moment acutely in danger of being lost forever.[2] In this context, it is important to note that *language* is not just about using a specific tongue. Language is about culture, an entire worldview, it is about imagining the futures of peoples. Language is politics,

1 UNESCO Bangkok, *Why Language Matters for the Millennium Development Goals* (UNESCO, 2012), p. 1.

2 S. Romaine, 'The Global Extinction of Languages and Its Consequences for Cultural Diversity', In H. Marten, M. Rießler, J. Saarikivi, and R. Toivanen (eds.), *Cultural and Linguistic Minorities in the Russian Federation and the European Union* (Multilingual Education, vol 13, Springer, Cham, 2015) pp. 31–46, https://doi.org/10.1007/978-3-319-10455-3_2.

and language is power. The most endangered languages are spoken by people who have the least political power to decide about their own situation, including the right to create a world where their specific language would enjoy the right to flourish. As UN Special Rapporteur on Minority Issues Fernand de Varennes recently noted:

> Language issues are at times among the main grievances that may contribute to toxic environments of exclusion and claims of discrimination in education that can lead to tensions and even conflicts between minorities and authorities, as shown unfortunately in different parts of the world.[3]

In this context, it becomes evident that when the right to use a language is not guaranteed to each and every person on the same basis, then language laws are needed to ensure a fair chance of survival even to the smallest language communities. After first presenting the chapter's theoretical stance, the role of human rights law standards in protecting and promoting minoritised languages will be discussed. In the next part, the present legal situation of certain minority languages in Finland will be presented. This will be followed by a question key to the last part of the discussion: What makes the Swedish spoken in the Åland Islands different from or similar to other minority languages in Finland, such as Inari Sámi and Karelian in the Finnish context?

It is apparent that the language situations differ markedly because the Swedish spoken in the Åland Islands has not been declared an endangered language, like Inari Sámi and various Karelian dialects. The paper will not so much seek to compare the different minority languages as test what can be learned from discussions on language and its preservation to better recognise language rights in different situations.

2 Theories and Methods

The main inspiration for this chapter comes from the life work of Tove Skutnabb-Kangas, who already in the 1980s began writing about how refusing people the right to speak their mother tongue was akin to racism.[4] The

---

3 UN Human Rights Council, *Report of the Special Rapporteur on minority issues, Education, language and the human rights of minorities*, Human Rights Council Forty-third session 24 February–20 March 2020 (Doc. A/HRC/43/47).

4 T. Skutnabb-Kangas, *Vähemmistö, kieli ja rasismi* [Minority, Language and Racism] (Gaudeamus, Helsinki, 1988).

concept proposed by her is called linguicism, meaning discrimination on the basis of one's mother tongue.[5] Another concept developed by her and Robert Phillipson was the term for linguistic genocide, linguicide.[6] Whereas both terms have their uses, they have been rejected by some sociolinguists as too harsh and straightforward in their condemnation.[7] Also, studies show that 'killing a language' may also be a way to give birth to another.[8]

Both concepts, whether overly harsh or not, are of relevance to this chapter. We will look more closely at the international standards, considering whether they give grounds to hinder linguicism and remedies for overcoming or compensating for discrimination on the basis of language. We will also look at concrete cases of minority languages in Finland, asking whether it is relevant to discuss measures taken to hinder linguicism and linguicide in different parts of the country.

Brief definitions of mother tongues by Skutnabb-Kangas:[9]

Criterion	**Definition**
Origin	The language one learned first
Identification	a. The language one identifies with
a. Internal	b. The language one is identified with as a
b. External	native speaker by others
Competence	The language one knows best
Function	The language one uses most

5 T. Skutnabb-Kangas, *Linguicism. The Encyclopedia of Applied Linguistics* (Blackwell, Malden, MA, 2015), DOI: 10.1002/9781405198431.wbeal1460.

6 T. Skutnabb-Kangas and R. Phillipson, 'Linguicide and Linguicism' (Papers in European language Policy. ROLIG papir 53. Roskilde: Roskilde Universitetscenter, Lingvistgruppen, 1995) pp. 83–91.

7 See discussions in D. Beck and D.Y. Lam, 'Language Loss and Linguistic Suicide: A Case Study from the Sierra Norte de Puebla, Mexico' (Toronto Working Papers in Linguistics 27, 2008) pp. 5–16; D. Crystal, *Language Death* (Cambridge University Press, Cambridge, 2014); S. May, *Language and minority rights: Ethnicity, Nationalism and the Politics of Language*, 2nd ed. (Routledge, London, 2012).

8 See R. Toivanen and J. Saarikivi, 'Introduction to New and Old Language Diversities: Language Variation and Endangerment in Changing Minority Communities', In R. Toivanen and J. Saarikivi (eds.), *Linguistic genocide or superdiversity? New and old language diversities* (Linguistic Diversity and Language Rights 14, Multilingual matters, Bristol, 2016) pp. 1–18.

9 T. Skutnabb-Kangas, *Bilingualism or not - the education of minorities* (Multilingual Matters, Clevedon, Avon, 1984) p. 18.

In the early model devised by Tove Skutnabb-Kangas, the big question was about identities, identification and language competences, where she made a key observation that became one of the fundamental components of her language theory: A person's knowledge of a language can be quite different from how they identify with the same language. Her vigorous research in several language communities in different parts of the world backed up her views that it is not the fault of a speaker if the language disappears or if they did not have the chance to learn it. The right to one's language became for her an essential topic and gave rise to an important question: Who has the right to learn the heritage languages of one's family, and who will not have such a chance? It is a question of equality and equity in the modern world.[10]

One central claim made by Tove Skutnabb-Kangas and her colleague and husband Robert Phillipson, in a study published in 2023,[11] is that it is possible to identify with a language that one does not even master. They write:

> It is possible to have a mother tongue that one does not have (any or 'full') competence in. (…) It could also have legal consequences in land claims by Indigenous peoples where lack of language competence is used against the claimants. When attempts by the state at forcible assimilation have led to a language being neglected (endangered, in need of revitalisation), we should use only a mother tongue definition by internal identification, when demanding full linguistic human rights (LHR) for individuals and collectivities, regardless of whether the individuals are receptive (understand) or productive users, or non-users of the language.[12]

With this idea, developed by Skutnabb-Kangas and Phillipson based on ethical and long-term research among endangered language communities, they do not wish to enter into or engage with political debates on who belongs to what minority but simply to underline that, from the perspective of linguistic human rights, it is not the fault of a particular person if for reasons such as racism and discrimination their ancestors discontinued using a specific language. People today are not responsible for a language loss that took place before their time,

10 For a more extensive list of Tove Skutnabb-Kangas's speeches and writings, see <http://www.tove-skutnabb-kangas.org/en/index-en.html>, last visited 30 October 2023.

11 T. Skutnabb-Kangas and R. Phillipson, *The Handbook of Linguistic Human Rights* (Wiley Blackwell, 2023), DOI:10.1002/9781119753926.

12 *Ibid.*

and they can very well identify with a language as their mother tongue even if that is only what they feel. Nobody can take that away from them.

Thus, the current academic discourse about language rights explores the dynamic interplay between language legislation and its potential to stimulate the vitality of minority languages. Additionally, it assesses the constraining ramifications inherent in legal frameworks when they are fashioned in a manner that ostensibly curtails the domain of language utilisation. The 'living' conditions of languages have dramatically changed through literacy, formal education, standardisation, mass media, social media, urbanisation, changes in livelihoods, increased mobilisation, centralised states and nationalist identities.[13] One of the consequences of what academics term modernisation is a restriction of language use through different means, leading people to abandon their mother tongues; the resulting threat posed to language diversity has emerged as a pervasive concern across the globe.

3 Right to Language: Legal or Moral Obligations?

Language serves as both an object of and a tool for legal and judicial activities.[14] Laws can dictate language choices at state and regional levels, regulating language use in contexts like administration and court proceedings, in institutions, such as parliaments and schools, in the media and even in public and private settings, like businesses, thus illustrating the close, reciprocal relationship between language and law.[15] Language determines participation in lawmaking and enforcement efforts, affecting citizens, parliamentarians, officials and judges. Legal measures can constrict or broaden linguistic space, establishing hierarchies and power imbalances in terms of symbolic recognition, resources, and access to various domains.[16]

Language legislation has historically served as a tool for control and dominance, impacting Indigenous peoples, minorities and former colonies.[17] Instances of forbidding public use of a language still persist today, with

13 R. Toivanen and J. Saarikivi, *supra* note 9, p. 1.

14 K. Henrard, 'Linguistic Human Rights in Relation to the Administration of Justice: A European Perspective', in T. Skutnabb-Kangas and R. Phillipson, *supra* note 11, pp. 227–234.

15 J. Jackson-Preece, *Minority language rights in Europe today* (Populaçao e Sociedade, Specia, 2006).

16 Henrard, *supra* note 14.

17 For an overview, see, e.g. J. Laakso, A. Sarhimaa, S. Spiliopoulou Åkermark, and R. Toivanen, *Towards openly multilingual policies and practices: Assessing minority language maintenance across Europe* (Multilingual matters, Bristol, Linguistic Diversity and Language Rights 11, 2016) p. 3ff. https://doi.org/10.1080/14664208.2016.1264744.

countries like France, Greece and Turkey reluctant to acknowledge linguistic minorities. For example, France's Conseil Constitutionnel[18] deemed the European Charter for Regional and Minority Languages incompatible with its constitutional principles. However, language can also empower, as seen in the case of Sámi language revival through legislative efforts in Norway, Sweden and Finland.[19]

It is noteworthy that law and legal theory can often be dismissed as irrelevant or mere 'moralism' by non-lawyers,[20] who might criticise language rights theory for being insufficient. Francois Grin suggests that justifying minority language protection as part of broader claims to 'diversity management' requires more than the moral arguments typically used for rights-based claims.[21] Grin emphasises that such efforts at protecting minority languages must also demonstrate technical feasibility, effectiveness and fairness in distribution. While Grin does not deny the importance of linguistic rights, he appears hesitant to rely solely on legal rights arguments. He underlines that purely utilitarian cost-effectiveness arguments miss two key points. First, they confuse language legislation with individual or collective language rights. Language legislation extends beyond language rights, which are specific legal claims that do not necessarily override all considerations of fairness and appropriateness. This observation has sparked a discussion on 'linguistic justice', recognising that language laws and policies influence not only social cohesion and economic efficiency but also the legitimacy of societal and political structures, fairness perceptions and inclusion for speakers of diverse languages and identities.[22]

Critics of language protection theories, including legal ones, overlook another key aspect. In democratic societies, as well as internationally, legislation serves a crucial purpose. It legitimates expectations and recognises persons with diverse backgrounds. This recognition effect empowers individuals and groups by making their claims visible and accepted. Legal acknowledgment itself holds empowering value, as it brings the claims and their proponents into the public eye. When the law neglects such claims, those persons may feel marginalised and powerless. Additionally, the law institutionalises

18 Conseil Constitutionnel, *Décision No 99–412 DC, 15 juin 1999* (Recueil p 71 JO 18.6.1999) p. 8974.

19 U. Aikio-Puoskari, 'Linguistic Human Rights of Indigenous Sámi in the Finnish Education System', in Skutnabb-Kangas and Phillipson, *supra* note 11, pp. 477–491.

20 See more on this in Laakso et al., *supra* note 17, p. 55.

21 F. Grin, 'Linguistic human rights as a source of policy guidelines: A critical assessment', 9 *Journal of Sociolinguistics* pp. 448–460 esp. p. 451, https://doi.org/10.1111/j.1360-6441.2005.00300.x.

22 See H. de Schutter, 'Language policy and political philosophy: On the emerging linguistic justice debate', 31:1 *Language Problems and Language Planning* (Jan 2007) pp. 1–23, https://doi.org/10.1075/lplp.31.1.02des.

the results of discussions, disagreements and compromises about resource allocation and accommodation among conflicting interests. Language-related decisions, including resource allocation and status, are also institutionalised within legal frameworks. Law plays a dual role by recognising languages (shaping identity through its 'expressive' dimension) and regulating their practical functions (essential for communication through its 'functional' dimension).[23] This impacts speakers' chances and motivation to use their language.

According to Kaarlo Tuori, law in Habermasian thought is connected with morality through its foundational justification, extending beyond just its moral dimension. The link between positive law and morality hinges on rational discourse, fundamental to democratic decision-making practices.[24] This discourse, particularly at the parliamentary stage and when preparing legislation, encompasses discussions of effectiveness, feasibility and fairness. Tuori asserts that the main role of (positive) law is to stabilise societal expectations of behaviour. Language rights, similarly, aim not to override all societal needs but to recognise and advance legitimate expectations for protection among diverse language speakers. In this context, legal analysis concerns itself less with philosophical and moral underpinnings, focusing more on practical considerations than political theory.[25]

However, exceptions exist in attempts to bridge the gap between options for regulating the legitimisation of a language and broader societal debates on fairness and justice.[26] Notably, Robert Dunbar has observed increasing dialogue on the nature and theoretical basis of viewing linguistic rights as human rights.[27] Presently, legal scholars employ the terms 'language law', 'language rights' and 'linguistic justice'. 'Language law', or 'linguistic regimes', as

23 See P.A. Kraus, *A Union of Diversity: Language, Identity and Polity-Building in Europe* (Cambridge University Press, Cambridge, 2008). https://doi.org/10.1017/CBO9780511491993.

24 K. Tuori, *Critical Legal Positivism* (Ashgate, Aldershot 2002) p. 84; J. Habermas, *Between Facts and Norms: Contributions to a Discourse Theory of Law and Democracy* (The MIT Press, Cambridge, MA 1996) pp. 107–109.

25 A. Patten, 'The Justification of Minority Language Rights', 17 *Journal of Political Philosophy* (2009) pp. 102–128, https://doi.org/10.1111/j.1467-9760.2008.00321.x.

26 A. Spiliopoulou Åkermark, *Justifications of Minority Protection in International Law* (Kluwer Law International, den Hague, 1997); S. Spiliopoulou Åkermark, 'Shifts in the Multiple Justifications of Minority Protection', 7:1 *European Yearbook of Minority Issues Online* pp. 1–18, https://doi.org/10.1163/22116117-90001627201O); A. Mowbray, *Cases, Materials, and Commentary on the European Convention on Human Rights*, 3rd ed. (Oxford University Press, Oxford, 2012).

27 R. Dunbar, 'Minority Language Rights in International Law', 50:1 *International & Comparative Law Quarterly* (2001) pp. 90–120, esp. p. 93, doi:10.1093/iclq/50.1.90.

demonstrated by Markku Suksi's work,[28] examines domestic approaches to language concerns. Suksi's analysis of Finland, for instance, highlights various parallel regimes for different languages.[29] Finland, constitutionally a bilingual country (Finnish and Swedish), safeguards the Sámi languages through dedicated legislation (The Sámi Language Act), and other minority languages also enjoy different types and levels of legal protection. Suksi notes that the distinct regimes showcase how "a single country, even a small one, can simultaneously employ different linguistic regimes for numerous groups".[30] His has an argument in favour of nuanced and varied solutions on the basis of the needs of the individuals and groups concerned as well as wider societal considerations and needs, following balancing deliberation. For authors like Dunbar and de Varennes, both the foundation or justification for as well as the contents of specific linguistic rights require further analysis and therefore need to be looked at within the broader context of comprehensive language policies and regulations.[31]

In the context of this chapter, the focus is on constitutional human rights guarantees, existing legislation, litigation outcomes and non-discrimination theory, but also on understanding the systemic aspects of legal and institutional frameworks. Whereas the legal right to a language is perhaps just one aspect of protecting and fostering minority languages, its role should not be underestimated, even with respect to more morality-based societal debates.[32]

4 The Finnish Law Protecting Language/s in Åland and Elsewhere in Finland

The official languages of Finland are Finnish and Swedish. According to the Constitution of Finland,[33] public authorities must ensure the educational and societal needs of the Finnish- and Swedish-speaking population on equal

28 M. Suksi, 'Functional Autonomy: The Case of Finland with Some Notes on the Basis of International Human Rights Law and Comparisons with Other Cases', 15:2–3 *International Journal on Minority and Group Rights* (2008) pp. 195–225. https://doi.org/10.1163/157181108X332604.

29 *Ibid.*; see also in this volume (see Chapter 4 by Suksi).

30 Suksi, *supra* note 28, p. 238.

31 Dunbar, *supra* note 27; F. de Vareness, 'Linguistic Human Rights Challenges in the Work of the UN Special Rapporteur on Minority Issues', in T. Skutnabb-Kangas & R. Phillipson, *supra* note 11, pp. 183–194.

32 Laakso et al., *supra* note 17.

33 The Constitution of Finland, 11 June 1999 (731/1999, amendments up to 817/2018 included).

grounds. The state must ensure that, for example, public services are effectively available in accordance with the language law requirements.

The Constitution also mentions the right to use and maintain the Sámi language, sign language and Romani language. The Language Act,[34] Sámi Language Act,[35] Sign Language Act,[36] and Language Skills Act[37] regulate linguistic rights more specifically. Interestingly, no Romani Language Act exists, nor are any serious attempts being made to adopt such an act.

People belonging to minorities have the right to enjoy their own culture, practise their own religion and use their own language according to Finnish law. Finland is committed particularly to protecting and promoting regional languages and minority languages as well as the rights of their users, a position visible in its commitment to the Council of Europe treaties, the Framework Convention on National Minorities and the so-called European Language Charter.[38] The languages include Swedish as a second domestic language, the Sámi languages, the Romani language, the Karelian language, Russian, Estonian, Tatar, Yiddish and sign language. These linguistic rights impose obligations on the authorities, such as arranging public services in a person's own language. Linguistic rights are often a prerequisite for the realisation of other rights, too, including, for example, educational and social rights as well as legal protection.[39]

4.1 *Åland Islands and the Situation with Swedish in Finland*

The Åland Islands are a very specific part of Finland, consisting of more than 6500 islands and a population of approximately 30 000 persons. A 1921 case decided by the League of Nations established the islands as an autonomous, demilitarised area of Finland, located between Finland and Sweden. The bilingualism of mainland Finland does not apply to the Åland Islands, which are entirely Swedish speaking, meaning it is the exclusive official language of the islands.[40] This policy dictates that Swedish is to be utilised by all local, municipal and national institutions on the islands. As per the Autonomy of Åland Act,

34 Language Act (423/2003).

35 Sámi Language Act (1086/2003).

36 Sign Language Act (359/2015).

37 Language Skills Act, Act on the Knowledge of Languages Required of Personnel in Public Bodies (424/2003).

38 Treaties.

39 Laakso et al., *supra* note 17.

40 S. Spiliopoulou Åkermark, 'The Åland Islands Question in the League of Nations: The ideal minority case?' in *Redescriptions – Yearbook of Political Thought, Conceptual History and Feminist Theory*, vol. 13 (2009), 195–205, http://doi.org/10.7227/R.13.1.10.

any correspondence between the Finnish Government and Åland authorities must take place in Swedish. Moreover, any interactions involving individuals fluent in Finnish and Åland authorities must also be in Swedish. Nevertheless, Finnish individuals possess the right to employ Finnish when managing their personal affairs in front of a court of law or other central governmental bodies in the Åland Islands.[41]

The self-governance of the Åland Islands has often been cited as a success story, a conflict-free solution to minority language rights matters. Spiliopoulou Åkermark has even argued that the case of the Åland Islands has strongly influenced the way we understand minority language protection as a central issue of peace and security and (territorial) self-governance,[42] as opposed to within the framework of emancipation and self-expression of identity, or as human heritage, as it is dealt with in the works of, for example, Tove Skutnabb-Kangas.

4.2 *Sámi Languages and Inari Sámi in Finland*

The Inari Sámi people are one of the Indigenous peoples of Finland. Indigenous peoples' rights in Finland are protected by the Constitution of Finland (1999) and the law on the Sámi Parliament (1995).[43] The Inari Sámi language, which is one of the Sámi languages spoken in Finland, is protected and promoted through the Sámi Language Act (*Saamen kielilaki* in Finnish).[44] The Sámi Language Act recognises the importance of preserving and developing the Sámi languages, including Inari Sámi, and it aims to ensure the linguistic rights of Sámi speakers in Finland.

The Sámi Language Act grants certain rights to speakers of Sámi languages. Some of the key provisions of the act include:

- Right to use Sámi languages: The act guarantees the right to use Sámi languages, including Inari Sámi, in dealings with authorities and courts in the Sámi homeland.
- Education: The act ensures the availability of Sámi language education at different levels, from early childhood education to higher education. This includes education in Inari Sámi where applicable.
- Public services: Public services and communication from authorities should be available in the Sámi languages, including Inari Sámi, in the Sámi homeland.

41 Suksi, *supra* note 28.

42 Spiliopoulou Åkermark, *supra* note 40, p. 197.

43 The Constitution of Finland, *supra* note 34; The Act on Sámi Parliament 1995.

44 Sámi Language Act, *supra* note 35.

- Media and culture: The act promotes use of the Sámi languages in the media and cultural activities.
- Place names: The act addresses the naming of places in the Sámi homeland, with the aim of preserving and promoting Sámi names, including Inari Sámi names.

The Inari Sámi language has always been a rather small language, with researchers estimating that it never had more than 1000 speakers.[45] Still, Inari Sámi language activism is today an international example of a successful grassroots movement to save an endangered language.[46] The Inari Sámi language became seriously endangered in the 20th century, which made its extinction by the 1990s, at the latest, seemingly inevitable.[47] The impending decline was successfully reversed through conscious, community-driven efforts. The key factors in this language reversal process have been language nests for young children, where the Inari Sámi language is taught in an immersive fashion, native language instruction in schools and intensive language learning for adults. The primary responsibility for the revitalisation efforts has been shouldered by *Anarâškielâ servi*, the Inari Sámi Language Association, established in 1986. In the book *Revitalising indigenous languages: How to recreate a lost generation*, the authors show how parents of small children and a few Inari Sámi language activists started a daycare with the aim of reviving the Inari Sámi language in the 1980s.[48] They founded the Inari Sámi Language Association, which later received significant financial support from the Finnish Cultural Foundation. With this support, the association launched the first Inari Sámi language nest in 1997: it still continues to operate.[49] The association was successful in turning itself "into an engine for the revitalization of the Inari Sámi language",[50] which today encompasses not only early childhood but also adult education.

According to Annika Pasanen's long-term research on Inari Sámi revitalisation efforts,[51] there were only three people under the age of 30 who spoke Inari Sámi as their first language when the first language nest started operating. The language nest marked the beginning of the revitalisation of the Inari

45 M-L. Olthuis, 'Uhanalaisen kielen elvyttäminen: esimerkkinä inarinsaame', [Revitalization of an Endangered Language: The Case of Inari Sámi], 107 Virittäjä (2003) pp. 568–579, as cited in Pasanen 2015, p. 84, see note 51.

46 M-L. Olthuis, S. Kivelä, and T. Skutnabb-Kangas, *Revitalising indigenous languages. How to recreate a lost generation* (Multilingual Matters, 2013).

47 *Ibid.*

48 *Ibid.*

49 U. Aikio-Puoskari, *supra* note 19, pp. 477–491, esp. p. 480.

50 *Ibid.*

51 A. Pasanen, *Kuávsui já peeivičuovâ. 'Sarastus ja päivänvalo'. Inarinsaamen kielen revitalisaatio* [Dawn and Daylight': The Revitalization of the Inari Sámi Language], (Uralica Helsingiensia 9, Helsinki, 2015).

Sámi language, which has since led to the beginning of more general Inari Sámi language instruction in 2000, new types of language training for adults and the possibility to study Inari Sámi as a major subject at the University of Oulu since 2015.[52]

Thus, the situation of a minority language like Inari Sámi is fundamentally different from that of Swedish in Finland, including the Åland Islands, since it was originally spoken only around Lake Inari in northeastern Finland. Though speakers of Inari Sámi can now be found everywhere, the number of speakers remains low, consisting only of an estimated 500 persons.

4.3 *Karelian in Finland*

Karelian is an autochthonous language in Finland, which means that it has been spoken for as long as the Finnish language. Nevertheless, it does not enjoy the same standard as a national language, as do the two official languages of Finland, Finnish and Swedish. Neither does it enjoy a similar level of recognition as the Sámi languages, which are governed by the Sámi Language Act. Karelian is not mentioned in the Constitution of Finland (1999) by name, but it is covered by the general formulation extending minority rights to "the Roma and other groups, [who] have the right to maintain and develop their own language and culture" (section 17).

The Karelian homeland has historically been divided between neighbouring states: first between Sweden and the Novgorodian Republic, then between Sweden and the Russian Empire, and since WWII between Finland and the Soviet Union/Russian Federation.[53] According to Anneli Sarhimaa, Karelians have been subjected to both Finnish and Russian nationalism. For this reason, they never developed into an independent nation but remained a regional minority in both countries.[54] According to estimates, approximately 11 000 people in Finland speak the Karelian language.[55] Sarhimaa writes that Karelian is currently endangered in Finland due to interrupted language transmission across generations, declining numbers of speakers, usage and interaction issues, limited public use, low private domain interest, ineffective language

---

52 Aikio-Puoskari, *supra* note 19.

53 H. Karjalainen, U. Puura, and R. Grünthal, *Karelian in Russia: ELDIA Case-Specific Report*, Studies in European Language Diversity 26 (Wien: ELDIA, 2017), https://phaidra.univie.ac.at/o:314612.

54 A. Sarhimaa, 'Language Endangerment and Linguistic Human Rights of a Cross-Border Minority: Karelian in Russia and Finland', in Skutnabb-Kangas & Phillipson, *supra* note 11, pp. 517–531, esp. p. 518.

55 A. Sarhimaa, *Vaietut ja vaiennetut: karjalankieliset karjalaiset Suomessa* [The Silenced and the Quieted: Karelian-Speaking Karelians in Finland], (Suomalaisen Kirjallisuuden Seura, Helsinki, 2017).

policies and limited Karelian language resources.[56] In addition, the political sensitivity of cross-border relations and suspicion regarding the loyalty of Karelians towards Finland has resulted in racism, which has consequently silenced many Karelian-speaking families, at least in public.[57]

In Finland, the existence of Karelian speakers was officially recognised only in the year 2009. Finland added Karelian to the list of languages to be monitored by the Council of Europe before ratifying the European Charter for Regional or Minority Languages (ECRML). According to Sarhimaa,[58] most Finns are not aware of the existence of a separate Karelian language that is not the same as the eastern Finnish dialect known as the Karelian dialect. They may not even know that Karelian speakers are currently struggling for the future of their language.

5 Minorities and Multilingualism: Is the Law Suitable to Protect Multilinguals and People Who Have Lost Their Languages?

Tove Skutnabb-Kangas and Robert Phillipson have proposed several theses about mother tongues:[59]

1. An individual can have at least two, possibly three, mother tongues ('bilingualism/ multilingualism as a mother tongue').
2. A person's mother tongue can vary depending on what definition is used.
3. A person's mother tongue can change during her/his lifetime, according to all definitions, except for a mother tongue defined by origin (the only exception is for the Deaf, as explained below).
4. Mother tongue definitions can be organised hierarchically in relation to the extent to which they respect linguistic human rights.

Even if they do not yet know (much of) a language, Deaf persons and Indigenous peoples have the right to claim a sign language or an ancestral language as their mother tongue on the basis of simply identifying with it.[60]

In this chapter it has been argued that language laws can only help to a certain degree in fostering and supporting language maintenance and revitalisation

---

56 Sarhimaa, *supra* note 54, p. 519.

57 U. Savolainen, 'The Return: Intertextuality of the Reminiscing of Karelian Evacuees in Finland', 130:516 *Journal of American Folklore* (2017) pp. 166–192, https://doi.org/10.5406/jamerfolk.130.51.

58 Sarhimaa, *supra* note 55.

59 T. Skutnabb-Kangas and R. Phillipson, *The Handbook of Linguistic Human Rights* (Wiley Blackwell, 2023), DOI:10.1002/9781119753926, p. 5.

60 T. Skutnabb-Kangas, *Linguistic Genocide in Education – or Worldwide Diversity and Human Rights* (New York, 2008).

efforts. Law can also be particularly inhibiting towards new speakers and language communities when it does not understand the contexts and histories of assimilation. According to sociologists and language historians, the importance of a language may be unknown to legal scholars and practitioners, but lawyers may also be reluctant to address the societal complexities and moral dilemmas that emerge when assimilated language communities engage in claiming their language rights or when language speakers do not agree on the language variants that should be protected.

All these situations and complexities exist in the Finnish language realm, whether among Finnish speakers, national minorities or new (migrant) minority language speakers. At the same time, the right to a language, the right to even several mother tongues, is a strong human right. The act of implementing laws that protect the right to a language requires concerted efforts by language communities, speakers and non-speakers alike, scientists and decision makers (often guided by lawyers). Whereas extending the same level of protection, including financial and structural support, to all language variants may not be realistic, any state will profit from an engaged civil society and from all members of society engaging with the debate about what languages to recognise in that country.

Tove Skutnabb-Kangas's lifework was to convince lawyers, politicians and language speakers that all language communities are entitled to the necessary linguistic human rights through state-financed education, which enables them to acquire full spoken and written skills in the mother tongue(s).

The previous discussion may give rise to a certain question about language politics. Since the Swedish language is the only actively spoken language in the Åland Islands, islanders can be insensitive to the importance of also fostering linguistic diversity in those places.

Inari Sámi has always been a small language group, and the area of Inari has always been a crossing point for people from various linguistic backgrounds. This may be the reason why the Inari Sámi often have a more positive attitude towards newcomers and other languages. At the same time, the community has faced strong assimilation measures that almost led to the total extinction of the language. Still, the culture has remained strong especially among fishers and reindeer herders. Due to the long period of assimilation, many Inari Sámi have been refused membership in the Sámi Parliament, leading to a denial of their right to vote or be voted into the Sámi Parliament,[61] which could lead to linguicide. The Inari Sámi have chosen the strategy of keeping language

61 R. Toivanen, 'Protecting Indigenous Identities? An example of cultural expertise on Sámi identity', 54:2–3 *Legal pluralism and critical social analysis* (2022) pp. 210–230, https://doi.org/10.1080/27706869.2022.2151167.

revitalisation separate from ethnic identification, adopting the ideology that whoever opts to learn Inari Sámi is doing the language community a big favour.

Then again, Karelians have long fought for recognition of a language separate from an eastern Finnish dialect also called the Karelian dialect. The several different language variations of Karelian have also been the subject of heated debate as to which variation should receive financial support for revitalisation efforts. The debates, including among Karelians themselves, have been fierce and many activists have been targeted on social media and elsewhere for their views. At the same time, Karelian speakers clearly believe that whatever variant of Karelian is promoted, the language as a whole will then have a better future.

When it comes to language laws, the 1920 Self-Government Act for the Åland Islands provided guarantees for the preservation of the Swedish language, culture and local traditions of the Åland Islands, making Åland a unilingual Swedish-language region in the otherwise bilingual country of Finland.[62] The Indigenous Sámi languages are likewise protected by a language law, but many Inari Sámi do not think that the Sámi Parliament gives their language enough attention or resources, and some wish for a separate law for Inari Sámi. Karelian associations have also demanded their own law, one that would protect and promote Karelian language and culture. Language laws are important, but as already pointed out, laws also have a coercive role in possibly limiting language variations, linguistic change and the inclusion of new speakers. In this regard, the Åland law on self-governance has been a good source of inspiration for many minority activists and lawyers in Finland because it also addresses culture and local traditions as part of what needs to be protected. At the same time, following the earlier argument made by Sia Spiliopoulou Åkermark, it would be time to start thinking about rights to language and culture as human rights that promote emancipation and not so much as guarantees for social peace and security.

62 M. Suksi, 'Finnish and Swedish as National Languages of Finland: A Linguistic Human Rights Success Story – Why and How?', in Skutnabb-Kangas & Phillipson, *supra* note 11, p. 448.

CHAPTER 18

Language Discrimination in Europe: Surprisingly Strict and Promising Lessons from Finland

Axel Hjo

1 Introduction: the Prospect of New European Discrimination Standards

The post-war shift from local collective minority protection, such as territorial autonomy, towards a universal individual human rights paradigm has posed a challenge to many states. In terms of linguistic minority rights,[1] the shift has created an intriguing normative paradox of equality: how and to what extent should nation-states treat language groups differently to guarantee their equal treatment?

A vague European answer could be found by looking at the Council of Europe (CoE) and the principle of non-discrimination. The principle is laid out in, *inter alia*, the European Convention on Human Rights (ECHR) Article 14 in relation to other convention rights. Additionally, Protocol 12 to the convention, specifically Article 1 (P12–1) para 1, states that the enjoyment of *any right set forth by law* shall be secured without discrimination on any ground, such as language or ethnicity.[2] The term "shall be secured" indicates that the right includes both a negative and positive obligation for the Member states. This implies that the article not only regulates public conduct but, to a certain extent, also addresses private conduct.[3] Furthermore, para 2 explicitly clarifies that no one may be discriminated by a public authority.[4] This means that even if there is no right set forth by law, public authorities are obligated to refrain

1 By *minority* I mean minority *de facto* (by number) and not according to any legal or conceptual classifications.

2 Although a variety of international legal instruments could shed light on potential language discrimination rights, complaints and remedies, this limited article will focus on the interrelationship between European, Finnish and Åland legal standards. This choice is motivated by the caution paid in general to European standards by legislators, courts and administrations in Åland and Finland.

3 See on positive obligations, e.g., ECtHR. *J.D and A. v. the UK*, App nos. 32949/17 and 34614/17. 24 October 2019, para 84–85.

4 For a parallel within the EU legal order, see the European Charter on Fundamental Rights, Article 21.

DOI:10.1163/9789004691117_020

from discrimination when exercising their public power. However, not all Member states of the Council of Europe have ratified Protocol 12, thus limiting the relevance of this question and the content of this book section primarily to those states who have ratified the protocol.[5]

Although European non-discrimination standards are also developed within the EU framework, this book section will exclusively focus on the interrelated ECHR framework, as interpreted by the European Court of Human Rights (ECtHR).[6] This delimitation is motivated by the unique nature of P12–1. Thus, based on its wording, the standard provided by P12–1 seems to possess extensive applicability and could be a relevant norm in many matters of linguistic discrimination. However, the crucial factor for the relevance of this standard lies in the interpretation of the term "discrimination" within the context of European law.[7]

Strategic interests of the nation-states suggest a rather limited concept. Europe is a flower field of minority languages. Hence, an expansion of European constitutional standards on substantive language policy could potentially open a pandora's box for minority groups seeking to contest national language regulations and policies.[8] Not surprisingly, European institutions, including the ECtHR and the Court of Justice of the European Union (CJEU), have demonstrated a cautious approach. The courts have traditionally afforded member states significant discretion in matters regarding minority language policy and

5 Finland already ratified Protocol 12 in 2004, entering into force in 2005. Finland is still the only Nordic country that has ratified the Protocol. By the 12th of May 2023, 19 other Member States of the Council of Europe had ratified the Protocol: Albania, Andorra, Armenia, Bosnia and Herzegovina, Croatia, Cyprus, Georgia, Luxembourg, Malta, Montenegro, Netherlands, North Macedonia, Portugal, Romania, San Marino, Serbia, Slovenia, Spain and Ukraine. Council of Europe, Treaty Office: https://www.coe.int/en/web/conventions/full-list?module=signatures-by-treaty&treatynum=177, accessed 17 May 2023.

6 On the interdependence of EU- and ECHR standards on discrimination, *see*, S. Besson, 'Evolutions in Non-Discrimination Law within the ECHR and the Esc Systems: It Takes Two to Tango in the Council of Europe', 60:1 The *American journal of comparative law* (2012) pp. 147–80. https://doi.org/10.5131/AJCL.2011.0018, and more generally CoE, and FRA. *Handbook on European Non-Discrimination Law*. Publications Office of the European Union (2018).

7 The ECtHR has repeatedly emphasized that the term "discrimination" in P12–1 is to be interpreted in alignment with the court's jurisprudence on the identical term found in ECHR Article 14, see, e.g., ECtHR. *Paun Jovanović v. Serbia*. App no. 41394/15, 7 February 2023, para 74.

8 Opportunities for safeguarding minority rights are more easily found in the jurisprudence of ECtHR, particularly when raising core questions of other convention rights. Notably, this includes, but not limited to, ensuring equal rights in political participation during elections and parliamentary processes under ECHR Article 10 in ECtHR. *Affaire Mestan v. Bulgaria*. App no. 24108/15. 2 May 2023, paras 60–64.

regulation.[9] Whether this caution has evolved or could face challenges, particularly in relation to P12–1, arises when member states themselves explicitly codify linguistic rights.[10]

The general aim of this book is to find new ways to expand the room of manoeuvre for the Åland autonomy through international law. As this article aims to demonstrate, strict national implementation of emerging non-discrimination standards, combined with old national categorical linguistic rights, may contribute to establishing previously unexplored possibilities for enforcing minority language rights for Swedish speakers in Åland and Finland.[11] It should be stressed that this concise study is of a purely heuristic and instrumental nature, with the primary aim of exploring the possibilities of discrimination standards as alternative tools for enforcing linguistic minority rights. The unique insights gained should therefore be approached with a critical mindset and considered as suggestions for further inquiry. Nevertheless, these suggestions might extend their relevance beyond Swedish speakers in Åland and Finland. The lessons could perhaps serve as inspiration for regulating and litigating linguistic rights elsewhere. This is especially pertinent for those seeking to develop regional collective minority rights through the individual human rights paradigm in general and side by side with European discrimination standards in particular.[12]

Yet, the primary question this article seeks to answer is whether the implementation of European non-discrimination standards in Finland has facilitated

---

9 Further on historical cautiousness and developments, *see*, N. Noémi, 'Language Rights as a Sine Qua Non of Democracy – a Comparative Overview of the Jurisprudence of the European Court of Human Rights and the Court of Justice of the European Union' *EPLO Publications* (2018), especially at p. 5 and P. McDermott, 'Language Rights and the Council of Europe: A Failed Response to a Multilingual Continent?'. *Ethnicities* 17:5 (2017) pp. 603–26. https://doi.org/10.1177/1468796816654725. On minority rights and the ECtHR more broadly, *see* R. Medda-Windischer, 'The European Court of Human Rights and Minority Rights' 25:3 *Journal of European Integration*, (2003) p. 249–71, https://doi.org/10.1080/0703633032000133583.

10 Generally, on the late development of discrimination standards, *see e.g.*, Rubio-Marín, Ruth, and Mathias Möschel. 'Anti-Discrimination Exceptionalism: Racist Violence before the ECtHR and the Holocaust Prism' 26:4 *European Journal of International Law* (2016) pp. 881–99. https://doi.org/10.1093/ejil/chv058. https://doi.org/10.1093/ejil/chv058.

11 Although the same discrimination standards could potentially also be used by Finnish speakers to claim in Åland the likeliness of succeeding with such claims seem limited, as long as there is a limited amount and scope of codified linguistic rights for Finnish speakers in Åland.

12 In this article I use the terms *Åland* and *Finland* to point to exclusive and separate jurisdictions. When referring to the two jurisdictions collectively, I use the term "the Republic of Finland".

a more accessible enforcement of minority language rights for individuals in Åland and Finland. While increased enforceability might not grant greater flexibility to the public authorities in Åland, it could provide more effective tools for individuals in Åland and Finland to strengthen their linguistic rights through legal avenues. Such collective legal actions have the potential to exert pressure on Finnish authorities to start securing the most fundamental prerequisite for both the autonomy and the Finnish sovereignty of the islands: the status of Åland as unilingually Swedish.

2 Declaratory Linguistic Rights with Little Real Enforcement

Although Finland has several *de facto* minority languages, this book section will be delimited to studying Swedish as an officially recognized minority language in Finland.[13] The main reason for this limitation is the research interest of this book being centred around Åland. Furthermore, the linguistic rights of Swedish speakers in Finland prescribed by law are strong and categorical in theory, making them a notable European example that highlights the potential influence discrimination standards could have on the enforcement of such rights.

Swedish is an official language in Finland, which according to the Finnish Constitution Section 17 is formally equal to Finnish.[14] In numbers, Swedish is a minority language spoken by roughly six per cent of the population. Furthermore, the official bilingualism of the young Finnish state was a prerequisite for the League of Nations when deciding to include the Swedish-speaking people in the Åland Islands under Finnish sovereignty in 1921.[15] It was probably difficult to see how a unilingual Finnish state could have bound itself to international and constitutional obligations to secure Swedish as the only official language in Åland, without ceding all legislative, administrative, and administrative and judicial power to the Åland autonomy.

At the time of writing, the right for individuals to use and be addressed in the Swedish language within the Republic of Finland historically derives from at least two constitutional sources and two sources of international law. Besides the bilingualism proclaimed by the Finnish Constitution, the Åland Autonomy

13 *Cf*, R. Hiltunen, *Country report : Non-discrimination : Finland 2022* (European Commission, Brussels, 2022), p. 5.

14 *Finlands grundlag* (FFS 731/1999) [Constitution].

15 *See*, M. Suksi, 'Finnish and Swedish as National Languages of Finland', In T. Skutnabb – Kangas and R. Phillipson (eds.), *The Handbook of Linguistic Human Rights* (Wiley Blackwell, Oxford, 2022) p. 448.

Act Section 36 derogates from the Finnish Constitution by stating Swedish as the only official language in the Åland Islands.[16] These provisions are to be read in close conjunction with the decisions of the League of Nations regarding the Åland Islands in 1921 and the bilateral agreement between Sweden and Finland regarding the protection of the Swedish language and culture in the Åland Islands.[17]

Regarding Finland, the right to use Swedish as a minority language has been operationalised though the Act on Language and a myriad of other specialized statutes.[18] The Act on Language provides Swedish speakers extensive rights to communicate with authorities in Swedish, especially if the authority is classified as bilingual, a status held by many central authorities. However, since the Åland Autonomy Act contains special constitutional rules regarding linguistic rights in the Åland Islands, the Finnish Act on Language is not considered applicable in Åland or to individuals from Åland in contact with Finnish authorities.[19] Consequently, individuals from Åland can assert their right to use and be addressed in the Swedish language directly based on the language provisions outlined in the Åland Autonomy Act, in conjunction with the relevant sources of international law.

However, Swedish speakers, both in Finland and Åland, share two common problems. The first problem is factual and regards the constant failure of compliance with linguistic rights, undermining Swedish as an official language in practice. The second problem, which is of particular interest to this book section, relates to the historical absence of effective enforcement mechanisms. Neither the Finnish Language Act nor the Åland Autonomy Act provides any mechanisms for individuals seeking to enforce their linguistic rights through legal channels such as courts or tribunals.[20] The general legal requirements for initiating penal or tort claims against authorities based solely on linguistic

16 *Självstyrelselag* (*FFS 1114/1991*) *för Åland*, for the original operationalisation of the Swedish language as the only official language in Åland Islands see Articles 29–31 the first Åland Autonomy Act of 1920, *lag* (*FFS 124/1920*) *om självstyrelse för Åland.*

17 *See*, in this book chapter 4; M. Suksi, *supra* note 11, p. 448.

18 *Språklagen* (*FFS 423/2003*). According to Suksi, there is no directly applicable and enforceable constitutional right to use one's language in the Finnish constitution, M. Suksi, *supra* note 11, p. 450 *see further* on linguistic policy, M. Ackrén, 'The Åland Islands : 100 Years of Stability' In C.H. Fong and I. Atsuko (eds.), *The Routledge handbook of comparative territorial autonomies* (Routledge, New York, 2022) pp. 110–122, and more comprehensively on linguistic rights in Finnish legislation, K. Myntti, *Finlands språklagstiftning* (Institutet för mänskliga rättigheter vid Åbo Akademi, Åbo, 2015).

19 RP 92/2002 rd, s. 31.

20 The special rules on language are regulated in the Åland Autonomy Act, *självstyrelselagen* (*FFS 1991/1144*), Chapter 6.

rights have been sparingly granted and have seldom, if ever, resulted in successful actions towards authorities or other private actors failing to perform their obligations under the legislative framework on linguistic rights. Thus, pursuing performance actions have not historically been a viable option for individuals, neither has filing declaratory actions to courts been a very promising or frequently used alternative.[21] Could the reason for the lack of litigation of linguistic rights be rooted in the presumption that Finnish public authorities are notoriously good at respecting and securing linguistic rights? Probably not.[22]

Rather than resorting to litigating, many individuals have found filing complaints to one of two Finnish ombudsmen to be a popular way for seeking justice and correcting deficient public practices concerning linguistic rights.[23] Nevertheless, it is important to note that both the Parliamentary Ombudsman (*Justitieombudsmannen*) and the Chancellor of Justice (*Justitiekanslern*) can only provide advisory opinions. Neither ombudsmen are competent to formally declare public practice deficient or to determine performance remedies. However, these opinions are generally respected by the authorities and function as a *de facto* source of public law. Despite the dominance of these declaratory enforcement mechanisms, the absence of performative enforcement has given the linguistic rights prescribed by law a declaratory character *de facto*.

The prominent status of the ombudsmen in the Finnish legal system might explain why individuals tend to avoid the courts in matters of linguistic rights. For those primarily seeking a general change of public practice rather than specific retribution, lodging a complaint to one of the ombudsmen could be a strategic choice. This process is cost-free, and legal counsel is not necessarily needed as the ombudsman undertakes the investigation. However, Finnish administrative courts do also have a duty to investigate such cases.[24]

A more important reason for refraining from litigation could stem from the potential burden of court costs, in combination with both procedural and

21 *Cf*, R. Hiltunen, *Country report: Non-discrimination: Finland 2022* (European Commission, Brussels, 2022), p. 45.

22 Concerns have been raised regarding the enforcement of linguistic rights for Swedish speakers, *see, e.g.*, the 2022 Annual Report of the Non-Discrimination Ombudsman, *Diskrimineringsombudsmannens årsberättelse* 2022, p. 51; CoE. *Evaluation by the Committee of Experts of the Implementation of the Recommendations for Immediate Action contained in the Committee of Experts': fifth evaluation report on Finland.* 7 October 2020, pp. 11–13; A. Jonsson, 'Konsten Att Olovligen Ta Makten Av En Autonomi' *Tidskrift utgiven av Juridiska föreningen i Finland*, (2021), *passim*; The Finnish Chancellor of Justice, OKV/945/70/2020.

23 *See, e.g.*, The Parliamentary Ombudsman Decision EOAK/2756/2021 of 2nd September 2022.

24 The duty is prescribed by the Act on Administrative Procedure, *lagen* (*FFS 2019/808*) *om rättegång i förvaltningsärenden*, Article 37.

substantive requirements of presenting evidence of a certain severity of negative impact following from a specific breach of linguistic rights. Such requirements theoretically implies a *consequential understanding of linguistic rights*. From this perspective, individual linguistic rights are breached only if there is both a deficient language practice and the deficit also has a negative impact on another right of the individual beyond mere communication in a certain language. For instance, if medical treatment is provided by using the wrong language and causes a misunderstanding, which in turn results in an injury, only then the linguistic right is enforceable. On the contrary, if there is only a misunderstanding but no consecutive injury, there is no breach of the linguistic right. In other words, from a strict consequential perspective, linguistic rights do not contain absolute rights to understand and be understood; rather, they encompass a relative right to avoid negative impacts from misunderstandings due to improper choice of language. As regards minority linguistic rights in European law, as interpreted by European institutions, this consequential perspective has had at least some legitimacy and explanatory value.[25]

3 The Prosperous Marriage of Young European Non-discrimination Standards and Old Finnish Linguistic Rights

Concerning the historical consequential reasoning regarding linguistic rights and discrimination, its defence could be attributed to the absence of a general prohibition against language discrimination in ECHR Art. 14, which served as the primary legal ground before the introduction of P12–1 in the contracting states. Article 14 requires a connection to another convention right to be applicable. In contrast, P12–1 applies to "any right set forth by law". Therefore P12–1, widened the scope substantially to other rights prescribed by law, whether at the national or international level. The question is whether this new requirement also lends itself to a more *formalistic understanding*. By "formalistic", I mean discrimination standards that solely assess whether legal rights – which aim to establish objective criteria for differential treatment based on legal grounds such as language – are fulfilled. On the contrary, consequential reasoning would focus more on whether differential treatment had a real adverse impact on an applicant compared to another person in a real comparable

25 As demonstrated, for instance, by the longstanding leading case on language discrimination, ECtHR (Plenary). *Case Relating to Certain Aspects of The Laws on the Use of Languages in Education in Belgium v. Belgium*. App nos. 1474/62; 1677/62; 1691/62; 1769/63; 1994/63; 2126/64. 23rd July 1968.

situation. Formalistic reasoning would occur by examining only whether a positive right to equal treatment, as set forth by law, was breached or not. This approach creates a presumption, based on the law, that others would be treated as set forth by law, i.e., in a differing manner.

There are two crucial questions for the Swedish speakers in Åland and Finland. The first question revolves around whether their linguistic rights, according to national legislation, qualify as "any right set forth by law" according to P12–1. The answer is probably yes. It is hard to see why codified linguistic rights would not fall within the criteria of "any rights set forth by law" under P12–1. Presumably, both national linguistic rights and anti-discrimination norms share a common purpose: to establish objective criteria for differential treatment, limiting subjective and arbitrary discretion based on language.

The second question pertains to how the criterium "discrimination" is to be understood. This criterium is just as essential as it is problematic because it introduces an element of circular reasoning. The title of P12–1 "general prohibition of discrimination" implies that the Article aims to define what discrimination is. Yet, by explicitly including the term "discrimination" as a criterium within this definition, the reasoning inherently becomes circular.[26] However, the interpreters of the article, the ECtHR in particular, cannot be blamed for this conceptual deficit in the language of the convention, a deficit caused by the drafters of the article and, ultimately, by the contracting parties. Nevertheless, discrimination emerges as a key concept requiring interpretation.

Not very surprisingly, the ECtHR has solved this issue by interpreting the term discrimination in P12–1 in accordance with its prior interpretation of the ECHR, Article 14, although – or perhaps because – this Article suffers from the same kind of circular deficit.[27] Consequently, the ECtHR has found it necessary to develop its own concept of discrimination for Article 14 and declared that the same conceptual framework should be used analogously as for discrimination in P12–1.[28]

In the recent case *Paun Jovanović v. Serbia* decided in February 2023, the ECtHR found a violation of P12–1 due to language discrimination. The definition used in the case therefore serves as a natural starting point for an up-to-date insight in the ECtHR methodology on language discrimination. The case involved a lawyer speaking *Ijekavian*, one of the two variants of the Serbian

26 This interpretation derives from the title of P12–1, "General prohibition of discrimination", reflecting my understanding of its objective.

27 A similar circular relationship between the title and the wording of the article applies to Article 14 of the ECHR, where both explicitly reference the term "discrimination".

28 *See*, ECtHR. *Paun Jovanović v. Serbia*. App no. 41394/15. 7th February 2023, para 74–75.

language officially used domestically. The lawyer was warned by an investigating judge not to use this language, despite having an undisputed the right to do so according to national law. The lawyer representing the other party, who spoke the other version of the Serbian language, received no warning. The key legal question was whether refusing an advocate to use a language permissible by national law before the court, while defending a client, constituted discrimination under P12–1. The conclusion of the ECtHR was affirmative. When justifying the judgement, the ECtHR reiterated a general three-step methodology for evaluating discrimination, referring to previous case law.

Firstly, different treatment must occur based on a status, predominantly one of those grounds of discrimination explicitly mentioned in Article 14 or P12–1, such as language. Secondly, the difference in treatment must occur in contexts that are substantially similar. Lastly, the different treatment could perhaps be justified by pursuing a legitimate aim and demonstrating a reasonable correlation of proportionality between the means employed and the aim sought to be realised.[29]

The Finnish definition of the standard, in relation to direct discrimination, differs slightly from the one prescribed by the ECtHR. The most striking difference is that the Finnish Act on Discrimination, Article 8, defines direct discrimination as occurring when "a person is treated less favourably than another is, has been or would be treated in a comparable situation due to circumstances of the personality of the person."[30] This implies that an actual difference in treatment between two real persons in real situations is not strictly necessary. Furthermore, if it is reasonable to assume that different treatment *would have occurred* for a hypothetical person in a hypothetically similar situation, the criteria for discrimination are fulfilled according to the Act on Discrimination, Article 8. The ECtHR does not provide such explicit guidance on whether hypothetical comparisons are accepted.[31] So, why does the Finnish legislator opt for a stricter standard? The reason given in the preparatory work is the ambition to codify a general act on discrimination, implementing several international documents on discrimination, *inter alia*, the European directive on equal

29 Having laid out these three general criteria, this is also the method by which the ECtHR conduct a detailed analysis of the case, *see*, ECtHR. *Paun Jovanović v. Serbia*. App no. 41394/15. 7th February 2023, para 80–92.

30 My translation of the original text: "Direkt diskriminering ska anses förekomma när någon på grund av en omständighet som gäller honom eller henne som person behandlas på ett ofördelaktigare sätt än någon annan har behandlats, behandlas eller skulle behandlas i en jämförbar situation."

31 On the comparable situations criteria in EU-law and ECtHR case-law respectively, *see further* CoE and FRA, *Handbook on European Non-Discrimination Law*, p. 23 ff.

treatment, which is limited to racial and ethnic discrimination.[32] Article 2 in this directive employs a similar wording to that of the Act on Discrimination, Article 8, also allowing for the consideration of hypothetical comparisons.

Racial and ethnic discrimination is generally considered as one of the most severe grounds of discrimination, obviously according to the EU legislators but also the strict standard applied by the ECtHR in cases involving racial and ethnic discrimination, compared to, e.g., language discrimination.[33] However, the Finnish implementation has, to some extent, broadened this strict standard to encompass other grounds of discrimination, including language discrimination. Consequently, Finnish legislators have merged limited in scope yet strict EU-law with general but vague case-law from the ECtHR, establishing legislation that is both strict and general in prohibiting discrimination. The relevance of this observation is further confirmed when studying the Finnish implementation of reasonable justifications, which determine whether different treatment is legitimate and non-discriminatory.

In the case *Paun Jovanović v. Serbia*, the ECtHR offered another important clarification regarding the margin of appreciation left to the member states when applying the general standard to the case:

> Lastly, the margin of appreciation [...] could only have been of relevance in terms of possible linguistic policy choices, as regards how to legally regulate the use of an official language in court proceedings, but not in a situation where, such as in the present case, there was a failure on the part of a judge to implement the undisputed interpretation of the already existing legislation on this matter.[34]

This conclusion was not a part of the general considerations, and in principle, one could question the relevance or transferability to other cases. Nevertheless, the conclusion may indicate that the margin of appreciation is not just limited to cases when there is a clear and undisputed national linguistic right being violated. Furthermore, the cited statement suggests that whenever there is a clear right according to national law, the threshold for proving a reasonable justification could be high, requiring *ex ante* justifications for the different

32 RP 19/2014 rd, at p. 73 referring, *inter alia*, to the European Council Directive 2000/43/EC of 29 June 2000 implementing the principle of equal treatment between persons irrespective of racial or ethnic origin.

33 ECtHR (GC). *Biao v. Denmark*. App no. 38590/10. 24 May 2016, para 94.

34 ECtHR. *Paun Jovanović v. Serbia*. App no. 41394/15. 7 February 2015, para 92.

treatment to allow a margin of appreciation. In other words, justifications that contradict national law and policy considerations are unlikely to be classified as reasonable if presented *ex post*.

This strongly echoes the formalistic understanding of available reasonable justifications codified in the Finnish Act on Discrimination, *Diskrimineringslagen* (*FFS 2014/1325*), Article 11, para 1, which states: "Different treatment is not discrimination if the treatment is justified by legislation, has a legitimate aim and the means to reach this aim are proportional in relation to the aim sought to be realized."[35]

This Finnish interpretation of "reasonable justifications" for different treatment, which includes criteria of formal legality and being prescribed by legislation, appears to extend beyond the interpretation of the same concept by the ECtHR. The ECtHR usually needs to take different regulative strategies into account, especially in common-law countries that may rely more on court developed norm-production than legislation. Thus, one might perceive the Finnish implementation as an over implementation of P12–1.[36]

Nevertheless, both the case *Paun Jovanović v. Serbia* and the Finnish implementation illustrate the potential strength of European discrimination standards when combined with undisputed, clear and categorical linguistic rights. In the absence of any exceptions prescribed by law, either in legislation or following from other legal sources, it becomes challenging to argue that other objective criteria could reasonably justify why those rights are not respected. Otherwise, ostensibly reasonable justifications, such as lack of human resources or time, simply appear questionable when national law does not allow for such considerations. Two recent examples from Finland confirm this formalistic line of argument.

---

35 My translation. The original wording of the Discrimination Act, Article 11, para 1 reads: "*Särbehandling är inte diskriminering, om behandlingen föranleds av lag och annars har ett godtagbart syfte och medlen för att uppnå detta syfte är proportionerliga.*" In the same Article, para 2, a reservation to para 1 is stipulated for unregulated situations where different treatment aims to protect human rights in a proportional manner. However, the reservation does not apply to public authorities and a couple of other situations, giving the reservation limited applicability. For an example of justifying different treatment motivated by rights protection, see ECtHR. *Adam and others v Romania*. App no. 81114/17. 13th October 2020, para 85 ff.

36 As previously mentioned in *supra* note 27, one possible explanation is that the Finnish Discrimination Act also implements other international instruments regarding non-discrimination. This implementation, at least to some extent, explains the emphasis on formal legality.

4 The Finnish Turn towards Formal Legality and Strict Equality in Practice

This section will present two distinctive examples.[37] These examples do not originate from court rulings, and their normative status – as sources of law – is therefore limited. The motivation for discussing them is simple: court cases regarding language discrimination are hard to find. Moreover, the selected examples illustrate the emergence of easily accessible and specialized institutions, along with cost-effective procedural avenues that the Finnish legislator has established for individuals who may lack the will or resources to turn to the traditional courts.

The first case was brought before the National Non-Discrimination and Gender Equality Tribunal (hereinafter the tribunal) (*Diskriminerings- och jämställdhetsnämnden*). The tribunal is not a court in the formal sense but consists of several highly qualified jurists, and has the competence to declare behaviour to be discriminatory. It can instruct public authorities to stop and refrain from such discriminatory actions, combined with the authority to impose penalties (*vite*) in the event of persistent discrimination. From June 2023, the tribunal has also been empowered to recommend compensation (*diskrimineringsgottgörelse*). However, to obtain an enforceable decision, the applicant must turn to the courts. Yet, if the tribunal has declared discrimination to have occurred, the declaration can be used as a decent prognosis of how the courts would likely assess the case.

The tribunal investigates the case without charging any fees, and there is no risk of the applicant bearing process costs. Furthermore, discrimination cases before courts and other law-applying authorities are to be decided with a somewhat reversed principle concerning the burden of proof, as stipulated in the Discrimination Act, Article 28. If the applicant can provide enough evidence to establish a presumption of discrimination, the burden of proof shifts to the defendant to show that different treatment either did not occur or that the difference was justified. This slightly reversed burden of proof is also in line with the case law regarding the burden from the ECtHR.[38] In summary, initiating a process before the tribunal is inquisitory, cheap, and involves minimal risks, but offers substantial potential benefits for an applicant.

37 For a general oversight in English regarding Finnish discrimination law, see R. Hiltunen, *Country report: Non-discrimination : Finland 2022* (European Commission, Brussels, 2022).

38 *See*, e.g., ECtHR. *Timishev v. Russa*. App nos. 55762/00 and 55974/00. 13th December 2005, para 57; ECtHR (GC). *Biao v. Denmark*. App no. 38590/10. 24th May 2016, para 114.

The first example from 2019 is a case brought before the tribunal concerning a parking fee, regulated under general contract law in Finland (*the parking case*).[39] The applicant, who spoke Swedish, had parked a car in a private parking lot where information about parking terms and conditions was provided in both Swedish, Finnish, and English. While the Finnish signs clearly stated that a special certificate was required to park without paying a fee, the Swedish and English signs did not specify any such certificate. The parking company (defendant) insisted that the applicant pay the fee based on the terms and conditions provided in Finnish. The applicant refused and turned to the tribunal, arguing discrimination had occurred and requesting the tribunal to compel the parking company to cease the discriminatory behaviour.

The legal question at hand was whether it classifies as direct discrimination under the Finnish Discrimination Act, Article 10, when a private entity – appearing to provide customer service in both Finnish and Swedish – requires a customer to fulfil a contractual duty specified only in the national language not spoken by the customer, in this case, Swedish.

The tribunal affirmed the question positively. It pointed out that although the Finnish Language Act does not apply to private entities, the defendant's language for communication and information was Swedish, English, and Finnish, according to the signs provided on-site.[40] The tribunal stated that individuals proficient in any of the three languages should be considered in comparable situations, having received information from the defendant in a contact language comprehensible to the applicant. Consequently, the tribunal argued that by exclusively providing information regarding a crucial contractual condition in Finnish, the defendant had treated the Swedish-speaking customer differently, presenting sufficient evidence to establish a presumption of discrimination. This hypothetical difference in treatment, based solely on the information available from the signs and not on a comparison with the situation of another present real person, distinguishes the case from *Paun Jovanović v. Serbia*. In the latter case, the ECtHR could compare the actual behaviour

39 Due to personal data considerations, the case was anonymised when requested from the National Non-Discrimination and Gender Equality Tribunal. The anonymised version excluded an official archive number but was given by the tribunal in 2020, and a summary was referred here: https://www.yvtltk.fi/sv/index/materiaalit/tapausselosteet/fallbeskrivningar2020.html#, accessed 30 May 2023. On the legal classification of parking relations as general contracts, see e.g., HD 2010:23, especially para 15.

40 *Språklagen* (FFS 2003/423). The fact that parking is not regulated by legislation *prima facie* suggests that P12–1 to the ECHR is not directly applicable to the case, as parking itself hardly qualifies as "any right seth forth by law" under the Article.

of the Serbian court towards the two different lawyers involved, obviating the need for hypothetical comparison.

However, the most relevant part of the *parking case* to this book section pertains to the justification test conducted by the tribunal. The tribunal observed that there was no legislation regulating parking situations in Finland. Consequently, there were no applicable legitimate aims under the Finnish Discrimination Act, Article 11, para 1, requiring grounds of justification to be prescribed by legislation. Additionally, the defendant had neither presented arguments nor proved evidence demonstrating any unprescribed grounds of justification related to the protection of human rights, under Article 11, para 2.

This case implies three important observations. Firstly, even outside the scope of special linguistic rights, private entities purporting to use multiple languages for information and communication place individuals from those language groups in a comparable situation under discrimination law. Secondly, the failure to provide equal information to individuals in comparable situations could constitute discrimination under Finnish law, at least when attempting to impose and enforce contractual obligations. Thirdly, the absence of reasonable justifications prescribed by formal legislation substantially raises the threshold for justifying differential treatment between language groups.[41] In essence, this reflects a formal understanding of discrimination, focused on the general contact- and information language, and formal reasonable justifications, as opposed to a free assessment of real and case-specific circumstances.

However, the decision of the tribunal was neither later confirmed nor repealed by a court, indicating its limited normative value as a formal source of law. Nevertheless, in my view, the Tribunal's legal reasoning is closely aligned with relevant legislation, well-structured, and seems to be in accordance with the methodological standards practised by the ECtHR. All in all, the decision appears methodologically persuasive. If my evaluation of the methodology is accurate, this is good news for Swedish speakers, particularly those seeking to assert their right to Swedish information on par with the Finnish information offered by private entities appearing to be bi-lingual in general.

Furthermore, another decision from the tribunal in 2021, *the custody case,* highlights potentially even more favourable outcomes concerning public authorities because they often have an explicit obligation by legislation to

41 The observation, regarding the difficulty in successfully proving reasonable justifications when no such justifications are prescribed by law is partly confirmed by the Supreme Administrative Court of Finland in HFD 2021:8. The case regarded indirect differential treatment, which according to the Discrimination Act, Article 11, can be justified even without a basis in formal law. Even so, the court did not accept the justifications suggested by the defendant.

provide services and information in Swedish.[42] The applicant was a Swedish-speaking minor, whom the police had temporarily taken in custody for sobering up. Although the minor had asked the police to speak Swedish, the police had on several occasions used Finnish in their interactions. The relevant question of law was whether it constitutes discrimination under Finnish Law when a public servant provides information in only one of the two official languages of Finland to an individual in a vulnerable situation, notwithstanding explicit requests to receive information in the other official language.

The tribunal reached a positive conclusion to the question. The tribunal argued that the police were obliged under national legislation to provide information in Swedish. Furthermore, the tribunal stated, the police had provided partial information in Swedish and had access to Swedish speaking personnel, placing the applicant in a situation comparable to that of a Finnish speaker. Since the police were exercising public authority (*offentlig myndighet*), any legitimate justification of different treatment must be prescribed by legislation. According to the tribunal, no such justifying legislative provisions were applicable in this case. On the contrary, the tribunal noted that the police is a bilingual authority obligated by the Act on Legislation, Article 23, to provide information in the language preferred by the client.

The most important insight derived from this case is as follows: If a bilingual Finnish public authority has Swedish-speaking personnel available, it places individuals from both language groups in a comparable situation. *E contrario*, this also poses a potential limitation on the general value of legal relevance of the case to other cases. The tribunal never assessed a situation in which such resources were unavailable, because the prevalence of Swedish-speaking personnel was undisputed. If, on the night of *the custody case*, the police did not have Swedish-speaking human resources available, one might question whether a Swedish speaker had been in a comparable situation to a hypothetic Finnish speaker. However, in the *parking case*, discrimination was found without a comparison with a real person, just by the fact that the information given to a Swedish speaker was not the same compared to a hypothetical Finnish speaker.

Indeed, while a bilingual authority is obligated to consistently offer bilingual information, one could question if such obligations, as prescribed by language legislation, proposing that people with different languages *should be* in a comparable situation, also imply that they *are* in comparable situations within

42 The National Non-Discrimination and Gender Equality Tribunal, Decision no 616/2018, 24 June 2020. The decision of the tribunal was recently confirmed by the Administrative Court of Helsinki in decision no 1064/2024.

the specific context of applicable discrimination law. A more general way to frame this question is whether legal norms themselves are enough to establish necessary legal facts (*rättsfakta*).

Although the answer to this question does not seem entirely clear according to Finnish law, lacking confirmation in either preparatory works or case law, the general tendency towards a formal and legalistic understanding of comparable situations seems difficult to ignore.

Concerning the available grounds of justification for different language information in Finland, the tendency towards formalism is already indisputable: the criteria prescribed in the Discrimination Act, Article 10, para 1, are absolute and precise, and the exceptions stipulated in para 2 are interpreted narrowly by the tribunal in linguistic cases, with reference to the Constitution.

5 Conclusion and European Outlook

The research question explored in this book section was whether the implementation of European standards of non-discrimination in Finland has facilitated the enforcement of minority language rights. Altogether, a positive answer seems plausible regarding the duties of public authorities. Furthermore, from the *parking case* suggests that the overly loyal implementation of European discrimination standards could have introduced entirely new linguistic rights for individuals approaching private entities professing bilingual communication but failing short in practice. Consequently, the recent marriage of old categorical linguistic rights with new enforcement mechanisms related to discrimination appears to be a promising development for Swedish speakers in both Åland and Finland who seek to enforce their linguistic rights. This may come as a somewhat unexpected turn for Swedish speakers in Åland and Finland, given the historical declarative character of their linguistic rights. However, it raises the question: Could the strict Finnish formalistic approach also reveal a new potential line of interpretation and argument as regards to European non-discrimination standards for linguistic minority rights?

As a starting point, a formalistic approach to discrimination requires making hypothetical assumptions when evaluating whether different treatment would have occurred to a person in a comparable situation, as prescribed by the Directive on Equal Treatment, Article 2, the Finnish Discrimination Act, Article 10, as evidenced by the tribunal's practical application in both the *parking case* and the *custody case*. A brief look at ECtHR case law shows that hypothetical comparison of different treatment in comparable situations could be accepted.[43] However, such comparisons are so far accepted primarily in cases closely connected to discrimination grounds subject to the ECtHR's strict standard, such as racial and ethnic discrimination.[44] Although there is some overlap between ethnicity and language, the European stance on embracing hypothetical comparisons in relation to language discrimination remains uncertain. Nevertheless, in principle, the gateway to hypothetical comparisons and formalistic reasoning is not closed for European human rights advocates.[45]

A formalistic approach could at least have some persuasive strength to the logical mind of a judge, particularly when framing a linguistic right and a potential justification to depart from the same right as a conflict of norms. In conflict with a clear and categorical linguistic right prescribed by national law, one can argue that any reasonable justifications to depart from this right should also have a legal basis in a legal source possessing at least the same hierarchical status in the legal system to serve as an acceptable *ex ante* justification. This purely formalistic argument, rooted in the hierarchy of norms, could perhaps support human rights advocates looking for a European pathway to cast doubt on any deficient *ex post* explanations for differential treatment.

On one hand, it would appear coherent to consider codified linguistic rights and to position them within the hierarchy of norms when interpreting and applying European prohibitions against language discrimination. On the other hand, as the Finnish implementation of European discrimination standards illustrates, exclusively accepting reasonable justifications prescribed by law could have fundamental and unpredictable consequences for the legal order.

---

43 See, ECtHR (GC). *Biao v. Denmark*. App no. 38590/10. 24 May 2016, para 91, showing even general policies could constitute discrimination regardless of effect, and ECtHR. *X and others v. Romania*. App nos. 73548/17 45521/19. 31 May 2022, para 77 ff illustrating that even the failure to prevent discrimination could constitute a violation of P12–1.

44 As demonstrated in ECtHR (GC). *Biao v. Denmark*. App no. 38590/10. 24[t] May 2016, para 94.

45 For further general reflections on the future role of the ECtHR in discrimination cases, see C. Danisi, 'How Far Can the European Court of Human Rights Go in the Fight against Discrimination? Defining New Standards in Its Nondiscrimination Jurisprudence' *International Journal of Constitutional Law* (2011) https://doi.org/10.1093/icon/mor044. https://doi.org/10.1093/icon/mor044, pp. 793–807.

CHAPTER 19

International Relations of the Åland Islands

Assessments and Ambitions as Expressed by the Parliament's Autonomy Committee

Susann Simolin

1 Introduction

In a globalised world where policy areas are affected by events which respect no borders and where decision-making happens at multiple levels, no political entity remains unaffected or can ignore developments in their surroundings. This is true not least for sub-state entities with legislative power, which as the world has become increasingly internationalised have needed to strengthen their capacity to manage impact from abroad as well as their international presence. As international relations are often regarded as a core area in relation to the state's sovereignty, states are in general eager to retain their competence in this domain, rather than devolving it. Nonetheless, the practice of sub-state entities acting in an international arena – practices which are commonly referred to as "paradiplomacy" – has become increasingly normalised.[1]

The autonomy of the Åland Islands in Finland is no exception in this regard. While the autonomy system was originally designed to focus on governance of local matters on Åland, and the Åland authorities in the 1920s had few contacts beyond Finland,[2] the impacts of developments at an international level are today clearly visible. A reading of contemporary annual reports of the Åland Government shows a profound awareness of international developments (such as migrations flows, the COVID-19 pandemic, a deteriorating security situation, and – not least – EU regulations) which have an impact on Åland and affect its competence areas, financial situation, and policies. They also provide proof of Åland participation across borders, especially in the Nordic and European co-operation projects.

1 N. Cornago, "On the Normalization of Sub-State Diplomacy" 5 *The Hague Journal of Diplomacy* (2010); J.A. Schiavon, *Comparative Paradiplomacy* (London, Routledge, 2019).

2 *For an overview of the development of the international contacts of the Åland Government see* S. Simolin 'Ålands självstyrelse i en föränderlig omvärld – 100 år av omvandling från lokal till internationell och global aktör', in S. Spiliopoulou Åkermark (ed.), *Styr ålänningarna sitt öde? Demokratiperspektiv på Åland* (Mariehamn, Cavannus förlag, 2021) pp. 23–49.

 | DOI:10.1163/9789004691117_021

While previous research has mostly explored the legal and formal dimensions of Åland's competences and participation within international relations,[3] mainly relative to its participation in the EU and the Nordic co-operation,[4] single case studies focusing on the international relations of Åland beyond the legal and formal level or explicitly using the lens of paradiplomacy[5] remain rare.[6] This chapter adds the perspective of how the leadership of the Åland autonomy – its parliament and government – govern Åland's international relations, and investigates whether they consider the scope of Åland's international activities and legislative and administrative competences in this field as sufficient, or in need of expansion or improvement. The chapter provides an overview of the legal acts and policy documents in which the international competences, activities, priorities, and positions of the Åland Parliament and Government are expressed. Subsequently, it zooms in on a particular set of documents, namely the parliament's Autonomy Committee's commentaries of the Åland Government's yearly reports on autonomy politics and external politics respectively, during the last eight years.[7] Based on the findings in these commentaries, it is discussed what needs and wishes for new activities or expansion of international contacts and competences

3 *See for instance* M. Suksi, *Sub-State Governance through Territorial Autonomy. A Comparative Study in Constitutional Law of Powers, Procedures and Institutions* (Springer-Verlag, 2011); Silverström, S, 'The Competence of Autonomous Entities in the International Arena – With Special Reference to the Åland Islands in the European Union', *International Journal on Minority and Group Rights* 15:2–3 (2008), pp. 259–271. https://doi.org/10.1163/157181108X332622.

4 K. Creutz and S. Spiliopoulou Åkermark, 'The Faroe Islands, Greenland and the Åland Islands In Nordic Cooperation', 69 *FIIA Report* (2021), The Finnish Institute for International Affairs; S. Stephan, 'Making Autonomies Matter: Sub-State Actor Accommodation in the Nordic Council and the Nordic Council of Ministers An Analysis of the Institutional Framework for Accommodating the Faroe Islands, Greenland and Åland within "Norden"', *European Diversity and Autonomy Papers* (2014) https://www.eurac.edu/en/institutes-centers/institute-for-comparative-federalism/pages/edap; S. Stephan 'Regional Voices in the European Union – Regions with Legislative Power and Multi-Level Governance. Perspectives for the Åland Islands', 1 *Report from the Åland Islands Peace institute* (2010); S. Simolin 'Att påverkas och påverka – Ålands ambitioner och självbestämmande inom EU' 2 Report from the Åland Islands Peace institute (2021).

5 *For a discussion on the concept of paradiplomacy*, see Schiavon, *supra note 1*. p. 6.

6 *See however* E. Hepburn, 'Forging Autonomy in a Unitary State: The Åland Islands in Finland' 12:4–5 *Comparative European Politics* (2014) pp. 468–487; P. Joenniemi, 'The Åland Islands: Neither Local nor Fully Sovereign' 49:1 *Cooperation and Conflict* (2014) pp. 80–97; B. Bartmann, 'In or Out: Sub-National Island Jurisdictions and the Antechamber of Paradiplomacy', in G. Baldacchino and D. Milne (eds.), *The Case for Non-sovereignty: Lessons from Sub-national Island Jurisdictions* (Routledge) Issue 386, pp. 53–71; C. Cantir, 'Kin states in Sub-state Diplomacy Conflict Dynamics' 16:1 *Foreign Policy Analysis* (2020) pp. 59–77.

7 Commentaries are written in Swedish and all quotes from the documents have been translated specifically for this chapter.

are expressed by the authorities. In essence, the main questions analysed are, what needs and desires for a) new or expanded direct international contacts and b) new or expanded legislative competences in the field of international relations are expressed by the autonomy's leadership?

2 Legislation, Policies and Procedures Which Govern Åland's International Relations

The legislative competences of the Åland Parliament are regulated in the Autonomy Act,[8] which is of a constitutional nature and can only be amended with the consent of both the Parliament of Åland and that of Finland. The state is responsible for foreign affairs, and originally, the competences of the autonomy focused solely on matters internal to Åland. However, with the new Autonomy Act of 1951, the Åland Parliament was authorised to approve of international treaties containing provisions involving repeal or amendments of provisions in the Autonomy Act for these to enter into force within the region.[9]

In connection to Finland's accession to the EU, the Autonomy Act was amended to contain provisions concerning Åland's participation in EU matters. Åland's main avenue for participation goes via participation in work at the national level, but in some instances it may also act directly in contact with EU institutions.[10] For instance, Åland may make direct contact with the Commission in matters falling within the powers of Åland and concerning the implementation of decisions made in the European Union.[11] In addition, the Åland Government has the right to designate a candidate who shall be nominated to one of Finland's seats in the advisory body the Committee of the Regions.

Åland's participation in the Nordic co-operation is not codified in the Autonomy Act but in a law issued by the Åland Parliament; the Law on the Åland Delegation in the Nordic Council.[12] The Nordic co-operation includes Denmark, Norway, Sweden, Finland, Iceland, and the autonomous territories, which besides Åland are Greenland and the Faroe Islands in Denmark. Nordic

8 *Autonomy Act 1991*. Självstyrelselag för Åland, 16.8.1991. FFS 1991/1144, Unofficial translation in English: https://www.finlex.fi/fi/laki/kaannokset/1991/en19911144_20200098.pdf.

9 *Autonomy Act 1951*. Självstyrelselag för Åland 28.12.1951. ÅFS 5/1952; Autonomy Act 1991 sec. 59.

10 *Autonomy Act 1991*, chapter 9a.

11 *Autonomy Act 1991*, sec. 59b.

12 Åland Parliament, *Law on the Åland Delegation in the Nordic Council* (Landskapslag om Ålands delegation i Nordiska rådet) (1984:25).

co-operation is governed by the Helsinki Treaty and includes legal, cultural, social, and economic co-operation, as well as co-operation on transport and communications and in environmental protection.[13] The Åland Parliament and the Åland Government elect representatives to the parliamentary body of the Nordic co-operation, the Nordic Council. The government representatives can also take part in the work of the Nordic Council of Ministers. The representatives from the Åland Parliament and Åland Government together form the Åland delegation to the Nordic Council, which issues an annual report to parliament concerning issues of core interest in the Nordic co-operation. This report is complemented with the report of Finland's delegation to the Nordic Council, of which the Åland delegation is a part. In addition, the work in the Nordic Council is guided by a policy document produced by the Åland delegation to the Nordic Council, which covers the years 2020–2023 and includes political priorities.

While Åland has few competences which are related to security politics or defence,[14] this field is nevertheless of great importance for the islands due to their demilitarised and neutralised status. Although Åland is not a party to the international and bilateral treaties entrenching the demilitarisation and neutralisation regimes, the autonomy has over time developed its actorness and actively monitors the status. The Åland Government has issued a policy on Åland's demilitarisation and neutralisation (*Policy för Ålands demilitarisering och neutralisering, 2015*), which is to function as an internal manual, guiding the approach of the authorities of the autonomy.

The work of the Åland Parliament, including regarding international matters, are regulated in the Parliament Act and the rules of procedures.[15] For each election period, the Åland Parliament appoints an autonomy political committee[16] (*självstyrelsepolitiska nämnden*), which manages questions concerning Åland's constitutional position and external relations, as well as matters concerning the European Union. The government is required annually to submit to the parliament reports on substantial matters of autonomy politics and EU issues. The report on EU issues may be included in a report on the government's external politics, which has been the practice since 2014. These two

13 *Treaty of Co-operation between Denmark, Finland, Iceland, Norway, and Sweden* (*the Helsinki Treaty*). This Treaty was signed on 23 March 1962 and entered into force on 1 July 1962, and has since been revised several times.

14 However, Åland has some competences within public order and security (Autonomy Act section 18, mom 6), and authority over the Åland Police.

15 Åland Parliament, *Parliamentary Act* (Lagtingsordningen för Åland); 2011:97; Åland Parliament, *Rules of Procedure* (Arbetsordning för Ålands lagting) (2015:87).

16 Henceforth called "the Autonomy Committee" or simply "the Committee".

annual reports from the government, the report over questions of importance to the autonomy (*redogörelse över självstyrelsepolitiska frågor*) and the report on its external policy (*meddelande om landskapsregeringens externpolitik*), are debated in parliament and are commented by the Autonomy Committee through commentaries (*betänkanden*).[17]

None of the documents discussed above cover comprehensively the overall aims and strategies of the Åland Government and Åland Parliament in the field of international relations. In the absence of such an overarching strategy for the international relations of the Åland Islands, this chapter focuses on the commentaries of the Åland Parliament's Autonomy Committee. The commentaries analysed here cover government reports for the mandate periods 2015–2019 and 2019–2023.

3 The Format and Substance of Reports and Commentaries on Autonomy Politics and External Relations

The distinction between "autonomy politics" and "external politics" might not be self-explanatory, as the government report regarding questions of importance to the autonomy also contains international questions, in particular those related to security matters.

Autonomy political issues of an essential nature include, in the committee's opinion, the Autonomy Act, the status of the Swedish language, the relationship with Finland and Sweden, demilitarisation and neutralisation, as well as the Right of Domicile, business rights, and land acquisition.[18] In its annual report on external politics, the government focuses on the EU and the work in the Nordic Council of Ministers,[19] but it also mentions other arenas for bilateral or international co-operation. The report on external politics discusses both the priorities of the government and how the Åland administration manages the effects of international pressures, such as EU regulations. The reports on

---

17 The reports of the Autonomy Committee (*betänkanden*) will be referred to as "commentaries", to clearly distinguish them from the government reports and thus facilitate reading. In the text the commentaries are referred to by policy area and the parliamentary year they were issued, for instance: Commentary on External Politics 2020–2021, Commentary on Autonomy Politics 2020–2021.

18 Commentary on Autonomy Politics 2020–2021.

19 The work in the parliamentary body, the Nordic Council, is covered in the yearly report of the Åland delegation to the Nordic Council mentioned above, but which is not included in the materials for this analysis.

external politics cover the activities which have occurred during the preceding year as well as outlining priorities for the year to come.

The Autonomy Committee has itself noted that there is a need to clarify the structure and boundaries of the external politics report in relation to the report on autonomy politics. The Committee has contemplated if it might be wise to merge the two, different, government reports into one, so that all matters concerning external relations are consolidated into one document.[20] It has also expressed concern that the reports over external policy are normally treated in Parliament first in June, thereby limiting the possibilities for the Parliament to affect the governments priorities for the current year. However, to date, the practice of delivering separate reports on autonomy politics and external politics, as well as delivering a report on external politics which covers both the past and current year, has continued unabated. While the commentaries do not summarise the overarching goals and priorities of Åland regarding its external relations, they do highlight the issues related to external relations which are considered essential for the autonomy and can be understood to convey "the view of the autonomy".

The relations between Åland and Finland are frequently discussed in the Committee's commentaries and, even though this chapter focuses on the international – not national – level, this dimension cannot be neglected for three reasons. Firstly, it might be essential to understand this dimension to be able to assess the stances of the Åland authorities when it comes to Åland's international relations. Secondly, some dimensions relative to the relations Åland-Finland include an international aspect. Thirdly, it can be considered that for Åland – understood as a political entity in its own right – "external politics" include both relations with the state and with actors beyond the national level.

Contact with the state authorities is Åland's most important arena for "external politics" and the Committee frequently emphasises the importance of good contacts between Åland and Finland. The views of the government and the Committee on the state of relations between Åland and Finland vary over the years, with a low point in its commentary on Autonomy Politics 2016–2017, where the Committee maintains that "The (Åland) government states that there has been a fundamental change in how the mainland views Åland's autonomy, which is also reflected in how Åland is treated. The willingness to develop the autonomy so that Åland residents are assured the opportunity

20 Commentary on Autonomy Politics 2020–2021.

to organise their lives as freely as possible for a region that is not a separate state[21] seems limited, as does the knowledge of the background of the autonomy and the Autonomy Act." While later commentaries display a less gloomy view, some concerns are repeated. For instance, regarding the revision of the Autonomy Act, the committee is not satisfied with the lengthy process (which started in 2010 and has not yet been concluded), nor does it find that the state is prioritising the revision sufficiently. It appears that the Committee does not find that the state is sufficiently open to the development of the autonomy.[22]

At a general level, the Committee, in relation to the revision of the Autonomy Act, in its commentaries promotes "development" of the Åland autonomy system and a more flexible system for taking over competences. In the process for the revision, the Åland authorities have called for enhanced competences for Åland.[23] This shows that, at a general level at least, to some extent expansionist tendencies exist. However, the question in this chapter concerns the potential expansionist tendencies specifically in the field of international relations. Within the revision process, strengthened competences for Åland in this realm have been discussed. A parliamentary committee, consisting of representatives both from Åland and the state, in 2017 issued a proposal for a new Autonomy Act, which included extended authority for Åland to negotiate and implement international obligations, as well as greater opportunities to influence the preparation of matters decided by the institutions of the European Union.[24] However, in its commentaries the Committee does not specifically discuss these requests in relation to the revision process.

4 Calls for Expanding Direct International Contacts

The clearest and most consistent claim made regarding direct contacts in the international arena, concerns Åland's wish for a seat in the European Parliament, a Member of the European Parliament (MEP). This claim has

---

21 This expression is paraphrased from preparatory works for the first Autonomy Act 1920. *Finnish Government Bill 73/1919*. (Regeringens proposition till riksdagen nr 73/1919 angående lag om självstyrelse för Åland). https://www.lagtinget.ax/sites/www.lagtinget.ax/files/rp_73_1919.pdf.

22 Commentary on Autonomy Politics 2022–2023.

23 Simolin, S. 'The Aims of Åland and Finland Regarding a New Act on the Autonomy of Åland: An Analysis of three Parliamentary Committee Reports (2010–2017)', 2:1 *Journal of Autonomy and Security Studies* (2018) pp. 8–48. https://jass.journal.fi/article/view/142854.

24 *Åland självstyrelse i utveckling. Ålandskommitténs 2013 slutbetänkande – Ahvenanmaan itsehallinnon kehittäminen.* Ahvenanmaa-komitean 2013 loppumietintö. The permanent address of the publication is http://urn.fi/URN:ISBN:978-952-259-600-0 (pp. 20, 32).

been repeated since prior to Finland's accession to the EU.[25] In its commentaries, the Committee supports and encourages the government's intentions to direct requirements towards the state concerning an Åland MEP, emphasising that Åland has a legitimate claim and that promises have been made at the state level which should be fulfilled. It also highlights that this issue could be brought to international attention.[26] The Autonomy Committee encourages the Åland Government to call on the Finnish Government to initiate the legislative measures required for Åland to form its own constituency in the European Parliament elections.[27] The latest twist in the struggle for an own MEP is that the parliament's speaker's conference on 6 September 2023 proposed that the Åland Parliament should bring an initiative to the Finnish Parliament.[28] The aim of the initiative is to bring about an amendment to the Electoral Act[29] so that Åland constitutes a constituency in the elections to the European Parliament, thus guaranteeing a seat in the European Parliament.[30]

For the Åland autonomy, relations with the EU are mostly managed through co-operation with the state in the national preparation of EU issues, and in government reports and the Autonomy Committee commentaries, the dimension of contacts with the state are also more frequently covered than the direct contacts Åland has with the EU. In the government documents it is furthermore often the activities the administration needs to take to meet EU requirements which are in focus, rather than the opposite direction – what stances Åland takes in this field. However, the Committee also encourages the Åland Government's proposal to work more actively with contacts with MEPs, to take part in the open consultations of the EU Commission, and in addition points to the importance of making direct contact with the Commission in matters of importance.[31] Åland has a representative in Brussels, who is employed by the Åland Government and is stationed at Finland's Permanent Representation in Brussels. The Committee believes that this arrangement is working well, but also notes that the tasks assigned to the representative are extensive. "Therefore, the committee requests the Åland Government to investigate and consider

25 For an overview, see S. Simolin, 'Att påverkas och påverka – Ålands ambitioner och självbestämmande inom EU', 2 *Report from the Åland Islands Peace institute* (2021).

26 See for instance the Commentary on External Politics 2020–2021 and 2015–2016.

27 Commentary on External Politics 2015–2016.

28 The Åland Parliament presidium petition no. 4/2022–2023. § 22 of the Autonomy Act grants Åland the right to propose initiatives to the Finnish Parliament.

29 Parliament of Finland, *Electoral Act* (Vallag), FFS 714/1998.

30 Commentary on External Politics 2022–2023.

31 Commentary on External Politics 2015–2016.

whether the Ålandic representation at Finland's Permanent Representation in Brussels should be strengthened."[32]

Another wish for expanded participation concerns the International Maritime Organization (IMO), an intergovernmental UN body for maritime affairs, of which Finland is a member and where Åland can participate in the preparation of positions and in the Finnish delegation at meetings. Even if merchant shipping falls under Finland's jurisdiction, shipping issues are essential for the Åland region and the Committee is of the opinion that the Åland Government should therefore consider applying for associate membership of the IMO.[33] In this context, the Committee emphasises the importance of Åland actively participating in international co-operation and working for Åland to become a subject instead of an object.

A third but more vaguely expressed wish for direct international contacts concerns Sweden. Government reports and commentaries repeatedly return to concerns over a perceived lack of commitment from national Finnish authorities regarding the preservation of the Swedish language in Finland, as well as deteriorating knowledge of the Swedish language within Finland's state apparatus. To ensure that the state authorities can maintain communication in Swedish with Åland in the manner required by the Åland Autonomy Act, the Committee suggests either that Åland be made a hub for Swedish language administration in Finland or for Åland to deepen contacts with Swedish authorities. It is however not clarified how or by whom the Committee finds this should be done.[34]

Contacts with Sweden are considered important not only for cultural and linguistic reasons but also for the economy. In its Commentary on External Politics 2020–2021, the Committee covers all these dimensions, maintaining that "For Åland, the ongoing pandemic and the introduction of border restrictions have been particularly challenging in relation to Sweden, not only because the free movement of labour and trade exchange has been negatively affected, but also because the linguistic and cultural connections with Sweden has become more difficult."[35] The Committee repeatedly calls on the Åland Government to work for the development and strengthening of co-operation and contacts with Sweden. Åland has previously maintained an office in Stockholm with one member of staff, but as it has been discontinued, the Committee encourages the government to consider the importance of

32 Commentary on External Politics 2018–2019.

33 Commentary on External Politics 2017–2018.

34 Commentary on Autonomy Politics 2018–2019.

35 Commentary on External Politics 2020–2021.

formalised and structured co-operation with Sweden, including representation in Sweden.[36]

The Nordic co-operation is considered by the Committee as an important arena for external politics for Åland, as active work in the Nordic area gives Åland good opportunities to influence the content of politics, and as the contacts that are created with parliamentarians and ministers are valuable.[37] Given this assessment of the importance of Nordic co-operation, questions about Nordic co-operation are less frequently discussed in the commentaries than might be expected. However, the parliamentary aspects of work within the Nordic context is covered in the annual report of the Nordic delegation, which is not discussed here. Furthermore, since Åland has taken part in Nordic co-operation since 1970, the forms of participation are established and the Committee might not see a need to discuss it. However, in one commentary the Committee highlights that the Åland Government does not actively participate in the work with legislative harmonisation (MR-LAG). This is because the work of the Council of Ministers mainly concerns issues outside Åland's legislative authority. The Committee, however. "… believes that it is valuable to participate in Nordic co-operation also in areas outside of Åland's direct jurisdiction and therefore encourages the Åland Government to participate in Nordic co-operation also in areas that do not directly fall within Åland's jurisdiction."[38]

5 Calls for Enhanced Competences

While, as described above, the autonomy has some ambitions to reinforce its direct contacts at the international level, when it comes to Åland's competences in the international field the autonomy seems to be less ambitious. Overall, in its commentaries, the Committee makes no general or explicit calls for extended legislative competences for Åland in the field of international relations. However, in some instances it highlights how in situations when Finland and Åland are affected by developments in the surrounding world 1) there is a need for Åland to have more influence at a national level, 2) that Åland's competences in such situations must be respected by the state, 3) that the Åland Government needs to use fully the room for manoeuvre it has within Åland's competences, 4) that there is a need for clarifications of the exact division of

36 Commentary on External Politics 2018–2019.
37 Commentary on External Politics 2017–2018.
38 Commentary on External Politics 2017–2018.

Finnish and Åland competence, and/or 5) that the Åland authorities themselves need to stay vigilant or improve their routines.

In relation to the COVID-19 pandemic in 2020, the Finnish Government from mid-March to May enacted emergency powers legislation and imposed a set of restrictions. The Autonomy Committee highlights how in this situation it was on several occasions unclear what legislation would apply in Åland and how the responsibilities, for instance relative to preparedness (*beredskap*), population protection (*befolkningsskydd*), and disease control (*smittskydd*), were to be divided between Åland and Finland. The Committee concluded that Åland's position during exceptional circumstances must be investigated.[39]

The Committee maintains that the long-term closure of the border with Sweden, which the Finnish Government decided on due to the COVID-19 pandemic, hit Åland extremely hard. According to the Committee, due to the great importance of shipping and tourism for Åland and Åland's insular location, the closing of the border with Sweden has meant that Åland's economy has been hit much harder than the economies of Finland and Sweden.[40] It is also noted that the border closure was not preceded by political contacts on the Nordic level, nor was the (Åland) government's statement obtained in accordance with Section 33 of the Autonomy Act – something which the committee finds serious. In the Committee's opinion, these events demonstrate a need for increased Åland influence over border issues.[41]

The committee also discusses that when during the COVID-19 pandemic, schools were temporarily closed on the mainland (Finland), and despite the lack of legal basis pertaining to Åland, the Åland Government accepted the state's wishes and closed schools on Åland. The Committee "... has no objections to such a precautionary measure being taken but believes that the Åland Government should in the future make use of the void provided by the lack of provisions in the Autonomy Act and the Emergency Act (*beredskapslagen*).[42] The void should also be used in connection with possible future states of emergency due to, for example, pandemics or climate crises." Furthermore, the committee maintains that "... it is important that the Autonomy Act is complied with even in crisis situations".[43]

One area where the Committee sees a need to ensure Åland's influence is participation at the national level in the preparation of EU issues. In this

39 Commentary on Autonomy Politics 2021–2022.

40 Commentary on External Politics 2020–2021.

41 Commentary on Autonomy Politics 2020–2021.

42 Parliament of Finland, *Law on Emergency* (Beredskapslag) (2011/1552).

43 Commentary on Autonomy Politics 2020–2021.

context the main issue concerns language. The Committee urges the Åland Government to (once again) inform the Finnish Government about Åland's language rights in the preparation of EU matters and to demand that the Finnish Government continuously informs the relevant civil servants about Åland's position in EU matters, as well as ensuring that relevant documents are translated in a timely manner.[44] The Committee also encourages the Åland Government to strengthen routines for internal work within Åland. It maintains that the number of EU-matters of interest to the region is substantial, while the resources available to the Åland government are limited, and it welcomes the Åland Government's initiative to oversee and potentially improve the internal routines. In relation to the management of EU matters, it also urges the Åland Government to more actively keep the Åland Parliament informed, and it encourages the committees in the Åland Parliament – including itself – to more frequently seek to be informed by the government of developments relative to EU matters.[45]

The reports and commentaries also show that Åland is impacted by wider developments in the surrounding world. For instance, in 2015–2016 the Committee highlights that Åland has to some extent seen the repercussions of the current security policy situation in Europe, as several refugees came to Åland in connection with the migration crisis. The Committee notes that, just as in the surrounding regions, the preparedness for this type of event was not very strong, and maintains that "The events thus meant a useful reminder of the need to upgrade preparedness for major unforeseen events."[46] Also, the Russian invasion of Ukraine has impacts on Åland's economy and security political situation, not least due to Finland's subsequent decision to accede to NATO. Both in relation to deepening military co-operation between Finland and Sweden, and in relation to Finland's negotiations for NATO-membership, the Committee supports the Åland Government's efforts to have Åland's demilitarised and neutralised status retained and confirmed.[47] It is emphasised that Åland "must remain demilitarised and neutralised regardless of the commitments that Finland otherwise undertakes", and the Committee encourages the government to be vigilant in this regard.[48]

In the commentaries, the Autonomy Committee maintains that the political leadership in Åland maintains good contacts and continuous dialogue with

44 Commentary on External Politics 2021–2022.
45 Commentary on External Politics 2020–2021.
46 Commentary on External Politics 2015–2016.
47 Commentary on Autonomy Politics 2015–2016.
48 Commentary on Autonomy Politics 2021–2022.

Finland's foreign policy leadership, as well as with Swedish leadership. As regular meetings are held with the Finnish leadership of the defence forces and border security, and there are contact groups at the civil service level with both the Ministry of Foreign Affairs and the Ministry of Defence, the Åland leadership is assessed to have a comprehensive understanding of the international environment. However, the Committee emphasises that, regardless of Åland's participation, "… the primary responsibility for respecting Åland's special status and upholding Finland's international commitments lies in Helsinki."[49]

6 Discussion

International developments affect sub-state entities, which need to at the least monitor, and preferably participate in and try to affect, their environment beyond state borders. The Åland autonomy has a limited scope of competences in international or semi-national (European Union) matters, and in many cases, especially regarding EU issues, participates in national work "via" the state. It can still be maintained that Åland actively participates in international co-operation at multiple levels, and that it works actively with "external politics", which is considered here to include both relations with the state and beyond state borders.

At a political level, there is no overarching and long-term strategy or policy document which guides Åland's international activities and priorities. Rather, these are discussed in several different documents where administrative activities and political priorities are sometimes mixed. These documents are part of the communication between the government and the parliament, rather than targeting the public. This can be compared to for instance the Finnish Government Report on Finnish Foreign and Security Policy, which is issued every four years, or with the Government of Greenland's Foreign Policy Report.[50] These reports present explicitly both the goals of foreign policy and the strategies planned for achieving these goals. The comparison may at first glance seem unfair, as Finland is a sovereign state and Greenland has a more extensive room for international manoeuvre than has Åland. Nevertheless, Åland de facto performs external politics, it discusses its activities in reports in this field, and there should not be any formal hindrances for Åland to issue a more comprehensive strategy.

49 Commentary on Autonomy Politics 2022–2023.

50 Last issued in 2024.

If the ambitions and goals for the international activities of the Åland Government and the Åland Parliament were to be more clearly defined, including how different activities within the area of international relations are prioritised in relation to one another and potentially synchronised to achieve these goals, it would also aid in assessing what needs the Åland authorities may potentially see for enhanced activity, capacity, and competences in this field. Potentially is an important word here, as an autonomy does not necessarily see a need to expand its competences or room for manoeuvre, generally or in specific policy fields.

In its commentaries, the Committee makes no explicit calls for extended legislative competences in the field of international relations. In several instances, the Committee takes a more defensive stance, aiming to protect or clarify the competences Åland already has, and to secure influence in national processes. The agenda is more ambitious concerning direct international contacts. The most consistent claim for a need for new international contacts relates to the question of a seat for Åland in the European Parliament. Other expansionist tendencies relate to participation in international organisations, where the Autonomy Committee wishes for enhanced membership in the IMO, and supports strengthening of already existing contacts, for instance with Sweden or within the EU.

The Autonomy Committee does not itself make any grand assessment or compare the scope and depth of Åland's competences and participation in international matters with that of other sub-state entities. However, in two of its commentaries it discusses how the Danish autonomies, the Faroe Islands and Greenland, are represented abroad, as well as how other regions are represented in Brussels. The Faroe Islands and Greenland also appear in one commentary relative to the overall stance of Finland vis-à-vis Åland. In this context, the Autonomy Committee refers to Denmark's relationship with its autonomies as a model: "In Nordic contexts, due to the Faroe Islands' application for full membership in the Nordic Council, there is no longer talk of the autonomous areas but rather of 'the small countries'." According to the Committee, this reflects the seemingly more generous attitude that the Danish state exhibits toward its small "countries", the Faroe Islands and Greenland.[51] Åland's authorities have so far not made a similar claim for full membership in the Nordic Council. In general, the Ålandic competences, direct international contacts and ambitions are more limited and modest than those of its Nordic sister autonomies.

51 Commentary on Autonomy Politics 2016–2017.

It should be mentioned that not all claims known to have been made or implemented are commented in the Committee commentaries. One such issue, which appears in the government programme, in government reports on external relations, and has been discussed within the process of revision of the Autonomy Act, is the question of establishing a supervisory function for the autonomy system, with an international organisation replacing the original role of the League of Nations.[52] Another issue not commented on is UNESCO, to which Åland became an associate member in 2021. In addition, associate membership in the WHO is mentioned by the government in its report, but not commented on by the Committee.

There may be several reasons why the Autonomy Committee expresses no claims for expanded competences. A first potential reason is that the committee is happy with the status quo and sees few needs for expansion. This might be the case when it comes to the field of security politics, where the process of Finland acceding to NATO may have provided an opportunity to demand an expanded role for the Åland Government in the monitoring of developments which – as the consequences of NATO membership are to date rather inconceivable – might in the future affect the status of Åland.

A second reason might be that Åland considers the possibilities to expand its competences in the international field as unrealistic. The Committee appears to perceive that the state is hesitant when it comes to expansion of Åland's competences in general. It might consider the defence and clarification of the competences Åland already has in an ever-changing environment as more important than efforts to expand into new fields.

Thirdly, any expansion of competences and activities in the realm of international relations would have an impact on the use of the administration's already rather stretched resources. So, a third explanation may be that the Committee is simply realistic in its assessment of how much the autonomy can manage. The list of international arenas where the autonomy takes part is already rather extensive, and judging from the government reports and Committee commentaries the impact of external regulations and shocks on most policy areas of the administration of the Åland Islands is extensive and requires resources. The resources and capacity of the administration might simply not be sufficient to expand into new fields or arenas.

---

52 Åland Government Programme for 2019–2023: "Based on the Åland Committee's report (33/2017), the question of which international organisation could function as recipient of the right of complaint that the Åland people possess in accordance with the Åland Agreement and Finland's other international obligations is investigated".

7 Conclusions

The Commentaries show that the Åland authorities are performing a rather demanding balancing act between the wish for self-determination and the practicalities of capacity, resources, and the willingness of Finland to expand Åland's room for manoeuvre. It also balances between the internal and the external, the boundaries between which are increasingly blurred with intensified internationalisation, not least within the European co-operation. In general, many of Åland's international relations are performed in close co-operation with the state and partly managed at a national level, which is why relations with the state are crucial also in this arena. It can also be concluded that external shocks, such as the COVID-19 pandemic and a deteriorating security situation with the Russian invasion of Ukraine and Finland's subsequent decision to accede to NATO, affects Åland and can stress the autonomy system. It seems in this volatile environment that the Åland authorities are taking a pragmatic stance, not expressing overly ambitious goals for expanding the autonomy's international room for manoeuvre, but rather focusing on performing its duties and clarifying and protecting the competences and undertakings Åland already has. Put more briefly, for the Åland autonomy, international relations are important, but overall, significantly expanding these relations seems not to be a main priority.

CHAPTER 20

Military Service and NATO Membership

Gun-Mari Lindholm

1 Historical Background

Following the slow melting away of the ice sheet in the Baltic region, the first skerries of Åland rose from the sea. The earliest inhabitants thrived on fishing and hunting. Seal was a precious game that offered food and the raw materials for clothing and tools. Moreover, it produced seal oil and furs, valuable items to trade. The Åland Islands' strategically important location in the Baltic Sea has since ancient times meant that the region's great powers have shown them a special interest. Already during the Viking Age, the islands were an important trading point for merchants in the crossroads of the trade routes; one north-south trading furs and salt, and one east-west trading some items as far afield as Byzantium, today's Istanbul. Archaeological finds giving evidence for this trade, such as Arabic silver coins, are not unusual in Åland.[1]

In the beginning of the 18th century Sweden's time as a great power in the Baltic region had ended. Åland was exposed to severe raiding by the Russians, and a large part of the population took refuge on the Swedish mainland during the troubled times. In connection with the Napoleonic Wars, Sweden also waged war against Russia. Russia occupied Åland in 1808, but an uprising of the local population defeated the occupying Russian force, retaking the islands. However, already the following spring, Russia again had control of Åland, and the war soon ended with a Swedish defeat. The peace treaty explicitly stated that even Åland was now subject to Russian sovereignty, thus Åland and Finland were separated from the Swedish realm.

The Russians immediately realised the strategically important location of the Åland Islands and began planning an extensive fortification on the main island. The fortress of Bomarsund would serve as a naval base to protect the approaches to St. Petersburg and to secure Russia's access to the Baltic Sea, and thus the world's oceans. During the Oriental War,[2] the not-yet-completed naval base was attacked by French and British forces, which razed the fortress

1 Mats Dreijer, *Den historiska bakgrunden till Ålands självstyrelse*, (Åländsk Odling, Mariehamn, 1971).

2 Also called the Crimean War 1853–1856.

to the ground. At the peace negotiations in Paris in 1856, Åland's statehood was discussed. During the on-going war, the Allies had offered the Åland Islands to Sweden, which, citing its neutrality, refused. Through the peace treaty, Russia was forced to accede to a convention on the demilitarisation of Åland, meant to weaken Russia's position of power in the Baltic region. The so-called Åland Servitude formed an integral part of the peace treaty of 1856.

2 The 1921 Convention on the Demilitarisation and Neutralisation of the Åland Islands

The Council of the League of Nations' decision in 1921 on the statehood of Åland included, in addition to the nationality guarantees, a demand that the Åland Servitude of 1856 should be strengthened and supplemented with the neutralisation of the Åland Islands. Neutralisation means that all military activities within a certain territory are prohibited for all warring parties in accordance with an agreement. Should a belligerent party direct activities towards a neutralised area, it constitutes a violation of international law.

At this time, the future Soviet Union did not have a recognised government and did not participate in the negotiations leading to the Åland Convention. Although the Soviet Union later became a member of the League of Nations, it did not accede to the convention, nor did it consider itself bound by it. In connection with the 1940 peace treaty between Finland and the Soviet Union, the parties concluded a separate treaty on the demilitarisation of the Åland Islands in which the Soviet Union had its interests considered. The content of the treaty is identical to the 1921 Åland Convention, except that it does not contain neutralisation and it entitles the Soviet Union to maintain a consulate on Åland with the special task of monitoring compliance with the treaty. As the war continued, Finland fortified Åland and notified the parties to the 1921 convention in the prescribed manner.

In the 1947 peace treaty that ended the Second World War, it was stipulated that "the Åland Islands remain demilitarised according to the current state of affairs".[3]

According to the Autonomy Act every Åland man is exempted from the otherwise compulsory conscription. Instead, Ålanders are expected to serve in the pilot and lighthouse service, a requirement that was never enforced. The reason for this was a consequence of the nationality guarantees, which make

3 <www.kulturstiftelsen.ax/internationella-avtal/webbversion/1947-fredsfordraget-i-paris-alandsbestammelser/>.

Swedish the only official language in Åland, while the language of command in the Finnish military is Finnish.[4]

3 My Experiences in My Roles as Minister and Speaker

During my time as Minister of Civil Affairs in the Åland Government, as well as speaker and deputy speaker of the Åland Parliament, we had annual gatherings with representatives from the Finnish Government, the Finnish Navy and the Finnish Border Guard. The meetings were to discuss previous agreements and how they had been complied with since we last met, as well as the current situation in our border areas. The meetings were always held in good understanding and were experienced by me as very informative.

The Border Guard (a branch of the Finnish military) felt that they needed to teach their new recruits to patrol, and become familiar with, Åland waters, but from the Åland perspective the military presence was perceived as problematic. Patrolling the borders is not an issue for Åland. However, concerns are raised when military ships penetrate further into the inner waterways and come close to land.

For my own part, I usually say that when you see the Sea Patrol, as they used to be called, in your own home waters, you feel safe, while it is the opposite when you see a military ship patrolling the same waters. You get worried. They don't belong in our waters.

4 The Finnish Border Guard

The situation has developed to the point where the Sea Patrol has been transformed into the Coast Guard, a section of the Finnish Border Guard, which today has increasingly military features and is part of the Finnish military. Those who work in the Border Guard have undergone training in the Finnish military and belong to the reservists in the military. This means that even those who work in the Coast Guard in the waters around Åland will play an active role in the event of external threats and war.

Much has changed recently regarding the powers of the Finnish Border Guard and the military presence in our waters and inland bays. Increasingly, the Åland police ask the Border Guard for assistance in their police work. This applies especially in the archipelago, where no police officers work daily, but even on mainland Åland you can see border guards working on shore duty.

4 The Self-Government Act for Åland (1144/1991).

When I, as a child, more than 50 years ago, was out fishing with my father, both he and my mother probably felt safe knowing that the Sea Patrol was present in the outer archipelago and also in our home waters. The officers of the Sea Patrol, at that time, were Ålanders with a good knowledge of both the people and the waters they sailed. They were familiar with the local population. Today it is very different. Along with the general process of centralisation, the Coast Guard has disappeared from the more peripheral stations, which of course has significance for the security of the archipelago's population in emergency situations.

Today, it is not unusual for those who are on duty in Åland to come from different places in Finland, which of course means that they have little knowledge of life in the archipelago and of Åland as an autonomous entity. In the past, most people knew each other because it was usually Ålanders working in the Sea Patrol and could follow an archipelago resident from the cradle to the grave.

5 The Home Guard and Reservist Association

In the wake of Russia's war against Ukraine more people have taken an interest in defence, also in Åland. Active politicians, leading civil servants and other people have signed up and participated in the military's basic courses.

A reservist association has been formed in Åland mainly comprising people who were not born in Åland, and who underwent military training in their youth and believe that they are needed in the defence of Åland. The formation of the reservist association has not gone unnoticed in the Åland public debate.

...

The Åland newspaper 15 June 2022:[5]

> The Ministry of Defence gives the green light for the Åland reservist association (…) "The Ministry of Defence has a positive attitude towards increasing interest in voluntary defence throughout Finland," the ministry writes in its statement.

The Åland newspaper on 23 April 2023:

> "The reason why the march has been organised is simply that we want to organise an event for our many members. We have not organised

5 All quotes are translated from Swedish to English by the author.

> anything before and this is a good place to start, says the association's chairman, Jonas Back. Inspiration has been drawn from similar events that are organised in Finland. (…) The events mainly take place this week in Finland, but in Åland we chose to march now because it suits our members best."

In April 2023, I submitted an article to the media which was published in the Åland newspapers as well as in the leading Finnish-Swedish newspaper Hufvudstadsbladet:

> When our safety is threatened, we help each other!
>
> National Veterans Day is celebrated on April 27 every year in honour of Finnish war veterans and in memory of the end of the war and the coming of peace. For me and my family, it is an annual reminder of the struggle of all young men in the war, of wounds that never healed, of mothers who lost their sons, of mothers who put their young children on a train to an unknown destination in a foreign country. People had to leave their homes and were forced to flee. The war tore families apart. In a war there are only losers.
>
> To me, the war meant that an uncle who was a sailor was imprisoned in a concentration camp, a father who as a young man at the front had to lift his dead friends onto the bed of a truck. The visible wounds healed, the invisible ones never.
>
> The war in Ukraine has touched us all. As fellow human beings, we have helped those affected in various ways and to the extent that we could.
>
> The unrest has led to renewed mobilisation even on the Islands of Peace, the demilitarised Åland Islands. Reservists march and Ålanders attend the defence training association's courses and learn, among other things, how to plant mines. I hope that their commitment will instead be turned to the voluntary organisations that exist in our civil society and thus follow the purpose of the Self-Government Act concerning the work obligations of the Ålanders.
>
> Columns are written about why Finns should risk life and health for Ålanders. According to the Åland Convention of 1921 Finland has undertaken primarily to defend the demilitarisation of Åland, and, if necessary, the other signatory powers will take over.
>
> All acts of war on Åland during wartime constitute a violation of international law as Åland is neutralised. This has become even clearer with Finland's membership in NATO, which both President Niinistö and former Minister of Defence Enestam meritoriously clarified.

It is valuable that many people get involved in civil preparedness tasks such as in the Red Cross, in volunteer fire brigades, in sea rescue, and in many other associations with the aim of helping others when needed. We experienced the strength of the small community during the winter storm Alfrida 2019. Neighbours helped each other, fire brigades, electricity and forestry companies worked around the clock, younger people helped older people, those with electricity offered food, heat and a sauna to those without. It showed cohesion and solidarity, as we all did what we could. We must manage and develop that; we must train volunteer forces that are prepared for various forms of crises.

True to my habit, I will wear my grandmother's iron ring today. She received it as a replacement for her gold wedding rings, which she gave to the state during World War II so they could buy weapons.

It is my memory of a war with only losers.

Gun-Mari Lindholm.

In 21 June 2023, the local newspaper Åland referenced a report from the Peace Institute's seminar on demilitarisation. Sia Spiliopoulou, Director of Åland Islands Peace Institute:

> When it comes to the Ukraine war, it's mostly the military that speaks out. The media seems to forget diplomacy. Then we usually get the counter question that Russia has violated international law, isn't it naive that we should respect international law? However, if someone drives too fast we don't abolish the whole traffic legislation, but we do realise how important the laws are. If we scrap all the rules, rogue states will have free rein. I think we are already talking as if the war is here, but it is not. We will support Ukraine in every possible way, but we cannot waive our obligations. Finland is not at war and there is no war in the Baltic Sea.

She warns of chaos if international agreements are ignored:

> Many diplomats and lawyers are worried about the consequences if we stop caring about concluded agreements. Especially for small players, the agreements are very important. It can become a domino effect.

In the same article, the issue of the reservist association is raised. Sia Spiliopoulou Åkermark says:

> ...that demilitarisation and neutralisation are strongly connected with self-government and the protection of the Swedish language. (...) In

> different phases, Åland has been pressured by various actors to renounce either demilitarisation or self-government. One needs to understand that if Åland's demilitarisation is called into question, it can also have consequences for the self-government and vice versa.

During the lecture, Sia Spiliopoulou Åkermark was asked to give her view on the Åland reservist association:

> It is complex and important to discuss. It is quite natural that the Ukraine war makes people worried and angry and that a feeling of wanting to do something grows. That is why it is good that it is completely voluntary to do military service, if you so wish. We should also be generous with the freedom of association, which is a democratic right. I believe and hope that they have a true sense of patriotism and want to help the state. But there are people who are over-interested in the military and it can be a slippery slope. Now, I'm not a psychologist but one can get into a spiral thinking where nothing other than violence is seen as a solution to violence. What the defence wants is a strong will to defend, not those who want to use violence when violence is not needed. It is clear that reservist training cannot be arranged on Åland.

She highlights civil preparedness on Åland, which is Åland's responsibility:

> I would call for some kind of watchdog concerning Åland's civil preparedness. Which organisations exist? You can get involved in so many ways. Here there are, for example, the Red Cross, the volunteer fire brigade, the Åland Sea Rescue, Save the Children. During, for example, the Estonia disaster and the storm Alfrida we saw how Åland society can respond when there is a crisis.

In general, everyone has an interest in resolving conflicts as quietly as possible. "If you talk as if there is already a war, the risk of the use of violence is significantly higher. It is important to keep the tension level as low as possible" says Sia Spiliopoulou Åkermark.

6 NATO Membership

During Finland's application to NATO, Åland's special status within Finland caused a heated debate in Finnish newspapers. The debate ranged from abolishing the demilitarisation and closing the Russian consulate in Mariehamn to the more moderate question whether Åland's demilitarisation and neutralisation would in any way be compromised by the Finnish NATO membership.

Finnish Foreign Minister Pekka Haavisto chose to have a representative for Åland in the Finnish delegation to participate in the negotiations for NATO membership. Anton Nilsson, the Åland Government's Minister Counsellor to the EU, participated in the negotiations.

Anton Nilsson writes in an article in the Åland newspaper in September 2023:[6]

> Sometimes those who defend demilitarisation and neutralisation are accused of being naïve. Nothing could be more wrong. On the contrary, it is a very dangerous path to even consider shaking off internationally binding agreements. What is naïve, on the other hand, is to think that we would become safer by seriously impairing our ability to maintain two out of three legs of our security policy. In this context, it is also worth mentioning that it is of course good that Ålanders also feel a desire to contribute in some way when there is uncertainty in the world. But it is extremely important to do so in a way that does not risk challenging the framework of demilitarisation and neutralisation.

President Sauli Niinistö's speech at the opening of the Finnish Parliament in April 2023:[7]

> Åland's position has been brought up in the discussions here in Finland. I would like to point out that it is more stable now than perhaps ever: an act of aggression towards Åland would be a declaration of war against NATO. It is clear that the situation of the region is given special attention in NATO's joint defence planning. We have always regarded the binding effect of multilateral international agreements as a condition of life for small countries. It is good to hold on to that idea. However, changing circumstances and the rapid development of military technology may affect the actual application of existing agreements.

6 Ålandstidningen, 9 september 2023.

7 Republikens president Sauli Niinistös tal vid riksmötets öppnande den 13 april 2023 – Tasavallan presidentti Sauli Niinistö.

7 Defence Training and Conscription

The annual musters are important occasions for the Armed Forces because it provides an opportunity to meet conscripts in person. At conscription, the conscript's fitness for service is determined. The conscripts are heard about wishes regarding the service and decisions about the service are made. With the call-up, every young person gets the opportunity to discuss with representatives of youth work about, among other things, the upcoming service, their own everyday life, future plans and other issues that they are thinking about.

The Finnish conscription act states that completion of conscription includes conscription service, rehearsal exercise, extra duty and duty during mobilisation, as well as participation in mustering and inspection of fitness for duty.[8] It also refers to the exemption for Åland in the Autonomy Act, where it states that persons carrying an Åland citizenship are exempted from military duty. Instead, they are obliged to conduct lighthouse and pilot service, which provision is obsolete today, and civil duties in case a conforming law in both the Åland and Finnish parliaments is passed.[9]

A working group appointed by the Finnish Ministry of Defence for the development of the conscription system came up with its proposal in January 2024. The working group proposes: "… that for all 17-year-olds there should be a common defence day that is carried out in the educational institutions. During the day, the young people should receive information about defence, conscription and overall security. The goal of the defence day is to increase young men's awareness of the obligations that apply up to the age of conscription, and young women's awareness of the possibilities of applying for service."[10]

The working group's proposal is that the rally should be held throughout Finland, also on Åland. Implementing the working group's proposal on Åland would be a breach of the self-government. Because Åland is demilitarised we are not included in Finland's general military conscription. Åland has legislative competence in both education and healthcare. This makes it impossible for the Finnish working group's proposal to apply in Åland when it comes to militarising education in the manner proposed, and for all 17-year-olds to undergo a health examination for recruitment purposes.

The working group's proposal has been received in different ways among official representatives and the general population in Åland. The Åland Government, via the Premiere Minister Katrin Sjögren, expressed its position

8 Conscription Act (1438/2007).

9 The Self-Government Act for Åland (1144/1991).

10 <www.defmin.fi/sv/teman/utveckling_av_varnplikten#9e33e0db>.

in the Åland newspaper on 2 February 2024: "I am completely convinced that we will find solutions that work within the framework of the demilitarisation and the Åland jurisdiction" she writes, and continues: "If the proposal becomes a reality, the plan might have to consider Åland in a different manner … My view is that the Ministry of Defence and the working group definitely have control over the demilitarisation and the laws and agreements that apply," writes Katrin Sjögren.

If we Ålanders think it would be wise to offer our young people information about civil preparedness work, we can do it ourselves. We can put together material containing significant information regarding civil preparedness work and offer the schools the opportunity to inform their students about it. The material could contain, for example, information about demilitarisation and neutralisation and what this means both in peacetime and in the event of war. It could further contain information about the third sector's important work in civil preparedness work, about the Red Cross, about the important work of volunteer fire brigades, about maritime rescue, about energy supply and so on, but also about the authorities' responsibilities and about the duties of the health and medical services. It could give a deeper insight into our society and perhaps also interest young people in taking part in various activities.

If the working group's proposal goes ahead and becomes a bill, it must also be approved by the Åland Parliament. At that stage, the Swedish Parliament will have an important role to play in standing up for the self-government as well as Åland's demilitarisation, considering that Sweden was a party to the Åland Agreement of 1921.[11]

---

11 The Åland Agreement of 1921 between Sweden and Finland on the nationality guarantees for the Åland people as part of the decision by the League of Nations in 1921.

CHAPTER 21

Åland: Sport Organisations and Sport Events

Bogi Eliasen

A substantial part of the identity of countries, nations and peoples is built on participation in sports.[1] Athletes and sports teams are identified as coming from or representing a country in international competitions, regional and world championships and the Olympics. Åland is not a sovereign state but, based on a special international agreement, it is a country recognised in international law as a subject and not merely as an integrated part of Finland like any other Finnish region.

In this paper, the Faroe Islands and a number of other countries and territories will be examined with the purpose of describing the membership opportunities of non-sovereign entities in international sport organisations and events. How and where the Faroe Islands have obtained international sport membership will be identified, plus some reflections on where this has not been achieved. The paper can also be seen as providing an overview of the possibilities that Åland has for achieving membership in international sport so that Åland athletes and teams may compete under their own flag if and when they so desire.

1 Functional Sovereignty Approach

In the post-Westphalian world of globalism it is common to work with a concept of functional sovereignty, meaning that countries with formal power over a specific policy area are admitted to membership in inter-governmental organisations which are involved in the same field of activity. This is the case with e.g. the Faroese membership of the International Maritime Organisation (IMO), the Food and Agriculture Organisation (FAO) and the United Nations Educational, Scientific and Cultural Organisation (UNESCO). Among other inter-governmental organisations which use this approach are the World

1 For an earlier article on a similar topic, see Bogi Eliasen, "Non-Sovereign Polities and Their Access to the International Community" in Sjúrður Skaale (editor), The Right to National Self-Determination. The Faroe Islands and Greenland, Leiden: Martinus Nijhoff Publishers, 2004, pp. 179–203.

Trade Organisation (WTO), the World Meteorological Organisation (WMO), the International Labour Organisation (ILO) and the World Health Organisation (WHO). Also the International Criminal Police Organization (Interpol) and the Organisation for Economic Co-operation and Development (OECD) could be mentioned as international organisations where the functional approach is employed.

In international relations it is generally understood that non-sovereign but overseas polities will not disrupt territorial integrity by gaining membership in sport organisations in their own right. The support of the so-called metropolitan state is required, which for the Faroe Islands means the agreement of Denmark. When the polity has metropolitan acceptance to membership, most organisations will accept the application.

2 What Is a Country?

In the context of sport organisations, and seen from a Faroese point of view, there has been an ongoing discussion about what is a territory and what is a country. The general understanding of territory is a colony, as can be seen in the process of decolonisation at the United Nations, with its lists of non-self-governing and trust territories. The Faroe Islands have never been on such a list because they have always been considered a country in the Danish Commonwealth (rigsfællesskabet). The Faroes have furthermore a very long parliamentary tradition, which, it is claimed, is the oldest in the world.

Historically, the Faroe Islands have never been fully integrated into Denmark but remained a people and a proper country in the Danish Commonwealth. This is underscored in the most important bilateral treaties, where it is stated that the Faroes and Denmark are equal parties in this commonwealth.[2] Access to international cooperation and membership of inter-governmental organisations underscore that the Faroe Islands are recognised as a country in

2 The Foreign Policy Act of the Faroe Islands, no. 80 of 14 May 2005, on the Conclusion of Agreements under International Law by the Government of the Faroes. The Act is based upon a Treaty between the Government of the Faroes and the Government of Denmark as equivalent Parties; for full text see "https://www.government.fo/en/foreign-relations/constitutional-status/the-foreign-policy-act". See also Act no. 79 of 12 May 2005 on the Assumption of Matters and Fields of Responsibility by the Faroese Authorities. It is based upon a Treaty between the Government of the Faroes and the Government of Denmark as equivalent Parties; for full text see "https://www.government.fo/en/foreign-relations/act-on-assumption-of-fields-of-responsibility". All websites referred to in this article were visited on 20 December 2023.

international law and by international governmental bodies. In international law the Faroe Islands are thus a subject of international law.[3]

3 Compared to the Cook Islands

Free Association is a model developed in the UN decolonisation process as one of the results that can flow from a colony's exercising of the right of self-determination. It was created as a middle course between secession and integration. Several former island colonies, like Micronesia and the Cook Islands, are in free association with the former colonial powers – in the two instances mentioned with the United States and New Zealand, respectively.[4]

Free association provides for, or can lead to, formal sovereignty within the UN decolonisation framework. It has been argued that the Faroe Islands actually enjoy free association with Denmark. By contrast, while geographically separate and to a large degree self-governing, the Åland Islands have so far been seen as an autonomous territory. With the achievement of sovereignty, the right to membership in international or regional sport bodies is likely to follow when other practical requirements have been fulfilled.

4 Differing Requirements

There is no common approach to the membership policies of international sport federations regarding non-sovereign polities. The break-down of the Soviet Union shocked the system established after World War II. The aftermath witnessed several secessions, civil wars and secessionist movements, many of which approached inter-governmental and non-governmental organisations in order to obtain membership as a part of their struggle for the restoration of old states or the creation of new ones. This was especially the case for former Soviet republics and Eastern European countries.

Already prior to the breakdown of the Soviet Union, most sport federations were open to polities which met an administrative standard, generally understood to mean an approved local or national body organising competitions

3 Gudmundur Alfredsson, "The Faroese People as a Subject of Public International Law" in Føroyskt Lógar Rit – Faroese Law Review, vol. 1, no. 1, January 2001, pp. 45–57.

4 Gudmundur Alfredsson, A Step in the Decolonisation Process: Free Association, Nasiffik Working Paper No. 1, Nasiffik – Centre for Foreign and Security Policy at Ilisimatusarfik (University of Greenland) and the Danish Institute of International Studies (DIIS), Nuuk, May 2023, 6 pages; available on line at "https://www.diis.dk/en/research/a-step-in-the-decolonisation-process-free-association".

according to the accepted rules of regional and/or global sport organisations in the respective field. Some federations, like those for volleyball, handball and table tennis, have kept that practice, while others, like the World Athletics (formerly known as the International Amateur Athletic Federation or IAAF), are only open to countries with a recognised international profile. Others, like basketball, require IOC (Olympic) membership.

5 Comparing Åland with the Faroe Islands and Cook Islands

The comparison between the Faroe Islands, Cook Islands and Åland in the context of international sports memberships, set forth in the following table, helps to illustrate what is possible. Åland has participated in the international Island Games since 1985. It is the only international competition that Åland currently participates in. Participation in the International Islands Games does not require sovereignty or statehood.[5] The differences between Åland and the Faroe Islands are also interesting, even striking, as both are self-governing Nordic polities. To broaden the comparison, the following table also shows memberships acquired by the Cook Islands.

Faroe Islands	Cook Islands	Åland
NatWest Islands Games. Will be hosted by the Faroes in 2027.		NatWest Island Games
ENGSO (European Non-Governmental Sports Organisation)		
IBF (International Badminton Federation)	IBF	
ITTF (International Table Tennis Federation)	ITTF	
EVBU (European Volleyball Confederation)	IVBF	
FIFA (World Football Association)	FIFA	
IHF (International Handball Federation)	IHF	
IPC (International Paralympic Committee)		
IJF (International Judo Federation)	IJF	

5 For information about the International Island Games Association (IIGA), see their website at "https://www.iiga.org/".

(*cont.*)

Faroe Islands	Cook Islands	Åland
FINA (Fédération Internationale de Natation)	FINA	
FITA (Fédération Internationale de Tir à l'Arc)		
UEC (European Cycling Union)		
International Triathlon	International Triathlon	
International Shooting Sports Federations		
	International Golf Federation	
	World Sailing Organization	
	International Tennis Federation	

The Faroe Islands have had a long-standing application for membership in the International Olympic Committee (IOC). Even given that the Faroes were eligible for IOC membership prior to the change of rules in 1992 and had submitted the application before that change, the Faroes have not been successful in gaining admission. A resulting complication is that, for example, Faroese swimmers, who can participate in international competitions representing the Faroe Islands, need to be part of the Danish team if they want to participate in the Olympic Games.

While it will be difficult to obtain a full membership of IAAF (World Athletics), it should be possible for the Faroe Islands to obtain membership of Nordic Athletics, as it is up to the member countries to decide. While the Faroe Islands have pushed for Nordic Athletics membership for many years, it has yet to be realised. Nordic Athletics does not have a formalised organisation but rather a Nordic Handbook entitled 'Rules and Regulations covering the Meetings and Competitions between the Nordic Athletic Federations', which provides the framework for collaboration.[6] It is quite clear that the will of the

6 The Rules and Regulations covering the Meetings and Competitions between the Nordic Athletic Federations are available at "https://fri.is/wp-content/uploads/2022/03/Nordic-Handbook-updated-June-2021.pdf".

five Nordic states is the decisive factor whether the Faroe Islands, Åland and Greenland can participate under their own flags in Nordic championships.

6 Concluding Remarks

The Faroe Islands have been an independent country for at least 1200 years and for the last 1000 years as an independent or separate country, first within the Kingdom of Norway and later as part of the Commonwealth of Denmark.

The Faroes have the support of the so-called metropolitan state, Denmark, both when it comes to membership of international sports federations as well as in many inter-governmental organisations. Thus the membership of the Faroe Islands in any particular organisation would not constitute a precedent for secessionist regions as the Faroes already constitute a country in their own right, have metropolitan state acceptance, are located overseas, and will not disrupt the territorial integrity of the state.

When inter-governmental organisations allow certain countries membership, it should be natural for international sport organisations to follow the same approach, as many of them already do. In order to gain membership of additional organisations, such as IAAF, Åland and the Faroe Islands would have to enjoy the support of Finland and Denmark, respectively, and underlining that Åland and the Faroe Islands are countries and not territories. As concerns participation in Nordic Athletics cooperation, the possibility for the Faroe Islands, Greenland and Åland rests on the will of the current participating countries, that is Finland, Sweden, Norway, Denmark and Iceland.

When we look at other continents in the world the openness of non-sovereign polities for membership in sport organisations and events is wider than is generally the case in Europe. The criteria for membership are also different between sports associations, be they regional or global and depending on the type of sport.

If a wish arises from Åland to participate as a country in international sports, this article and the accompanying annexes show some clear precedents. Although the membership window in Europe is narrower than in the rest of the world, there are openings and they could be actively pursued. One place to start could be in the specific sports in which Åland participates as part of the International Island Games.

The following annexes contain lists of non-sovereign countries which are members of a series of sport organisations. The lists are indicative rather than exhaustive.

Annexes

1

IAAF – world athletics, with 213 member countries and territories at 2010:[7]
Aruba – Dutch commonwealth
Anguilla – British Overseas Territory
British Virgin Islands – British Overseas Territory
Bermuda – self-governing British Overseas Territory
Cayman Islands – self-governing British Overseas Territory
Montserrat – self-governing British Overseas Territory
Puerto Rico – unincorporated territory of the United States classified as a commonwealth
Turks & Caicos Islands – self-governing British Overseas Territory
US Virgin Islands – organised, unincorporated United States territory
Gibraltar – self-governing British Overseas Territory
Hong Kong – special administrative region in China
Macao – special administrative region in China

2

European Non-Governmental Sports Organisation (ENGSO):[8]
Faroe Islands FAROESE CONFEDERATION OF SPORTS AND OLYMPIC COMMITTEE – autonomous territory of the Kingdom of Denmark
Greenland SPORTS CONFEDERATION OF GREENLAND – autonomous territory of the Kingdom of Denmark

3

IBF (International Badminton Federation):[9]
Aruba – Dutch commonwealth
Macau – special administrative region in China
Bermuda – self-governing British Overseas Territory
Cayman Islands – self-governing British Overseas Territory
Norfolk Island – external territory of Australia
Cook Islands – free association with New Zealand
Curaçao – constituent country of the Kingdom of the Netherlands

7 See "https://worldathletics.org/about-iaaf/structure/member-federations/europe".
8 See "https://engso.eu/our-network/members/".
9 See "https://corporate.bwfbadminton.com/about/membership/".

Puerto Rico – unincorporated territory of the United States classified as a commonwealth
Saint Helena – British Overseas Territory
Falkland Islands – British Overseas Territory
Faroe Islands – autonomous territory of the Kingdom of Denmark
French Polynesia – overseas collectivity and an overseas country of the French Republic
Gibraltar – self-governing British Overseas Territory
Greenland – autonomous territory of the Kingdom of Denmark
Guam – territory of the United States
Hong Kong – special administrative region in China

4

EBF (European Badminton Federation):[10]
Gibraltar – self-governing British Overseas Territory
Faroe Islands – autonomous territory of the Kingdom of Denmark
Greenland – autonomous territory of the Kingdom of Denmark

5

ITTF (International Table Tennis Federation):[11]
Anguilla – British Overseas Territory
American Samoa – unincorporated territory of the United States
Aruba – Dutch commonwealth
Bermuda – self-governing British Overseas Territory
Bonaire – special municipality of the Netherlands
Cayman Islands – British Overseas Territory
Cook Islands – free association with New Zealand.
Curacao – constituent country of the Kingdom of the Netherlands
Falkland Islands – British Overseas Territory
Faroe Islands – autonomous territory of the Kingdom of Denmark
Micronesia – UN member State in free association with the USA
Guernsey – self-governing British Crown dependency
Greenland – autonomous territory of the Kingdom of Denmark
Gibraltar – self-governing British Overseas Territory
Guam – territory of the United States
Hong Kong – special administrative region in China
Isle of Man – self-governing British Crown dependency

10 See "http://badmintoneurope.com/CMS/?cmsid=239&pageid=4651".
11 See "https://directory.ittf.com/#/home".

US Virgin Islands – organised, unincorporated United States territory
British Virgin Islands – British territory
Jersey – self-governing British Crown dependency
Saint Maarten – constituent country of the Kingdom of the Netherlands
Marshall Islands – UN member State in free association with the US
Northern Mariana Islands – unincorporated territory and commonwealth of the United States
Norfolk Island – external territory of Australia
New Caledonia – overseas territory incorporated by France
Niue – self-governing island country in free association with New Zealand
Puerto Rico – unincorporated territory of the United States classified as a commonwealth
Tokelau – dependent territory of New Zealand
Wallis and Futuna – French overseas territory

6

IVBF (International Volleyball Federation) and EVBU (European Volleyball Confederation):[12]
Faroe Islands – autonomous territory of the Kingdom of Denmark
Gibraltar – self-governing British Overseas Territory
Greenland – autonomous territory of the Kingdom of Denmark

7

Asian Volleyball Confederation:[13]
American Samoa – unincorporated territory of the United States
Cook Islands – free association with New Zealand.
Guam – territory of the United States
Marshall Islands – UN member State in free association with the United States
Niue – self-governing island country in free association with New Zealand
Northern Mariana Islands – unincorporated territory and commonwealth of the United States
Macao – special administrative region in China
Hong Kong – special administrative region in China

12 See "https://www.fivb.com/en/thefivb/directory/europeanvolleyballconfederation" and "https://www.cev.eu/team/13000-faroe-islands".
13 See "https://www.fivb.com/en/thefivb/directory/asianvolleyballconfederation".

8

The North, Central America and Caribbean Volleyball Confederation (Norceca):[14]
US Virgin Islands – unincorporated United States territory
Netherlands Antilles – Saba, Sint Eustatius, Sint Maarten, Aruba, Bonair and Curaçao, all Dutch territories
Montserrat – British Overseas Territory
Puerto Rico – unincorporated territory of the United States classified as a commonwealth
Cayman Islands – self-governing British Overseas Territory
British Virgin Islands – British territory
Bermuda – self-governing British Overseas Territory
Aruba – Dutch commonwealth
Anguilla – British Overseas Territory

9

Fifa (Fédération Internationale de Football Association) and UEFA (Union of European Football Associations):[15]
American Samoa – unincorporated territory of the United States
Anguilla – British Overseas Territory
Aruba – Dutch commonwealth
Bermuda – self-governing British Overseas Territory
British Virgin Islands – British Overseas Territory
Cayman islands – self-governing British Overseas Territory
Cook Islands – free association with New Zealand
Curacao – constituent country of the Kingdom of the Netherlands
Faroe Islands – autonomous territory of the Kingdom of Denmark
Gibraltar – self-governing British Overseas Territory
Guam – territory of the United States
Hong Kong – special administrative region in China
Macau – special administrative region in China
Montserrat – British Overseas Territory
New Caledonia – overseas collective owned by France
Puerto Rico – unincorporated territory of the United States
Turks and Caicos Islands – self-governing British Overseas Territory
US Virgin Islands – unincorporated United States territory

---

14 See "http://www.norceca.net/41%20Affiliated%20Federations/Federation%20Afiliated.htm" and "https://www.fivb.com/en/thefivb/directory/norcecavolleyballconfederation".

15 See "https://www.fifa.com/about-fifa/associations".

10

IHF (International Handball Federation) and AHF (Asian Handball Federation):[16]
Hong Kong – special administrative region in China
Macao – special administrative region in China

11

The European Handball Federation (EHF):[17]
Faroe Islands – autonomous territory of the Kingdom of Denmark

12

North America and the Caribbean Handball Confederation (NACHC):
British Virgin Islands – British Overseas Territory
Cayman Islands – self-governing British Overseas Territory
Greenland – autonomous territory of the Kingdom of Denmark
Guadeloupe – overseas department and region of France
Martinique – overseas department and region of France
Puerto Rico – unincorporated territory of the United States classified as a commonwealth

13

Oceania Continent Handball Federation (OCHF):
American Samoa – unincorporated territory of the United States
Northern Mariana Islands – unincorporated territory and commonwealth of the United States
Cook Islands – free association with New Zealand
Guam – territory of the United States
Marshall Islands – in free association with the United States
New Caledonia – overseas territory of France

14

IPC (International Paralympic Committee):[18]
Aruba – Dutch commonwealth
Bermuda – self-governing British Overseas Territory
Faroe Islands – autonomous territory of the Kingdom of Denmark
Hong Kong – special administrative region in China

16 See "https://www.ihf.info/federations" and "https://www.ihf.info/federations".
17 See "https://www.ihf.info/federations".
18 See "https://www.paralympic.org/teams-npc".

Macao – special administrative region in China
Puerto Rico – unincorporated territory of the United States classified as a commonwealth
US Virgin Islands – unincorporated United States territory

15

IJF (International Judo Federation):[19]
American Samoa – unincorporated territory of the United States
Aruba (Suspended) – Dutch commonwealth
Cayman Islands – self-governing British Overseas Territory
Cook Islands – free association with New Zealand
Curacao – constituent country of the Kingdom of the Netherlands
Faroe Islands – autonomous territory of the Kingdom of Denmark
French Polynesia – overseas collectivity and an overseas country of the French Republic
Guadeloupe – overseas department and region of France
Guam – territory of the United States
Hong Kong – special administrative region in China
Macau – special administrative region in China
New Caledonia – overseas territory of France
Niue – self-governing island country in free association with New Zealand
Northern Mariana Islands – unincorporated territory and commonwealth of the United States
Puerto Rico – unincorporated territory of the United States classified as a commonwealth
Réunion – overseas department and region of France
Saint Maarten – constituent country of the Kingdom of the Netherlands
US Virgin Islands – unincorporated United States territory

16

FINA (Fédération Internationale de Natation):[20]
Anguilla – British Overseas Territory
Aruba – Dutch Commonwealth
Bermuda – self-governing British Overseas Territory
Cayman Islands – self-governing British Overseas Territory
Curacao – constituent country of the Kingdom of the Netherlands

---

19 See "https://www.ijf.org/countries".

20 See "https://www.worldaquatics.com/members/national-federations?region=all&country=".

US Virgin Islands – unincorporated United States territory
British Virgin Islands – British Overseas Territory
Saint Maarten – constituent country of the Kingdom of the Netherlands
Puerto Rico – unincorporated territory of the United States classified as a commonwealth
Turks and Caicos islands – self-governing British Overseas Territory
Hong Kong – special administrative region in China
Macau – special administrative region in China
Faroe Islands – autonomous territory of the Kingdom of Denmark
Gibraltar – self-governing British Overseas Territory
American Samoa – unincorporated territory of the United States
Cook islands – free association with New Zealand
Guam – territory of the United States
Marshall Islands – in free association with the United States
Northern Mariana Islands – unincorporated territory and commonwealth of the United States

17

FITA (Fédération Internationale de Tir à l'Arc):[21]
Bermuda – self-governing British Overseas Territory
British Virgin Islands – British Overseas Territory
Curacao – constituent country of the Kingdom of the Netherlands
Falkland Islands – British Overseas Territory
Faroe Islands – autonomous territory of the Kingdom of Denmark
Hong Kong – special administrative region in China
Macau – special administrative region in China
Niue – self-governing island country in free association with New Zealand
Norfolk Islands – external territory of Australia
Puerto Rico – unincorporated territory of the United States classified as a commonwealth.
US Virgin Islands – unincorporated United States territory

18

European Cycling Union (UEC):[22]
Faroe Islands, UEC Associate Member (article 6) – autonomous territory of the Kingdom of Denmark

21 See "https://www.worldarchery.sport/members".
22 See "https://www.uec.ch/en/national-federations".

19

International Golf Federation:[23]
Bermuda – self-governing British Overseas Territory
Cayman Islands – self-governing British Overseas Territory
Cook Islands – free association with New Zealand
Guam – territory of the United States
Hong Kong – special administrative region in China
Puerto Rico – unincorporated territory of the United States classified as a commonwealth
Turks and Caicos – self-governing British Overseas Territory
US Virgin Islands – organised, unincorporated United States territory

20

World Sailing Organisation:[24]
American Samoa – unincorporated territory of the United States
Aruba – Dutch commonwealth
Bermuda – self-governing British Overseas Territory
British Virgin Islands – British Overseas Territory
Cayman Islands – self-governing British Overseas Territory
Cook Islands – free association with New Zealand.
French Polynesia – an overseas collectivity of France
Guam – territory of the United States
Hong Kong – special administrative region in China
Macau – special administrative region in China
Montserrat – British Overseas Territory
Netherland Antilles (Curacao And St Maarten) – Dutch territories
Puerto Rico – unincorporated territory of the United States classified as a commonwealth
Turks and Caicos – self-governing British Overseas Territory
US Virgin Islands – unincorporated United States territory

21

International Tennis Federation:[25]
American Samoa – unincorporated territory of the United States
Anguilla – British Overseas Territory

---

23 See "https://www.igfgolf.org/about-igf/nationalmembers/".
24 See "https://www.sailing.org/inside-world-sailing/organisation/governance/world-sailing-membership/".
25 See "https://www.itftennis.com/en/about-us/organisation/member-associations/".

Aruba – Dutch commonwealth
Bermuda – self-governing British Overseas Territory
British Virgin Islands – British Overseas Territory
Cayman Islands – self-governing British Overseas Territory
Cook Islands – free association with New Zealand
Curacao – constituent country of the Kingdom of the Netherlands
Guam – territory of the United States
Hong Kong – special administrative region in China
Macau – special administrative region in China
Marshall Islands – in free association with the United States
Norfolk Islands – external territory of Australia
Northern Mariana Islands – unincorporated territory and commonwealth of the United States
Puerto Rico – unincorporated territory of the United States classified as a commonwealth
Dutch Antilles (St. Maarten) – constituent country of the Kingdom of the Netherlands
Turks and Caicos – self-governing British Overseas Territory
US Virgin Islands – unincorporated United States territory

22

International shooting Sports Federations:[26]
Aruba – Dutch commonwealth
Cayman Islands – self-governing British Overseas Territory
Faroe Islands – autonomous territory of the Kingdom of Denmark
Guam – territory of the United States
Hong Kong – special administrative region in China
Macau – special administrative region in China

23

International Triathlon:[27]
American Samoa – unincorporated territory of the United States
Aruba – Dutch commonwealth
Bermuda – self-governing British Overseas Territory
British Virgin Islands – British Overseas Territory
Cayman Islands – self-governing British Overseas Territory
Cook Islands – free association with New Zealand

26 See "https://www.issf-sports.org/theissf/organisation/member_federations.ashx".
27 See "https://triathlon.org/federations".

Faroe Islands – autonomous territory of the Kingdom of Denmark
Guam – territory of the United States
Hong Kong – special administrative region in China
Macau – special administrative region in China
Northern Mariana Islands – unincorporated territory and commonwealth of the United States
Puerto Rico – unincorporated territory of the United States classified as a commonwealth

CHAPTER 22

The Stalled Faroese Constitutional Project: Lessons to Be Learned

Bárður Larsen

1 Introduction

The Faroese constitutional project was initiated in 1999 and abandoned in 2018. Even if its levels of activity varied, the Faroese committee was more or less active from early 1999 until late 2006, close to eight years in all. If we include the subsequent process in parliamentary committees and activities attached to the Prime Minister's office, the process lasted for about 19 years in its entirety. Compared to the average duration of processes of constitution-making that have varied between five weeks and up to two to three years, the Faroese process exceeded every normal time frame. The excessive length of the process, and the fact that it was not successful, suggests that some things ought to have been done differently. Here, a few reflections will be put forward about what might be learned from this effort. First, however, the reader needs a short introduction to where we are in the political and constitutional landscape when we talk about a Faroese constitution.

2 Overview of the Faroese Constitutional Position

The people of the Faroe Islands are traditionally considered to be descended from Norwegian settlers dating back to the beginning of the ninth century AD, even if more recent evidence suggests that there were also Scottish and Irish Celts among the ancestors. Probably as early as 1035, the Islands acquired the status of a tributary of the Norwegian king, but still enjoyed a position of a somewhat distinct political and legal entity.

When the Kingdoms of Norway and Denmark entered into a monarchical union in 1380, the Faroe Islands gradually came under the growing influence of the dominant state within that union, Denmark. When the Danish–Norwegian union was abolished in 1814 with the Treaty of Kiel, the Faroe Islands remained under the Danish crown together with Iceland and Greenland, while Norway entered a new union with the Kingdom of Sweden.

The decisive integration of the Faroe Islands with the Danish state would only happen later, in conjunction with the rise of modern Danish democracy and developments around, and in the aftermath of, the Danish Constitutional Convention that worked between late 1848 and early 1849. The Faroe Islands did not, like other counties in the Kingdom, get to elect their own representative to the Constitutional Convention, but were represented by an official elected by the King. Regardless, the constitution was enacted and announced as the law of the land, also in the Faroes.

The 'Faroese question' was not decided at the Constitutional Convention itself but awaited the enactment, a year and a half later, in late 1850, of a special electoral law on Faroese representation in the Danish Parliament that provided for the Faroe Islands to be represented in the *Rigsdag* by two members. Again, the Faroese people were not represented in the assembly that decided the representative question.

In 1852, the old Faroese parliament, the *Løgting*, was restored by Danish parliamentary law and given the status of a county council.

Between 1940 and 1945, the Faroes were separated from the rest of the Kingdom, as Denmark was occupied by Nazi Germany, and the Faroes by Great Britain. This autonomy during the war years resulted in a mindset where a return to the *status quo ante bellum* was not an option. However, negotiations between representatives of the Faroese Parliament and the Danish Government that were carried out between January and March in 1946 did not lead to agreement on a new future arrangement. This stalemate resulted in a referendum being held on 14 September 1946, in which the Faroese were asked to choose between a governmental proposal for internal autonomy or secession. In this referendum, the proposal for secession received a tiny majority of 50.7 per cent (5660 votes) while the government's proposal got 49.3 per cent (5499 votes). The voter turnout was 67.5 per cent. Following controversies in the aftermath of the referendum, the acting Danish Prime Minister recommended to the King on 24 September to dissolve the Faroese *Løgting* and call for a re-election.

Following a new election to the *Løgting* on 8 November 1946, the pro-independence wing lost its majority. New negotiations on a future constitutional arrangement were initiated, and the majority of the Faroese delegation eventually accepted a new Danish proposal for a Home Rule Act that entered into force on 1 April 1948. The proposal was adopted by the Unionist Party, the Social Democratic Party, and the old, small, Self-Government Party, while it was wholeheartedly rejected by the large minority constituted by the People's Party (*Fólkaflokkurin*).

The Home Rule Act divided governmental functions between the Faroese Home Rule authorities and the Danish metropolitan authorities. Home Rule officials could exercise enumerated competences on a 'List A' of special competences, while there was also a 'List B' of competences for which it was to be decided through negotiations whether and to what extent these could be transferred to Faroese authority. The metropolitan officials then retained authority over the competences that either had not been transferred or were inherently metropolitan affairs, not included on either of the lists A or B.

No formal changes occurred in the relationship between Denmark and the Faroe Islands for the next 50 years. After an economic crisis in the 1990s that had put some strain on the relationship, the three political parties most favourable to self-government – the Republican Party, the People's Party, and the old Self-Government Party – received a majority of 18 of the then 32 members at the election to the *Løgting* on 30 April 1998. A coalition was formed in May, 1998, with the express intention of establishing the Faroe Islands as an independent sovereign state.

Negotiations between the Faroese and Danish governments began early in the year 2000 and ended in the fall of the same year. They did not lead to any agreement. Following a new election to the *Løgting* in early 2004, a coalition was formed among the Social Democrats, the Unionist Party and the People's Party, and the agenda for independence was taken off the table. Instead of independence, the new Faroese coalition and the Danish government negotiated a kind of reconstruction of the relationship between the Faroe Islands and Denmark within the existing state.

As a result, the existing Home Rule Act was changed by means of two supplementary acts. One of these was the Danish parliament's Act no. 578 of 4 June 2005 on the transfer of powers and competences to the Faroese Home Rule government, and the other was Act no. 579 of 24 June 2005 concerning the conclusion of agreements under international law by the Home Rule government, both acts entering into force on 29 July 2005.

With these acts, the permanent competences of the Danish authorities were reduced in number, and the enumerated lists of A and B competences were replaced by a so-called 'negative list' containing only a few enumerated core areas of particular importance for the state, namely 1) the metropolitan constitution, 2) citizenship, 3) the Supreme Court, 4) foreign, security and defence policy, and finally 5) currency and monetary policy. This implies that the Faroe Islands according to the 2005 arrangement were positioned to develop a high level of autonomy.

The Danish Constitution was not originally put before the Faroese voters, and in the referenda on the two most recent formal constitutional amendments the electoral turnout in the Faroes was, in 1920, only 24.9 per cent of the eligible voters as compared with 49.6 per cent of the voters in the Danish

Kingdom as a whole, while in 1953, the Faroese voter turnout was a mere 8.7 per cent as compared with 59.1 per cent in the Kingdom as a whole.[1] One might infer from this that the Faroese did not really consider the Danish Constitution to be "theirs" and aspired to a constitution of their own, whether outside (sovereign state) or, especially later, within (sub-state) the wider Danish constitutional frame.

3 The Constitutional Project 1999 to 2018

The Constitutional Project began in the aftermath of the formation of the Faroese governmental coalition from April 1998. Originally the project was seen solely as a necessary instrument to establish a Faroese independent state. The law setting up the first Constitutional Committee was promulgated as Faroese Parliamentary Law no. 10 from 11 February 1999. The Committee was seated shortly thereafter.

The members of the Committee were representatives from, and chosen by, the political parties (two members from each of the four parties with four or more representatives in the Faroese *Løgting*, and one member each from parties with three or fewer representatives). In addition, there was one representative of the Faroese government chosen by the Prime Minister (*løgmaður*) and also five persons with education in social science (in a broad sense, also encompassing law), chosen by the Minister on Self-government. The mandate was to deliver a draft constitution on the governmental rules and basic rights and duties of Faroese citizens. The Minister on Self-government was given authority to elaborate on the mandate of the Committee.

The Constitutional Committee was supposed to deliver a report to the government (specifically, the Minister on Self-government) that included a draft constitution by 1 June 2000 at the latest. The Committee did not deliver on time, not least due to the controversy related to the independence negotiations. The law on the Constitutional Committee was thus changed with Law no. 78 from 8 May 2001 in order to postpone the deadline so that the committee could hand the government a preliminary report by 1 August 2001, and a final report by 31 December 2001 at the latest. The Committee could not deliver within that deadline either. The chairman of the Committee then decided

1 H.A. Sølvará, 'Direct Democracy in the Faroe Islands: A comparative study of referendums in a Faroese context', in volume 63 *Fróðskaparrit – Faroese Scientific Journal*, (2016) pp. 49–102. <doi.org/10.18602/fsj.v63i.85>.

unilaterally to hand the Minister on Self-government a report, within the deadline of 31 December 2001, on what the Committee had been working on so far.

The project now stalled somewhat but again, in 2003, an amendment to the law on the constitutional committee was enacted as Law no. 79 from 8 May 2003. A new deadline for proposing a draft constitution was set for 25 April 2004. New in this law was that the chairman got explicit authority to interpret the Committee's mandate. The same law expanded the Committee so as to include eight members with social-scientific education, and the Prime Minister (*løgmaður*) and the speaker of the Faroese Parliament (*Løgtingsformaður*) were appointed to the Committee *ex officio*.

Once again, the Committee did not manage to produce a common draft within the deadline. The chairman was again obliged to deliver his own report so as to respect the legally prescribed deadline. That report, containing a draft constitution, was written by himself, the Committee secretary, and the deputy chairman. This draft Faroese constitution was delivered to the Prime Minister on 25 April 2004 and was presented as a working paper, as it was not an official draft sanctioned by the whole Committee.

The chairman had interpreted the mandate – to deliver a constitution for the Faroe Islands (to propose an *uppskot til grundleggjandi stjórnarlóg fyri Føroyar*) – broad enough to merit a new and broader title, '*stjórnarskipan*'. This is somewhat equivalent to the English 'Constitution' or the German '*Verfassung*' rather than the narrower, more legalistic '*grundlóg*' (basic law), that, in the Danish tradition – perhaps somewhat surprisingly to an English speaker – carries with it to a higher degree the connotation of independence. This change of title could be seen as indicating a firmer commitment to the drafting of a constitution that would be appropriate for the Faroese polity regardless of whether or not it became an independent state. This must be understood in the light of the fact that a new coalition, more friendly to retaining the union with the Danish state, had been formed in early 2004, following Faroese parliamentary elections in late 2003.

By Act no. 72 of the Faroese Parliament from 23 May 2005, yet another final deadline for the submission of the official draft was set at 31 December 2006. On 18 December 2006 the Committee finally handed the Prime Minister a draft constitution.

The draft constitution of December 2006 is close to the version included in the chairman's report from 2004, mainly drafted by the late Kári á Rógvi, former secretary and vice-chairman to the Committee, and former professor at the University of the Faroe Islands. The 2006 draft contained 82 sections and 3380 words, compared to the 100 sections and 3831 words in the draft from 2004. The new draft had the form of a full, traditional constitution with preamble, governmental rules, and basic rights. Its underlying vision can be said to be reflected in the provisions that declare adherence to these basic values and principles:

1. the principle of popular sovereignty as chief principle of political and constitutional legitimacy in the Faroe Islands, and the related principle of self-determination of the people;
2. the continuity of the Faroese polity within the Danish realm;
3. the self-definition of the Faroese inhabitants as a people and as a nation, and the self-definition of the polity as a land.

Expressions of the principle of popular sovereignty are found in different parts within varying contexts. First it is found in a general form in the preamble sounding like this (this and later English texts are translated by the author):

> We, the People of the Faroe Islands, enact this, our Constitution. It shall form the basis of our Government and be the Charter that shall insure our Freedom, Safety and Prosperity.

Then it is implicitly present in the right to terminate the arrangement with the Danish state in this wording in section 1, subsection 1:

> Any federal or quasi-federal arrangement can be abolished as specified in this Constitution.

Finally, it is expressed in the procedural rules on how to federate with other Lands and Kingdoms, including how to terminate federal arrangements (i.e., implicitly the right to secede from the Danish Kingdom), as in section 79, subsection 2:

> If the Faroe Islands decide to federate with other Lands or Kingdoms, the Faroese *Løgting* shall enact this according to the procedures of ordinary law but with an absolute majority, before the matter shall be put before the People to vote in a referendum with simple majority at least half a year later. The same procedure shall be employed if the Faroe Islands decides to opt out of a federation with other Lands or Kingdoms.

Content that expresses the idea of a continuous Faroese polity within the Danish realm, formerly Norwegian realm, and the principle of popular sovereignty and self-determination, are provisions in the preamble with this wording:

> We built this Land in ancient times and governed ourselves with a *Løgting*, Laws, Rights, and Duties. We have held the *Løgting* until this day and organised ourselves according to the needs of the People of the entire Land. The Faroe Islands have for centuries cooperated with other lands and empires. Nothing can, however, extinguish the self-government of the Land or our Self-determination.

Also, the text at the end of the preamble, originally placed as the final section 100 in the 2004 draft, is worth mentioning:

> This Constitution takes precedence over laws. No law or custom can be thought to be valid merely because it is older than this Constitution or has been tolerated for a long time.

This text can be interpreted as a supremacy clause incompatible with the relations between the Faroes and Denmark, and that seems to be how the Danish Ministry of Justice, in a memorandum from June 2010, did interpret a similar text in the 2010 draft. A better interpretation is arguably that the clause must be understood as applying within the Home Rule sphere rather than understanding the draft constitution in itself as a secessionist instrument.

Finally, section 1, subsection 1, should be mentioned as it contains a provision defining the polity and the people:

> The Faroe Islands are a Land and the Faroese people a Nation.

It is fair to say the central vision driving the Committee was the wish to reach a Faroese consensus on the right to self-determination in a broad sense (i.e. also encompassing external self-determination and the right to secede from the Kingdom of Denmark), the procedures on how to opt out of the Danish Kingdom if and when the Faroese chose full independence, and finally how to define the polity of the Faroe Islands and its relation to Denmark.

After the Constitutional Committee delivered its report on 31 December 2006, the Prime Minister's Office handed the draft over to the *Løgting*. In April 2007, an *ad hoc* parliamentary committee (the so-called 'Section 25 Committee') with two members each from the four big political parties and one member each from the two small political parties, ten members all in all, was seated. The committee's mandate expired and was renewed several times at the end of each parliamentary session until a proposal for a draft constitution finally was put before the *Løgting* on 6 March 2010 (Parliamentary Case no. 140/2009).

In June 2010, the Danish Ministry of Justice issued a memorandum presenting a heavy critique of the 2010 draft. The Ministry seemed to be reading the draft constitution, with references to *inter alia* popular sovereignty, as aspiring toward being the most basic legal source, thus giving the impression that it would take precedence over the Danish Constitution. This could, according to the Ministry, create uncertainty about the constitutional status of the Faroe Islands.

The draft of March 2010 was re-submitted to the parliament in August 2010 (as Parliamentary Case no. 11/2011), again put before yet another *ad hoc* parliamentary committee. That committee held meetings from October 2010 to June 2011 when its mandate expired at the end of the parliamentary session, mainly due to disagreement on the questions related to the preamble and section 1 on how to describe the identity of the polity, the people, and their relation to Denmark.

There was now little or no activity until a new coalition was formed after parliamentary elections in September 2015. The project was now resumed on the basis of the 2010 draft. The project was to be in the hands of the Prime Minister's office, working together with the leaders of the political parties.

A draft was finally presented to the *Løgting* (Parliamentary Case no. 19/2017) in July 2017. The proposal was opened to public commentary, with a deadline of 25 August 2017. 124 comments were delivered, mostly from individuals, but to a lesser degree also from private associations and public authorities. Approximately ten per cent of the comments focused on matters of collective identity, self-determination, and relations to Denmark, close to 40 per cent concerned religious rights, and more than half of the comments covered all remaining topics, but with a dominant focus on political and civil rights. This indicates that the population did not have as narrow a view of the constitutional project as the politicians did, the latter almost exclusively focusing on collective identity, self-determination, and the relation to Denmark.

The Danish Prime Minister's Office also submitted a commentary. It referred to a then recent memorandum from the Ministry of Justice, now expressing a less worried opinion than previously about the relation between the draft and the Danish constitution, as a new text in section 57 had ensured that the new constitution would be administered in accordance with existing constitutional arrangements unless and until a decision were eventually made to establish the Faroe Islands as an independent state.

After the 25 September deadline, the draft was again submitted to a new parliamentary *ad hoc* committee. After a series of meetings from November 2017 through 2018, the committee was still not able to fulfil the promise of the coalition and to submit, by the spring of 2018, a draft to the population as part of a ratification process. No explanation was given for this failure, and the constitutional project has not subsequently been resumed.

4 Lessons Learned

4.1 *The Identity of the Final Interpretive Authority*

As was highlighted in a classical constitutional commentary, a law might be written with the greatest care by the most learned persons, and have undergone the most mature deliberation, but its provisions will remain unclear and obscure until their meaning has been ascertained and determined by adjudication.[2]

In the context of rights, new constitutional systems have sometimes dealt with the challenge of a new beginning by importing constitutional doctrine from countries that are politically and culturally close or countries which, for other reasons, have influenced their legal elites.[3] With respect to the most political parts of a constitution, there are notable historical examples of judges deriving broad principles from the constitutional text in an effort to establish the authority of the new system within a polity that has ratified that text.[4] Thus, it is to a significant extent in the hands of the interpreter to create a constitution in practice. The identity of the final interpretive authority is therefore, or ought to be, regarded as a question of central importance.

Therefore, it is strange that the actors involved in the Faroese constitutional project showed a persistent lack of interest in the identity of the final interpretive authority. Only in the very early stages did this question receive moderate attention, but for the most part it was just presumed that the identity of the judges and court system was of little importance. That this presumption is an example of juristic naivety is easily illustrated by court cases that ignore the possibility of developing independent Faroese interpretations by

2 James Madison, 'The Federalist nr. 37', in Alexander Hamilton, James Madison & John Jay, *The Federalist Papers*, Oxford World Classics (Oxford University Press, 2008) pp. 177–78.

3 Catherine Dupré, *Importing the Law in Post-Communist Transitions – The Hungarian Constitutional Court and the Right to Human Dignity* (Hart Publishing, 2003), especially pp. 54–55 and p. 65, and Richard J. Goldstone, 'The First Years of the South African Constitutional Court', vol. 42 *The Supreme Court Law Review*, (2008) pp. 30–31.

4 See Michael W. McConnell, 'John Marshall and the Creation of a National Government', vol. 27 *Journal of Supreme Court History* (2002) pp. 273–285, especially p. 280; and Ditlev Tamm, 'The History of the Court of Justice of the European Union Since its Origin', in Allan Rosas et al. (eds.), *The Court of Justice and the Construction of Europe: Analyses and Perspectives on Sixty Years of Case-law* (Springer, 2013) pp. 9–35, especially p. 23.

dint of simply presuming full convergence between provisions in the Faroese Instrument of Government and similar provisions in the Danish constitution.

4.2 *Constitution-Making without Time Constraint*

Comparatively and historically speaking, there seems to be a robust connection between constitution-making and times of crises. A constitution-making project needs, so to speak, to have its back against the wall, or else it will likely never reach a conclusion. Originally, the Faroese constitutional project seems to have acquired momentum from the Faroese economic crisis of the early 1990s that had led to both administrative reforms and a new Instrument of Government and stimulated a movement for independence. Since the momentum for independence was lost in the early years of the new millennium, and since the constitutional project was redefined from being primarily an activity conducing to the establishment of an independent state into a broader, sub-state constitutional project, the urgency for constitution-making decreased, and momentum faded. This likely contributed to the culture of indecision and inconclusiveness that came to mark the project.

Given the absence of such preconditions as external crises, and the difficulty of arguing for the necessity of a constitution without the prospect of an independent state, it is worth reflecting on whether and how, a momentum might have been, or might sometime be, generated by a firmer commitment to the legally stipulated deadlines.

4.3 *The Institutional Grounding of the Process*

The members elected to the constitutional committees from 1999 to 2006 were (with the exception of the Prime Minister and the Speaker of the Faroese Parliament, serving as *ex officio* committee members from 2003 onwards) chosen at the full discretion of the appointing authority, i.e. the political parties for the political members, and the Minister on Self-government – later Prime Minister – for the members with social scientific education. There were no provisions concerning the duration of the appointments, the independence of the appointed members, nor any rules establishing a 'veil of ignorance' to weigh against any of the short-term interests of the persons involved.

My personal recollection from committee meetings was that the members with social science backgrounds – when they were in the plenary forum with the politically appointed members – were inclined to assume a passive role as listeners, while the politically appointed members assumed a more active role, and also seemed to see themselves as having a higher degree of legitimacy. Such a division of roles struck me as more appropriate for public officials and politicians in the ordinary administration than for actors putatively involved in constitution-making. The explanation might be related to the weak mandate of the non-political members of the committee.

Independence and competence did not improve as the constitutional project continued in parliamentary *ad hoc* committees during 2006–2007. Such committees had only one jurist acting as secretary out of a secretariat that included four jurists in the Faroese Parliament: hardly a suitable institutional setup for drafting a constitution.

The same is fair to say about the period, from 2015 to 2017, when the project was continued through the Prime Minister's office together with the leaders of the political parties. Two changes to the draft during this phase illustrate the importance of ensuring protection against the self-interested strategic thinking of politicians. In the 2010 draft, which formed the basis of the constitutional process between 2015 and 2017, there was a minority protection clause, ensuring that a one-third minority of the parliament could demand, for up to a week after enactment, that a law be submitted to a consultative referendum. There was also a safeguard against an overly fragmented ministerial structure, restricting the maximum number of ministers, in addition to the Prime Minister, to seven. This was arguably a rational provision for a tiny society. Nevertheless, both of these important provisions were taken out of the 2017 draft.

Arguably, the nascent constitution ought to have been drafted by an independent assembly of some size and competence, elected for that purpose only, and presented for ratification through a procedure wherein the influence of institutional and (short term) political interests was limited.

4.4 *The Reluctance to Accept a New Constitutional Beginning*

To enact a new constitution is in some sense to initiate a new normative order. Thus, if constitution-making is to be reasonably genuine, there must be some acceptance of the idea of a new legal beginning. This must be the case within a sub-state context as well as in a more comprehensive constitutional deliberation, as a sub-state constitution implies a new normative order within the larger constitutional frame, rather than just a continuity at the sub-state level.

The Faroese constitutional project seemed far from such ideals of constitution making. The project was continuously, and in many contexts, haunted by a reluctance to accept the idea of a new beginning. One important example shall be mentioned.

There was repeated, and entrenched, insistence that the new Faroese constitution had to be enacted according to the amendment procedure specified in the Instrument of Government from 1995. Voices to that effect came from the governmental secretariat, from private lawyers, and – most persistently – from the secretariat of the *Løgting*, which repeatedly recommended to the Speaker that the draft should be renounced for violating the Instrument of Government.

This might be thought surprising, taking into account that the Instrument of Government only resembles a constitutional charter in the section on the governmental apparatus, while the Faroese draft constitution was a much fuller constitution, covering not only governmental rules but also provisions on credo or collective identity and basic rights. Amendment procedures for existing constitutional texts will have authority over the enactment of later texts only if the latter differ from the original to such a modest extent that one can still talk about them as amended versions of the same document. In case of a new constitutional charter, however, the procedure for textual innovation is thought to lie beyond the compass of the former constitutional document and must be derived from some constituent authority external to that document.[5]

This adherence to the amendment procedures of the 1995 Instrument of Government is difficult to account for, but it might have to do with the fact that the doctrinally educated Faroese jurists saw themselves as part of a Danish interpretive community and felt more comfortable with the maintenance of a well-known procedural hierarchy than with the theoretically challenging effort of creating an innovative Faroese (sub-state) constitution.

4.5 *Too Much Focus on Identity Constitutionalism*

The one-sided focus on the constitution as an expression of credo and collective identity might also be part of the explanation for the stalled efforts, overweighing the fact that the drafts of 2004 and 2017 contained, respectively, 100 and 58 sections and were therefore among the shortest constitutional documents on record. For although both drafts were phrased in abstract language at the level of high principle, thereby deferring many troublesome decisions that could be left to future resolution, the excessive focus on the difficult questions of how to identify the Faroese people and the Faroese polity, and especially the question of how to describe the relationship of the Faroe Islands to metropolitan Denmark – matters that the Faroese population and politicians were, and are, rather ambivalent about – might have raised what were *prima facie* low decision costs to problematic levels. The public commentaries to the 2017 draft, mentioned above, suggest that only a tiny minority agreed that the

5 See Walter F. Murphy, 'Merlin's Memory: The Past and Future Imperfect of the Once and Future Polity', in Sanford Levinson (ed.), *Responding to Imperfection: The Theory and Practice of Constitutional Amendment* (Princeton University Press, 1995) p. 177. <doi.org/10.1515/9781400821631>.

questions of identity and status were the most important matters upon which to focus.

5 Conclusion

In this essay, we have briefly described and evaluated the abandoned Faroese constitutional project 1999–2017. A number of factors have been mentioned that either contributed to that failure or at least to the weakening of the process.

One very obvious shortcoming was the persistent lack of interest – difficult to fathom – in the question as to who would have final interpretive authority. The possibilities for establishing regular Faroese courts or a Faroese constitutional court were not examined. Given that the introduction of a new constitution hardly makes any sense without making clear the identity of the ultimate authority for its interpretation, the ostensible constitution-making project would appear to have lacked a level of seriousness that degraded the efforts of the potential Faroese constitution-makers.

Another problem seems to be a culture of indecision and inconclusiveness. Probably because the economic crisis in the Faroe Islands in the 1990s, from which the project originally got its momentum, was, over the period 1999–2017, fading into the past, the impetus for the constitutional project faded correspondingly. It seemed hard to find any alternative source of urgency and motivation. A constitution not seen as an instrument for establishing an independent state was probably an insufficient inducement to push the project to conclusion.

Further, a committee chosen at the full discretion of the appointing authority, the later – even weaker – *ad hoc* parliamentary committees, and the process around the Prime Minister's Office did not secure the competence and independence that one would think essential for constitution-making.

In addition, the Faroese jurists involved showed a surprising reluctance to accept the very idea of a Faroese (sub-state) constitution.

And finally, excessive focus on the issues of collective identity and the relationship with Denmark seems to have increased decision costs to heights that posed an obstacle to ever accomplishing the introduction of a Faroese (sub-state) constitution.

Bibliography

Maria Ackrén, *Territoriella autonomier i världen* (Ålands Fredsinstitut, Mariehamn, 2005).

Maria Ackrén, 'Åland och EU', 2008:5 *Finsk tidskrift* (2008), pp. 235–242.

Maria Ackrén, *Successful examples of minority governance: the cases of the Åland Islands and South Tyrol* (The Åland Island Peace Institute, Mariehamn, 2011).

Maria Ackrén och Bjarne Lindström, 'Autonomy development, irredentism and secessionism in a Nordic context', 4:50 *Commonwealth & Comparative Politics*, Routledge, London (2012) pp. 494–510.

Maria Ackrén, 'The Åland Islands: 100 years of stability', in C.H.Brian Fong and Atsuko Ichijo (eds.), *The Routledge Handbook of Comparative Territorial Autonomies* (Routledge, London, 2022), pp. 107–118.

Christer Ahlström, *Demilitarised and neutralised territories in Europe* (Ålands Fredsinstitut, Mariehamn, 2004).

Olgun Akbulut and Elcin Aktoprak (eds.), *Minority Self-Government in Europe and the Middle East*, Brill (2019).

Nicolò Paolo Alessi, 'Joint Bodies – a Key Factor for Successful Autonomous Systems? The Cases of the Italian Special Regions and the Åland Islands', 5:1 *Journal of Autonomy and Security Studies*, (2021), pp. 8–25. Retrieved from https://www.jass.ax/index.php/jass/article/view/51.

Gudmundur Alfredsson, 'A Frame with an Incomplete Painting: Comparison of the Framework Convention for the Protection of National Minorities with International Standards and Monitoring Procedures' in *International Journal on Minority and Group Rights*, vol. 7, issue 4, 2000, pp. 291–304.

Gudmundur Alfredsson, 'The Faroese People as a Subject of Public International Law', 1:1 *Føroyskt Lógar Rit – Faroese Law Review* (2001) pp. 45–57.

Gudmundur Alfredsson, 'Minority Rights: Norms and Institutions' in K. Boyle (ed.), *New Institutions for Human Rights Protection* (Oxford University Press, 2009), pp. 175–206.

Gudmundur Alfredsson, 'Peoples' in A. Peters (ed.), *Max Planck Encyclopedia of Public International Law*, Oxford University Press, on-line – updated in 2022.

Anthony D'Amato, *The Concept of Custom in International Law* (Cornell University Press, Ithaca and London, 1971), pp. 264–271.

Björn Arp, *International norms and standards for the protection of national minorities, Bilateral and Multilateral Texts with Commentary* (Martinus Nijhoff, Leiden, 2008).

Andreas Backfolk, *FN:s definition av begreppet "ursprungsbefolkning" ur ett åländskt perspektiv* (Åländsk utredningsserie, Mariehamn, 1998:1).

Andrés B. Baka, 'The Convention and the Protection of Minorities under International Law', in Ronald St. J. Macdonald, Franz Matscher, Herbert Petzold (eds.), *The European System for the Protection of Human Rights*, (Martinus Nijhof, Leyden, 1993) pp. 875–888.

James Barrows, *The Aland Islands Question: Its settlement by the League of Nations* (Yale University Press, New Haven, 1968).

Barry Bartmann, 'In or Out: Sub-National Island Jurisdictions and the Antechamber of Paradiplomacy', in Godfrey Baldacchino and David Milne (eds.), 386:2006 *The Case for Non-sovereignty: Lessons from Sub-national Island Jurisdictions* (Routledge, 2006) pp. 53–71.

Mikaela Björkholm, *Ålandsöamas demilitarisering och neutralisering* (Meddelande från Ålands kulturstiftelse, Åbo Akademi, 1990).

Mikaela Björkholm och Allan Rosas, *Ålandsöarnas demilitarisering och neutralisering* (Åbo Akademis förlag, 1990).

Gustav Blomberg, *The Åland Example Applied: a case study of the autonomous region of muslim Mindanao* (Ålands fredsinstitut, 2015).

Ove Bring, *Ålands självstyrelse under 80 år: erfarenheter och utmaningar* (Ålands landskapsstyrelse, Mariehamn, 2002).

Ove Bring, 'Åland som internationellt objekt idag och i framtiden', *Vitbok för utveckling av Ålands självbestämmande* (Ålands framtid, Mariehamn, 2017) pp. 33–49.

Philip Marshall Brown, 'The Åland Island Question', 15:2 *The American Journal of International Law* (1921) pp. 268–272.

Thomas Buergental, *International Human Rights in a Nutshell*, Second Edition, (West Publishing Co., St. Paul, 1995).

Cristian Cantir, 'Kin states in Sub-state Diplomacy Conflict Dynamics' 16:1 *Foreign Policy Analysis* (2020) pp. 59–77.

Maria Carlsson, *Åland och den europeiska konventionen angående skydd för de mänskliga rättigheterna och de grundläggande friheterna, till den del konventionen berör undervisningsspråket och rörelsefriheten* (M. Carlsson, Mariehamn, 1991).

Matthieu Chillaud, *Les Iles Åland en mer Baltique* (L'Harmattan, Paris, 2010).

Committee report No 24/1919 to the Government from the Committee on the Drafting of Proposals for County Self-Government, Administrative Courts of Lower Instance, and re-districting of current counties and administration (Justitieministeriet, Helsingfors, 1919).

Congress of Local and Regional Authorities, 32nd Session, Local and regional democracy in Finland, Monitoring Committee, CG32(2017)08 final, 28 March 2017 pp. 20/45.

James Crawford, *Brownlie's Principles of Public International Law* (9th edn., Oxford University Press, 2019).

Katja Creutz and Sarah Stephan, 'Making Autonomies Matter: Sub-State Actor Accommodation in the Nordic Council and the Nordic Council of Ministers, An

Analysis of the Institutional Framework for Accommodating the Faroe Islands, Greenland and Åland within "Norden"', *European Diversity and Autonomy Papers* (2014) https://www.eurac.edu/edap.

Andreas Dahlén, *Den åländska hembygdsrättens omgestaltning: från jordförvärvsrätt till regionalt medborgarskap* (Lunds Universitet, 2007).

Yoram Dienstein, *The Models of Autonomy*, (Transaction Books, New Brunswick and London, 1981).

Yoram Dienstein, 'Autonomy regimes and international law', 56 *Villanova Law Review* (2011), pp. 437–454.

Karl Doehring, 'Das Gutachten des Generalsekretärs der Vereinten Nationen über die Fortgeltung der nach dem ersten Weltkrieg eingegangenen Minderheitenschutzverpflichtungen', 1954:15 *Zeitschrift für ausländisches öffentliches Recht und Völkerrecht* (1954), pp. 521–540.

Krzystof Drzewicki, 'The Lund Recommendations on the Effective Participation of National Minorities in Public Life – Five Years After and More Years Ahead', 12:2–3 *International Journal on Minority and Group Rights* (2005) pp. 123–131.

Krzystof Drzewicki, 'A Constitution for Europe: Enshrining Minority Rights. Words Can Make Worlds of Difference', *OSCE Magazine* (March 2005) pp. 19–21.

Krzystof Drzewicki Drzewicki, 'A Constitution for Europe: Enshrining Minority Rights. Words Can Make Worlds, The OSCE High Commissioner on National Minorities – Confronting Traditional and Emerging Challenges', in Stanislaw Parzymies (ed.) *OSCE and Minorities. Assessment and Prospects* (Warsaw: Wydawnictwo Scholar, 2007) pp. 14–16.

Krzysztof Drzewicki, 'European Systems for the Promotion and Protection of Human Rights', in Catarina Krause and Martin Scheinin (eds.), *International Protection of Human Rights: A Textbook* (Åbo Akademi University, Institute for Human Rights, Åbo, 2009) pp. 365–388.

Robert Dunbar, 'Minority Language Rights in International Law', 50:1 *International & Comparative Law Quarterly* (2001) pp. 90–120.

Jorri Duursma, 'Fragmentation and the intemational relations of Micro-states', *Cambridge Studies in International Law* (Cambridge University Press, 1996).

Martin Ekman, *Det självstyrda och demilitariserade Ålands gränser: historiska, geovetenskapliga och rättsliga synpunkter* (Ålands Högskola, Mariehamn, 2000).

Bogi Eliasen, 'Non-Sovereign Polities and Their Access to the International Community' in Sjúrður Skaale (ed), *The Right to National Self-Determination. The Faroe Islands and Greenland* (Martinus Nijhoff Publishers, Leiden, 2004) pp. 179–203.

Jannika Enegren-Åberg, 'En utredning om gränserna för Ålands demilitarisering', 2006:18 *Justitieministeriets arbetsgruppsbetänkande* (Helsingfors, 2006).

Susanne Eriksson, *Islands of Peace: Åland's autonomy, demilitarization and neutralization* (Åland Islands Peace institute, Mariehamn, 2006).

Niklas Fagerlund, *Ålands folkrättsliga status och* EG (Meddelande från Ålands högskola, Mariehamn, 1993).

Rolf Einar Fife, *Et komparativt perspektiv: Bestemmelsene om begrensning av militær virksomhet på Svalbard i helhold til artikkel 9 i Traktaten av 9. Februar 1920 om Spitsbergen* (Utrikesministeriets publikationer 1/2006, Helsingfors, 2006).

A Gross, 'Positive experiences of autonomous regions as a source of inspiration for conflict resolution in Europe', 9824 *Political Affaires Report* (Council of Europe, 2003).

Henrik Gustafsson, 'Drei Autonome Regionen in Nordeuropa : Die Åland-Inseln', 1985:3/4 *Ausblick Zeitschrift für Deutsch-Skandinavische beziehungen* (1995) pp. 1–3.

Kenneth Gustavsson, *Ålandsöama – en säkerhetsrisk? Spelet Om Den Demilitariserade Zonen 1919–1939* (PQR, Mariehamn, 2012).

Lauri Hannikainen, *Cultural, linguistic and educational rights in the Åland islands* (The Advisory Board for International Human Rights, Helsinki, 1992).

Lauri Hannikainen, *Ahvenanmaan itsehallinnon ja ruotsinkielisyyden kansainoikeus-delliset perusteet* (Institutet för mänskliga rättigheter vid Åbo Akademi, Åbo, 1993).

Lauri Hannikainen, 'The Continued Validity of the Demilitarised and Neutralised Status of the Åland Islands', 54 *Zeitschrift für ausländisches öffentliches Recht und Völkerrecht* (1994) p. 614.

Lauri Hannikainen and Frank Horn (eds.), *Autonomy and Demilitarisation in International Law: The Åland Islands in Changing Europe* (Kluwer Law International, The Hague, 1997).

Lauri Hannikainen, *De folkrättsliga grunderna för Ålands självstyrelse* (Institutet för mänskliga rättigheter vid Åbo Akademi, Åbo, 2004).

Hurst Hannum and Richard B. Lillich, 'The concept of autonomy in international law', 1980:4 *The American Journal of International Law* (Cambridge University Press, 1980).

Hurst Hannum, *Procedural Aspects of International Law: Autonomy, Sovereignty, and Self-Determination: The Accommodation of Conflicting Rights* (2nd ed). (University of Pennsylvania Press, 1996).

Sten Harck, Åland Islands, in Anne Peters. (ed.), *Max Planck Encyclopedia of Public International Law* (online edn., OUP, January 2008).

Eve Hepburn, 'Forging Autonomy in a Unitary State: The Åland Islands in Finland' 12:4–5 *Comparative European Politics* (2014) pp. 468–487.

Charles Herford, *The Case of German South Tyrol against Italy* (G. Allen & Unwin, London, 1927).

Rainer Hofmann et al., 'Introduction', in Rainer Hofmann et al. (eds.), *The Framework Convention for the Protection of National Minorities* (Brill, Nijhoff, Leiden, Boston, 2018), pp. 3–21.

Rainer Hofmann, Moritz Malkmus, Alexander Heger, 'The Åland Islands in International and European Union Law: Present Situation and (Potential) Problems', 2024:1

Research Paper of the Faculty of Law of Goethe University Frankfurt/M (Frankfurt, 2024).

Marine Holm-Johansson, 'Vissa äganderättsbegränsningar på Åland och Europakonventionen om mänskliga rättigheter' 1992:5 *Tidskrift utgiven av Juridiska Föreningen i Finland* (Helsingfors, 1992) pp. 329–350.

Marine Holm-Johansson, *Förhållandet mellan självstyrelselagen och grundlagen*, Promemoria 2020-09-01 (Ålands landskapsregering, Mariehamn, 2020).

Lars-Ingmar Johansson and Peter Wahlberg (eds.) *International Treaties and Documents Concerning Åland Islands 1856–1992*, (Ålands kulturstiftelse, Mariehamn, 1993).

Harry Jansson (ed), *Vitbok för utveckling av Ålands självbestämmande* (Ålands framtid, Mariehamn, 2017).

Harry Jansson and Johannes Salminen (eds.), *The second Åland Islands question. Autonomy or independence?* (Julius Sundblom Memorial Foundation, Mariehamn, 2002).

Ida Jansson, *Att sätta självstyrelsens gränser* (Olof M Janssons Stiftelse, Mariehamn, 2020) https://www.olofmjanssonsstiftelse.ax/app/uploads/2020/09/att-satta-sjalv styrelsens-granser.pdf.

Pertti Joenniemi, 'The Åland Islands: Neither local nor fully sovereign', 49:1 *Cooperation and Conflict* (2014) pp. 80–97.

Axel Jonsson, 'Konsten att olovligen ta makten av en nordisk autonomi', 2/2021 *Tidskrift utgiven av Juridiska Föreningen i Finland* (1992) pp. 87–110.

Antero Jyränki, 'Autonomy of the Åland Islands: A Federal Element in the Constitution of a Unitary State?', in Kirsi Pohjolainen (ed.), *Constitutionalism in Finland – Reality and Perspectives* (Finnish Society of Constitutional Law, Helsinki, 1995).

Anna Khakee, *Vad avgör en autonomy regions grad av autonomi? En jämförande studie mellan Färöarna och Åland* (Lunds Universitet, 1992).

Love Kellberg, 'Ålandsöarnas internationellrättsliga ställning', 59 *Svensk Juristtidning* (1974) p. 190.

Ruth Lapidoth, Autonomy: *Flexible Solutions to Ethnic Conflicts* (United States Institute of Peace, 1997).

Bardur Larsen, 'Problemet med den ubekymrede retliga transplantation', 2022:6 *Juristen* (København, 2022) pp. 251–263.

Göran Lindholm, 'Bakgrunden till Ålands folkrättsliga ställning', 1982:1–2 *Nordisk tidskrift för internationell ret* (Copenhagen, 1982).

Bjarne Lindström, *De legala och politiska förutsättningarna för Europas autonomier: En jämförande studie* (Olof M Janssons stiftelse, Mariehamn 2020) https://www.olofm janssonsstiftelse.ax/app/uploads/2020/11/omj22020.pdf.

Bjarne Lindström och Göran Lindholm, *Den åländska autonomins framtidsförutsättningar: En studie av självbestämmandets legala och politiska utveckling* (Olof M

Janssons stiftelse, Mariehamn, 2021) https://www.olofmjanssonsstiftelse.ax/app/uploads/2021/05/862-olof-m-slutmanus3majmed-parm-winter.pdf.

Bjarne Lindström and Göran Lindholm, *The future conditions for the Åland Autonomy: A study of the legal and political development of Åland's self-determination* (Olof M Janssons stiftelse, Mariehamn, 2021) https://www.olofmjanssonsstiftelse.ax/app/uploads/2021/11/2164-olofm-nr-4-2021.pdf.

Bjarne Lindström, 'State Integration vs. Minority Protection through Regional Self-Determination: The Åland Case', 30:1 *International Journal on Minority and Group Rights* (Brill Nijhoff, Leiden Boston, 2023) pp. 110–131.

Bjarne Lindström, *The political and legal prerequisites for autonomies in Europe: A comparative study* https://www.olofmjanssonsstiftelse.ax/app/uploads/2023/10/cmc-11654-paper-autonomy-in-europe-061023.pdf.

John Loughlin & Fairmah Daftary, *Insular Regions and European Integration: Corsica and the Åland Islands Compared* (European Centre for Minority Issues, Helsinki & Mariehamn, 1999).

Tarja Långström, *Transformation in Russia and International Law* (Martinus Nijhoff Publishers, Leiden, 2003),

Philip McDermott, 'Language Rights and the Council of Europe: A Failed Response to a Multilingual Continent?'. *Ethnicities* 17:5 (2017) pp. 603–26. https://www.doi.org/10.1177/1468796816654725.

Roberta Medda-Windischer, 'The European Court of Human Rights and Minority Rights' 25:3 *Journal of European Integration*, (2003) pp. 249–71. https://www.doi.org/10.1080/0703633032000133583.

Tore Modeen, *De folkrättsliga garantierna för bevarandet av Ålandsöarnas nationella karaktär/ La protection du caractère national des Iles d'Aland en droit international* (Ålands kulturstiftelse, Mariehamn, 1973).

Tore Modeen, *International Protection of the National Identity of the Aland Islands, The Scandinavian Studies in Law 17* (Stockholms Universitet, 1973), pp. 175–210.

Tore Modeen, 'UNESCO-konventionen mot diskriminering inom undervisningen och Ålandsöarna', 1976:3 *Tidskrift för Juridiska Föreningen i Finland* (Åbo Akademi, 1976) pp. 140–166.

Nagy Noémi, 'Language Rights as a Sine Qua Non of Democracy – a Comparative Overview of the Jurisprudence of the European Court of Human Rights and the Court of Justice of the European Union', *EPLO Publications* (2018).

Georg Nolte, 'Some Observations on the 1920 and 1921 Expert Reports Regarding the Åland Islands Question', in Donath P.B. et al. (eds), *Der Schutz des Individuums durch das Recht* (Springer, Berlin, Heidelberg, 2023), pp. 93–100.

Deborah Paci, 'The Åland Island Question: Irredentism and Autonomism in the Archipelago of Peace', 40:85 *Revista Brasiliera de História*, (Sao Paulo, 2020).

John Packer, 'The OSCE High Commissioner on National Minorities', in G. Alfredsson et al. (eds.), *International Human Rights Monitoring Mechanisms. Essays in Honour of Jacob Th. Möller* (The Hague-Boston-London, Martinus Nijhoff Publishers, 2001) pp. 641–656.

Norman Padeldorf, & Gösta Anderson, 'The Åland Question', 33:3 *The American Journal of International Law*, (New York, 1939) pp. 465–487.

Sten Palmgren, 'The Autonomy of the Åland Islands in the Constitutional Law of Finland', in Lauri Hannikainen and Frank Horn (eds), *Autonomy and Demilitarisation in International Law: The Åland Islands in a Changing Europe* (Kluwer, The Hague et al., 1997), pp. 85–97.

Sten Palmgren, 'De statsrättsliga garantierna för Ålands självstyrelse', 2020:6, *Tidskrift för Juridiska Föreningen i Finland* (Åbo Akademi, 2020) pp. 689–715.

Sten Palmgren, *Ålands självstyrelse. En introduktion for statsrådets tjänstemän*, (Justitieministeriet, Helsingfors, 2023).

Alan Patten, 'The Justification of Minority Language Rights', 17 *Journal of Political Philosophy* (2009) pp. 102–128, https://www.doi.org/10.1111/j.1467-9760.2008.00321.x.

Matti Pellonpää, 'Economic, Social and Cultural Rights', in Ronald St. J. Macdonald, Franz Matscher, Herbert Petzold (eds.), *The European System for the Protection of Human Rights* (Martinus Nijhof, Leyden, 1993) pp. 855–874.

Alan Peters (ed.), 'International Court of Justice (ICJ)', *Max Planck Encyclopedia of International Procedural Law* (online edn., OUP, June 2018).

Yannick Poullie, 'Åland's Demilitarisation and Neutralisation at the End of the Cold War – Parliamentary Discussions in Åland and Finland 1988–1995,' *International Journal on Minority and Group Rights 23* (Brill Nijhoff, Leiden Boston, 2016) pp. 179–210.

Ulla Aikio-Puoskari, *Linguistic Human Rights of Indigenous Sámi in the Finnish Education System* (University of Lapland, Rovanniemi, 2011).

Steven R. Ratner, 'Does International Law Matter in Preventing Ethnic Conflict?', 32:3 *New York University Journal of International Law and Politics* (2000) pp. 668–673.

Holger Rotkirch, 'The Demilitarization and Neutralization of the Åland Islands: A Regime "in European Interests" Withstanding Changing Circumstances', 23:4 *Journal of Peace Research* (1986).

Claudio Scarpulla, *The constitutional framework for the autonomy of Åland: a survey of the status of an autonomous region in the throes of European integration* (Meddelande från Ålands Högskola, Mariehamn, 2002:14).

Harald Christian Scheu, 'The heritage of the League of Nations' minority protection system', *Hungarian Journal of Legal Studies 61* (2020), pp. 356–371.

Sören Silverström, 'The competence of autonomous entities in the international arena: with special reference to the Åland Islands in the European Union', 2008:15 *International Journal on Minority and Group Rights* (Brill Ninjhoff, 2008) https://www.doi.org/10.1163/157181108X332622.

Susann Simolin, 'The Aims of Åland and Finland Regarding a New Act on the Analysis of three Parliamentary Committee Reports (2010–2017)', 2:1 *Journal of Autonomy and Security Studies* (2018) pp. 8–48. https://www.jass.ax/volume-2-issue-1-simolin>.

Susann Simolin, 'The Aims of Åland and Finland Regarding a New Act on the Autonomy of Åland: An analysis of three parliamentary committee reports (2010–2017)', *Journal of Autonomy and Security Studies* 2 (2018), pp. 8–48.

Susann Simolin, 'Ålands självstyrelse i en föränderlig omvärld – 100 år av omvandling från lokal till internationell och global aktör', in Sia Spiliopoulou Åkermark (ed.), *Styr ålänningarna sitt öde? Demokratiperspektiv på Åland* (Mariehamn, Cavannus förlag, 2021) pp. 23–49.

Susann Simolin, 'Autonomies interacting with the EU: Exploring variations between the Åland Islands, South Tyrol and the Faroe Islands', 4 *Report from the Åland Islands Peace Institute* (Mariehamn, 2021).

Susann Simolin, 'Att påverkas och påverka – Ålands ambitioner och självbestämmande inom EU', 2021:2 *Report from the Åland Islands Peace Institute* (Mariehamn, 2021).

Anna-Lena Sjölund, 'EU-rätten och behörighetsfördelningen mellan riket Finland och landskapet Åland', 2016:1 *Rapport från Ålands fredsinstitut*, (Mariehamn, 2021).

Tove Skutnabb-Kangas, *Linguicism. The Encyclopedia of Applied Linguistics* (Blackwell, Malden, MA, 2015).

Tove Skutnabb – Kangas and Robert Phillipson (eds.), *The Handbook of Linguistic Human Rights* (Wiley Blackwell, Oxford, 2022) https://www.doi.org/10.1002/9781119753926.

Sia Spiliopoulou Åkermark, *Justifications of Minority Protection in International Law* (Kluwer Law International, den Hague, 1997).

Sia Spiliopoulou Åkermark, 'The Åland Islands Question in the League of Nations: The ideal minority case?' in 2009:13 *Redescriptions – Yearbook of Political Thought, Conceptual History and Feminist Theory*, (2009), 195–205, https://www.doi.org/10.7227/R.13.1.10.

Sia Spiliopoulou Åkermark, *Justifications of Minority Protection in International Law* (Kluwer Law International, den Hague, 1997).

Sia Spiliopoulou Åkermark (ed.), *The Åland Example and Its Components – Relevance for Conflict Resolution* (Ålands Fredsinstitut, Mariehamn, 2011).

Sia Spiliopoulou Åkermark, 'Ålands Demilitarisation and Neutralisation: Continuity and Change', in S. Spiliopoulou Åkermark (ed.), *The Åland Example and Its Components: Relevance for International Conflict Resolution* (The Åland Islands Peace Institute, Mariehamn, 2011) p. 50.

Sia Spiliopoulou Åkermark *Towards Openly Multilingual Policies and Practices Assessing – Minority Language Maintenance Across Europe*, co-authored with J. Laakso, A. Sarhimaa & R. Toivanen (Multilingual Matters, Bristol, 2016).

Sia Spiliopoulou Åkermark, Saila Heinikoski and Pirjo Kleemola-Juntunen, *Demilitarization and International Law in Context: The Åland Islands* (Routledge, New York, 2018).

Sia Spiliopoulou Åkermark, 2021:3 *EU och lagberedningen* (Ålands fredsinstitut, Mariehamn, 2021).Sia Spiliopoulou Åkermark, 'Shifts in the Multiple Justifications of Minority Protection', 7:1 *European Yearbook of Minority Issues Online* pp. 1–18, https//www.doi.org/10.1163/22116117-90001627201O.

Sara Stephan, 'Regional Voices in the European Union – Regions with Legislative Power and Multi-Level Governance. Perspectives for the Åland Islands', 2010:1 *Report from the Åland Islands Peace institute* (Mariehamn, 2010).

Markku Suksi, 'Lagstiftningskontroll och rättsskipning i autonomier', 2015:1 *Tidskrift för Juridiska Föreningen i Finland* (Åbo Akademi, 2015) pp. 27–55.

Markku Suksi, *Double enumeration of legislative powers in a sub-state context: a comparison between Canada, Denmark and Finland* (Springer, New York, 2018).

Markku Suksi, *Ålands konstitution: en sammanställning av material och tolkningar i anslutning till självstyrelselag för Åland* (Åbo Akademi, 2005).

Markku Suksi, 'Functional Autonomy: The Case of Finland with Some Notes on the Basis of International Human Rights Law and Comparisons with Other Cases', 15:2–3 *International Journal on Minority and Group Rights* (2008) pp. 195–225. https://www.doi.org/10.1163/157181108X332604.

Markku Suksi, 'What Can We Learn From the Åland Islands Case?' in Daniel Thürer and Zdzislaw Kędzia (eds.), *Managing Diversity. Protection of Minorities in International Law* (Zurich, 2009) pp. 147–173.

Markku Suksi, *Sub-State Governance through Territorial Autonomy* (Springer Verlag, Heidelberg, 2011).

Markku Suksi, 'Autonomy', in Anne Peters (ed.), *Max Planck Encyclopedia of Public International Law* (Online edn., OUP, 2021).

Jan Sundberg, *Det åländska självstyrets kvaliteter* (Svenska Litteratursällskapet i Finland, Helsingfors, 2021).

Jan Sundberg och Stefan Sjöblom, *Det åländska självstyrets kvaliteter. Demokrati, resurser och kompetens* (Svenska litteratursällskapet i Finland, Helsingfors, 2021).

Johan Otto Söderhjelm, *Démilitarisation et neutralisation des Iles d'Åland en 1856 et 1921.* (Helsingfors, 1928).

Christian J. Tams, Malgosia Fitzmaurice (eds.), *Legacies of the Permanent Court of International Justice* (Brill, Nijhoff, Leiden, Boston, 2013).

Teija Tiilikainen, *The Åland Islands, Finland and European Security* (Åland Islands Peace Institute, Mariehamn, 2002).

Daniel Thürer, Thomas Burri, 'Self-Determination', in Anne Peters (ed.), *Max Planck Encyclopedia of Public International Law* (Online edn., OUP, December 2008).

Reetta Toivanen and B. Bergholm, 'Narratives on 'refugee knowledge' in the institutions of Europe', in M. Kmak & H. Björklund (eds.), *Refugees and Knowledge Production: Europe's Past and Present* (*Routledge* 2022).

Reetta Toivanen, 'Protecting Indigenous identities? An example of cultural expertise on Sámi identity'. 54(2-3) *Legal pluralism and Critical Social Analysis*, (2023).

Reetta Toivanen and C.P. Krieg, C. P., *Situating Sustainability: A Handbook of Contexts and Concepts*. (Helsinki University Press, 2021).

Arthur Tollet & John Uggla, *Lagstiftningen angående självstyrelse för Åland, jämte tillhörande författningar* (Holger Schildts förlag, Helsingfors, 1930).

Charles de Visscher, *Theory and Reality in Public International Law* (Princeton University Press, Princeton, 1968).

Alan Watson, 'From Legal Transplants to Legal Formants', 43:3 *The American Journal of Comparative Law* (1995) pp. 469–476.

Helena Wisthaler, *Minorities and immigration: frameworks of exclusion and inclusion in Åland and South Tyrol compared* (Åland Islands Peace Institute, Mariehamn, 2014).

Sir Michael Wood, 'Special Rapporteur of the International Law Commission on the "Identification of customary international law"', 2018:2 *Yearbook of the International Law Commission* (2018).

Selected Åland Related Instruments

Åland Autonomy Act, English version, https://www.lagtinget.ax/sjalvstyrelsen/sjalvstyrelselagen, also available at https;//www.finlex.fi/en/laki/kaannokset/1991/en19911144.pdf>.

International Treaties and Documents Concerning Åland 1856–2009, Peter Wahlberg and Lars Ingmar Johansson (eds.) (Ålands kulturstiftelse, Mariehamn, 2018) also available at https://www.lagtinget.ax/sjalvstyrelsen/internationella-avtal-0.

Finnish Government: *Proposition till Riksdagen angående lag om självstyrelse för Åland.* (Helsingfors 1919) Rd. - Sv. – Prop. No. 73.

Ålandsfrågan Inför Nationernas Förbund: La Question Des Îles d'Aland, Aktstycken 1920:1 (Utrikesdepartementet, Stockholm, 1920), 234–279.

Åländska skattegruppens betänkande, Olsson-kommittén, Justitieministeriet, (Helsingfors, 1994).

Åland Government, *Betänkande från parlamentariska kommittén om förslag till reformering av självstyrelsesystemet och självstyrelselagen för Åland* (Åländsk utredningsserie, Marieham, 2010:2).

Åland självstyrelse i utveckling. Ålandskommitténs 2013 slutbetänkande – Ahvenanmaan itsehallinnon kehittäminen. Ahvenanmaa-komitean 2013 loppumietintö. https://www.urn.fi/URN:ISBN:978-952-259-600-0.

Åland Government, *Slutrapport från parlamentariska kommittén för fortsatt arbete med ett nytt självstyrelsesystem* (Åländsk utredningsserie, Mariehamn, 2013:2).

Index

www.ingramcontent.com/pod-product-compliance
Lightning Source LLC
Chambersburg PA
CBHW071230230926
51849CB00001B/65
9789004691100